FIRMS AND INDUSTRIAL ORGANIZATION IN JAPAN

Firms and Industrial Organization in Japan

Yoshiro Miwa
Professor of Economics
University of Tokyo

NEW YORK UNIVERSITY PRESS
Washington Square, New York

First published in the U.S.A. in 1996 by
NEW YORK UNIVERSITY PRESS
Washington Square
New York, N.Y. 10003

Library of Congress Cataloging-in-Publication Data
Miwa, Yoshiro, 1948–
Firms and industrial organization in Japan / Yoshiro Miwa.
p. cm.
Based on the author's Nihon no kigyō to sangyō soshiki, published
in 1990
Includes bibliographical references and index.
ISBN 0–8147–5551–8
1. Industrial management—Japan. 2. Industrial policy—Japan.
I. Title.
HD70.J3M58188 1996
658'.00952—dc20 95–42222
CIP

Printed in Great Britain

Contents

v

List of Figures and Tables

Preface and Acknowledgements

I wrote this book primarily for two groups of people. One group consists of those scholars and students interested in industrial organization and economic theory, including the theory of the firm and the market. The other group are the comparativists interested in Japan. Unlike most books on the Japanese economy, this volume argues that nothing is peculiar to Japan. Many argue that Japan is different, and there exists a huge collection of stylized facts about the Japanese economy. However, most of these alleged facts are either non-existent or based on shaky ground.

For a long time Japan has been in a world of exchange by agreement rather than by coercion, where the costs and benefits of agreement determine its scope. It is my purpose to demonstrate that the standard principles of economics explain the dominant patterns of Japanese economic phenomena. The principles are not those anyone invented to explain Japan. Indeed, they were not invented to explain any particular society. This is my central point. I argue below that the essence of the underlying mechanism of the Japanese economy closely resembles the *essence* of the underlying mechanism in *most* other economies. I wish to deal only with Japan, and only with the basic contours of firm behaviour and the function of markets. That I consider challenge enough. Readers are not expected to have much or any knowledge of Japan, particularly the *stylized facts* and anecdotes about the Japanese economy. However, a basic knowledge of economics and a strong dose of logic, even in the flood of strange tales and anecdotes, is required.

In the process of writing this volume, I have incurred a large intellectual debt to many senior scholars, mostly Japanese, upon whose pathbreaking work I draw heavily and some of whom are still entirely against my arguments. The citations should make this debt clear, but lest there be any doubt I gladly acknowledge their contribution. In alphabetical order, with (as we shall do throughout the book) given names first and family names last, they are: Ken'ichi Imai, Keimei Kaizuka, Tadao Kiyonari, Kazuo Koike, Ryutaro Komiya, Yutaka Kosai, Yoshikazu Miyazaki, Hideichiro Nakamura, Takafusa Nakamura, Kohnosuke Odaka, Yoshio Sato, Mikio Sumiya, Toshimasa Tsuruta, Masu Uekusa, and Kozo Yamamura.

Much of this book (Part I to Part III) is based on my Japanese book, *Nihon no Kigyo to Sangyo Soshiki (Firms and Industrial Organization in Japan)*, published in 1990 by the University of Tokyo Press (Miwa 1990a).[1] That book is a collection of academic papers each of which challenged many aspects of what I call below the conventional view of the Japanese economy.

A long time has passed since the first paper was published in 1977. Over that period many friends at many institutions, besides some of the senior scholars cited above, shared their ideas with me, both in conversation and through their gracious comments on my drafts. Those who were particularly generous with their time and thoughts include: Takahiro Fujimoto, Akira Goto, Leslie Hannah, Juro Hashimoto, Motoshige Itoh, Hideki Kanda, Yoshitsugu Kanemoto, Motonari Kurasawa, Masahiro Okuno-Fujiwara, Hiroyuki Odagiri, Tetsuji Okazaki, Mark Ramseyer, Shizuki Saito, Paul Sheard, John Sutton, Haruhito Takeda, Kazuo Wada, Rhuhei Wakasugi, Peng Xu and Noriyuki Yanagawa. In addition, I received many helpful comments from participants in numerous conferences and workshops. I could not have completed this work without the assistance of many people both in industry and in government who were generous with their time and frank in expressing their views.

I gratefully acknowledge the permission of the University of Tokyo Press and the Academic Press Inc. of Tokyo to refer to my earlier works. I received financial support from a number of sources: the Ministry of Education (Monbusho) Grant for Scientific Research, the Japan Economic Research Center Grant, the Seimei-kai Grant of Mitsubishi Bank and the University of Tokyo Research Fund Grant of the Economics Department. My secretaries Nobuko Kubo and Yuriko Hiratsuka contributed much in completing both the Japanese book and this one, and David W.Lane, Karl Ruping and Shigeo Hirano did great work in editing my English. I am happy to thank them all.

Last but not least, I thank my wife, Kazuko, for her understanding and forgiveness through the many evenings and weekends lost while writing this book. It is to her that I affectionately dedicate this book.

YOSHIRO MIWA

1 Introduction and Summary

1.1 INTRODUCTION

Fifty years have passed since the end of the Second World War in 1945, and almost 40 years have passed since the 1956 *Economic White Paper* solemnly declared: 'No longer are we in the *postwar* age. We are now facing a new, different situation'. But, as far the basic views of Japanese firms, industries and the economy are concerned, the postwar age has not yet ended, and we still find ourselves insisting strongly and repeating softly that we are no longer in the *postwar* age. The view of the Japanese economy dominant in the 1950s and 1960s (hereafter referred to as 'the conventional view of the Japanese economy' or simply 'the conventional view') still implicitly and often explicitly dominates the way Japan is viewed in the 1990s both at home and abroad. The conventional view was not effective in analysing the Japanese economy in the 1950s and 1960s and is even less effective when applied to the present economy. We are no longer in the postwar age. We should put an end to the anachronistic conventional view which was invented for postwar Japan. Now we should begin a new study of the Japanese economy based upon a critical review of the past literature and the conventional view.

Today the industrial success of the Japanese economy gathers world wide attention, and many people are interested in the causes and underlying mechanism of its economic development. The interest tends to centre on firms, industries and the role of the government. This interest naturally stimulates interest in the historical process. As I will describe shortly, the 1950s and 1960s are the so-called '*High-Growth Era*' of the Japanese economy after which Japan has grown to having the second largest economy among Group of Seven (G7) countries. However, during this time the literature and related documents on the Japanese economy were dominated by the conventional view. The recent literature is about the same. A simple, but basic, question arises immediately: how have vital firms and industries grown, given the conditions assumed in the conventional view? This leads to a second question: how has the industrial success been attained? Further, much of the discussion about today's Japan depends primarily on the conventional view, implying both that it was effective for the 1960s and that it still is effective today. The conventional view of the Japanese economy is composed of two basic components.

1. The view that the *Japanese economic system* played a critical role in Japan's economic development. This system can be described by certain keywords, such as monopoly capital, finance capital, dual structure,

1

exploitation, *keiretsu* loan, loan-concentration mechanism, corporate groups, main banks, *keiretsu* control, *keiretsu* transaction, subcontract (*shitauke*), subordination or dependence (*reizoku*), small business or small and medium firms (*chusho kigyo*), modernization, burden-shifting (*shiwayose*).

2. The view that, under the guise of 'industrial policy', the Japanese government has intervened heavily in (or guided and led) the private sector, which has contributed much to Japan's industrial success.

Neither component is very persuasive. In the first two parts of this book, I conclude that the Japanese economic system, which is based on a mixture of ill-defined terms and vague arguments, gives a false image of the Japanese economy which is distant from reality. In Part III, I conclude that industrial policy was ineffective and did not contribute much to the industrial success because its influence on business activities has never been substantial.

It is a touchstone of accepted economics that all explanations must run in terms of the actions and reactions of individuals. It is my purpose to demonstrate that Japan has for a long time been 'a world of exchange by agreement rather than by coercion [where] the costs and benefits of agreement determine its scope' (Stigler, 1992, p. 456) and that the standard principles of economics explain the dominant patterns of the Japanese economic phenomena. It is only recently that many economists have begun to talk about the Japanese economy using the standard principles of economics. Prior to the change, before the 1970s for instance, dreadfully dogmatic Germanic theory or Marxian economics dominated discussions of the Japanese economy. (Frequent use of terms such as 'monopoly capital' and 'finance capital' symbolizes this tradition.) Those who subscribed to such theories failed to recognize that the economic phenomena could have occurred as a result of exchange by agreement, not coercion. The dominance of Germanic or Marxian theories has a long history, which is not limited to economics and dates back to the turn of the century. These theories influenced not only academics in other fields of social sciences but also those outside academics, such as journalists, politicians, lawyers and bureaucrats. Even business leaders shared the view when they talked, not about their own business, but about the Japanese economy as a whole. Thus the Germanic or Marxian theories have become so ingrained that they still permeate the conventional view of the Japanese economy. Even today most Japanese, particularly those who are over 40, strongly sympathize with those theories.

I see the problem created from the influence of these theories as being twofold. First, by using such keywords, many unconsciously accept these theories as valid for the present Japanese economy. Thus my argument faces strong resistance from many sides, which, however, is seldom understandable. Second, most of the keywords invented in the 1960s, which are still used in current talk about the Japanese economy, are products of these theories and reflect the belief that economic phenomena are a result of exchange by coercion, not agreement. Because of this, most of the literature on the Japanese economy from the 1950s and 1960s is incomprehensible. The literature hardly explains why coercion might occur and how it could work, but rather assumes *a priori* that it does. The term 'dual structure' is one example. As I will discuss in the next two chapters, many argue that the Japanese economy operates with a dual structure system where the small firm's freedom of choice is strictly limited and large firms exploit them, but I could never find a persuasive explanation why such a system might occur.[1] In Chapter 3, I critically examine the persuasiveness of their argument, and instead show how competitive markets have worked well and therefore economic phenomena could be explained as a result of the voluntary choice of participants.

Studies of the Japanese economy abound, but few provide a good introductory overview. This is partly because interest in Japan's economy has intensified as its industrial success has become well-known since the 1970s and especially in the 1980s. Interest in Japan is predicated upon a taste for the exotic and the expectation at home and abroad that Japan is and should be different from Western countries. The strong demand for the Japan-is-different-view has been satisfied by those with similar beliefs. As will be shown below, there are many stylized facts on Japan's economy, most of which are vague, ill-defined and supported by few firm empirical grounds. Before introducing my argument, this chapter has two preliminary sections: first, an overview of Japan's economy and industry in the half-century after the Second World War and, second, comments on five basic misconceptions of the Japanese economy.

1.2 A BRIEF OVERVIEW OF JAPAN'S POSTWAR ECONOMIC HISTORY

As shown in Tables 1.1 and 1.2, Japan's 1990 GDP was more than half that of the USA and was larger than the remaining Group of Seven industrialized nations'. Japan's per capita income was the highest of the Group with Germany. In 1980 the situation was almost the same. Even in 1970, at the mid-way point between 1945 and today, Japan's GDP exceeded that of all the G7 countries but the USA, and per capita income was catching up with that of Europe. In 1960, however, Japan's GDP was less than a tenth of that of the USA and slightly larger than that of Italy and Canada. Its per capita GDP was the smallest of all the G7 countries, only a third that of the UK, Germany and France.

Although Japan's per capita income grew the fastest among the G7 countries from 1973,[2] its growth rate was even higher in the 'high-growth era' of 1951–73. Table 1.3 shows the five year average real growth rate of GNP between 1945 and 1980.

The Japanese economy has grown at a remarkably rapid speed, not only since the war but also before. Between 1913 and 1929, for example, Japan's real per capita income increased by 46 per cent, compared with the 36 per cent growth over the same time period in France, the second fastest-growing

Table 1.1   GDP at current prices in Group 7 countries (US$ billion)

	Japan	USA	UK	Germany	France	Italy	Canada
1990	2932	5522	983	1496	1195	1095	572
1980	1036	2626	524	821	656	396	253
1970	197	974	120	187	149	94	84
1960	43	504	72	73	62	35	38

Source: Bank of Japan, *Comparative Economic and Financial Statistics*.

Table 1.2   Per capita GDP in Group 7 countries (US$ 100)

	Japan	USA	UK	Germany	France	Italy	Canada
1990	237	221	171	237	211	190	215
1980	89	115	94	133	122	70	106
1970	19	47	22	31	29	17	39
1960	5	28	14	14	14	7	21

Source: Bank of Japan, *Comparative Economic and Financial Statistics*.

Table 1.3   Real GNP growth rate in Japan, 1945–80 (five-year average, per cent)

1945–50	1950–55	1955–60	1960–65	1965–70	1970–75	1975–80
9.4	10.9	8.7	9.7	12.2	5.1	5.6

Source: Adapted from Kosai (1981, p. 2, Table 1).

country among today's G7 members.[3] As shown in Figure 1.1, only in 1957 did real per capita income exceed the 1939 prewar peak. Total GNP topped the prewar level in 1954.[4]

As shown in Table 1.4, postwar Japan's industrial success can be characterized by the machinery industries, whose ratio of exports to total exports of all industries in 1970 was 46.3 per cent, almost double the 25.3 per cent of 1960, and four times the 10.5 per cent of 1950.

Rapid growth of the machinery industries began in the prewar period; the ratio of machinery exports to total exports was already 13.0 per cent in 1940. As shown in Table 1.5, production of machinery items reached its peak before the Second World War and rose rapidly again after a wartime lull. Different products emerged successively, starting with electric fans, sewing machines and binoculars, followed by cameras, radio receivers, monochrome televisions, bicycles, clocks and watches, and then by motorcycles, three-wheeled trucks, ships, cars and various other kinds of electrical and industrial machinery.

Table 1.4 Export component ratios of Japan, 1900–1990 (per cent)

	1900	1910	1920	1930	1940	1950	1960	1970	1980	1990
Marine products	1.8	1.6	0.9	2.6	2.9	3.6	3.2	1.6	0.5	0.3
Tea	4.4	3.3	0.9	0.5	0.7	0.6	0.2	0.0	0.0	0.0
Coal	9.8	3.4	2.3	1.5	0.2	0.0	0.0	0.0	0.0	0.0
Copper	6.3	4.6	0.7	1.5	0.3	0.0	0.0	0.0	0.0	0.0
Cotton yarn	10.3	9.8	7.8	1.0	1.6	2.1	1.3	0.1	0.0	0.0
Cotton fabric	2.8	4.5	17.2	18.5	10.9	24.8	8.6	1.0	0.3	0.0
Silk yarn	21.8	28.4	19.6	28.4	12.2	4.7	2.2	0.0	0.0	0.0
Silk fabric	9.1	7.2	8.1	4.5	1.0	2.7	1.3	0.1	0.0	0.0
Non-cellulosic fibre fabric	—	—	—	2.4	3.6	6.0	5.3	3.5	1.4	0.7
Pottery	1.2	1.2	1.6	1.8	1.7	2.2	1.7	0.7	0.3	0.2
Cement	0.1	0.3	0.5	0.7	0.4	0.7	0.6	0.2	0.2	0.1
Machinery	0.0	0.9	2.6	1.4	13.0	10.5	25.3	46.3	46.4	75.0
(Ships)	0.1	0.1	0.8	0.4	1.0	3.2	7.1	7.3	2.7	1.9
Steel	—	—	0.7	0.6	—	8.7	9.6	14.7	8.8	4.4
Others	32.4	34.8	37.1	34.6	51.5	33.4	40.7	31.8	42.1	19.3

Source: Adapted from T. Nakamura (1993, p. 43, Table 16).

6

Table 1.5 Production of selected goods, 1935–53

	Sewing machines	Electric fans	Radios	Ships (tons)	Three-wheeled trucks	Binoculars	Bicycles	Cameras	Clocks and watches
1935	12 301	43 562	153 974	174 067	9 837	81 700	903 000	95 326	4 183 000
1936	40 924	42 228	427 287	274 784	12 557	79 200	1 055 000	154 648	4 864 000
1937	53 133	46 918	406 753	483 548	15 233	99 500	1 090 000	178 321	5 114 000
1938	104 204	43 575	604 463	464 679	10 450	45 600	1 080 000	187 569	3 814 000
1939	132 997	58 302	740 356	391 679	7 953	62 500	950 000	205 522	3 384 000
1940	154 402	64 780	852 903	401 866	8 113	60 000	1 245 000	218 659	3 424 000
1941	142 317	55 828	917 001	466 249	4 503	56 400	185 000	203 011	2 935 000
1942	51 129	41 200	841 301	547 051	3 721	35 200	181 000	133 854	1 582 000
1943	25 573	45 240	741 816	1 030 601	2 259	36 100	70 000	57 588	808 000
1944	16 047	2 360	262 372	2 198 790	1 338	60 000	65 000	29 548	413 000
1945	2 150	1 240	87 529	632 005	686	14 400	20 000	13 082	98 000
1946	36 912	66 282	672 676	143 860	3 647	37 836	—	24 145	714 000
1947	133 949	74 329	772 428	83 565	7 432	31 158	—	51 772	1 599 000
1948	165 726	72 167	769 730	162 898	16 852	47 623	337 000	53 016	2 404 000
1949	274 468	95 703	702 327	163 980	26 727	97 356	552 000	83 243	3 051 000
1950	493 038	118 804	281 602	229 761	35 503	115 970	981 000	117 481	2 331 000
1951	1 030 289	173 903	399 943	454 149	43 717	176 180	987 000	213 840	3 050 000
1952	1 260 293	290 879	929 126	627 064	62 262	179 510	1 019 000	357 918	3 803 000
1953	1 318 059	434 585	1 391 031	521 759	98 405	212 704	1 184 000	663 484	4 673 000

Source: Ministry of International Trade and Industry, *Kokogyo Seisan Shisu* [*Production Indexes of Mining and Manufacturing Industries*] (1955); Adapted from Miwa(1993a, p.137).

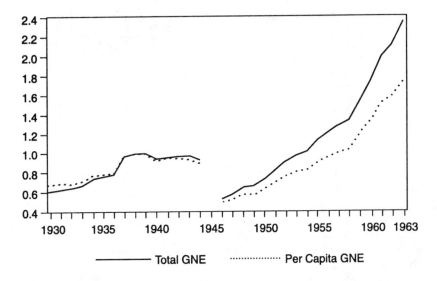

Source: *Kokumin Shotoku Tokei Nenpo* (*National Income Statistics Yearbook*), Economic Planning Agency, 1963.

Figure 1.1   Total and per capita Gross National Expenditure (GNE) at current prices in 1934–6 (1939 = 1)

The car industry is one example of the machinery industry's success.[5] As shown in Table 1.6, Japan's total production in 1955 was only 20 000 when Toyota launched its first true car, the Crown. Production grew to approximately 700 000 cars in ten years, 3 000 000 cars in 15 years, and in 1971 more than 1 000 000 cars were exported.[6] As shown in Chapter 4, the basic features of today's motor industry were clear before 1970.

Thus, by 1970, before the first oil crisis in 1973, the Japanese economy had grown to a size big enough to gather worldwide attention. This is the first reason why my focus in the first three parts of this book centres primarily on the 'high-growth era' of 1951–73, particularly the 1960s. The average growth rate in the process was quite high, and per capita GDP was also catching up with that of Europe. The basic features of Japan's industrial success had become clear, as symbolically shown in the figures for 1970 – 46.3 per cent in Table 1.4, the ratio of machinery exports to total exports, and 3 178 708 and 22.8 per cent in Table 1.6, the figure for Japanese car production and its export ratio. For the next 25 years the Japanese economy as a whole and each individual industry, particularly the machinery industries, grew steadily along the same line of growth as in the preceding decades.

Table 1.6   Japanese car production and exports

Year	Production	Exported (%)
1947	110	0.0
1948	381	0.0
1949	1 070	0.0
1950	1 594	0.0
1951	3 611	0.0
1952	4 837	0.0
1953	8 789	0.0
1954	14 472	0.0
1955	20 268	0.0
1956	32 056	0.1
1957	47 121	0.9
1958	50 643	4.7
1959	78 598	6.2
1960	165 094	4.2
1961	249 508	4.6
1962	268 784	6.0
1963	407 830	7.7
1964	579 660	11.6
1965	696 176	14.5
1966	877 656	17.4
1967	1 375 755	16.2
1968	2 055 821	19.8
1969	2 611 499	21.5
1970	3 178 708	22.8
1971	3 717 858	34.9
1972	4 022 289	35.0
1973	4 470 550	32.5
1974	3 931 842	43.9
1975	4 567 854	40.0
1980	7 038 108	56.1
1985	7 646 816	57.9

Source: Nihon Jidosha Kogyokai (Japan Automobile Manufacturer's Association), *Jidosha Tokei Nenpo*; adapted from Miwa (1990a, p. 68, Table 4.1).

1.3   FIVE MISCONCEPTIONS OF THE JAPANESE ECONOMY

Talk about today's Japanese economy is full of misconceptions, upon which not only political debates but also academic works heavily depend. Most of these misconceptions prevailed in the 1960s, and survive even today, often with only cosmetic changes, like *keiretsu* loan to main bank relationships (see Chapters 5 and 6). Many people adopt them as stylized facts without close examination of whether these 'facts' ever really existed. They were misconceptions even in the 1960s. Many argue, for instance, that industrial policy was tremendously effective in the 1960s, and that it is still effective although diminishingly so. But if industrial policy was ineffective in the 1960s, as I believe, then it cannot be effective today. Thus, for an accurate understanding of the current Japanese economy, it is essential to understand the Japanese economy in the 1960s, for which a critical examination of the literature of the time is crucial. This is the second reason for my focus in the first three parts centring primarily on this period.

A reader may be happy enough not to have any such misconceptions. But the world is full of talks and articles based, often unconsciously, on these misconceptions, and this happy reader like little Red Riding Hood has no way to defend herself against them. Therefore, as a beginner's guide to studying today's Japanese economy, I point out five basic misconceptions: the dominance of large firms, the dominance of corporate groups, the effectiveness of industrial policy by the strong government, the argument that all trade relationships are long term and exclusive, and the important role of cross-shareholdings among firms.

The stylized misconceptions are contrasted with the facts. I show what the facts are, and why and how the conventional view is full of misconceptions. Introductory explanation is minimized, and detailed discussion can be found below.

The Dominance of Large Firms

Misconception 1: Japan's economy is dominated by large firms.

Fact 1: Japan's economy is dominated by small- and medium-sized firms (hereafter, small business).

The first misconception is a mixture of three components: (1) each large firm is really gigantic; (2) large firms occupy the dominant portion of the Japanese economy; (3) each large firm or group of large firms subordinate and exploit many small business under *keiretsu* relationships, making their presence and power much larger than their size, as measured by the number of employees, alone suggests. However, all three components are wrong.

Each large firm is really rather slim. In discussing Japanese firms and industrial organization most have in mind such firms as Toyota, Nissan and Honda in the motor industry and NEC, Hitachi and Sony in electronics. Some may think that Toyota's unique 'Just-in-time' production-system or *kanban*-system is common throughout the Japanese economy. A comparison of large Japanese firms and their American and European counterparts reveals that Japanese firms are rather small and have far fewer employees in relation to sales.[7] Table 1.7 gives some statistics. For example, in 1991, Toyota's annual sales amounted to about half those of General Motors (GM) and a third more than Volkswagen's, but Toyota employs less than one-tenth (72 000) the number of GM workers (751 000) and less than one-third the number of Volkswagen workers (266 000).

Table 1.7   A comparison of size of large firms: American, European and
              Japanese

American		European		Japanese	
General Motors		Volkswagen		Toyota	
[N]	751		266		72
[S]	124 705		50 290		68375
General Electric		Philips		Hitachi	
[N]	284		240		82
[S]	60 236		33 282		31 337
Du Pont		ICI		Toray	
[N]	133		128		10
[S]	38 695		23 321		4782
Dow Chemical		Bayer		Mitsubishi Chemical	
[N]	62		162		10
[S]	18 807		27 941		5 804

Note: Sales are converted at the nominal exchange rate of 31 Dec. 1991.
[N]: Number of employees (thousands) in 1991.
[S]: Sales (US$ millions) in 1991.
Source: Toyo Keizai Shinpo-sha, *Kaisha Shikiho*, 3 (1992, Tokyo).

Small business occupies the dominant portion of the Japanese economy.
Most Japanese firms are small, most Japanese workers are employed by small
firms, and more than half of value added in the corporate sector is produced
by small firms. Such dominance of small firms in Japan has a long history,
and their share in the corporate sector has not changed for at least 30–40
years.[8] The total number of establishments in the whole private sector of
Japan (not including agriculture and fishery) was 6.5 million in 1991, and
99.1 per cent of them were small businesses. The total number of employees
there was 55 million, and 79.2 per cent of them were in small business.
Limiting our attention to the manufacturing sector, we find almost the same
picture. There were 857 000 establishments in 1991, and 99.4 per cent of them
were small businesses. The total number of employees was 14.1 million, with
73.8 per cent in small business. The corresponding figures in the manufacturing sector in 1957 were 99.6 per cent and 72.3 per cent, respectively, which
suggest the stable predominance of small business. Throughout these 30–40
years, more than 55 per cent of the value added has been produced in the
small business sector.[9]
     The profit rate of small businesses has been much higher than that of large
firms, and the number of small businesses has constantly increased (see Table
2.1, and Table 3.1.) This implies that neither subordination nor exploitation
of small business existed even in the 1950s and 1960s, and that many new
entrants have found small business promising.

The position of large firms in Japan's economy is symbolized by the following figures on the largest firms. In 1984, the largest 100 firms accounted for 20.7 per cent of Japan's private non-financial sector's total assets. There has been a weak downward trend since 1967, when the percentage was 25.6 per cent.[10] When the subsidiaries of these 100 firms (those with a shareholding of more than 50 per cent) are included, the 1984 figure increased to 24.8 per cent. The corresponding 1984 figure in manufacturing was 33.0 per cent and there has also been a downward trend since 1967, when it was 37.2 per cent.[11] As shown in Scherer and Ross (1990, p. 63, Table 3.3), the 1985 employment of Japan's top ten and top 20 leading companies as a percentage of total industrial employment was 7.3 per cent and 9.9 per cent, respectively, remarkably lower than nine other nations, including the USA (13.1 per cent and 18.6 per cent, respectively) which was the lowest among these nine nations.

The Dominance of Corporate Groups

Misconception 2: There is a small number – say, six – of corporate groups (kigyo shudan). Mitsui, Mitsubishi, and Sumitomo are the representative. Member firms of each group form a tight organization and take concerted action, as if each member is a division of the whole. A large bank is at the core of each group and has a close 'main bank' relationship with the other members. Those corporate groups dominate the Japanese economy.

Fact 2: However 'corporate group' is defined,[12] the number is greater than six. No group of this type was tightly connected, or took such concerted action, particularly in making management decisions, even in the 1960s – the heyday of the corporate-group-view. The role of main banks is exaggerated. The dominance of these corporate groups in the Japanese economy is an exaggeration, too.

Part II of this volume is entirely devoted to the analysis of the issues related to this misconception. What follows is an overview of seven aspects of this larger issue, each of which is quite ill-defined: historical importance, the role of the presidents' meeting (*shacho-kai*), the large bank's dominance in the capital market, main bank's monitoring function, large bank's role as the head of a corporate group, the corporate group's dominance in the Japanese economy, and the argument that the system of corporate groups and the main banks is the secret of Japan's industrial success.

Many argue that the number *six* is of historical importance, for 'six major industrial groups', descendants of the prewar *zaibatsu*, dominate the Japanese economy. In fact only three of these groups, Mitsui, Mitsubishi and Sumitomo, are usually regarded as ex-*zaibatsu*. The other three have no such historical background (see the second part of Section 7.2 below).

The presidents' meeting is often recognized as functioning as the headquarters of each group. No evidence is available to evaluate the role of these meetings, but they are said to occur only once a month for two hours. The commonsense view is that one hour is for lunch and general conversation and the other is for a lecture, often invited from outside the group. Member firms in each group in 1990 ranged between 20 and 47 (32 on average), too many for complicated business talks. The starting date of these meetings ranges between 1951 and 1978, with a median of 1963, 18 years after the end of the Second World War (see Chapter 7, and especially Table 7.1).

It is widely believed that six large banks (Mitsui, Mitsubishi, Sumitomo, Fuji, Sanwa and Daiichi Kangyo), one at the heart of each major corporate group, dominate Japan's capital markets. Japan has a wide variety of financial institutions. In 1963, for instance, there were 13 city banks (including the six banks noted above), 65 regional banks, seven trust banks, and three long-term credit banks, in addition to many smaller institutions, including 17 042 deposit taking post offices. The 13 city banks together held 41.8 per cent of the total assets of private financial institutions.[13]

Many argue that, in Japan, each firm has a main bank which monitors the firm as a representative of other lenders and plays a central bail-out role when the borrower falls into a state of insolvency. Clear definition of the main bank and hard evidence for its activity do not exist, making debate impossible. Whatever your definition of a main bank may be, see the last two sections of Chapter 6 below.

It is often believed that each large bank functions as the head of a corporate group subordinating other member firms with loans, shareholding, and seconded directors, for which such terms as *keiretsu* control and *keiretsu* relationship are used. A large firm usually borrows less than 20 per cent of its total needs from one bank (see, for instance, Tables 6.5 and 6.6), and borrows from that bank's competitors as well. The Anti-monopoly Act limits shareholding by a bank to 5 per cent of any firm, and well-run firms usually have no directors seconded from or controlled by outside stakeholders such as a main bank acting as a monitoring agent (see Chapters 6, 7, and 11 for details).

'Six major corporate groups' are regarded as dominating the Japanese economy. Their presence is exaggerated. Taking the presidents' meeting members as defining a corporate group, of the whole Japanese economy in 1990, the six groups (excluding banks and insurance company members) accounted for 13.6 per cent of total assets, 15.2 per cent of sales, 13.7 per cent of income before income taxes and extraordinary items, and 4.1 per cent of employment. The number of employees of all member firms in three ex-*zaibatsu* groups – Mitsui, Mitsubishi and Sumitomo – was 637 000 (see Tables 7.1 and 7.2), fewer than the 751 000 of General Motors (see Table 1.7). As pointed out in Chapter 7, however, aggregating the individual firms' figures is hardly justifiable.

It is often insisted that the system of corporate groups and main bank relationships is the secret of Japan's industrial success. Its importance is exaggerated. Even where the conventional view of corporate groups and main banks is justified, their contribution to Japan's industrial success remains an open question. At a minimum they generate 'distortions' in the economy. Japan's industrial success is so remarkable that many tend to search for unique institutions and arrangements and make illogical conclusions, ignorant of the *post hoc, ergo propter hoc* fallacy (see Part II).

The Effectiveness of Industrial Policy

Misconception 3: Under the guise of industrial policy, one of the main engines of industrial success, the Japanese government has used strong powers to intervene in the private sector.

Fact 3: The strength of state powers of intervention is a matter of definition. Outside regulated industries, the government rarely intervenes, however, and the net contribution of industrial policy to Japan's industrial success is negligible.

The third misconception is composed of five parts: a big government, a government organization suitable for 'targeting policy', a strong government like those in socialist countries, a magnificent capability on the part of the government to beat the market and a big contribution to Japan's industrial success. All are examined in Part III of this volume, which is entirely devoted to industrial policy. Note that the effectiveness of industrial policy is not a black-and-white affair, but a 'grey' matter to varying degrees.

Many believe that Japan is highly bureaucratized and has a big government. Whether Japan is bureaucratized is a matter of definition, but its government is small in terms of both budget and the number of government employees per capita. As Pempel and Muramatsu (1993, p. 20) state,

> despite the fact that Japan is often thought of as a bureaucratized country, it actually has fewer public sector employees per capita than most other major industrialized countries . . . [G]overnment employees represent approximately 15–20 per cent of the total employment of the United States, France, Germany, and Britain; in Japan the figure is only 7.9 per cent.[14]

Furthermore, as a result of a series of administrative reforms, 'there has been almost no substantial growth in the number of Japan's national civil servants over the last three decades'.[15] They also point out that Japan maintains 'the lowest cost government among the industrialized democracies as a per cent of GNP' (p. 34). Japan's 1990 ratio of public expenditure to GDP was 32.4 per cent; in the USA the figure was 36.1 per cent, in France, 49.9 per cent, in Germany, 46.0 per cent and in the UK 42.1 per cent.[16]

Many argue that the Japanese government selects a group of industries of strategic importance: it designates an organization which is responsible for each industry and concentrates its effort on their development, which is often referred to as a 'targeting policy'. Since the Meiji era, almost every industry has had a government counterpart which devotes all its efforts to protecting, encouraging and supporting the firms in that industry. Examples include the steel industry section of the Ministry of International Trade and Industry (MITI) and the Securities Bureau of the Ministry of Finance (MOF). Almost all industries are systematically and continuously protected and supported by the government (see Chapter 8). Problems arise from the fact that nobody can protect and subsidize everybody. The vast number of small businesses has meant, for example, that policy developed by MITI's Small and Medium Enterprise Agency (SMEA) has been indiscriminate and thinly spread, as detailed in Chapter 3. Furthermore, targeted policies can be implemented only over the strong objection of the government sections and industries which are not selected.

It is often supposed that the Japanese government, like those in socialist countries, can intervene freely in the private sector and achieve almost all its aims. In postwar Japan, the government has never had such influence. Government power ebbed through gradual 'liberalization', and attempts to strengthen it have almost always failed. Today, as in other developed countries, government influence is strong in regulated industries like energy, transport, communications, financial intermediation and agriculture. However, state influence is weak in other industries, including most of manufacturing. Pressure to open the Japanese market mounted sharply towards the end of 1950s.[17] In June 1960, the Cabinet decided on a 'Trade and Exchange Liberalization Plan' and Japan's import liberalization greatly expanded in the first half of the 1960s (for details, see Komiya (1990), Chapter 1). During the process of liberalization, MITI provoked the 'new industrial order debate' and attempted in vain to strengthen its power by enacting the Specified Industries Act.[18]

Even when the law empowers the government to intervene in the private sector, it is often reluctant in using it. This point is developed in Chapter 10, where the case of the Petroleum Industry Act is examined in detail. The Act permits the government to intervene in individual refiners' decisions on production levels, pricing and investment. In the Idemitsu incident of 1963, MITI officials and the Chairman of the MITI's Petroleum Council tried without success to elicit Idemitsu's cooperation in output coordination. The case suggests four points: (1) even when the government has strong powers, 'self-coordination (coordination by themselves)' is normally chosen by the government as the basic approach to conflict resolution; (2) only when self-coordination fails does government intervene; (3) for government participation to achieve its goals, the active cooperation of the relevant firms is essential; (4) even when the government uses its power to coordinate private sector activity, it is not easy to actually attain its goals.

Many assume, often implicitly, that the government can beat the market at selecting industries and directing resources to them. But no evidence has ever been shown for this assumption, making debate impossible. In Japan and among Japanologists abroad, this argument, often called a 'signalling effect' view or a 'cowbell effect' view, is popular. This assumes that the government has incredible ability to select industries for 'targeting policy', and small businesses for small business policies, much like the ability of main banks to select which firms to lend to. Because of this capability the government is assumed to beat the market by inducing the private firms to cooperate for the policy target through policy intervention. This is almost equivalent to suggesting that the centralization of the economy improves efficiency, and also is close to the 'Japan-Inc.' view.[19] These arguments are still open to a careful investigation, especially with the collapse of a number of socialist economies since 1989. Note that, in Japan, strongly regulated industries are notoriously poor performers.

Industrial policy is widely believed to be the engine of Japan's industrial success. To test this assertion, we should conduct careful investigation on the net contribution of industrial policy to Japan's industrial success. Because government intervention generates 'distortions' in the economy, the key question is not whether industrial policy had a positive impact but whether the benefits covered the costs. (As will be shown in Part III, it neither had positive impact nor covered its cost.) To repeat an earlier assertion, Japan's industrial success is so remarkable that many tend to search for unique institutions and arrangements and make illogical conclusions, ignorant of the *post hoc, ergo propter hoc* fallacy.

All Trade Relationships are Long-term and Exclusive

Misconception 4: In Japan, trade relationships are long-term and exclusive; therefore it is hard to begin business with new partners or to enter new markets. Foreign firms feel this constraint strongly.

Fact 4: Trade relationships in many fields probably do have a long-term character. However, such relationships are not strongly exclusive, as evidenced by the many new entrants and competitive markets in Japan over the postwar period. Thus long-term relationships are not the main factor constraining the success of foreign firms in Japan. As in other countries, not all new entries succeed, and foreign firms are not the only firms to fail in Japan.

Many assert that the cooperative association of first-tier suppliers to Japan's car assemblers (*kyoryoku-kai*) is exclusive. Toyota's *Kyoho-kai* is a notable example. As discussed in the second part of Section 4.4, in 1987, 45 of 162 cooperative association members of Nissan, Toyota's arch-rival, also belonged to Toyota's *Kyoho-kai*.[20] Many suppliers, like Akebono Brake, Ichikoh Industries, NOK, Kayaba and Koito, belonged to cooperative associations of the 'Big 5' (Toyota, Nissan, Mazda, Mitsubishi and Honda) and other assemblers, and even Nihon Denso, the biggest car parts manufacturer in Japan, of which Toyota held 23 per cent of the stock, belonged to the cooperative association of every assembler except Nissan. As discussed in Chapter 12 of this volume, especially in Section 12.9, the predominance of stable, long-term inter-firm relationships with a non-exclusive characteristic is one of the most striking and important peculiarities of Japanese industrial organization.

The Important Role of Cross-shareholdings among Firms

Misconception 5: Most large Japanese firms are controlled by a group of directors and managers who are relatively independent of shareholders. Independence is assured by cross shareholdings (mochiai) by a group of stable and friendly shareholders (antei kabunushi), who may be other member firms in a corporate group. The antei kabunushi as a group hold the majority of stock in particular firms, and are loyal to the firms' directors. The power of other shareholders is consequently weak, and Japanese capitalism is therefore different from that in Western countries. However, the collapse of the recent 'bubble economy' has meant the diminution of cross-shareholdings, and convergence with the Western standard.

Fact 5: Though definitional problems remain, especially as to the meaning of 'control', many large Japanese firms are controlled by a group of directors. This is not because of cross-shareholdings, however, but is an outgrowth of the mechanism of organization. Antei kabunushi remain shareholders and choose to support the present directors, but the extent of their power is open to question. Whether Japanese capitalism differs from the Western variant is another question, and whether cross-shareholding is diminishing is yet another.

Many hold this misconception in spite of, or even because of, its extreme ambiguity. For the details, see Chapter 11 of this volume. Friendly shareholders (*antei kabunushi*) are still shareholders and no change has occurred in their legal position. As large shareholders, friendly shareholders can easily 'control' the firm's decision making if they decide to behave collusively and, for example, dismiss the board of directors. The fact that we observe no such case of collective action suggests that friendly shareholders choose to support the directors because it is profitable to do so. The power of directors comes first, and friendly shareholders are selected because they are supposed to be friendly to the directors. When once friendly large shareholders threaten the present management, the directors change their selection of the friendly shareholders. Cross-shareholdings or group share-holdings (for example, among 'corporate group' firms) are but a result of voluntary choice. Whether the organizational mechanism empowering the board of directors is peculiar to Japan is another question. On the significance of shareholders' power in the American corporation, Alchian and Demsetz (1972, p. 789) state: 'instead of thinking of shareholders as joint owners, we can think of them as investors, like bondholders, except that the stockholders are more optimistic than bondholders about the enterprise prospects'.[21] Whether cross-shareholdings are in the process of diminishing is not apparent.

1.4   PART I: SMALL BUSINESS AND DIVISION OF LABOUR

Part I focuses on Japan's small business or small and medium-sized firms (hereafter, small business), especially before 1970. This is for five reasons.

First, as shown above, Japan's economy has been dominated by small business. Second, Japan's industrial success depends more than anything else upon the success of machinery industries, especially those specializing in fabrication and assembly. As I will mention in detail below, in these industries small business have played essential roles within supplier–assembler relationships for division of labour, called subcontracting (*shitauke*). Third, in focusing on small business, I take issue with the conventional dual structure view, which asserts that, at least before 1970, small businesses were exploited and suffered from large firms' burden-shifting (*shiwayose*). By way of questioning this view I ask: (1) How could such exploited small businesses play essential roles? (2) How could exploited small businesses become as active and creative as they did? (3) Why did exploited small businesses increase both in number and production capacities rather than disappear? (I discuss these questions in Chapter 3.) Fourth, emphasis on small business allows investigation of the common view that even if large Japanese firms are actually rather slim and their total share of employment is rather small, they subordinate many small businesses under *keiretsu* relationships (this term is too vague to define here – see below) and so their presence is greater than their size alone suggests. Fifth, focus on small business also calls into question the role of government policy, for if Japan's success depends on both small business and industrial policy, small business policy must have contributed much. I shall examine whether this has been the case.

I focus on the period before 1970 for three reasons. First, as mentioned above, Japan's GDP in 1970 already exceeded all other G7 countries but the USA, and per capita income was catching up to that of Europe. The growth rate was much higher and the growth process more dynamic before 1970 than after. Japan's economy expanded after 1970, but only on the basis of earlier development. Second, the conventional understanding of Japan's economy prior to 1970 is symbolized by two terms, 'dual structure' and 'monopoly capital' (or *keiretsu*). Support for the dual-structure view weakened significantly by 1970, but most of the keywords of the time are still used in analysing the Japanese economy today. I argue that their continued usage is a source of misunderstanding and confusion about Japan today. In studying small business before 1970 I ask: Why and how did the dual structure collapse? Who destroyed it? What was the role of the government? Was the dual-structure view right? Third, as Chapter 4 details, in 1970 the Japanese motor industry, a symbol of Japan's industrial success, manufactured more than three million cars and exported nearly one million. In 15 years, production had grown from 20 000 units, and the basic features of today's car manufacturing system has become clear. Thus the development process of this industry by 1970 is worth attention.

The core of Part I is Chapter 4, where I examine the formation and workings of the inter-firm relationships for division of labor and the supplier–assembler relationships, otherwise known as subcontracting relationships. First, however, two chapters are devoted to debunking some common myths, since small businesses and their relationships with large firms are so deeply misunderstood. Chapter 2 is the gateway to Part I and with it the whole volume. Its focus is on the concept of dual structure and its validity, which I test by comparing the profit rate of large firms with that of small businesses. Under dual structure assumptions, large firms must be in an advantageous position relative to small businesses, and therefore should enjoy significantly higher profit rates. I show, however, that small business profit rates were double those of large firms and conclude that the dual-structure view of the economy before 1970 is totally wrong. By implication, policies enacted on the basis of such faulty analysis (including policies for small business) and current views of the Japanese economy that rely on the dual-structure conceptualization are also misguided.

Chapter 3 answers the three questions listed above related to my third reason for focusing in Part I on Japan's small business. I expand the conclusion in Chapter 2 on the details of the conventional view of dual structure, and closely examine the reality of small business and the effectiveness of policies for them before 1970 when the dual structure was thought to dominate Japan. The dual-structure view is ill-defined, and it basically recognizes Japan as a world of exchange, not by agreement but by coercion. Detailed refutation of the conventional view will be helpful for understanding the reality of small businesses and the role of policies for them. Two propositions follow the discussion: (1) a wide gap has existed between the image and reality of small businesses since the 1950s; (2) the image of small business has changed more radically than the reality. Thus the problem that small business policy was ostensibly designed to address did not exist. Therefore, if the elimination of the 'dual structure' is the standard for measuring the effectiveness of small business policy, the policy could not have been effective. So many new small businesses continuously started operations simply because entrepreneurs found the business promising. Neither miracles nor environmental factors, like history and culture, particular only to Japan have existed for small business. Chapter 3 also includes a critical review of the literature on small business and a detailed introduction to Japanese small business policy. There has been no miraculous small business policy, either.

Chapter 4 examines the formation and mechanism of supplier–assembler relationships or subcontracting relationships in the Japanese motor industry. I ask two questions: (1) Under what incentives have suppliers, particularly small businesses, joined and maintained their commitment to the relationship? (2) How has the system functioned? Supplier–assembler relationships in this industry are quite often long term, implying that participants commit in offering a kind of monopolistic position to the partner. How each participant has protected itself from the evils of monopoly is a third critical question. Because of its success, readers often assume that the motor industry was powerful and efficient from the start, and lack knowledge of the history of its development and success. In chapter 4 long sections are devoted to a critical review of the academic literature, industrial history and common misunderstandings of both.

Even those impressed by the description of the Japanese motor industry should not mistake its message: decentralization and the division of labour among independent firms is not effective everywhere, Toyota's production system is not easy to imitate and not the way to success for everybody. Part IV focuses again on organizations and inter-firm relationhips.

1.5 PART II: FINANCIAL MARKET

The three chapters in Part II investigate the loan-concentration mechanism, main banks and corporate groups, all facets of the conventional view of the postwar Japanese financial system. I conclude that the importance placed on them by the conventional view is wrong not only today but also for the period before 1970, when the dual-structure view was dominant. Coupled with the conclusion in Part I, this implies that the first basic component of the conventional view of the Japanese economy, the view that the Japanese economic system or the economic system peculiar to Japan played a critical role for its success, is totally wrong. Probably because of the dominance in Japan of dogmatic Germanic theory, mentioned above, the literature and discussion on the Japanese economy have been dominated by those focusing on financial factors, such as loans and shareholdings, financial institutions like banks, and financial markets like loan markets and stock markets.

The loan-concentration mechanism is a component, and for some the basis, of the dual-structure view. Loan concentration is directly related to small business, which has dominated the Japanese economy. Accordingly, Chapter 5 is the most important chapter in Part II. The loan-concentration view asserts that a *de facto* mechanism in the Japanese financial sector directed loans to large firms rather than small businesses, thereby harming the financial interests of small business. Such discrimination, called *keiretsu* loan, is supposedly more clear during periods of tight money policy and so-called 'burden shifting' or *shiwayose*. If Japan's financial markets were a world of exchange by agreement rather than by coercion and those markets were competitive, the loan-concentration mechanism could neither have worked nor existed. In Chapter 5, after showing why I think the loan-concentration view is unpersuasive and invalid even in the decade beginning in the mid-1950s, I review both the theory and the evidence for the conventional view, and conclude that the loan-concentration view is wrong.

While Chapter 5 focuses on small business, the next two chapters investigate the relationship between financial markets and large firms, the alleged beneficiaries of burden shifting. The loan-concentration view argues that large banks dominate the Japanese financial market and each large bank has a special relationship, an 'adhesion relationship', with a group of large firms towards which it directs its loans (*keiretsu* loans). The main-bank view argues that Japanese large firms have special long-term relationships, called main bank relationships, with one or more large banks, and that these relationships pervade the Japanese financial market influencing Japan's industrial organization. Each large bank has such a relationship with a group of large firms, otherwise known as corporate groups. The corporate group view asserts that these groups are important for understanding the Japanese economy. In reading Chapters 6 and 7 the reader should keep in mind that the firms under consideration are large and occupy a small portion of the Japanese economy. (Recall that even when we count all the firms with more than 300 employees as large firms, they employ only 25 per cent of the manufacturing workforce.)

Chapter 6 is almost a direct translation of a 1985 paper. (In Section 6.6, I comment on more recent literature on the main bank relationship.) In Chapter 6 I argue that the phenomena predicted by proponents of the main bank view for the decade preceding the mid-1980s are not in fact observed. In this respect I find that the main bank view resembles the dual structure view: both are asserted and supported without clear definition or evidence.

Readers who accept the arguments up to Chapter 6 need not read Chapter 7 on corporate groups. Though corporate groups and *keiretsu* are common parlance, the terms are seldom used with precision. In Chapter 7 I focus on the six major corporate groups, such as the Mitsubishi Group, the Mitsui Group and the Sumitomo Group. Recent studies in English distinguish three types of corporate groups or *keiretsu*;[22] of these, we study 'production' or 'vertical' *keiretsu* in Chapter 4. A brief note on 'distribution' *keiretsu* is given in Chapter 12, while 'horizontal' *keiretsu* are treated in Chapter 7. Like the concepts of a main bank and dual structure, the corporate group view suffers from poor definition and little evidence. Many simply conflate today's corporate groups with the prewar *zaibatsu*. They take the importance of firm's collective decisions and actions for the common goal as obvious, which makes empirical investigation difficult.[23] Since there is no agreement on the definition of the corporate group view, I use Miyazaki (1976) to illustrate what the view amounts to, and explain why I never take it seriously. I entitle the chapter 'An Anatomy and Critique of the Corporate-Group View', instead of 'Analysis'.

As basic information for Part II, note the following. First, the number of financial institutions has not been small, as mentioned above in Section 1.3. Second, even a large firm with close long-term links to one large bank does not borrow a very high ratio of its total borrowing from that bank. As will be shown in Chapter 6, such big *keiretsu* borrowers as general trading companies and real estate companies in the 1970s borrowed less than 20 per cent of their total needs from their main bank. Third, small businesses also borrow from large banks. As will be shown in Chapter 5, between 1963 and 1965, 35.6 per cent of total borrowing by small business in manufacturing came from city banks and another 26.0 per cent came from regional banks.[24]

1.6 PART III: INDUSTRIAL POLICY

Part III focuses on the role of the government, particularly the 'industrial policy', and examines the validity of the other basic component of the conventional view of the Japanese economy: the belief that under the guise of industrial policy the Japanese government has used strong powers to intervene in the private sector, which contributed much to Japan's industrial success. As mentioned in Section 1.3, this is one of the five basic misconceptions of the Japanese economy. Like other technical jargons invented for talks on the Japanese economy and critically reviewed in Parts I and II, neither clear definition of nor wide agreement on the concept of 'industrial policy' exists. As a result, under the title of 'industrial policy', many have talked about different matters. They discussed the effectiveness of industrial policy, caring little for the difference. For supporters of the 'Japan-is-different' view, and the 'Japan-Inc.' view, the importance of industrial policy is so obvious that they simply search for episodes and anecdotes consistent with this view. Accordingly, they tend to include a wider group of policy measures than is really covered by 'industrial policy'. Moreover, because of Japan's impressive industrial success, again many are inclined to search for something peculiar and make illogical conclusions.

To ask, 'Can industrial policy be effective in promoting the growth of the economy?' is almost the same as asking, 'Can the government do anything for the economic growth?' The answer to these questions is 'probably yes', which, however, is too general to draw a policy recommendation. Critical questions are 'How can the government promote the growth?' and 'Under what conditions can it be effective?' Therefore Japan's industrial policy attracts wide attention. Whether Japan's government policy contributed much to its rapid growth is another question. For this we have to carry out a carefully designed empirical examination.

A wide variety of topics on industrial policy are discussed at once, and two questions have to be distinguished: (1) What should the government do for industries to promote economic growth and productivity? (2) What could it do and did it actually do for that purpose? Many discuss market failures as the basis for industrial policy and search for anecdotes as evidence for its effectiveness, often backed up by the bureaucratized 'Japan-Inc.' view. However, as Stigler (1975, p. 113) pointed out, 'We may tell the society to jump out of the market frying pan, but we have no basis for predicting whether it will land in the fire or a luxurious bed'. Besides, policies are formed and carried out through the political process, and ideal policies, to answer the first question above, will not necessarily be chosen for four reasons. First, the government may not follow the target. It may prefer 'equity' to 'efficiency'.[25] Second, the government may not have the capability to beat the market, so that, not only the market but the government fails. As revealed by the recent collapse of socialist economies, the centralized economy is too complicated to be efficient. Third, environments function as strong restrictions to policy choices. For example, Japan's administration system inescapably results in indiscriminate policy decisions. As shown in Chapter 3, the government, with broad public support and enthusiastic political backing, has put much emphasis on policies for small business. But it has been too thinly spread and indiscriminate to be effective. Fourth, the government has neither strong powers to choose freely the ideal policies nor strong trust and support from firms and the public to carry out these policies.

Chapters 9 and 10 are the core of Part III, in which I investigate the details of one type of 'industrial policy', that for coordination within industry, particularly that for equipment investment coordination prior to 1970, the so-called 'heyday' of industrial policy. I look closely at what occurred in the industry and how government intervention influenced individual firms' behaviour and industrial performance. Chapter 9 is a detailed case study of the equipment investment coordination in the steel industry. Chapter 10 is a generalization of the conclusion of Chapter 9 into three types—output, price and investment—expanding reference also to oil refining. Chapter 8 is an introduction to these two chapters and explains the historical background of the policies for industries in the 1960s, listing several points for beginners to learn Japan's industrial policy.

Chapters 9 and 10 focus on the question of what the government could do and actually did do to promote growth and productivity increase, which is purely empirical. Coordination within industry and related policies have three characteristics. First, such policy does not require money, and can be carried out without outside budgetary check, for example, by the Diet and the Ministry of Finance. Second, it is essentially a cartel promoting and supporting policy. Therefore it was in the interest of the majority of incumbents and was the most popular type of policy intervention towards industry. Third, as discussed in Chapter 8, the central issue of the 'new industrial order debate' around 1960 was the role of this type of intervention, where MITI failed in the attempt to strengthen its power by enacting the Specified Industries Act. I focus on policies in the 1960s, since this decade is the heyday of industrial policy.[26] I conclude that the role of the policy and its contribution to Japan's industrial success even in the heyday were, at most, negligible.[27] The government has lost the power step by step with a series of 'liberalizations', which suggests that this conclusion also applies in the 1970s and onward.

In reading Part III, four points should be noted. First, I do not discuss 'targeting policy' in the 1970s, for instance, and whether my conclusion also applies to such cases is another question. My argument below, however, suggests that the factors conditioning policy for 'coordination within industry' also apply to industrial policy in general. For this, one has to examine carefully whether none of such factors as the characteristics of the administration system, the government's capability, and the government's power has functioned as a restriction on its effectiveness. We should be careful not to simply search for episodes of 'successful targeting policy' on the assumption that it was successful. The next question for those who believe it was successful is, 'Why has it occurred in Japan, not in socialist economies where the government has much stronger power?' Some may comment that Japan's R&D policy has enjoyed great success, referring to the VLSI Technology Research Association. But this is also an example of searching for an episode to fit an assumption. As Wakasugi (1986, pp. 146-66, especially p. 163) pointed out, this case was rather exceptional and on average, research associations established on the same law (the Mining and

Manufacturing Technology Research Association Act enacted in 1961) were neither productive nor efficient.

Second, any investigation into the role of government policy requires a careful identification of the policy's effect. Many talk about industrial policy without considering this point, which results in an overvaluation of the effect. Quite often firms talk about a cooperative action by themselves and then ask the government (their counterpart) to mask their action under the guise of 'policy'. In these cases the role of the government is only a veil, but many tend to include all related individual firms' actions in the policy evaluation. As shown below, in the cases of cooperation within industry, the role of the government was almost always passive and marginal. My negative conclusion is composed of two parts: (1) the government played a minor role; (2) trials for coordination did not last long and had no serious effects on individual firms' behaviour. Thus I conclude that the sum of the effect of policy and that of individual firms' coordinating behaviour was negligible.

Third, why Japanese industrial policy was ineffective is another question. The reasons must be multiple, such as the characteristics of the administration system and the powers of the government. Even when the government could overcome most of those factors which may function as a restriction on its effectiveness, the capability of the government must be the final barrier as the history of socialist economies proved. In the long run I believe no government is able to beat the market.

Fourth, 'industrial policy' is not peculiar to Japan. Whatever the title is, government intervention in industries was more usual and more forceful, at least in socialist economies, than in Japan. Also the term 'industrial policy' was so popular in the UK in the 1910s and 1920s as to lead to the publishing of a government report in 1918, 'Committee on Commercial and Industrial Policy after the War, *Final Report*',[28] for instance, and the Japanese term *sangyo seisaku* (industrial policy) was a translation in the 1960s of a French term, *'politique industrielle'*. It was the Prime Minister of the UK, John Major, who made the following comment at the CBI Annual Dinner on 18 May 1993:

> You create the world class companies. But in a thousand ways, the decisions that we take in Government can help you or hinder you. So we, too, are part of Britain's competitiveness. All our policies – not just our economic policy – need to be focused on the future strength of the British economy.

1.7 PART IV: INTRA-FIRM ORGANIZATION AND INTER-FIRM RELATIONSHIPS

Part IV focuses on intra-firm organization and inter-firm relationships in Japan. In Parts I to III, I assumed a neoclassical firm as the basic decision-making unit. This real world neoclassical firm is controlled by shareholders, who use the board of directors as their agent. This firm purchases factors of production other than 'capital' in the market. The firm's objective is to maximize profit under given constraints, such as the production function and demand conditions. Also I assumed zero transaction costs, unless otherwise stated. Transaction costs are not zero, however, and institutions do matter. If we are interested in the formation and function of firms, inter-firm relationships and the market, we must closely examine the validity of the above assumptions. Such an analysis is essential for understanding Japan's intra-firm organization and inter-firm relationships.

The predominance of small business and the slimness of large firms are the two basic facts of the Japanese economy. One possible source of Japan's industrial success is the effective use of inter-firm division of labour. There are several issues related to this observation. Who coordinates this division among individual agents and how is this accomplished? Are there any specific institutional arrangements which make this coordination easy? Why have these arrangements functioned particularly well in Japan?

Debate surrounding the Japanese economy is full of stylized facts, many of which are due to fundamental misunderstandings or are based on uncertain grounds. There is a strong temptation to depend on these misleading facts when explaining Japan's industrial success which often leads us to the 'Japan-is-different' view. Each of those conventional views and models of the Japanese economy, such as the dual-structure view, *keiretsu* 'loan' model, main 'bank' model and corporate 'group' model, is based on such stylized facts. Each of them also has its own specific view of the coordinating agent and related institutional arrangements. As shown above on both theoretical and empirical grounds, however, these views are incorrect. Some may argue that 'the market' alone can explain the coordination. The 'market' explanation is correct; however, it is almost always unsatisfactory and we want to proceed beyond this. As I mention in Section 11.2, economists do not have a highly developed theory either of the firm or of the market. Therefore it is sometimes misleading to analyse these issues with established standard economic models. However, I will approach these issues with theories that incorporate real world features of a firm, though such theories are still rudimentary. In this way we can begin to understand the organizational issues concerning the Japanese economy far better than when depending on the conventional view alone. This will, in return, contribute to the study of the firm and the market in general.

Part IV focuses on two specific aspects of Japanese firms: corporate governance in Japanese firms in Chapter 11 and inter-firm relationships in Chapter 12. To begin a study of intra-firm organization and inter-firm relationships, we need a definition of the firm. Therefore the discussion in Chapter 11 begins with three questions related to the definition. First, what are the boundaries of a firm? Second, who decides the boundaries and internal organization of a firm? Finally, how are these boundaries related to the legal definition of a firm? Underlying these is the basic question of Coase (1937): 'why [does] a firm [emerge] at all in a specialized exchange economy?'

My argument in Part IV is basically the nexus of contract theory associated with Jensen and Mechling (1976). The central point for organizational issue is, using Simon's (1976) words, who is 'the controlling group', that is, who has the power to set the terms of membership for all the participants. With the importance of employees' investment in organization-specific human capital formation, the body of employees takes this key position, and selects the directors as their representative. Other stakeholders such as friendly shareholders and friendly lenders rationally agree with the controlling group. Since a firm in the real world is a legal fiction, the legal boundary of a firm usually does not coincide with the boundary used by this controlling group in their decision making. A firm, for Coase in particular and economic analysis in general, is a set of activities and/or agents within this effective boundary, and therefore is different from a firm both in the real world and in statistics. Accordingly, many economic phenomena related to the organization must be re-examined, such as the predominance of small business and the slimness of large firms in the Japanese economy. For this controlling group the legal boundary is only one of the constraints for its decision making process and may not significantly affect the intra-firm organization and inter-firm relationship. The inside–outside distinction of a firm, as prescribed by Coase, depends on transaction costs. Here again the legal definition does not necessarily affect the economic definition of a firm. In this view, even for a firm owner–manager it is in their interest to be friendly to the body of employees. Therefore the question of whether the management is separated from control is irrelevant.

Since a firm is a legal fiction and its boundary is usually different from the effective boundary of the decision-making unit, the two basic facts of the Japanese economy do not necessarily imply that the effective boundary of the Japanese organization is small and that the Japanese economy is idiosyncratically decentralized. In Chapter 12 we consider how organizations and inter-organizational relationships form and function, how the economic activities within each firm are coordinated, and who assumes the leadership in designing the system for this coordination.

Most of this chapter is a series of case studies on inter-firm relationships from three points: (1) whether 'transaction costs', particularly for large Japanese firms, are lower than elsewhere. (2) whether these relationships fail to respond to changes in the market environment, like demand and technology and (3) whether new entry to some Japanese markets is more difficult than elsewhere, and even impossible in some cases, because of these relationships. I present five case studies from three industries. The first is the supplier–assembler relationships in the motor industry. The other four cases are from industries regarded as not so successful: one from the distribution sector and three from the textile industry. The basic objective of these case studies is to investigate Japanese inter-firm relationships in action, and apply to them now developing theories of the firm. In this manner we can reach an understanding of the organizational issues far better than with the traditional theories. In return this will contribute to the study of the firm and the market, because Japanese firms and their inter-firm relationships are a rich source of materials for the further research along this line.

Four observations follow these case studies. (1) An extensive division of labour with long-term relationships prevails throughout Japan. (2) These relationships are formed and maintained as a result of voluntary agreement of rational participants. A new entrant offering a profitable business opportunity in this manner develops such relationships with its trade partners. (3) 'Transaction costs' through these relationships are not particularly low for large firms in comparatively advantaged industries. (4) Firms within these relationships often fail to adapt to the environmental changes, partly because of these relationships. This can also be explained as the rational choice of related parties not to adapt. The last point is observed not only in rather comparatively disadvantaged industries but in advantaged industries as well. In Section 12.9, I discuss one most striking peculiarity of Japan's industrial organization, namely, the predominance of stable, long-term inter-firm relationships with a non-exclusive characteristic.

Part IV studies Japanese firms alone, but it is never argued that they are different in any sense from firms in other countries. The nature of the basic logic underlying the discussion in Part IV – that the fundamental factor which determines the form, character and workings of organizations is organization-specific human capital found in the body of employees–is technological and therefore not peculiar to any one country. When a crucial difference is observed between economies, it must be caused by some environmental factors, such as the legal system, history or culture. As I mention in Section 11.9, outside Japan we find the same type of observations and arguments on both the corporate governance of firms and the nature of economic organizations.

1.8   A PRIOR REJOINDER

Like my previous book in Japanese (Miwa, 1990a), this volume will arouse strong reactions from various sides, some of which will use expressions such as iconoclastic, controversial and eccentric. Mostly they arise because of the tradition mentioned in the first section of this chapter: it is only recently that many economists began to talk about the Japanese economy with the standard economics principles. This is a volume by an economist written primarily for two groups: for the scholars and students of economics and for comparativists interested in Japan. A prior rejoinder to some reactions will be helpful for better understanding of this volume and for avoiding confusions.

Some may complain that this volume does not talk about the secret of Japan's industrial success, and ask for an explanation for this omission. First, neither Japanese nor American firms (or firms in other countries) are particularly badly managed. The reason is straightforward: most badly managed firms either fire their managers and improve their performance, or go out of business. 'Elementary notions of comparative advantages suggest that some firms in any country will *always* be uncompetitive compared to firms in the same industry elsewhere' (Ramseyer, 1993, p. 2020). Therefore I take four out of five case studies in Chapter 12 from not so successful industries and conclude that we observe almost the same characteristics in inter-firm relationships in these industries as those in the successful motor industry. Second, I am part of the majority of economists, identified as the 'non-miracle-occurred' school by Chalmers Johnson (1982, p. 9). This school 'does not literally assert that nothing happened to Japan's economy, but they imply that what did happen was not miraculous but a normal outgrowth of market forces'. The following statement by Hugh Patrick, quoted in Johnson (1982, p. 8) represents this view:

> I am of the school which interprets Japanese economic performance as due primarily to the actions and efforts of private individuals and enterprises responding to the opportunities provided in quite free markets for commodities and labour. While the government has been supportive and indeed has done much to create the environment for growth, its role has often been exaggerated. (Patrick, 1977, p. 239)

This has led many, typically political scientists such as Johnson and David Friedman (1988), to ask who then led, or who made, such a miracle. These scholars will not accept the 'invisible hands' view suggested by economists as a persuasive answer. Readers who subscribe to this view are asked to consider a similar question put forward in the 1920s by non-Americans, such as Europeans or Japanese: who led, or what made, the miracle of the rapid growth of the American economy after the nineteenth century? My answer, like that of many economists, would be 'invisible hands'. Third, I simply do not have any clearer explanation of Japan's industrial success than the majority of economists, and I should say that I wish I had. Like most economists (and probably like most scientists), I will not claim to explain all aspects of Japanese economic phenomena.

In reading this volume (and the literature and discussions about the Japanese economy), it is important to keep in mind that in Japan people usually speak, write and document in Japanese, and only a small portion of this is translated into English. In addition, because of the above mentioned tradition, almost all the literature and materials in Japanese are still based on the view that Japan is a world of exchange by coercion rather than by agreement. Recent writings in English even by economists who read Japanese often follow the same line, by adopting the conventional view without careful examination. Some simply reproduce the conventional views and models of Japanese economic phenomena, while others reinterpret them through the standard principles of economics, resulting in only a cosmetic change, like *keiretsu* loans to main bank relationships. As shown in Chapter 6, in this case the phenomena to be explained never existed and the assumption underlying the argument was invalid. Thus they are like attacks with high-tech weapons on a sand castle or a mirage.

To readers who reply that, where there is smoke, there is fire, I would like to mention a Japanese proverb coming originally from China: 'One dog barks at a shadow, and a hundred dogs at the voice' (an approximate equivalent in English may be 'Much ado about nothing') and ask them to recall what the wrong dual-structure view was and what the fire was. My work on the corporate group model in Chapter 7 is analogous to examining the validity of the existence of UFOs. Others may respond as did Wallich and Wallich (1976, p. 253): '[I]t is tempting . . . to show that economics works in Japan as it does elsewhere. . . . [But a] triumphant finding that the laws of economics do apply to Japan and that, economically speaking, Japan after all is not very different may be misleading'. But what else can explain economic behaviour? Some search for differences in Japan, on the assumption that 'it is obvious that the system differs greatly from Western systems in both its structure and its behavior' (ibid.). This is what many supporters of the incorrect conventional view have done.

Readers may comment, 'why so much discussion and new literature on Japan's main banks and industrial policy?' My answer is threefold. First, many ignore the *post hoc, ergo propter hoc* fallacy. Second, strong demand for the discussion and literature exists among politicians, government officials, journalists and academics, particularly in the former socialist economies. It creates the supply, which the politicians and government officials in Japan support enthusiastically both on the belief of the effectiveness of government policy and for their own self-justification. Third, as is usually the case, the authors of the literature on main banks, for example, are only those who are interested in them. Thus, there now exist the 'main bank literature industry' and the 'Japan's industrial policy literature industry'.

Some may list 'important issues' and criticize this volume for ignoring them: it does not talk about the secret of Japan's industrial success; it does not fully investigate the labour market; it ignores important political factors; and it does not even investigate the basic question of why Japanese firms decided to subcontract rather than produce 'in-house'. In commenting on Professor John K. Galbraith's *The New Industrial State*, Solow (1967, pp. 100–101) used the distinction of big thinkers and little thinkers. Big thinkers made important decisions, such as what to do about Jerusalem, and how to deal with crime in the streets, while little thinkers made unimportant decisions, such as what job they should take, where they should live and how to bring up children. Economists are determined little thinkers, and this is a book not for the dinner table but for the desk.

1.9 CONCLUSION

Is the Japanese economy different from other economies? Are Japanese firms and industrial organizations different from those in other economies? Will studies of Japanese firms and industrial organizations provide something instructive for restructuring individual organizations and development of other economies? The answers are, of course, both yes and no.

As Coase (1988, p. 5) noted, the firm in economic theory has been a shadowy figure. Many argue, like Holmstrom and Tirole (1989, p. 63):

[F]irms have, as ever-developing institutions, played a central role in the growth and prosperity of a country's economy. In tandem with technological innovations, innovations in firm organization have enhanced welfare greatly. It would seem essential to understand the underlying forces behind such institutional dynamics, both for a proper appreciation of how institutions have conditioned economic development and for policy decisions that relate to institutional change.

It is my purpose to demonstrate that the standard principles of economics explain the dominant patterns of Japanese economic phenomena. The principles are not those anyone invented to explain Japan. Indeed, they were not invented to explain any particular society. Nowhere in this volume do I argue that Japan is different from other societies. My argument needs no jargon, including *keiretsu*, corporate groups, main banks and industrial policy, invented for and frequently used in the literature on the Japanese economy, except when I introduce and critically review the conventional view. Japanese firms and industrial organization deserve wide attention, not because of their *international competitiveness*, which is a ridiculous idea (on this point, see Krugman, 1994a), but because of the huge size of the economy and the history of its development. Most Japanese firms are well-run; most American firms are well-run. Most badly managed firms either fire their managers and improve their performance, or go out of business. Since the thirteenth century, when the descriptions of Cipango or Zipangu in Marco Polo's book *Il Milione* set a definite goal for Columbus in his journey, Japan has been a rich source of imagination and myth, particularly for Westerners. Even today Japan still remains full of misunderstanding and mythfication. I hope that this volume will push us in the direction of a fuller, more proper understanding of the Japanese economy.

I wish to deal only with Japan, and only with the basic contours of firm behaviour and market function, which I consider challenge enough. But this is not an area study. Every country has its peculiarity; so does every firm or group of firms. Hence each country, firm or group of firms can survive in a market economy. It is my hope that other scholars will provide comparable volumes for other economies, which will enable us to carry out comparative studies of firms and industrial organization. This is, of course, not for *international competitiveness*, but both for a deeper understanding of organizations and markets in action and also for the development of the theory of the firm and the market. The Japanese economy is distinctive enough to merit close investigation; so are other economies.

Part I
Small Business and Division of Labour

2 Monopoly, Corporate Profits and the Dual Structure

2.1 INTRODUCTION

The first half of the postwar period almost entirely corresponds to Japan's 'high growth era', 1951–73 (see T. Nakamura, 1993, p. 164). During this time, the economy grew at a stable annual average real rate of 10 percent, much faster than in the most recent decades, whose growth has itself been much higher than that of other OECD countries. Although interest in Japan's economy has intensified in recent years, the early postwar years remain worthy of study, partly because current economic strength is built upon earlier growth.[1] Furthermore, nearly all the keywords used to analyse the economy in recent years were employed in earlier postwar decades as well, implying that the conventional understanding of the economy in earlier years was and remains effective today. I will show, however, that the conventional wisdom was totally wrong, and that these same mistaken concepts applied to today's economy result in faulty understanding.

The heart of Japan's early postwar growth is the decade from the mid-1950s onward. At the time, the Japanese were divided over the causes and character of the rapid growth, the future of the Japanese economy and the role of government in the growth process. Debate was sharp and exuberant, but suffered from ill-defined terms and poor reasoning, even in scholarly treatments. Prominent terms of the day (or keywords) included: monopoly capital, dual structure, exploitation, subordination (or dependence), *shiwayose* ('using as a cushion' or 'burden-shifting'), finance capital, *keiretsu* loan, loan concentration, corporate groups, capital *keiretsu*, grouping (group-*ka*[2]), main bank, *keiretsu-ka*, *shitauke* (subcontracting), large enterprises versus small and medium-sized enterprises, modernization, and rationalization. It is uncontroversial to state that monopoly capital and dual structure were the most important among them. Despite strongly divided views on other subjects, all participants in these debates used these terms, thereby implying common acceptance of their validity.

Over the three decades since then, Japan has attained remarkable industrial success and has significantly raised its level of per capita income, industrial technology and its presence in the world economy. Views of Japanese economy among observers both at home and abroad have also changed. Several previously common terms of analysis have been dropped, but most are still popular and are used for industrial and policy analysis. These include: main bank, corporate groups, *keiretsu* loans, subcontracting (*shitauke*), burden-shifting (*shiwayose*) and large versus small and medium-sized enterprises (small business).

In this chapter, I focus on the keyword,[3] dual structure. I examine its validity by comparing the profit rate of large firms with that of small business. Under the dual structure large firms are expected to be in an advantageous position relative to small business, and therefore their profit rate should be significantly higher. However, the profit rate of small businesses has been much higher than that of large firms, even in the heyday of the dual-structure view in the 1950s and 1960s. Thus, in the following sections, I show empirically that the view of the economy in the 1950s and 1960s, which relied entirely on the concepts of a dual economy and monopoly capital for explanation, is wrong. I suggest that contemporary views of the Japanese economy which share reliance on the same use of terms are also faulty. Therefore I conclude that the policies for industries built on the basis of such faulty analysis, especially small business policy, are wrong. Section 2.2 defines the problem, section 2.3 discusses empirical tests and section 2.4 offers concluding remarks. This chapter is the gateway for the whole book.

2.2 DEFINING THE PROBLEM

The government's *Economic White Paper* in 1956 is famous for declaring 'no longer are we in the postwar age', and the next *White Paper* asserted the existence and emphasized the seriousness of the 'dual structure' of the Japanese economy. This argument gained immediate acceptance and 'dual structure' became one of the most popular phrases of the time. This view apparently struck a responsive chord among the public, and the term became a keyword in the study of the Japanese economy. The words 'dual structure' suggest two distinct sectors in the economy, one consisting of small, traditional enterprises (hereafter, small business) with low productivity and low wages, and another consisting of large firms with modern technology, high productivity and high wages.

Closely related to 'dual structure' is the view that large firms in the modernized industrial sector subordinate, control and exploit small businesses in the traditional sector. This view assumes that large firms had and could exercise power to exploit small businesses, whose freedom of choice was tightly restricted and likened to a 'hold-up' situation. Large firms were called 'monopoly capital'. Many Japanese recognized this situation as a social problem to be solved by government intervention, such as through policies for small business.[4]

The Japanese supported this view unanimously and strongly. With the exception of Ryutaro Komiya (1961a, 1961b, 1962), no article challenged this view until Miwa (1988), upon which this chapter is based.[5] Komiya (1962) attacked the dual-structure view by testing the hypothesis that, when 'monopoly' or 'monopoly capital' had and could exercise power to exploit small business, their profit rates should be significantly higher than that of small business. He found that in 1953–59 the average profit rate (net profits before tax divided by paid-in capital) of large firms – firms with more than 100 million yen in capital – was lower than that of any other class of firms, and that there was a wide difference in profit rate between large firms and small businesses.[6]

Unanimous support for the dominant view precluded serious debate over the causes and functions of the 'dual structure', and there remained untouched a wide variety of views and models of Japanese economic phenomena related to this view. Four advantages for large firms can be distinguished as part of the dual-structure view.[7] However, Komiya's rebuttal of the dual-structure view as a whole may also invalidate each corollary argument.

1. A 'loan-concentration mechanism', making the profit rate of large firms higher than that of small business, was established as a result of both *keiretsu* loans (where large banks loan preferentially to closely related large firms) and the government subsidies and preferential loans for large firms.[8]
2. Large firms enjoy advantages in the labour market, making their profit rate higher than that of small business.[9]
3. Large firms exploit their advantageous position for high profit rates by purchasing products from low-wage small business and selling their own products at higher prices than small business.
4. The markets small business dominate are easy to enter and more competitive than others, driving profit rates down relative to large firms.

Unanimous and strong support for the dual-structure view does not mean that it is well-defined or coherently expressed. The definition of large firms is critically important in order to distinguish large firms from small businesses, but no authoritative definition existed until the adoption of the Small and Medium-sized Enterprise Basic Act in 1963.[10] Komiya (1962) divided firms into six classes in terms of their paid-in capital. His conclusion does not depend on the definition of large firms: whatever the line between large firms and small businesses may be, the average profit rate of large firms is lower than that of small businesses.

Komiya (1962) immediately elicited wide attention and a sharp reaction from the supporters of the dominant view,[11] but I find that it had little impact either on views of the Japanese economy or on small business policy debates.

Following Komiya (1962), therefore, I carry out the same test for 1960–84 below and find that the same conclusion holds during this period also. Komiya's findings cover rather a short period in the 1950s, the early stage of the 'high growth era', and have been criticized as being a result of chance. My finding implies that his conclusion is robust and applies not only throughout the 'high growth era' but also beyond. This strongly suggests that some of the conjectures favouring the higher profitability of large firms are invalid, which in turn implies that the dominant view of the time, which remains as the conventional view today, is totally wrong.

2.3 FIRM SCALE AND PROFITABILITY, 1960–84

The Small and Medium-sized Enterprise Basic Act was enacted in 1963 with broad public support and enthusiastic political backing. Ironically, however, with rapid economic growth in the 1960s, support for the dual-structure view weakened rapidly. By 1970, the *Small Business White Paper* was subtitled: 'The Transformation of the Dual Structure and the Variety of Small Business Problems'. Either the conditions facing small business or the public's image of small business had changed.[12]

Three positions are identifiable in the literature. Position 1 asserts that the dual-structure view was valid in the 1950s and the first half of the 1960s but disappeared in the second half of the 1960s. Position 2 asserts that dual structure conditions existed throughout the period under study. Position 3 asserts that the dual-structure view has been invalid since the 1950s. Positions 1 and 2 are further divided into two sub-positions.

Position 1: The dual structure was valid in the 1950s and the first half of the 1960s, but it changed rapidly. Hence the large firms' profit rate should be higher than small business's before the second half of the 1960s and the difference should disappear thereafter. *Position 1a*: Komiya's (1962) results are a matter of chance, and the remaining period to the mid-1960s should show that large firms have a higher profit rate. *Position 1b*: Komiya's (1962) results are based on biased data. As this bias holds throughout, the remaining years before the mid-1960s should show the same result as Komiya (1962) and large firms' profit rates thereafter should be much lower than those of small business.

Position 2: There has been no change in the seriousness of dual structure conditions. Hence the profit rate of large firms should be higher than that of small business throughout the period. *Position 2a*: Komiya's (1962) results were a result of chance, and the remaining period throughout should show the large firms' higher profit rate. *Position 2b*: Komiya's (1962) findings are the result of biased data. As this bias holds throughout, the remaining years should show the same result as Komiya (1962).

Position 3: The dual-structure view has been invalid since the 1950s. Throughout the remaining years, the profit rate of large firms should not be higher than that of small business.

See Table 2.1 and Figure 2.1. Following Komiya (1962), I use data from the Ministry of Finance, *Hojin kigyo tokei nenpo* (*Financial statement of incorporated business*, annual), which divides all incorporated business firms into six groups on the basis of their paid-in capital. Table 2.1 shows before-tax rates of profit on equity (paid-in capital) of corporate enterprises in all industries. Columns 2 to 6 show the five-year average of annual profit rates for each group. Columns 7 to 9 show the number of years of below-average profit rates for the periods 1960–84, 1960–74, and 1975–84. For readers' convenience, in column 1 I adopt Komiya's average profit rate for 1953–59. For 1960–84 I omit firms with less than 2 million yen in capital because they are too small, and divide firms with more than 100 million yen into two groups, firms between 100 million yen and one billion yen, and those over

Figure 2.1   Rate of profit on equity (paid-in capital) of corporate enterprises in Japan, before tax, all industries (per cent)

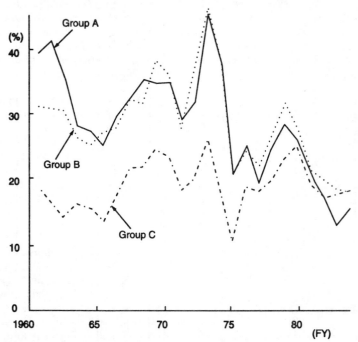

Group A: Enterprises with 5–10 million yen in capital
Group B: Enterprises with 10–50 million yen in capital
Group C: Enterprises with more than 1 billion yen in capital

Source: Adapted from Miwa (1990a, p. 13, Figure 1.1).

one billion yen.[13] Figure 2.1 shows the annual profit rate for three selected groups. Small businesses are represented by Group A and Group B firms with 5–10 million yen and 10–50 million yen of paid-in capital, respectively. Large firms are represented by Group C: firms with more than 1 billion yen in paid-in capital.[14]

Table 2.1 and Figure 2.1 show that Komiya's (1962) result for the 1950s holds also for the 1960s and 1970s. Only after the first oil crisis does change begin to appear, but its direction is contrary to the intuitive view that the relative profitability of small business improved after the mid-1960s. As Figure 2.1 shows, small business profit rates were almost twice as high as those of large firms in the 1960s and 1970s.

Table 2.2 uses after-tax profit rate data instead of before-tax rate data as in Table 2.1, and Table 2.3 uses data for manufacturing only instead of the data

Table 2.1 Rate of profit on equity (paid-in capital) of corporate enterprises in Japan, before tax, all industries

Firm size by equity (¥ million)	Profit rate (5-year running average)						Number of years below average profit rate		
	1953–59	1960–64	1965–69	1970–74	1975–79	1980–84	1960–84	1960–74	1975–84
2–5	22.4	32.4	30.7	34.6	22.2	16.1	7	0	7
5–10	20.9	34.1	31.4	35.4	23.0	17.8	6	0	6
10–50	21.2	28.7	31.2	35.5	24.4	20.9	1	0	1
150–100	18.7	25.3	26.7	30.4	23.1	24.4	2	0	2
100–1000	} 13.1	20.5	23.3	25.6	22.0	22.3	12	10	2
1000+		16.2	19.8	21.3	17.8	19.5	23	15	8

Note: Figures for 1953–59 are adapted from Ryutaro Komiya (1962, Supplemental Table A).
Source: Ministry of Finance, *Hojin Kigyo Tokei Nenpo (Financial Statement of Incorporated Business)* (Tokyo: Ministry of Finance, annual); adapted from Miwa (1990a, p.13, Table 1.1).

Table 2.2 Rate of profit on equity (paid-in capital) of corporate enterprises in Japan, after tax, all industries

Firm size by equity (¥ million)	Profit rate (5-year running average)						Number of years below average profit rate		
	1953–59	1960–64	1965–69	1970–74	1975–79	1980–84	1960–84	1960–74	1975–84
2–5	8.3	16.5	18.2	20.3	11.0	4.8	6	0	6
5–10	8.1	17.2	18.3	20.1	11.1	7.4	3	0	3
10–50	9.3	14.5	17.8	18.6	11.3	8.4	2	0	2
50–100	8.9	13.0	14.3	14.9	8.3	9.1	10	7	3
100–1000	} 7.5	0.9	12.7	12.4	7.7	8.3	17	13	4
1000+		9.9	12.7	12.5	7.5	8.7	22	15	7

Note: Figures for 1953–59 are adapted from Ryutaro Komiya (1962, Supplemental Table B).
Source: Ministry of Finance, *Hojin Kigyo Tokei Nenpo (Financial statement of incorporated business)* (Tokyo: Ministry of Finance, annual); adapted from Miwa (1990a, p. 15, Table 1.2).

Table 2.3 Rate of profit on equity (paid-in capital) of corporate enterprises in Japan, before tax, manufacturing

Firm size by equity (¥million)	Profit rate (5-Year running average)						Number of years below Average profit rate		
	1953–59	1960–64	1965–69	1970–74	1975–79	1980–84	1960–84	1960–74	1975–84
2–5	23.5	34.0	30.1	33.3	22.3	13.4	6	0	6
5–10	20.4	36.0	33.1	35.2	23.7	18.2	4	0	4
10–50	22.4	30.7	31.8	35.3	24.2	21.4	1	0	1
50–100	19.2	27.2	27.6	31.1	19.1	24.5	2	0	2
100–1000	} 17.0	20.9	24.7	26.2	21.5	22.8	8	7	1
1000+		18.3	21.2	22.0	16.8	18.5	25	15	10

Note: Figures for 1953–59 are adapted from Ryutaro Komiya (1962, Supplemental Table A).
Source: Ministry of Finance, *Hojin Kigyo Tokei Nenpo (Financial statement of incorporated business)* (Tokyo: Ministry of Finance, annual); adapted from Miwa (1990a, p.15, Table 1.3).

in Table 2.1 for all industries. Neither requires any modification of the above results.

Positions 1a and 2a should be rejected because we obtained the same result for the 1960s as Komiya did for the 1950s. Positions 1a and 1b should be rejected because we obtained the same results for the 1970s as for the 1950s and 1960s.

Positions 2b and 3 remain. Although our tables and figure do not help validate either one, I opt for Position 3 for three reasons: (1) the difference in the profit rate in the 1960s and 1970s is too big to be attributed to alleged data bias;[15] (2) the observed change around 1980 is inconsistent with constant data bias; (3) support for the dual-structure view in the 1970s and 1980s disappeared almost entirely. Hence I reject position 2b and accept Position 3, that is, the dual-structure view has been invalid since the 1950s.[16]

2.4   CONCLUDING REMARKS

The conclusion that the dual-structure view has been invalid since the 1950s leads us directly to reject the view common even today that at least until around 1970 large firms occupied an advantageous position in the Japanese economy relative to small business. Three implications follow.

1. The framework implicitly assumed operative in debates, discussion and even academic research of the era is fatally flawed. It is therefore important to examine closely the validity of the basic framework and assumptions of the arguments in the literature and documents of the time.
2. The thinking behind economic policy of the time, such as that towards small business, was rooted in the dual-structure view, so we must re-examine the appropriateness and effectiveness of policy with this problem in mind.[17]
3. The basic concepts and keywords used in popular debate and research reflect the dual-structure view. Though some are obsolete, most, including terms like main bank, *keiretsu* loans, corporate groups, subcontracting, burden shifting and large firms versus small business, remain as the keywords of discourse for industrial and policy analysis. It is important to examine the definition of such concepts and phrases clearly in order to clarify their meaning. We cannot be too careful in seeking to avoid the unconscious acceptance and intrusion of the dual-structure view in contemporary analysis of Japan's economy.

3 The Image and Reality of Small Business and Small Business Policies

3.1 INTRODUCTION

The Japanese phrase *chusho kigyo* (small- and medium-sized enterprises or small business, hereafter small business) rings heavy and serious for Japanese, especially for social science scholars. At any given time, however, the images brought to mind by the phrase have varied widely, and the dominant image among them has also varied greatly over time.

In the 1980s, two small business images were dominant. The first, which became prominent gradually among small business specialists, emphasizes small business vitality and creativity in their contribution to Japan's rapid economic growth. The emergence of this view paralleled and was backed by two worldwide trends. First, from the 1970s interest in and research on small business grew everywhere. Second, Japan's industrial success, and the recognition that a huge number of small businesses supported it and made it possible, gained worldwide attention. The other dominant image of small business in the 1980s was clearly revealed in media coverage of the rapid yen appreciation after the September 1985 Plaza Accord.[1] Given the common view that small businesses were especially vulnerable to and seriously damaged by yen appreciation, the phrase 'small business in distress through yen appreciation' quickly gained acceptance among the media and society at large.[2]

This chapter answers the following questions. How were the two images of small business related? Why could they coexist? Why did they coexist? Why has the relative strength of public support for each image changed? How big was the scale of this change and how widespread? Has a gap existed since the 1950s between the 'image' and 'reality' of small business? Has the change in the popular image reflected the change in small business realities? How?

What sort of small business policy can be considered appropriate? How accurately has the heated controversy over the means and ends of small business policy reflected both the popular images and the economic reality of small business and the changes therein? Have policies been responsive to changing reality? Has small business policy been appropriate and effective? How has small business policy contributed to Japan's rapid growth?

Two propositions follow from discussions of these questions (1) a wide gap has existed since the 1950s between the popular image and the economic reality of small business; (2) the popular image of small business has changed more radically than reality has, and the change in the 1980s in the image only reduced the gap between them. In short, the problems that small business

41

policy was designed to address, namely the elimination of the 'dual structure', did not exist. If the elimination of the 'dual structure' is the standard for measuring small business policy effectiveness, the policy could not have been 'effective'.

Following Chapter 2, we go into the details of the 'dual structure' and the image and reality of small business therein. We also discuss the position of small business, particularly in the 1960s, in the Japanese economy, and the means and ends of policies used to influence small business. Detailed refutation of the conventional view will be helpful for understanding the reality of small business and the role of policies for them. Section 3.2 introduces three representative images of small business at the beginning of the 1970s, and comments on the recent trend among small business specialists to re-examine their past methods and research. Section 3.3 is a brief review of changes in the images of small business and the accompanying controversies. Section 3.4 examines the gap between these images and reality. The 'dual-structure view' is so ill-defined that I show here three other reasons than that shown in Chapter 2 for the invalidity of this view. Section 3.5 discusses what small business policy was and what the implication of the gap for the policy is. Section 3.6 offers concluding remarks.

The conclusion of this chapter implies that the conventional view of the position of small business in the Japanese economy is totally wrong. The view that large firms have subordinated and controlled small business, and that as a result their relative importance in the Japanese economy is materially much greater than their share of employment and value added suggests, is but an illusion. Accounting for the true source of small business vitality, however, leads directly to Chapter 4: a close examination and revaluation of the supplier–assembler (buyer) relationships or subcontracting (*shitauke*) system.

3.2   DEFINING THE PROBLEM

Three Representative Images of Small Business

Figure 3.1 shows the result of an 'Image Survey of Small Business', carried out in December 1971 by MITI's Small and Medium Enterprise Agency of Japan and quoted in its 1972 annual report to the Diet, *White Paper on Small and Medium-Sized Enterprises in Japan* (hereafter, *Small Business White Paper*), p. 259. The subjects of the survey were financial institutions, large enterprise managers and small business owner-managers. As shown in Section 3.3, the survey was conducted at a time when the dominant image of small business among scholars and bureaucrats – and therefore the direction of small business policy and the weight placed on each policy objective – began to change.

The survey classified a wide variety of images into three categories, represented in Figure 3.1. Image 1 is straightforward and represented by such phrases as 'private firm', 'family-run enterprise', and 'one-man enterprise'. Image 2 is gloomy and closely related to the dual-structure view, as it is

Figure 3.1   Three images of small business

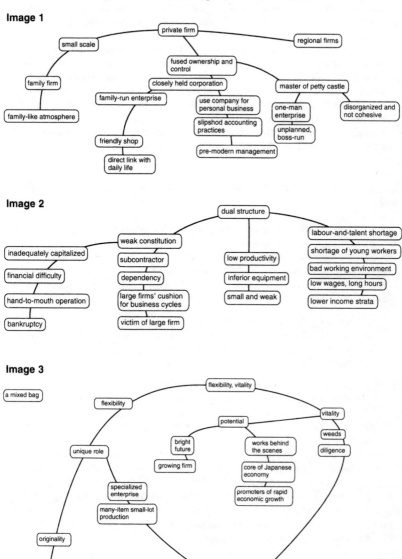

Source: Small and Medium Enterprise Agency, 'Image Survey of Small Business', Dec. 1971; adapted from 1972 *Small Business White Paper*, p. 259.

represented by the phrases such as 'subcontractor', 'dependency', 'hand-to-mouth operation' and 'small and weak enterprises', Image 3 reflects the view of independent and active small business, and is represented by 'flexibility', 'vitality', 'weeds' and 'core of Japanese economy' (ibid., pp. 260–1).

As noted in Section 3.1 above, Image 3 became common among scholars in the 1980s. Among the general public, however, Image 2 remained dominant into the 1980s. Thus, in the 1980s, a gap existed between the academics' views of small business and those of the public. By contrast, Image 2 was strongly supported by scholars rather than by the public in the decade after the mid-1950s, when the dual-structure view was gaining support.

The discussion that follows focuses mainly on the changing images among scholars; views held by the public are touched upon in Section 3.5.

The Recent Trend among Scholars towards Re-examining Views of Small Business

Discussion in this section focuses upon the small business under the subcontracting system (*shitauke*)[3] for several reasons. First, a focus on the subcontracting relationships shows clearly the changing image of small business among scholars. Furthermore, the recent increase in interest in Japan's small business is centred on those engaged in subcontracting relationships. This is shown by the claim that the

> subcontracting system began to be valued as a well-functioning inter-firm communication system based on highly advanced social division of labour, which is one of the causes of the supremacy of Japanese industry. (Nakamura, 1985, p. 90)

By contrast, it was as a 'small manufacturing workshop problem' that the public in Japan first paid attention to small business. Nonetheless, since the 1920s, when small business[4] became a subject of general interest, the centre of this attention was the subcontracting system. Thus, subcontracting relations have been of interest to both the public and academics.

The 1984 annual meeting of the Japanese Association for Small Business Studies chose as the common topic for discussion 'Today's Small Business under the *Shitauke* System and Distribution *Keiretsu-ka* (*keiretsu* control)'. This choice symbolically revealed that the image of subcontracting relationships dominant among scholars has greatly changed. This is indicated by the statement in the foreword of the meeting proceedings by Professor Taikichi Itoh, Association president, who argued:

> The problems in subcontracting manufacturing system have been at the core of the controversy among scholars since the prewar period, as they were regarded as representing the gloomy situation of small business. At the start of the postwar period also, the subcontracting system was criticized as the symbol of the 'dual structure' and the exploitation through burden shifting (*shiwayose*). However, unexpectedly, Western countries

began to pay attention to this system in the process of trade conflicts debates, recognize it as the secret of international competitiveness of Japanese industry, and finally study it for their own efficiency improvement. We chose the problems of the subcontracting system as the common topic, the story of which developed like that of Andersen's 'Ugly Duckling', in order to re-examine it closely. We have to look straight at reality and must be free from the views dominant in the past. (Itoh, 1985, p. i)

Ironically, it is this Association which attracted those who in the 1950s and 1960s most enthusiastically criticized the subcontracting system as the symbol of the dual structure and exploitation through burden shifting. Naturally, there were keen conflicts of opinion and heated discussion on the common topic. This statement, however, leaves many questions unanswered, which are essential in understanding both the changes in the images among scholars of small business engaged in subcontracting relationships and the actual situation of small business in the 1950s and 1960s. (1) What are 'the problems in the subcontracting system' and 'the views dominant in the past'? (2) Is the object of re-examination limited to the subcontracting system in recent years, or is there an intent to return to the 1960s and even to the 1950s, when most scholars and the public strongly supported the dual-structure view? (3) At that time dual structure was logically thought to be 'structural', that is, persistent and resistant to even strong policy intervention. Does this modern re-examination question even this basic assumption? (4) If the re-examination extends only to a certain point of time, like the second half of the 1960s or the beginning of 1970s, why? What has happened to small businesses and what kind of 'structural' change has occurred to the economy at this moment? (5) Do they frankly admit that they did not understand and expect such an efficiency–improving function from the system?

It is too demanding to ask that the Association's meeting transcripts satisfactorily answer these questions, since they have only begun their re-examination and there were acute differences of opinions and hot debate over this very topic.[5] Below I answer these questions and show that the dual-structure view of the economy dominant in the 1950s and 1960s is entirely wrong.

3.3 HISTORY OF THE CHANGE IN SMALL BUSINESS IMAGE

In this section, I briefly review the evolution of the dominant small business image among academics. As the conventional view of small business has been both controversial and the basis of small business policy, these controversies over the dominant small business views are also reviewed here. My treatment is divided into three stages. The first covers the 'original' view of small business problems and the second covers the late 1950s, when small business problems emerged in economic policy debates embodied in the popular phrase 'dual structure'. Finally, I examine the period around 1970 when the goals behind small business policy seemed to change radically.

The Original Image

The question, 'Why have small businesses attracted so much academic attention, and from what standpoint have they been studied?' must be answered by any review of the literature. However, I am puzzled to find that there was originally little agreement on the definition of a small business.[6] I choose Nakayama (1948) as the main reference for this subsection,[7] and draw the original image of small business for the following discussion.

Nakayama (1948) emphasizes the importance of the relation of small business study to economic policies:

> At the start, small workshops gathered wide attention as a social problem, since they suffered from disadvantages of small scale and irrational management, and were expected to be defeated and selected out of the market by large firms with modern capitalistic management. However, small business remained and were not extinguished. The study of this process led us to the discovery of the social system of subordination (*juzoku*), which is the essence of the small business problems.[8]

In Nakayama's view, small business attract public attention because they suffered from a 'problem', whose essence was 'subordination'. Therefore the objective of small business policy was to respond to the problem of subordination.

Even absent clear definition of the 'problem' or 'subordination', there were many opinions about the percentage of small businesses which did not suffer from the 'problem' and about the effectiveness of policies to eliminate 'subordination'. At least until around 1965, however, both scholars and the public supported the view that most small businesses did have a 'problem' and suffered from 'subordination'.

The Dual-structure View

Several important events in small business policy occurred in the early postwar period. The Small and Medium Enterprise Agency (SMEA) was created in 1948 as an extra-ministerial bureau of the Ministry of International Trade and Industry (MITI), and two public lending organizations for small business, the People's Finance Corporation (PFC) and the Small Business Finance Corporation (SBFC) were founded in 1949 and 1953, respectively. Together with the Central Cooperative Bank of Commerce and Industry, founded in 1936, the latter two corporations became the principal means by which the government channelled loans to small business. However, it was not until the late 1950s that small business policies drew public attention.

As mentioned above in Section 2.2, the government's 1956 *Economic White Paper* declared, 'No longer are we in the postwar age', and the next *White Paper* asserted the existence and emphasized the seriousness of the 'dual structure'. Many of its general remarks were devoted to the analysis of dual structure, and the importance of small business policy was strongly affirmed. 'Full employment', it argued, 'which is the final objective of the Japanese economy, is not only to decrease the number of fully unemployed but also to dissolve the dual structure through the modernization and growth of the economy' (*Economic White Paper*, 1957, pp. 36–7). The labour force was expected to grow rapidly over the following decade, and the government concluded that, because it was hard to pull even the smallest firms out of the dual structure, policies would focus instead on the modernization of medium-sized firms in the pre-modern sector. The National Income Doubling Plan for 1961–70, adopted by the government in December 1960, clearly followed this approach.

In the mid-1950s, the wide agreement on the seriousness of the small business 'problem' mentioned by Nakayama demanded policy redress. Once the government had settled on small business policy's direction and instruments, however, criticism erupted on all sides. Most scholars, who emphasized the issue of 'subordination', demanded policies to deal with the 'problem', and criticized the proposed policies as irrelevant to the main issues.[9]

In 1963, 15 years after the establishment of SMEA, the Small and Medium Enterprise Basic Act was enacted with broad public support and enthusiastic political backing. The Act ordered the government to conduct fact-finding surveys on small business and submit to the Diet an annual report entitled *White Paper on Small and Medium-sized Enterprises* or the *Small Business White Paper*, describing small business trends and the measures taken to assist them. From this date, small business policy was carried out system-atically.[10]

The Dual-Structure Transformation View

Ironically, as economic growth in the 1960s exceeded even the most optimistic forecast, support for the dual-structure view weakened rapidly. Meanwhile, some small business drew public attention because of their remarkable success.[11] The 1970 *Small Business White Paper* symbolically entitled its second section 'The Transformation of the Dual Structure and Increasing Variety of Small Business Problems'. Either the situation surrounding small business or the public's image of small business had changed.[12]

The contemporary view of small businesses, which emphasizes their contribution to Japan's industrial success, developed out of the success of some small businesses in the 1960s. Kiyonari (1973), who strongly asserted that the traditional dual structure had disappeared, is its best-known exponent. He argued: Some people regard the deterioration of dual structure as obvious, and the others believe in the continuance. There seems, however, to be no room for debate between two parties' (Kiyonari, 1973, p. 3). Pointing out that one reason why two parties were arguing on different planes was the vagueness of the dual-structure view, he clarified his own definition of dual structure and argued:

> Dual structure is the structure on which such relations are reproduced as large firms accumulate capital by keeping and exploiting small business based on low wage labours . . . Small businesses are exploited by large firms under the dual structure. They can neither accumulate capital because of low profitability, nor get permission to drop away. Thus, between small business and large firms there lies a tall wall, hard to jump over, and small businesses form a class with fixed members like sediment at the bottom of the social ladder of the economy. They live in a vicious circle as low wages → survival of small business with potentially unemployed labour → too many tiny rivals → excessive competition → low profitability → no capital accumulation → low productivity → financial instability → excessive competition. (Ibid., pp. 3–4)

Later, he asserts:

> with rapid wage increases, mild inflation, and rapid economic growth, the dual structure has disappeared . . . In the process . . . small business found business opportunities and earned high incomes, and those who accumulated managerial resources and competence became independent . . . Small businesses depending on low wages and compensating for low productivity with longer working hours disappeared, and were replaced by many small businesses paying high wages justified by high productivity attained through highly specialized ability. Thus the dissolution process of dual structure has proceeded.[13]

Though there was no agreement or discussion on the first appearance of small business without the 'problem', by the early 1970s many became aware of the vigour and importance of these small businesses to the economy. The government also clearly expressed its intention of focusing small business policy on those firms without the 'problem'.

3.4 A GAP BETWEEN THE IMAGE AND REALITY OF SMALL BUSINESS

In this section, I investigate how and to what degree the change in the small business image held by scholars reflected the change in reality. The investigation also provides an evaluation of the effectiveness and appropriateness of small business policy.

Three basic questions for investigation are: Has the percentage of small businesses with the 'problem' fallen? Has the seriousness of the 'problem' of small business still with the 'problem' abated? Can small business policy assist their effectiveness and appropriateness? The investigation goes on to ask whether the 'dual structure' ever really existed and whether the 'structural changes' said to have caused the 'dissolution' of the 'dual structure' actually took place. I conclude that a wide gap has existed between the image and reality of small business and that the image of small business has changed more radically than the reality. Therefore the answers to the above three questions are all in the negative.

My analysis is directed against the view that large firms exploit small business either directly or indirectly, or use them as a cushion against market fluctuations. I use as the material for investigation Kiyonari's depiction of the dual-structure view. Roughly classified, four points emerge.

Logical Consistency

Is the dual-structure view logically consistent? How could large firms exploit small business for a long time? Standard economic theory argues that, in a competitive market with free entry and exit, the long-run profit rate cannot differ from the normal rate in either direction. The markets dominated by small business satisfy these conditions, as they are characterized by 'too many tiny rivals' and 'excessive competition'.[14] Theory implies that buyers (large car manufacturers engaged in supplier–assembler relationships with small business, for example) will be unable to purchase small business products (car components) when they exploit small business by driving their purchasing price below the market rate, which includes normal profits. Small businesses have responded to the demand of large firms for products, which indicates that small businesses have earned at least normal profits (and that, in case where there existed phenomena termed burden shifting, particularly under depression, small businesses have earned a premium for them). By definition this implies that small businesses have not been exploited.

The Japanese economy grew rapidly even before the 'dual structure' was 'dissolved', and both small businesses (suppliers) and large companies (assemblers) grew steadily. This implies that large firms provided a stable demand for products of rapidly growing small businesses at a price not less than the market rate. Such a fact is not consistent with the exploitation of small business.

High Profit Rate for Small Business

The argument that small business could not accumulate capital under dual structure exploitation because of low profitability suggests that the small business profit rate was lower than that of large firms under the 'dual structure'. On the basis of hypothesized dual structure conditions, therefore, we might predict that small business profit rates were lower than large firm profit rates before the first half of the 1960s, and that this discrepancy disappeared thereafter. As shown in the previous chapter,[15] this forecast

(Position 1 of Section 2.3) is not supported by the facts. This conclusion also is inconsistent with the argument that small businesses were exploited by large firms. The profit rate for small businesses was much higher than that for large firms at least until the first oil crisis, that is almost ten years after the 1970 *Small Business White Paper* announced the 'Transformation' of the dual structure following the alleged 'structural change'. Moreover, the direction of the observed change after the oil crisis was the opposite of that implied by the dual-structure view.

Consistent Increases in the Number of Small Businesses

Consistent increases have been observed in the number of small business throughout the period under study. As shown in Table 3.1 for all industries, between 1951 and 1986, before and after the time of the 'structural changes', the number of establishments of every size increased constantly. The annual business failure rate of small businesses—the ratio of annual small business failures to all small business—stabilized at around 4 per cent. Given expanding net numbers of small business, the 4 per cent failure rate implies that the annual business start-up rate exceeded 4 per cent.[16] This evidence too is inconsistent with the argument that small business was exploited, for rational entrepreneurs would not enter markets in which they would be exploited. Table 3.2 uses data for the manufacturing sector instead of all industries as in Table 3.1, but the result requires no modification of my conclusion.

Table 3.1   Number of establishments by employee size, private, non-agriculture (in 1000s)

	1–4	5–9	10–29	30–99	100–299	300+	Total
1951	2640	284	202	51	9	1	3187
1954	2634	369	216	54	9	3	3285
1957	2715	433	237	60	12	4	3461
1960	2727	463	271	80	16	5	3562
1963	2931	515	325	103	20	6	3900
1966	3083	607	388	122	24	6	4231
1969	3360	687	431	138	27	8	4650
1972	3676	763	482	154	31	8	5114
1975	3840	834	522	156	30	8	5389
1978	4105	956	583	167	31	7	5849
1981	4349	1056	640	183	33	7	6269
1986	4428	1118	705	199	36	8	6494

Source: Management and Coordination Agency, Statistics Bureau, *Jigyosho Tokei Chosa* (*Census of Establishments*) (Tokyo); Adapted from Miwa (1990a, p. 35, Table 2.1).

Table 3.2   Number of establishments by employee size, private, manufacturing (in 100s)

	1–9*	10–29	30–99	100-199	200–499	500+	Total*
1951	3155	569	164	26	16	8	3938
1954	3357	698	193	30	18	9	4304
1957	3430	866	266	41	24	11	4637
1960	3456	974	335	58	31	15	4871
1963	4155	960	391	71	38	18	5633
1966	4334	1072	406	77	40	19	5948
1969	4751	1148	418	84	46	23	6469
1972	5229	1200	441	88	47	22	7026
1975	5607	1190	420	81	43	21	7360
1978	5698	1203	405	79	40	18	7443
1981	2518	1293	412	82	42	19	4365
1984	2432	1293	416	88	44	19	4290

* Data for 1981 and 1984 exclude establishments with 1–3 employees.
Source: Ministry of International Trade and Industry, *Kogyo Tokei Hyo* (*Census of Manufacturers*) (Tokyo: MITI, annual); Adapted from Miwa (1990a, p. 56, Table 3.1).

A Loan-concentration Mechanism in the Financial Sector?

Although it is widely argued[17] that a 'loan- concentration mechanism' in the financial sector directed loans to large firms rather than small business–perpetuating the notion of 'dual structure'–such a mechanism in fact never existed.[18] This point is elaborated in Chapter 5.

From these four points[19] (or even just one or two), three propositions follow: the assertion that a large majority of small businesses were 'exploited' between the late 1950s and the early 1960s is inconsistent with reality; the assertion that they have been exploited in more recent years is likewise inconsistent with reality; and 'structural change', in the sense of a drastic reduction in the proportion of small businesses being 'exploited', never occurred.

These propositions answer the three basic questions presented at the outset of this section: (1) the percentage of small businesses with the 'problem' was not so high as the dominant view assumed, nor is there evidence indicating a further fall in the percentage; (2) as shown by the level and the direction of change of profit rates, for example, the disadvantageous position of small business relative to large firms did not abate, implying that the seriousness of the 'problem' afflicting small businesses still with the 'problem' has not eased; (3) as the position of small business in the economy did not change notably, small business policy cannot be judged effective. No ineffective policies can be appropriate. In short, the problem that small business policy was ostensibly designed to address did not exist. If the elimination of a non-existent 'dual structure' is the measure of small business policy effectiveness, the policy could not have been 'effective'.[20]

All this suggests that at least in the 1950s and 1960s there was a tremendous gap between the image of small business and reality, which confused small business studies, debates over small business policy and the policy itself. As mentioned above, in adopting the keywords of the time, we face the potential unconscious intrusion of the dual-structure view into the analysis of today's conditions. In the next section, I detail how, why and by whom the dual-structure view was supported.

3.5 SMALL BUSINESS IMAGE AND SMALL BUSINESS POLICY

Small Business Image among Non-Scholars

Some readers may argue that their understanding of small business differs from that discussed above, or that I focus only on successful small businesses. As mentioned in Section 3.2, since even small business specialists began only recently to re-examine their traditional views of small business, it is possible that the public still holds outdated views of small business. Four points account for their persistence: vagueness in the definition of small business which confuses all related studies and debates;[21] the tendency of individuals to form opinions from their own observations only, unaware of the divergence of their views from the average view;[22] the flood of studies on small business with the 'problem' which biases their image; and the confusion of the exploitation of small business with that of small business labour.[23]

A review of popular literature suggests two points. First, the popular image of small business has changed less than that held by scholars. The popular view has been a mixture of Figure 3.1's Image 1 ('private firm' and 'one-man enterprise') and the gloomy Image 2, closely related to the dual-structure view. In the 1950s and 1960s the relative weight of gloomy Image 2 was higher among scholars than among the public, but the situation has now reversed itself. Second, wide popular support for the dual-structure view politicized both small business studies and policy making. By providing a framework for debate, the dual-structure view strongly influenced both the formation and implementation of small business policy. The dual-structure view also biased the direction and even the results of small business research.

Images of Small Business among Scholars and Small Business Policies

Although many students of small business policy address 'policy ideals', 'policy targets' and 'policy measures', few consider 'policy effects'. Of those who do, Hajime Takaki, former chairman of the Central Cooperative Bank of Commerce and Industry, observed soon after the depression of the early 1970s:

There are so many different policy measures for small business that most of us would be amazed to discover how tiny the scale of each policy is. Policy efforts have been wide but thin. It is as though the government waters large flower pots with small sprinkling cans . . . In the present severe depression, there is a strong demand for small business policy in order to encourage their owners and managers . . . Each policy is well designed and sensitive, but, the scale of government's policies is too small to have any effect.[24]

A more conventional view, however, would be similar to that expressed by Yokokura (1988, pp. 533–4). First, until the 1950s, policies for small business were but one facet of social policy and consisted of financial and cartel policies. In the 1960s, small business modernization policies were but one facet of industrial policy.[25] In the 1970s and 1980s, modernization policies emphasized human resources, technology (information), and industrial adjustment, including policies assisting firms in changing their line of business. Second, small business policies were indiscriminate in focus and in the policy instruments they used. This was in part because of the great variety of disadvantages faced by small business, but was also due to operation of political–economic mechanisms. (For details on this point, see Chapter 8 of this volume.) Nonetheless, the indiscriminate use of small business policy, like the designation of industries under the Modernization Promotion Act of 1963,[26] inevitably weakened their collective impact. Finally, small business policies relied primarily on financing allocated by the market rather than competition-restricting measures or direct subsidies. Thus small business policies were indiscriminate but not particularly protective, unlike agricultural policies which depended on import restrictions and direct subsidies.[27]

A realization of the broad-based public demand for small business policy, and of the political implications of this demand,[28,29] is indispensable for the understanding of both the policies adopted and their indiscriminateness.[30] Note also that, especially in the 1950s, many scholars participated in lobbying for small business policies and conducted small business studies as part of their political efforts. This was later criticized as 'subordination of scholars to politics', but also explains why so few scholars examine the effects of small business policy.[31]

In addition to the above-mentioned obstacles to effectiveness, namely a faulty basis for policy and policy measures that applied thinly and indiscriminately, the following conditions also make small business policy ineffective. (1) In some cases, the direct competitors that policies strengthen small business against are themselves small businesses in the same industry rather than large firms. Therefore, even when small businesses are subsidized heavily, the resulting benefits are passed on to the buyers and consumers. (2) Direct intervention in a small/large firm relationship to excise 'subordination' and 'exploitation' is ineffective in the face of a constant stream of new entries with potentially similar troubles and also in the face of the possible reaction of large firms: a decision to produce previously subcontracted components 'in-house'. (3) Firms with inferior performance lack something more than capital. Weak management, market demand and technical know-how may all contribute to poor performance. This is true for small businesses and large firms. In such cases, centrally planned policies can have only limited effect.

Financing Policies for Small Business: An Example[32]

There is wide agreement that the most important measures for small business policy are financial.[33] Therefore special attention should be paid to the role of financing policies and the magnitude of their effects. Three government-affiliated financial institutions carry out government policies for small business finance: the People's Finance Corporation (PFC), the Small Business Finance Corporation (SBFC) and the Central Cooperative Bank of Commerce and Industry (CCBCI). All were established by the government to furnish small business with funds for business operations (often expressed as 'quantitatively to complement loans available from private banks') and to promote specific policies. Here I concentrate on the SBFC because it is the newest and has the most clearly specified policy-oriented character of the three.[34]

The government holds all SBFC stock, and all SBFC loanable funds come from the government's Fiscal Investment and Loan Programme.[35] Until the mid-1980s more than 80 per cent of SBFC loans were provided by its general loan system, with the remainder by a special loan system.[36] Consideration here centres mainly on the former. The SBFC provides its loans directly through its approximately 60 offices and indirectly through private financial institutions appointed as its agents, which number 846 (15 131 branches). In fiscal year 1989, 75.5 per cent of SBFC loans were made directly. SBFC offices and their agents are open to any small business, and borrowers may negotiate with them directly. They need not, in other words, obtain recommendations from third parties such as local governments, Boards or Chambers of Commerce and Industry, or other financial institutions. At the end of the 1989 fiscal year, loans made by the SBFC and its agents to small business had an average value of 32.18 million yen and an average term of 6 years and 11 months. Borrowers had, on average, 23.49 million yen in paid-in capital and 48 employees.

The SBFC's loan rate is its designated 'base rate', which is equal to the 'long-term prime rate' and was at 5.5 per cent at the end of 1992. As small businesses are not always able to borrow at this rate in the regular financial market, especially when the market is tight, SBFC loans necessarily include a subsidy to small business. That subsidy is proportional to the amount of loan. However, the subsidy is not large, as the discrepancy between the base rate and the market rate seldom exceeds 0.5–1.0 per cent. The SBFC and its agents check the loan applications and collateral presented by their borrowers so rigorously that small business owners sometimes say their requirements are more severe than those of private institutions. If a default occurs on an indirect loan, the agent bears 80 per cent of the loss. In sum, an SBFC general loan includes a subsidy, although the amount is small and loan standards are strict.

The effectiveness of the small business financing policies depends on the state of the capital markets and the relations between small businesses and large firms. If the capital markets are competitive, below-market loans are equivalent to a direct subsidy equal to the amount of loan multiplied by the difference between the loan rate and the market rate. If the capital markets are not competitive and small business cannot obtain loans at or even slightly above the market rate (capital markets are divided into markets for large firms and small businesses and there is a shortage of capital in the latter), government small business policies may have additional impact.

The government-affiliated financial institutions were established in order to complement financing available from private banks. The assumption was that small business faced strong quantitative constraints in financing which were thought to reflect the directing of loans to large firms. As will be shown in Chapter 5, this never occurred. As a result, below-market loans had no impact beyond the direct value of their subsidies.

In order to assess the policy impact of the loan subsidies, consider the ratio of small business policy loans to total small business loans. Yokokura (1988, p. 523) has shown that during 1960–80 the three government-affiliated financial institutions provided only 10 per cent of the total amount of funds small business borrowed from all financial institutions.[37] Therefore, when policy loans are provided at 1 per cent below the market rate, the average rate of total small business funds is lowered by only 0.1 per cent, which cannot be considered very significant.[38,39,40]

3.6 CONCLUDING REMARKS

Many new small businesses continuously started operations simply because entrepreneurs found the prospects promising. Neither miracle nor environmental factors peculiar only to Japan, like history or culture, for small business have existed. Small business policy has hardly been miraculous either.

At any time there is a wide variety of images of small business, and the dominant image has changed greatly over time. Although, at least among scholars and some government bureaucrats, the dominant image has begun to change drastically, the general public still holds fast to what Nakamura (1985, p. 1) stated:

There is among Japanese a robust conventional view that a huge number of small businesses is a manifestation of the historical backwardness of the Japanese economy. This view occupies the minds of so many Japanese and has them regard small business as backward, weak, unstable, always suffering from excessive competition, and being exploited by large firms.[41]

A wide gap has existed between the image and reality of Japan's small businesses and the image of small businesses has changed more radically than their reality has. The gap still exists, and the process of change continues slowly but steadily. At this moment, however, emphasizing solely the image of independent and active small business (Image 3 of Figure 3.1) and praising them with such phrases as 'wonderful small business', 'active small business', 'small business as a source of the international competitiveness of Japanese industry', and 'the secret of Japan's rapid economic growth' leads to undesirable results. First, the image of small business has changed more dramatically among scholars and bureaucrats than among the public, and even now the small business image dominant among Japanese is one of backwardness, weakness and instability (Image 2 of Figure 3.1). Promoting a totally different small business image, antithetical to the dominant one, will produce emotional reaction among the public. It will slow the disappearance of the gap between the image and reality by impeding the search for an exact understanding of reality through cool investigations. Second, though small business policy slogans have changed, in substance small business policy basically reflects the small business view dominant when the framework and the fundamental character of those policies were chosen. Without changing the small business image dominant among the public, evaluation and fundamental re-examination of small business policy cannot proceed, and therefore change in policy to reflect reality is impossible.

The wide gap that has existed between the image and reality of small business is a result of the false dual-structure view. Implied is a wide gap between the image and reality of other components of the dual-structure view and therefore in the Japanese economy itself. Specifically, a wide gap has also existed between the images and reality of the position of large firms, small business's relations with large firms, capital markets, the effectiveness of policies for industry and the causes of Japan's rapid economic growth.

The rapid growth and industrial success of the Japanese economy has drawn attention to the following kinds of question: (1) What are the causes and conditions for the rapid growth? (2) What are the necessary conditions and policies for creating active small businesses among a massive group of small businesses with the 'problem'? (3) How has Japan's inter-firm division of labour formed and what has made it possible? How does it function? (4) What are effective and appropriate policies for small business?

By the same token, putting forward a totally different view on other components of the dual structure will produce an emotional public reaction. Further, without changing the conventional view, we cannot examine the realities behind such questions. Since conventionally used keywords are closely related to the dual-structure view, we cannot ask effective questions without careful examination of their definition. For example, when we discuss small business in traditional terms, we put questions to active and successful small businesses only with implicit qualifications like 'although it is a small business'. Thus certain questions have always been asked, like 'How have small businesses overcome disadvantages?' or 'What should the government do for small business?' We have to put an end to such qualifications in our inquiries and ask more positive questions, such as 'What are the necessary conditions and policies for a huge number of active small business?'[42] or 'What is the desirable role of the government vis-à-vis industry?' as small size, as shown, is not by itself disadvantageous.

Many of the keywords used to study today's Japanese economy, such as corporate groups, capital *keiretsu*, *keiretsu* loan, distribution *keiretsu*, subcontracting, bargaining power and technological gap are closely related to small business with the problem of exploitation under the dual structure conditions. When we use such terms, we unconsciously assume, for example, that large firms enjoy the advantages stemming from their large size. However, we cannot be too careful in using them for analysis of today's Japanese economy if we hope to avoid the intrusion and unconscious acceptance of the dual-structure view.[43]

4 Supplier–Assembler Relationships in the Motor Industry

4.1 INTRODUCTION

Paralleling Japan's industrial success is the 'spreading awareness that a vast group of small businesses support it' (Sato, 1986, p. 152). Therefore, since the industrial success of Japan depends more than anything else upon the success of the fabrication and assembly-type industries, increased interest in small business is above all focused on those engaged in supplier–assembler (final manufacturer) relationships or subcontracting. This chapter examines the formation and workings of Japan's inter-firm relationships for division of labour, known as *shitauke*, or subcontracting. The motor industry is taken as the representative fabrication and assembly industry.

As Itoh noted (1985, p. i), the problem in the subcontracting manufacturing system has been at the core of the controversy among scholars studying small business since the prewar period (see Section 3.2 above). As shown in Chapter 3, however, a wide gap has existed between the image held of small businesses and their actual situation, and the image has begun to change only recently. This is also true for small business in subcontracting relationships. In particular, the portrayal of powerful large firms and weak small businesses that underlies the image is an unacceptable premise for this volume's research.[1]

Past studies of subcontracting and subcontracting relationships, however, have taken this assumption as their starting-point. Hence both the definition of these basic concepts and the identification of objects of research are also based on it. Thus we need reassessment and re-identification of our objects of study and our terms of analysis. When we use the phrase 'inter-firm relationship' in both the motor industry and textile industries subcontracting, we assume that the phenomena are similar in the two industries. If either the assumption is invalid or our concept of subcontracting is inappropriate, our conclusion will be wrong. Most past studies are based on an image related to control, subordination (dependency), exploitation, and burden shifting (*shiwayose*) and assume that subcontracting exists in many if not most industrial sectors and that the nature of subcontracting is invariable across sectors. Based upon this assumption, previous small business studies chose

58

issues such as the following for research: What are the means of control? How serious is the exploitation? How does burden shifting appear? How can government policies cope with such small business problems? Our conclusion in Chapter 3 that a wide gap has existed between the image and reality implies that the assumptions of prior studies are invalid and such research is fruitless.

This is not to say that a vast group of small businesses have not contributed greatly to Japan's industrial success, and that raising the question of the formation and workings of the inter-firm relationships is valueless or misguided. This chapter examines supplier–assembler relationships in the Japanese motor industry with aims totally different from the traditional ones. Primary emphasis is placed upon a detailed description and analysis of the causes, conditions and workings of supplier–assembler or inter-firm relationships in an industry which realized quick and remarkable success. The focus is placed on a series of questions related to the incentive system supporting supplier–assembler relationships in the industry: Why have so many small businesses in supplier–assembler relationships been so active and creative? Why have they made continuous commitments to relationships requiring a long wait for pay-offs? What have car assemblers done to further suppliers' creativity and commitment?

The industrial success of Japan, which by itself surprised and interested the world, depends more than anything else on the success of the fabrication and assembly-type industries, of which the motor industry is representative. Therefore the study of the success of this industry leads us to realize the basic conditions and the mechanism for Japan's rapid growth. The recent rise in the public interest in small business centres on supplier–assembler relationships, especially those in the fabrication and assembly-type industries in recognition of their key role in industrial success.

As much literature is based on the erroneous traditional view with ill-defined keywords, we need reassessment and re-identification of our objects of study and our terms of analysis, to which Sections 4.2 and 4.3 are devoted. Section 4.2 deals with definitional issues. Section 4.3 describes the industry history. The current success of Japan's motor industry often prompts the mistaken belief that it was powerful and efficient from the start. By way of disavowing this view, this chapter focuses on the hard road to the success. Sections 4.4 to 4.6 study the incentive mechanism. In Section 4.4, I point out four popular myths: assembler (final manufacturer) exploitation of suppliers, strong assembler support of suppliers, and the paucity of suppliers' voluntary efforts at self-involvement (in the first part); and the closed nature and exclusiveness of the *kyoryoku-kai*, the cooperative associations of first-tier suppliers (in the second part). In Section 4.5, I examine the structure and functioning of the incentive system supporting supplier–assembler relationships. In this industry, inter-firm relationships are quite often long term, which implies that participants commit themselves to offering a kind of monopolistic position to their partners. The measures adopted to protect partners from the evils of the other partners' monopolistic positions produced through long-term relations are discussed in Section 4.6. Section 4.7 offers concluding remarks.

4.2 DEFINITIONAL ISSUES

Supplier–Assembler Relationships rather than Subcontracting or *Shitauke* Relationships

The term 'supplier–assembler relationship' is used in the sections which follow in preference to such expressions as the subcontracting relationship, the *shitauke* relationship or the *shitauke* system, to denote the inter-firm relationships for division of labour. This choice needs comment. The Japanese term *shitauke* was used in past small business studies, but these, and even government statistics, are based on the erroneous dual-structure view. By rejecting this view, I also reject the term *shitauke*.

Watanabe's (1985) survey, 'The *Shitauke–Keiretsu* Relationship and Small Business', is an example of the traditional view. He avers: Focus of studies is on a form of interaction between small businesses and large firms, in particular in the manufacturing industries, and its related issues rather than the issue inherent in small businesses themselves (p. 389). He continues:

> Because of the seriousness of its quantitative importance and issues raised ... the *shitauke–keiretsu* relationship has been one of the most important research issues on small business. Of the 710 000 small businesses in manufacturing, about two-thirds were in the subcontracting (*shitauke*) relationship as the representative trade relationship in 1981 ... The ratio of small businesses whose sales from *shitauke* orders exceed 50 per cent is more than 80 per cent ... In other words, the subcontracting relationship is quantitatively, the representative activity for small business manufacturers. (pp. 389–90)

Note, however, that the figures Watanabe used to stress the quantitative significance for small business are from the *Preliminary Report* of the 1981 *Report of the Sixth Basic Survey of the Reality of the Manufacturing Industry, (Kogyo Jittai Kihon Chosa Hokokusho)*, a study which also reflects the dual-structure view. The definition of *shitauke* is ambiguous. Although it is explained in the sheets attached to the questionnaire as '*shitauke* is ordered directly by parent firms, with specifications of standards, quality, performance, form, design, and etc.', ambiguity still remains. Data are obtained in a sample survey by asking: 'Is your firm engaged in *shitauke* production? Answer "Yes" or "No". If "Yes", what is the number of parent firms, and what is the ratio of *shitauke* transactions to total sales?' Surprisingly and unfortunately, the corresponding figures in the final report of the 1981 *Survey* differ greatly from those in the *Preliminary Report*, that is, 710 807, 23.4 per cent (instead of two thirds), and 18.6 per cent (instead of over 50 per cent). (However, 615 226, 60.7 per cent and 49.0 per cent are the corresponding figures for the fifth *Basic Survey* in 1976, and 679 662, 55.8 per cent and 41.0 per cent for the seventh *Survey* in 1987. I believe that one basic reason for the instability of the figures is the ambiguity in the definition of *shitauke*.)[2]

Watanabe typifies the popular view of *shitauke*:

> . . . *shitauke* is not only the most important business relationship for manufacturing small businesses in quantitative terms but is also regarded as reflecting most succinctly the nature of Japanese small business with the 'problem'. Furthermore, the *shitauke* small businesses have been viewed as the main bearers of this 'problem'. Thus the *shitauke* relationship reveals most clearly such 'problems' as large firms shifting the burden of business hardships to small businesses (*shiwayose*), their exploitation of small businesses and their subordination of independent small businesses.[3,4,5]

A risk taken in choosing to use 'subcontracting' in place of the term *shitauke* is that subcontracting reminds some of certain contracts typical in such industries as construction and shipbuilding. Since here we are interested in the formation and workings of the inter-firm relationship for division of labour in the motor industry, the choice might distort readers' image of the object of the study in two ways. First, products in the industries where this particular form of subcontracting is popular are typically made to order, but cars are standardized and ready-made products. This suggests that the basic character of the transactions and relationships between assemblers and parts suppliers in the motor industry is not the same as that of parties to a typically understood subcontract. Second, 'subcontracting' derives from a prime contract, suggesting the necessary existence of the latter's strong leadership to elicit the former. Hence I choose 'supplier–assembler relationship' for convenience, as 'inter-firm relationship' seems too general while 'inter-firm relationship for division of labour' is too tedious.

Definition of the Problem

The definition of the Japanese motor industry requires clarification. I focus mainly on four-wheel cars, and exclude such products as trucks, buses, three-wheel trucks, motorcycles and so on from prime concern. I focus not only on car assemblers (that is, the firms in the final stage of production and marketing), but also on the firms which supply car parts to assemblers, firms which perform machining work for assemblers and parts suppliers, and firms which supply production materials to those firms.[6] In most cases, the activities and the nationality of shareholders in the firms are not limited to one country. Consequently, the definition of 'Japanese' is not always clear. My view, however, is that, although GM holds 41.5 per cent of Isuzu's stock and Ford holds 23.6 per cent of Mazda's stock, making each the largest shareholder in these firms, Isuzu and Mazda are both Japanese.

By the 'industrial success' of Japan's motor industry, I mean that it has acquired a large share of the world car market by supplying cars with qualities consumers want at a price they accept. Most people agree, I believe, that the basic reason for this success is simple. Japan's carmakers supplied cars with high reliability and fuel economy at lower prices than their competitors, thereby satisfying the basic demands of the average consumer in developed countries. Though they worked at the technological level of prewar and wartime industry, at the start of car production in 1945–55, Japanese carmakers still had many problems to overcome in both product quality and productivity.[7] In a short time, however, they attained high product quality and productivity, and expanded production and exports. This is the essence of Japan's 'industrial success' and the primary concern of the following sections is to answer the following questions: Who played the crucial roles in the process? How did they do it? How were inter-firm relationships for division of labour formed and how did they function?

Looking closely at the motor industry and at fabrication and assembly-type industry in general, we find its development characterized as a continuous accumulation of small innovations. For such a process to arise, however, it was important to solve two problems. First, incentives encouraging continuous improvement and creativity had to be developed for a large number of economic agents, both within a given firm and outside. Second, communication between actors had to be smooth and dense, and their creative activities had to be appropriately coordinated. The supplier–assembler relationship, as one of the key factors in the industrial success of Japan's motor industry, was by implication well-suited to solve these problems. Thus the following are the subjects of our primary concern: What incentive and communication systems were best able to stimulate actors to accumulate specialized skills and know-how and then to transfer and exchange them, thereby continuously improving quality? How was this system formed and maintained? Who took the lead?

Before going into detail, we should note five points. (1) The supplier–assembler relationship has not been equally effective for all car manufac-turers.[8] My account of the industry's history in Section 4.3 focuses mainly on Toyota, which is regarded as the most successful firm in the industry. Therefore lessons drawn from the experience of an outlier may not accurately explain the success of the industry as a whole. In Section 4.4 and thereafter, however, I focus on the mechanism common to all supplier–assembler relationships in the Japanese motor industry. In those sections, 'assembler' represents the assemblers in the industry in general. (2) I investigate neither why these supplier–assembler relationships were more effective for Toyota than for other Japanese assemblers nor why these relationships were more effective for Japanese assemblers than for those elsewhere. (3) I ask neither why Japanese assemblers chose to depend heavily on these supplier–assembler relationships over 'in-house' production nor why they chose their present production locations.[9] (4) I focus mainly on assemblers and machining firms. Among suppliers I choose machining firms rather than suppliers of unit parts (often called 'vendors'),[10] because a machining firm is more tightly related to an assembler[11] and therefore is closer to the public's view of a subcontractor. (5) The purpose of this chapter is not a complete study of factors supporting the industrial success of Japan's motor industry, but is limited to a study of the working mechanism of one such factor. Nor do I argue that this factor is the only or the most important one for industrial success.

4.3   INDUSTRIAL SUCCESS AND AN ILLUSTRATION OF THE PROBLEMS TO BE OVERCOME

The Reality of the Success

It is hard for readers familiar with the success of Japan's motor industry and its products to imagine the conditions facing the industry during its development. Eiji Toyoda, Chairman of Toyota Motor Corporation, states in his memoirs, 'Our first true car was the Crown, unveiled in January 1955' (Toyoda, 1987, p. 172). As shown in Chapter 1 (Table 1.6), the number of cars produced in Japan that year was only 20 000.[12] In ten years the number rose to 696 000, and in 20 years to 4 568 000, of which 40 per cent were exported.[13]

At the start of the development process, there was a tremendous gap in productivity and product quality between Japanese and foreign manufacturers, and protective policies were adopted:

> By adding import restriction through foreign currency quotas, a higher wall was erected to protect domestic cars from import competition. Foreign currency quotas were adopted after 1952–3 imports of European compact cars rose even under a forty percent tariff, and were reinforced by the general import restriction imposed to soften the recession of 1954. Specifically, foreign currency quotas for car imports decreased from US\$ 13.74 million in 1953 to US\$ 0.61 million in 1954 and US\$ 0.92 million in 1955, and the number of imported cars fell from 5900 in 1953 to 370 in 1954 and 545 in 1955. (Ueno and Mutoh, 1973, pp. 126–7)[14]

While the domestic market was protected from import competition, Japanese car manufacturers increased production and began and expanded exports. As shown in Table 1.6, the number of cars exported was near zero in the mid-50s but increased to more than 10 000 in 1961, passed 100 000 in 1965, and exceeded one million in 1971. As the export market was not protected from competition with non-Japanese manufacturers, this increase in exports implies that Japanese manufacturers achieved sufficient productivity and product quality gains in a short time, and at the same time overcame the disadvantage faced by new entrants in the world market. While productivity in other countries also increased with production expansion,[15] the productivity of Japanese manufacturers increased at a faster pace.[16]

A car is composed of over 5000 kinds and 20 000 pieces of separate parts through the joint efforts of a huge number of firms. Therefore dramatic quality improvement in the final product implies simultaneous dramatic quality improvement in parts, materials, machine tools and production equipment. As all these items were made in Japan, except for rare cases where import were permitted,[17] quality improvement and productivity gains were realized in areas from stamping and machining to production of tyres, bearings, glass, steel and machine tools.

Problems on the Road to Success

At the motor industry's beginning, the technical and management levels of suppliers were low. Honda's experience in building mass-production plant for motorcycle assembly illustrates the situation. In August 1960, Honda began production of its best-selling 'Super-Cub' motorcycle in Suzuka City, Mie Prefecture, 40 kilometres west of Nagoya. The Suzuka government asked Honda to choose local firms as suppliers but few met Honda's requirements in precision, cost and production capacity. 60 per cent of its 250 suppliers were located in Keihin District, an area near Tokyo and more than 400 kilometers east of Suzuka, and the shares of those in other industrial districts Osaka and Nagoya, followed. Four firms in Suzuka applied, but Honda accepted none of them. Eight in Kuwana area in Mie for three, and a large number in Mie only for ten. As Honda is famous for 'après guerre rationalism' and does not establish an inflexible *keiretsu* relationship, this story implies that, even with the advantage of low transport costs, local firms could not compete.[18]

Furthermore, the motor industry had requirements not so easily dealt with by suppliers at that time: (1) mass production; (2) complex assembly; (3) high precision fabrication; (4) high durability; (5) continual improvement in both parts quality and production process. Thus assemblers had to begin by raising the technical and management levels of suppliers instead of choosing them from a pool of capable firms. To be chosen as a supplier, a firm had both to change its managerial mindset and to restructure every aspect of management, including production, inventory, materials, quality control, product development, labour relations and accounting.[19]

Assemblers and suppliers must also establish and maintain good communication with each other in order to facilitate knowledge transfer, exchange of intention and the coordination of interests,[20] since such a huge number of firms share the production of parts for a car.[21] As shown in Table 4.1, the number of firms directly and indirectly in trade with an assembler (Toyota) exceeded 40 000 in 1977. Today's dense and good communication relationships between assemblers and suppliers are the product of hard efforts over a long period of time. Many people, including the managing directors of rival car manufacturers,[22] argue that there is a wide productivity gap both between Toyota and its rivals and between Toyota's suppliers and the suppliers of Toyota's rivals, and that this gap results from poor communication and cooperation. For this reason I focus on Toyota, for Toyota's success suggests the difficulty of the problems assemblers had to solve at the start. The principal means of cost reduction is through effective use of production facilities and the reduction of fixed costs, which have been realized by improving production process through changing the shapes and uses of tools and dies. The gap which remains between Toyota and its rivals implies that, even with continuous effort, it is not easy to reach the target level, and this is true for other firms even after observing the process through which one firm has succeeded. Toyota's rivals praise not only Toyota's level

Table 4.1 Specialization structure in motor industry, number of suppliers: the case of Toyota (total of establishments, 1977)

	Core components	Electric–electronic components	Drive, transmission and steering components	Suspension and brakes	Accessories	Chassis	Body parts	Others	Total
First-tier supplier	25	1	31	18	18	3	41	31	168
Second-tier supplier	912	34	609	792	926	27	1213	924	5437
Third-tier supplier	4960	352	7354	6204	5936	85	8221	8591	41703
Total	5897	387	7994	7014	6880	115	9475	9546	47308

Note: Each figure for second-tier and third-tier suppliers is a total of number. Estimate without double counting for second-tier is 4700 and third-tier 31600.
Source: Small and Medium Enterprise Agency, *Bungyo Kozo Jittai Chosa (Jidosha)* (*Survey of Specialization Structure (Motor Industry)*), 1977; adapted from the 1978 *Small Business White Paper*, p.168.

of achieved efficiency, but also the commitment made by Toyota and its suppliers to higher efficiency.

In sum, raising firms' technical and managerial abilities to required levels, establishing cooperative relations based on shared information among them, and using these attributes effectively for dramatic productivity increase and quality improvement is a long and hard process.

What follows is the essence of a comment made in an interview by Ryojiro Kojima, president of Kojima Press and chairman of *Tokai Kyoho-kai*. Kojima Press is regarded as one of Toyota's representative suppliers, Kojima's comment illustrates well the hard process of updating:

> Toyota production system reminds people of the *kanban* system, under which firms have simply made continuous efforts for the 'just-in-time, just-the-right-amount of requested parts' objective. Only recently have we at last scored satisfactorily. This system totally depends on the assumption that all the parts delivered with *kanban* are defect-free; otherwise each defective part stops the production line. As a car is composed of a huge number of parts, this happens very frequently. Thus 'just-in-time, just the right amount' is not an appropriate objective. The no-defect assumption naturally leads us to a no-inspection-on-delivery policy, which again assumes buyer's absolute confidence both in the relationship with a supplier and in technical and management capability for making a part without defect, which required two or three years of development, for instance. Therefore, such a system should be established step by step, not at once. (*1985 API Yearbook*, pp. 162–3)

An Illustration of the Development Process: the Case of Toyota[23]

The history of Toyota's development process[24] illustrates the difficulties faced by Japan's carmakers. On the basis of a first meeting in Tokyo in November 1939, Toyota and its suppliers formed a cooperative association (*kyoryoku-kai*), later reorganized in 1943 and named *Kyoho-kai*. This association was again renamed in 1946 *Tokai Kyoho-kai* when the *Tokyo* (later, *Kanto*) *Kyoho-kai* and *Kansai Kyoho-kai* were newly established, meaning that its members are located in Tokai District where Toyota is.[25]

In 1952–3 Toyota and 21 members of *Tokai Kyoho-kai* were subjected to the Small and Medium Enterprise Agency's *keiretsu* diagnosis.[26] A group from Aichi Prefecture's Manufacturing Industry Guidance Centre and Commerce Department visited each firm for a few days, going from factory to factory, along with representatives of Toyota's Purchasing Department.[27] The group produced a 'Factory Diagnosis Report' for each supplier, and a '*Keiretsu* Diagnosis Summary' for the *keiretsu* as a whole. Among their proposals was one 'to increase the number of personnel in the Purchasing Department and strengthen their technical guidance capability',[28] which, according to Wada (1991), was vital to the relationship between Toyota and its suppliers. At the time, only 40 employees in the parts and chassis sections within Toyota's Purchasing Department dealt with suppliers. And although suppliers were clamouring for technical guidance, only three out of 40 were responsible for technical guidance, and these were always busy handling design changes. The *Summary* also advised that the *Kyoho-kai*'s activity be shifted from promoting mutual friendship among members to improving management ability by holding seminars and factory visits. For Toyota itself, it was a wonderful opportunity to learn how to make a factory diagnosis. 17 members of *Tokai Kyoho-kai* participated in the second *keiretsu* diagnosis in 1954.[29]

After the *keiretsu* diagnosis, Toyota became more active in contributing to improvements in its suppliers' work process, and planned to introduce quality control into every step of the production process. In 1953, Toyota established a new section for quality control and a new Quality Control Committee within its Inspection Department. At the *Kyoho-kai*'s autumn meeting, Shoichi Saito, a managing director at Toyota, requested members' cooperation in implementing quality control (hereafter, QC) and in improving inspection and delivery. Toyota sent instructors to *Kyoho-kai* seminars on QC, and sent staff to visit suppliers' plants to survey their QC implementation. In 1954, Toyota's Inspection Department put an end to the distinction between 'in house' and purchased parts and abolished its QC section, instead transferring its function to the sections in charge of related technologies. Thus the Inspection Department came to be in charge of inspection of the whole production process from raw materials to assembly, and constantly gathered and disseminated information on quality to Toyota's every section and every supplier.

Despite these efforts, however, the frequency of stoppages on the production line due to defective parts increased in the process of rapid production expansion after 1956. As mentioned above, in 1958–9 Toyota needed special efforts to meet US Army quality requirements. In 1960 problems arose with the introduction of the new Corona model, and during 1960–2 Toyota was outstripped by Nissan in the domestic car sales race. These problems were expressed in remarks like 'the office can't keep up with the increase in production', or 'communication between sections isn't going as smoothly as before' and also resulted from a relaxing of control over suppliers. As a solution, Toyota in 1961 introduced a programme of total quality control (hereafter, TQC) and promoted company-wide QC as the backbone of management control. In 1963, inspection was transferred from the central Quality Control Department to each factory, and later evolved into a no-inspection-on-delivery policy. In 1964, a new Quality Control Head Office was formed, and the QC Department was renamed the Quality Guarantee Department. Activities related to suppliers were concentrated step by step in the Purchasing Department.

Toyota tried to spread QC consciousness not only within its own walls but also among its suppliers, which is a part of their attempt to establish and maintain good communication with each other in order to facilitate knowledge transfer, exchange of intention and the coordination of interests.

Between September 1960 and May 1961 personnel from both the QC Department and the Technology Section of the Purchasing Department visited and gave QC guidance to 68 suppliers. They graded[30] each supplier and classified them by QC level, applied different guidance to each and conducted short training courses accordingly between 1961 and 1962. Toyota also took an active part in seminars of the *Kyoho-kai* which had been an autonomous supplier organization. Toyota placed its own personnel in each of 11 new committees organized by *Kyoho-kai* in 1961, of which the Coordinating Committee for Rationalization, the QC Committee and the Technology Committee were the most important. The Coordination Committee, which consisted of a Toyota director, the head and section chiefs of Purchasing Department, and *Kyoho-kai* officials of section head rank or higher, carried out a survey of 56 *Tokai Kyoho-kai* member suppliers and inspection tours of individual factories.[31] The QC Committee was in charge of TQC education for the suppliers' top management, and the Technology Committee aimed at introducing and disseminating so-called 'value engineering' techniques.

Thus the *Kyoho-kai* and its committees were vitalized and worked closely with Toyota to implement TQC. The gradual but constant acceleration of this process was called the 'synchronization' of production schedules. In 1963, Toyota introduced a *kanban* system with some of its suppliers, and in 1964 it appealed to suppliers to increase the number of parts directly deliverable to the production line with on-the-spot inspection, as a step towards establishing a no-inspection-on-delivery system.[32] Toyota upgraded its internal structure and pushed forward the synchronization between production schedules of itself and its suppliers. Supplier evaluation was also systematized and a comprehensive evaluation system was in place in September 1966,[33] more than ten years after the *keiretsu* diagnosis.[34,35] Underlying this process is the incentive system discussed below.

4.4   INTRODUCTION TO JAPAN'S SUPPLIER–ASSEMBLER INCENTIVE SYSTEM

Sections 4.4 to 4.6 study the incentive system which supported productivity increases and product improvement in Japan's motor industry.[36] This section lays the groundwork for the next two sections. I first discuss three types of popular misunderstanding of inter-firm relations in Japan, namely the belief in the predominance of exploitation, strong assembler support for its suppliers, and a lack of voluntary efforts of suppliers. More time is then spent on a fourth mischaracterization: the closed nature and exclusiveness of the *kyoryoku-kai*.

Three Types of Popular Misunderstanding

First, the conventional view of the *shitauke* or the supplier–assembler relationship between small and large firms, characterized by such keywords as 'exploitation', 'burden-shifting' and 'subordination' or 'dependence', cannot explain productivity increases and product improvement among small businesses. Note that we are talking about the Japanese economy before 1970, on which, as was shown in the previous chapter, the dual-structure view is dominant even today. A rational reaction to the fact that 'exploited' firms continuously supplied rapidly expanded demands is to reject the assumption of small business exploitation. As shown in the next section, the active supplier contributions induced by the incentive system were one of the key factors in Japan's industrial success. This point is inconsistent with an assumption of small business exploitation.[37]

Second, although there has been a close relationship between an assembler and suppliers, the former's support to the latter was not critically important for increases in suppliers' productivity and quality improvement. For instance, a questionnaire in December 1963 (Mitsubishi Economic Research Institute, 1965) asked suppliers whether they were receiving support from a specific assembler. It requested answers of 'Yes' or 'No' to the existence of seven forms of 'cooperation' between assemblers and suppliers. Results are summarized in Table 4.2. No item received 'Yes' from a majority of respondents, and the highest ratio of '

'Yes' answers was for Technical Guidance, with 26 affirmative responses out of 56. Advance Payment received the lowest number of affirmative responses, at 3 out of 57. The order of other forms of assembler support was, from the lowest to highest: Personnel Interchange, Bank Loan, Lease and Disposal of Equipment and Tools, Investment and Materials.[38]

Third, suppliers took decisions for cost reduction and quality improvement voluntarily, rather than being forced to do so by an assembler. If requests were made by assemblers, they were accompanied by a commitment to a future relationship. The above questionnaire also asked suppliers the source of initiative behind their efforts to rationalize and reduce costs. From the following alternatives—(1) guidance from the 'parent company'; (2) own initiative; (3) others—47 of 58 respondents chose (2), eight chose both (1) and (2), and only three chose (1).[39]

Table 4.2 Support from an assembler (number of responses)

	Support	*No support*	*Total*
Personnel interchange	8	49	57
Investment	17	42	59
Advance payment	3	54	57
Materials	19	37	56
Technical guidance	26	30	56
Lease and disposal of equipment and tools	11	45	56
Bank loan	9	46	55

Source: Adapted from Mitsubishi Economic Research Institute (1965, p. 38).

We can easily find cases which suggest this outcome. For instance, Mr Endo, Nissan's senior managing director, was asked, 'Japanese parts suppliers have succeeded in production process improvement, but not yet in purchasing, indirect sections and management itself. Do you agree?' He responded: 'Yes, I agree ... We have achieved the objective for the production process. The next step is related to purchasing, financing and management itself. However, we cannot and will not do it as we will be unable to do it without going too far. Nobody can do such a job but they themselves ... We talk with them when requested, of course. For instance, we talked intimately on such important matters as their new plant investment in the USA' (*1987 API Yearbook*, pp. 65–6). Likewise, Yasusada Nobumoto, chairman of the Japanese Association of Automobile Parts Industry and president of Akebono Brake Industry, answered the following question, 'Although assemblers need cooperation of suppliers for their production in North America, they do not ask you to come together. Is this true?' with 'They do not ask. Asking to come together means the guarantee, to buy therefore, they cannot. When suppliers invest there, they say "welcome", but not "we will buy"' (*1987 API Yearbook*, p. 57).[40]

Cooperative Association (*kyoryoku-kai*)

Each Japanese assembler organizes its own first-tier suppliers' cooperative association (*kyoryoku-kai*). Toyota's *Kyoho-kai* and Nissan's *Takara-kai* and *Shoho-kai* are representative of the type. Let me make several comments on their actual role, as it is a big source of misunderstanding of Japan's industrial organization.

Sceptics may ask: Even if suppliers' voluntary decisions, rather than an assembler's strong guidance and support, were decisive, haven't cooperative associations played an important role? Haven't assemblers guided and strongly supported suppliers by controlling cooperative associations activities? Doesn't the Toyota case suggest this?

In response, let us first examine the history of Nissan's *Takara-kai* and *Shoho-kai* (equivalent to Toyota's *Kyoho-kai*). Nissan is Toyota's rival and during 1960–62 passed Toyota in the domestic car sales race.[41] In 1987, Nissan's *Takara-kai* had 104 members and the *Shoho-kai* had 58. Most large-scale parts suppliers belong both to the latter and to Toyota's *Kyoho-kai*. Therefore, compared with the average firm size of *Kyoho-kai* members, that of *Takara-kai* members is smaller and is also more closely connected with Nissan.[42] Nissan organized its *Takara-kai* in 1951, and began supplier education for the improvement of production and management technology thereafter. Starting with industrial engineering education for work standardization, they began QC education in 1958 and value analysis education in 1960. From April 1963, Nissan hoped to strengthen and change the basic character of the *Takara-kai* from an association for friendship to one for the improvement of management control.[43] Thus the role of Nissan's *Takara-kai* was smaller than that of *Kyoho-kai*, and that of *Shoho-kai* was smaller still.[44]

In the cases of Mazda, Mitsubishi and Honda, the role of cooperative associations is less impressive. Mazda organized a cooperative named *Toyu-kai* in 1952 of 20 first-tier machining firms (*50 Years of Mazda*, p. 310), but it organized the similar *Yoko-kai*, a cooperative association of vendors, only in May 1981, which 40 members of *Toyu-kai* joined (*1981 API Yearbook*, p. 85). Mitsubishi's *Kashiwa-kai* counts both vendors and machining firms as members. For vendors it serves as a forum for communication; its study group is organized only by machining firms (*1985 API Yearbook*, p. 94). Honda at first maintained an 'open policy' and has no cooperative association, but subsequently announced a purchasing policy 'to strengthen the relationship with firms which need Honda and Honda needs too' (*1981 API Yearbook*, pp. 93, 100). In 1987, Mazda's *Yoko-kai* had 177 members (60 in *Nishi-Nihon*; literally western Japan, but actually the district around Hiroshima where Mazda is located, 61 in *Kanto*, and 56 in *Kansai*), and there were 347 in Mitsubishi's *Kashiwa-kai*. Honda also produced a list of 300 main parts suppliers (*1987 API Yearbook*).[45]

Thus, compared with other Japanese carmakers, Toyota and its cooperative association is rather exceptional: the relationships among cooperative association members are closer, and Toyota was also the most active supporter of members' efforts at cost reduction and quality improvement. Toyota's influence over its suppliers is consequently stronger than that of the other assemblers over their suppliers. Therefore, even if a cooperative association has played an important role in influencing supplier behaviour and even if an assembler has guided and supported suppliers' voluntary decisions, as Toyota did, this was not true for Toyota before the mid-1960s, and until recent time for other assemblers either.[46]

Next, let us examine the closed nature of a cooperative association. I distinguish in this volume the closed nature of a cooperative from its 'exclusiveness', the former referring to the difficulty of new access to a cooperative and the assembler's high dependency on the purchase from cooperative members and the latter referring to the difficulty of joining more than two cooperatives. The cooperative association and its relationship with an assembler is regarded as a symbol of the 'Japanese-style' production system and is often called a 'production *keiretsu*' and criticized for its closed nature. Yet most of this criticism is based on misunderstanding. For an illustration, I again use Toyota as an example as it is thought to be the most 'closed'. First, an assembler normally transacts business directly with cooperative association members, but even Toyota has direct transactions with non-member firms, therefore it bought 20 per cent from non-members in 1967 (*1967 API Yearbook*, p. 312).[47] Second, though there is little turnover in cooperative association membership, not a few new members have been added. Of the 171 *Kyoho-kai* members in 1984, 153 had been members since 1973, 21 were new members and only three left.[48] As Wada (1991, p. 40) points out, in the process of production expansion in the 1960s, Toyota increased parts purchase without increasing the number of suppliers, which in turn accelerated the formation of a tiered inter-firm relationship.

Last, let us examine the 'exclusiveness' of the cooperative associations. Though the position as a cooperative member has been stable, the general membership is not always exclusive and the cooperative association is therefore not an exclusive organization. (I will return to this point in Section 12.9 below.) To illustrate, let us count the number of suppliers which are members both of Toyota's and of Nissan's cooperative associations. Given the two firms' long rivalry, one might expect this overlap to be small or non-existent. In 1987, however, seven of Nissan's 104 *Takara-kai* members and 38 of its 58 *Shoho-kai* members also belong to Toyota's *Kyoho-kai*. Firms which belong both to Nissan's *Takara-kai* and Toyota's *Kyoho-kai* are Ichikoh Industries, Usui Kokusai Sangyo, Sanoh Industrial, Topura, Fuji Bellows Fuji Vulbe and Marui Industrial. The list of joint members of Nissan's *Shoho-kai* and Toyota's *Kyoho-kai* includes, in addition to the manufacturers of glass, tyres, bearings and batteries, Akebono Brake, NOK, Kayaba, Kawashima Textile, Koito, Jidosha Kiki, Sumitomo Electric Industries, Chuo Spring, Tokico, Topy, Nifco, NHK Spring, NGK Spark Plug, Nippon Piston Ring, Matsushita Electric Industrial, Mitsuboshi Belting, Meiwa Industry, Yazaki Corporation, Riken and more (*1987 API Yearbook*). Corresponding numbers for 1967 were three out of 119 and 29 out of 40.[49] Many suppliers, such as Akebono Brake, Ichikoh Industries, NOK, Kayaba, Koito, Tokico, NGK Spark Plug, NHK Spring, Mitsuboshi Belting, and Yazaki Corporation belong to the cooperative associations of Japan's 'Big Five' carmakers (Toyota, Nissan, Mazda, Mitsubishi and Honda) and of other assemblers in 1987. Even Nihon Denso, the largest of the Toyota Group's firms, and one in which Toyota holds 23 per cent equity, belongs to cooperatives of all assemblers but Nissan.[50]

4.5 THE INCENTIVE MECHANISM BEHIND JAPAN'S INTER-FIRM RELATIONS

Throughout Japan's motor industry, from assembler to vendors and machining firm, all began almost simultaneous efforts to modernize and rationalize production equipment and management. These efforts were begun and maintained voluntarily, not at the behest of an assembler. As shown in Section 4.3, it took a long time to establish close cooperative relationships among firms and to make them effective sources of productivity growth and quality improvement. As suggested by the case of Toyota, at the beginning even assemblers did not clearly realize the importance of such efforts, therefore they also failed to realize what efforts should be made or how to make them. Realization was gradual and progress was a matter of trial and error. This point applies more strongly to suppliers, especially to small machining firms, who found it hard to understand what was required by an assembler and what type of efforts were necessary to succeed.[51]

Study of the mechanism supporting supplier–assembler relationships begin with the distinction between what each firm actually did in these supplier–assembler relationships and what functioned as an incentive and what type of incentives was provided by an assembler to induce greater supplier effort. It is also effective to distinguish between the starting stage and the developing stage of inter-firm relations.

The Starting Stage

To establish a mass-production car manufacturing system, an assembler first had to show suppliers with which it intended to develop longstanding relationships for division of labour the nature of the industry, the industry's growth potential and the role the assembler expected them to play. Next, assemblers had to indicate the level of technology and management to be achieved by suppliers (a temporary objective); persuade and induce suppliers to participate in this effort and to work towards their required role; and support supplier efforts and guide them towards effective goal achievement.

As mentioned in Section 4.3, the motor industry had production requirements which were not so popular at the time. Hence educating supplier, owners and managers about the meaning of their commitment to participation required a lot of time and energy, for it demanded a fundamental change in their minds. Suppliers also had to spend time and energy to understand these requirements and to upgrade their employees and equipment.

At the beginning, therefore, assemblers provided incentives for supplier efforts and gave them constant concrete guidance to achieve the required cost reduction, product quality and timely delivery.

The Incentive System at the Starting Stage

What incentive system made suppliers continuously commit resources to the relationship with an assembler? What the supplier realized (hereafter, 'skill') by its own commitment and with an assembler's support and guidance can be divided into two parts, the part (hereafter, assembler-specific) which is entirely lost or dramatically reduced in value when the trade relationship with the assembler ends, and the remaining part (hereafter, general).[52] Compared with the next stage of development, when the supplier is more strongly requested to invest in large-scale production equipment, especially in special purpose machinery, and to synchronize production schedules with the assembler, the relative share of the latter general skill is higher. This stage enables the suppliers to play a part in this modern mass-production, assembly-type industry and therefore makes it an attractive partner to other assemblers and even to firms in other assembly-type industries.[53]

The supplier's loss suffered in ending the relationship with the assembler depends on the size of commitment, the relative share of assembler-specific commitment and the length of time required to search for other purchasers.[54]

Note that supplier losses are relatively smaller than assembler losses, which are composed of the cost of securing alternative suppliers and costs imposed upon the smooth running of the production system during this period.[55] The fruit of the assembler's sustained efforts to support and guide the supplier's commitment to raise the 'skill' quality to the required level entirely disappears, and it is left to choose from three alternatives: to select and support another new supplier, to increase purchase from other existing suppliers, or to produce the required components 'in-house'.

Given the constraints on the assemblers, what incentive system is ideal and which was actually adopted? The assembler's objective is fourfold: to secure supplier participation, to maintain good relations with the supplier (to protect supplier defection), to induce continuous effort from the supplier to play its required role, and to establish close relations with a group of suppliers among which a well-functioning system for division of labour is organized.

The most fundamental problem for the assembler was in showing the potential profitability of the venture and persuading the supplier to participate. What the assembler had to show was fourfold: (1) that the motor industry had a bright future; (2) that this assembler would be a success in this industry; (3) that it would not adopt such opportunistic behaviour as to exploit after the supplier was committed (non-existence of hold-up problems), by assuring no *ex post* change in such contractual terms as price, quantity, lead-time for delivery, term of validity and so on; and (4) that it would provide appropriate and necessary support and guidance. At the starting stage of the motor industry, it was not easy to persuade suppliers on the first point, and it was much harder to persuade on the second point.[56] What it could do, therefore, was only to make a guarantee on (3) and (4) and accumulate their trust by its achievements.[57]

Thus an assembler had to develop a long-run programme, show it to suppliers and accumulate their trust by following it sincerely. A supplier, in contrast, was in a relatively advantageous position. First, as the process to meet the assembler's demand took a long time and could only be achieved on a step-by-step basis, the supplier could choose at each step whether to take the next one. Second, even if the relationship ended, the supplier would retain the skills accumulated over the time. As mentioned above, at this starting stage, the ratio of assembler-specific skill was low, and the assembler's loss would be larger than the supplier's.

The Developing Stage

By the end of the starting stage, a supplier had become a part of a modern, mass-production, assembly-type industry. The assembler's next objective was to request the supplier to restructure its production capacity to allow for dramatic expansion in production and to improve the efficiency of the whole division-of-labour production system. The assembler's request was fourfold: to expand production capacity by active investment and new hiring; to invest in modern, large-scale equipment for increased efficiency and precision; to contribute to the improvement of the whole production system through synchronization of production schedules and introduction of specific use machinery; and finally to coordinate the interests and efforts of the assembler and suppliers for common objectives.

As before, a supplier had to spend much time, energy and money, and proceeded in a step-by-step fashion. However, at this stage the supplier had to commit itself further to the trade relationship with the assembler, for the scale of investment in equipment and new hiring became immeasurably greater and the ratio of assembler-specific skill rose. To encourage this commitment, the assembler had to secure its own strong position in the market to present a rosy future for suppliers; define clearly what was essential to the improvement of the whole system in order to show suppliers objectives and the means to reach them with support and guidance; and design an appropriate incentive system for the suppliers.

The Incentive System at the Developing Stage

What was the incentive system that induced suppliers to maintain their efforts at the developing stage? While the ratio of assembler-specific skill and the supplier's potential losses from ending the relationship grew larger at this stage, the assembler's potential losses also grew. The higher a supplier's skill level, and the higher the ratio of assembler-specific skill,[58] the larger the assembler's potential cost. Similarly, the higher the assembler's purchase ratio of some specific part from the supplier, the larger would be the assembler's potential cost of securing alternative supply sources and the potential cost to the smooth running of the total production system from supplier defection during this period.

Why did suppliers decide to maintain and further commit themselves to the relationship? What incentive system elicited such decisions? A combination of four factors made it possible: (1) the reduction of supplier's risk by demonstrating *ex ante* a risk-sharing rule, or by fixing a compensation rule by convention;[59] (2) knowledge that the assembler's loss from ending the relationship with a supplier is tremendous; (3) the externalities of the assembler's action against a supplier: the assembler's knowledge that action taken against a supplier may adversely affect its relations with all other suppliers, and that the cost from the latter may exceed the direct cost of ending the original relation;[60] and (4) the assembler's efforts from the start to make a supplier realize and trust the long-term character of the relationship. This works as a guarantee to suppliers that the assembler will not take short-sighted action. Each concrete decision is supported by a common understanding that the relationship as a whole is established and maintained for the long-run interest of both parties. Thus suppliers recognize that assemblers will not risk the whole system for short-run gain.

The last of these factors applies more clearly to a vendor. Mr Endo, Nissan's executive managing director, stated in an interview:

We purchase from a vendor not parts but technology, parts as a result of the technology. We sign a contract to purchase the parts now, on the assumption that the supplier will improve their products with new ideas and better technology even when we use the similar parts for the next model. Thus we contract not only for parts now but also for research and development in the future. (*1986 API Yearbook*, p. 87).

Surrounded by the reassurance of these four factors, each supplier made successive decisions on three points relating to assembler requests for commitment: whether to comply with the request, under what conditions and to what degree. It was often hard for an assembler to observe and judge to what degree the supplier complied with its request, and a promise was not credible unless its implementation was observable. I will discuss this point in the next section, as the countermeasure to this situation was a part of the set of measures for efficiency improvement of the whole system. Remember, however, that, since longstanding relations with the assembler were also profitable to the supplier, the assembler must have placed trust in the supplier from early on. Assemblers made efforts to show this and to persuade the supplier that keeping its commitments was indispensable to that trust.

A supplier made commitments successively, and the effective periods of some commitments overlapped. Therefore, neither suppliers nor assemblers regarded individual requests and corresponding commitments as independent, but regarded them as interrelated. Hence, maintaining friendly, productive and mutually beneficial supplier–assembler relationships for division of labour was the basic safety device.[61]

4.6 TWO TOPICS RELATED TO THE INCENTIVE SYSTEM

Measures for Efficiency Improvement

In Section 4.5, I asked what had worked to reduce uncertainty between suppliers and an assembler, and concluded that maintenance of the relationships for the division of labour was the basic element to which the assembler devoted its effort. Readers may ask immediately how assemblers established and maintained *efficient* production systems through stable long-run relations when participating suppliers could thereby enjoy monopolistic positions unavailable through spot market transactions.[62] The revealed choice of assemblers for long-run relationships with suppliers implies their relative superiority to spot market transactions and 'in-house' production. Therefore the real question is how efficiency improvement could be achieved in such a relationship.[63] Five measures comprise the apparatus for efficiency improvement in the supplier–assembler relationship as a whole, that is, both in the relations between individual suppliers and an assembler and in those between the entire group of suppliers and an assembler.

First comes the use of competitive pressure and incentives for better performance. Each supplier always has rival firms within the system, including the assembler itself, with capabilities adequate to replace that supplier quickly should the need arise.[64] Toyota's 'two-vendor policy' is a famous example.[65] Even in cases where it takes a long time to secure alternative suppliers, or when ending the relationship with a given supplier risks reducing the efficiency of the whole system, with a careful long-run plan, and every necessary procedure and explanation to other suppliers, the assembler can use competitive pressure and replace the supplier if this is necessary and rational. The assembler can also increase the number of suppliers[66] within the system in order to reward good performers with a higher share of orders over time. Thus the use of competitive pressure can be an effective measure in the long run.

Second, direct intervention is taken to prevent waste. An assembler can reduce total production cost by asking suppliers for delivery at a price assemblers estimate as feasible,[67] and by preventing waste through guidance. This requires detailed information about the supplier's technology and management.[68] Though asking too much may hurt the smooth operation of the system, appropriate guidance for and intervention in the suppliers' production process can be effective.

Third, assembler guidance improves the whole production process. Guidance can encompass both the cooperative activities of all the suppliers and such individual decisions as choice of materials and materials suppliers, the choice of tools and machinery and their use, equipment layout, division of work and training method. Assembler guidance is the most effective diffusion route to suppliers of information and know-how regarding the most efficient use of up-to-date machinery.[69]

Fourth, assemblers urge suppliers to make efforts at improvement. The progress of production technology in the motor industry is largely based on accumulated efforts for improvement within the factories of both assemblers and suppliers. Suppliers contributed much in boosting efficiency and reducing the number of rejected articles.[70] Therefore, it is of critical importance to give suppliers the incentive to state their needs and to propose ideas for the improvement of the whole production process. In 1966, for instance, when Toyota set up a Purchasing Control Department and began to spread TQC know-how to principal suppliers, it introduced an incentive system: if a supplier's suggestion on the reduction of parts cost actually led to cost savings, Toyota would return to the supplier half the amount saved (see Wada, 1991, pp. 42–3). We have also heard of a complaint by an assembler of insufficient supplier effort. Following discussion of a die compensation scheme (see note 59), Nissan's Mr Endo requested suppliers to

> express frankly your opinion when some of our proposal on design changes are not so important for users, and to tell us how much even a slight change will cost when you have already completed the die. We ask you to give to our design section your information and know-how as manufacturers of specialized parts with expertise. (*1986 API Yearbook*, p. 98)

Fifth, assemblers work to improve the efficiency of the entire system of division of labour. This can be done, for example, by smoothing overtime flow of orders for parts delivery, thereby contributing to the effective use of supplier capacity by requiring the reorganization of their production system, and by increasing lot sizes through standardization and the use of common parts to reduce supplier's unit cost.

Taken together, these five measures supplement the incentive system and improve efficiency in the entire division of labour between assemblers and suppliers. Note that none of these measures can be effective without close cooperation with, and the active participation of, suppliers, and that these longstanding relations with the assembler are also profitable to the supplier.

Long-term Relationship with Flexibility or Long-run Flexibility

The second, third and fourth measures to enhance productive efficiency mentioned in the latter part of the previous section are based on the assumption that the supplier–assembler relationship is commonly understood to be established and maintained for the long-run interest of both assemblers and suppliers, or at least suppliers recognize and trust the assemblers' long-run behaviour. The former part of the previous section, on the other hand, argues that the competitive pressure can be effective in improving long-run efficiency. If so, what is the logical relation of these arguments and the meaning of the long run?

For an illustration of an assembler's problem, let me list the cases where it would reduce the volume of trades or end a relationship with a supplier unless the above-mentioned safety devices worked: (1) when a supplier falls below expectations in productive efficiency or research and development; (2) when a supplier is made obsolete, say through a change in materials from steel to plastic; (3) when depression necessitates a reduction in orders for a supplier owing to falling car production or a shift to 'in-house' production; (4) when an assembler wants to leave the market or close a factory. An assembler's problem is to choose a profit maximizing alternative, subject to a constraint: suppliers trust that assemblers will not take action to reduce trade or end relationships in the long run because of the huge costs imposed by the above devices.

Though all relationships between an assembler and its suppliers are longstanding, they are not identical in character. Assembler relationships with cooperative associations (*kyoryoku-kai*) members, for example, have higher priority than those with non-members. One assembler even ranked cooperative association members by importance,[71] and followed this ranking when allocating orders under conditions of falling demands.[72] In this way, the entire supplier–assembler system has flexibility. Note that the phrase 'long-term' trade relationship is used without a clear definition. There exists no common understanding of this term which is defined only as not being a 'short-term' or spot transaction (see Chapter 12 of this volume).[73] In what follows I do not present a clear definition of the term, but sketch an image of how the system's long-run flexibility is maintained.

When an assembler intends to reduce interaction or end its relationship with a supplier, it first must judge whether it has grounds to justify its action and persuade the other suppliers. When it correctly judges in the affirmative, its action will not have a big effect on the other suppliers' reaction. However, when it takes action without showing its necessity, by stimulating the distrust of the other suppliers it will suffer a long-run heavy loss. The same logic applies also in the case of an allocation of orders among suppliers, particularly given a shrinking number of total orders. Though a supplier is persuaded at the beginning of the relationship that it will not end without reason, the future flow of orders from the assembler remains uncertain. Like the other suppliers, it understands that the volume of orders, the profitability of the relationship, and its position and the assembler's ranking among suppliers depend entirely upon its own performance. Here the safety device works also when the assembler takes an action against the common understanding.

When assemblers shift from purchasing from the suppliers to 'in-house' production in order to maintain employment for their own workers, the supplier distrust which results and the accompanying collapse of active supplier cooperation will result in long-run heavy losses for the assemblers. If a factory shuts down without persuasive reason or in defiance of common understanding, suppliers at other plants will react sharply. A decision to leave one market (such as the car market) will damage supplier relationships in other market (such as bus or truck markets). Supplier reaction to, and therefore assembler costs stemming from, a given reduction in orders depends upon the way in which it is justified. Where assemblers act to inform suppliers of the reduction in orders as early as possible and otherwise ease the adjustment suppliers face, the costs to the assembler in lost supplier loyalty will be minimal.

To sum up, a group of firms in supplier–assembler relationships with an assembler are mutually dependent and form an organic whole.[74] An assembler, the core of the group, cannot costlessly replace suppliers without good reason. Assemblers can totally ignore these costs only when they leave the market entirely.

4.7 CONCLUDING REMARKS

If we can agree that the economic problem of society is mainly one of rapid adaptation to changes in the particular circumstances of time and place, it would seem to follow that the ultimate decisions must be left to the people who are familiar with these circumstances, who know directly of the relevant changes and of the resources immediately available to meet them . . . We must solve it by some form of decentralization. But this answers only part of our problem. We need decentralization because only thus can we ensure that the knowledge of the particular circumstances of time and place will be promptly used. But the 'man on the spot' cannot decide solely on the basis of his limited but intimate knowledge of the facts of his immediate surroundings. There still remains the problem of communicating to him such further information as he needs to fit his decisions into the whole pattern of changes of the larger economic system. (Hayek, 1945, pp. 524–5)

This statement, which Friedrich von Hayek wrote ten years before Toyota launched its first car the 'Crown', comes to mind at the end of this study of the formation and workings of Japan's supplier–assembler system. Manufacturers of such a complex object as a car face the same problem as Hayek illustrates. Their success is built on close, long-term relationships with many suppliers rather than upon 'in-house' production or spot transactions.

Japanese car assemblers began with suppliers lacking strong technological and managerial abilities but achieved productivity growth and quality improvement in a short time. Japan's assemblers and its suppliers have answered Hayek's challenge: induced by assemblers with recognition of the importance of a 'man on the spot', armed only with potential, suppliers have worked continuously, with originality and their best effort, and assemblers have created and provided information necessary to fit individual firms' decisions into the pattern of overall systemic change. This process required much time and close cooperative relationships with suppliers, and the variation among assemblers in their success at achieving this goal has resulted in the tremendous variation in their overall performance in the marketplace.[75]

Note that it is hard for Toyota's rivals to imitate the process leading to its success and harder still to achieve equal success by implementing it. The process is a collection of steps taken individually as the best response to the circumstances of the moment. Rivals, ignorant of the reasoning behind each step, faced risks in trying to copy them.[76] As mentioned above, even its Japanese rivals praise Toyota, suggesting that a wide gap still exists between them. Even Toyota's *Kanto Kyoho-kai* members did not clearly realize in the 1970s what had occurred in Toyota's *Tokai Kyoho-kai*.[77]

As also mentioned in Section 4.4, latecomers to the industry like Mazda, Mitsubishi and Honda have recently strengthened ties with suppliers. There are three reasons for this. First, the demand for frequent model changes and a rapid development process necessitates the incorporation of supplier ideas at an earlier stage of product development. Second, assemblers realize that they can reduce the cost of parts through communicating, asking advice and exchanging opinions at an earlier point in time.[78,79] Third, assemblers have realized that close relationships from an early stage of development with specialized suppliers are effective in incorporating rapid technological advances, like electronics, lightweight materials and many-item, small-lot production technology, into their products.

Though the changing character of the problems faced by assemblers may alter the appearance of Japan's supplier–assembler relationships, the basic problem they overcome and the mechanism supporting them will not change. Variation in assemblers' organizational performance continues to cause tremendous variation in their market performance.

Part II
Financial Market

5 Economic Analysis of the 'Loan-Concentration' Mechanism

5.1 INTRODUCTION

This chapter examines the 'loan-concentration' mechanism, often referred to as financial dual structure, dual structure in the flow of funds and financial burden shifting. The loan-concentration view asserts that a *de facto* mechanism in the Japanese financial sector directed loans to large firms rather than small businesses, thereby harming the financial interests of small business. Loan concentration is closely related to *keiretsu* loans, main banks and corporate groups, and has been accepted as a serious phenomenon since the second half of the 1950s. Together with the dual-structure view, the loan-concentration view has been the basis of small business policy, especially in the 1960s.

The basic questions I ask about the loan-concentration view are: (1) What is the reality behind the term? (2) Has the view been logically consistent and coherent over time? (3) Has the existence of the loan-concentration mechanism been proved persuasively? (4) Who created and maintained this mechanism and why? (5) Does the loan-concentration view take into consideration market forces, which often constrain the choice sets of economic agents? Examination of representative academic literature, such as Shinohara (1961) and Kawaguchi (1965, 1966), leads me to answer these questions in the negative for the decade beginning in the mid-1950s. I also present reasons why the loan-concentration view is unpersuasive. The loan-concentration mechanism is a component and for some the basis of the dual-structure view; thus the argument in this chapter is directly related to that of Part I.

Section 5.2 defines the problem: representative treatments and their place in the literature are explained and Section 5.3 lays out my seven reasons for their rejection. Section 5.4 examines the reality of the 'loan-concentration' mechanism, that is, the long-run structure and the short-run dynamic process over the course of trade cycles of loan concentration. Section 5.5 discusses the reality of the 'adhesion relationship' (*yuchaku kankei*) between large banks and large firms or *keiretsu* loans, which form the basis of the loan-concentration view. Section 5.6 examines the empirical evidence supporting the conventional argument. Section 5.7 offers concluding remarks.

5.2 DEFINITION OF THE PROBLEM

In a joint volume,[1] Yamashita (1985, p. 231) declares at the outset of the section entitled 'The Nature of Small Business Financial Problems': 'we recognize small business financial problems as serious since they are rooted in the dual structure, one of the basic features of Japan's economy'. Teranishi (1974, p. 51) also begins his 'Loan-Concentration, Credit Rationing, and Credit Limit' by arguing: 'we can sum up the main features of the financial side of the postwar Japanese economy with "the loan concentration to large firms through the predominance of indirect financing" '[2] Our first concern is how deeply the loan-concentration mechanism has taken root in the dual structure and whether loans been made to large firms rather than small businesses. I thought this mechanism never existed. No literature totally denies the existence of this mechanism and its relation to the dual structure, but little of the literature proves its existence clearly with careful investigation and hard evidence. Like the dual-structure view, a wide variety of views exists in regard to the loan-concentration mechanism, and sharp controversy over the various aspects of interpretation rapidly developed.[3] Nobody denies Kawaguchi's position as the most influential promoter of the loan-concentration view. I take Kawaguchi (1965) as representative of the field.[4]

Because of the dominance in Japan of dogmatic Germanic theory, mentioned in Section 1.1, the literature and debates over the Japanese economy have been dominated by focus on financial factors, such as financial phenomena like loans and shareholdings, financial institutions like banks, and financial markets like loan markets and stock markets. This literature focused on the loan-concentration mechanism. In addition to the five basic questions listed in the previous section, critical examination of the literature leads us also to an anatomy of the underlying traditional, dominant theory, recognizing economic phenomena not as a result of exchange by agreement but by coercion. The next two chapters investigate the relationships between financial markets and large firms, the alleged beneficiaries of burden shifting, thereby focusing on the other side of the loan-concentration mechanism. The main-bank view argues that Japanese large firms have special long-term relationships with one or more large banks, and that these pervade the Japanese financial market and therefore influence Japan's industrial organization. Each large bank has such a relationship with a group of large firms, called 'corporate groups' and the corporate-group view asserts that these groups are important for understanding the Japanese economy. If the loan-concentration mechanism never existed, as shown below, these two views lose their foundation. Hence this chapter is a basis for the next two chapters.

As with the dual-structure view, support among both academics and the public for the loan-concentration view had weakened rapidly by 1970. However, just like the keywords for the Japanese economy in the 1950s and 1960s, the loan-concentration view and related keywords are often used to describe Japan's economy today. Some, like Yamashita (1985, p. 232), insist that there has been no change: 'As the financial dual structure takes root in the real economy, it cannot be solved in a short time. It applies in today's low-growth era also. In fact, the problem was obscured by the high speed of growth in the high-growth era, but it was revealed as a serious problem in the low-growth era'.[5]

5.3 SEVEN REASONS FOR REJECTING THE LOAN-CONCENTRATION VIEW

There are seven reasons why I think the loan-concentration view unpersuasive and invalid even in the second half of the 1950s and the first half of the 1960s. If Japan's financial markets were a world of exchange by agreement rather than by coercion and those markets were competitive, as in other developed economies, the loan-concentration mechanism could neither have worked nor existed. Only my third reason below – the large number of financial institutions competing in the market – directly related to the second assumption. The first six reasons, including the third, are related to the validity of the implicit assumption of the loan-concentration view: Japan's financial markets were a world of exchange by coercion. Each asserts that observed facts are inconsistent with this assumption and therefore with the loan-concentration view. The seventh reason directly opposes the existence of burden-shifting.

First, as shown in Chapter 3, small businesses were more profitable than large firms and the number of small businesses has increased over time. Such facts are not consistent with the loan-concentration view, which implies a disadvantageous environment for small businesses, resulting in low profitability and decreasing numbers.

Second, though 'specialization' is the guiding principle of government policy toward financial institutions, 'specialization of city and regional banks resulting in the former concentrating on big business and the latter on other business is far from complete' (Wallich and Wallich, 1976, p. 281). As mentioned in Section 1.3, the phrases 'city banks' and 'regional banks' are colloquial, not legal, terms. Both city banks and regional banks are established under the same provisions of the Banking Act, and both have the same legal status and usually called 'ordinary banks'. Actually, different restrictions are not imposed on either group and as, shown in Table 5.1, as a proportion of their loans, city banks lent more to small businesses than regional banks in the 1960s. This is not consistent with the loan-concentration view, since a large bank in a special relation, called an 'adhesion relationship' (examined closely in Section 5.5), with a group of large firms could and did lend to small businesses, implying that banks behaved in a world of exchange by agreement rather than by coercion. The alleged phenomena could have occurred only when the 'adhesion relationship' was so special as to force those banks consistently to sacrifice their own profits by directing loans to large firms rather than small businesses.

Third, as also mentioned in Sections 1.3 and 1.5, the number of financial institutions has not been small, and even large firms in close, long-term relationships with large banks do not borrow exclusively from one bank.

Table 5.1   Loan shares of financial institutions (three-year running average except for 1966–7, per cent)

		Small businesses			Large firms	
	1957–59	*60–62*	*63–65*	*66–67*	*1963–65*	*66–67*
City banks (1)	} 78.7	69.3	35.6	36.5	66.4	67.9
Regional banks			26.0	24.2	10.3	10.7
Mutual loans & savings banks (2)	6.4	13.1	19.8	18.8	1.1	0.8
Public financial institutions (3)	6.1	6.9	7.3	10.1	6.0	7.4
Others (4)	8.8	10.7	11.4	10.5	16.3	13.6

Notes:
(1)   Also includes long-term credit banks and trust banks.
(2)   Also includes credit associations, credit cooperatives, Central Cooperative Bank of Commerce and Industry, etc.
(3)   Includes Small Business Finance Cooperation, People's Finance. Corporation, Japan Development Bank, Export–Import Bank of Japan, etc.
(4)   Includes individuals, corporations, credit companies, life insurance companies, etc.
Source: Bank of Japan, *Financial Statement of Small Business in Japan* for small business and *Financial Statement of Principal Enterprises in Japan* for large firms.

These facts are not consistent with the loan-concentration view, since the large number of competing financial institutions undermine the cartels among financial institutions necessary for the loan-concentration mechanism. Without effective cartels, each bank suffers a loss from 'adhesion relationship', creating profitable business chance for other large banks through arbitration.

Fourth, among all private financial institutions, asset shares of city banks decreased continuously, from 50.5 per cent in 1953 to 41.8 per cent in 1963 and 36.1 per cent in 1973.[6] The decline mainly reflects a government policy of allowing more new branches for non-city banks. Partly as a result of this policy, 'the city banks have been confronted during much of the postwar period with a demand for funds that they have not been able to satisfy from their deposits' (Wallich and Wallich, 1976, p. 284). Attempts by city banks to meet this demand through borrowing on the short-term money market, called the 'call market', in which other financial institutions place their surplus funds, and relending to industry were criticized as 'overloans' and strongly discouraged by the government. This is not consistent with the loan-concentration view, since these facts imply that a larger amount of funds actually remained in non-city banks which these banks chose to lend to large firms through large banks rather than to small businesses.

Fifth, large firms in 'adhesion relationships' with large banks could profitably relend to small business. As shown in Table 5.1, however, small businesses borrowed most of their funds from financial institutions and, as mentioned in Section 4.4, even suppliers in close relationships with a car assembler rarely received support in the form of advance payment or bank loans. Such facts are inconsistent with the loan-concentration view, since large firms did not profit through chances that must have existed under the loan-concentration mechanism.

Sixth, as illustrated by Figure 5.1, the proportion of equity to total capitalization of large firms was consistently higher than that of small businesses over time, and it gradually fell to the level of that of small businesses by 1970 as support for the dual-structure view weakened.[7] This fact is inconsistent with the loan-concentration view, since it was large firms that could make advantageous use of the financial market and this advantage is thought to have gradually disappeared by 1970.[8]

Seventh, data show the opposite to the loan-concentration view, particularly burden shifting during the tight-money periods. As shown below in Tables 5.4 and 5.5, large firms appear to have suffered more from the restrictive monetary policy than small business, and it is because not of restrictive policy but because of a worsening outlook for business and industry that small businesses postponed or reduced equipment orders.

Figure 5.1   The equity–total capitalization ratio, 1960–74 (per cent)

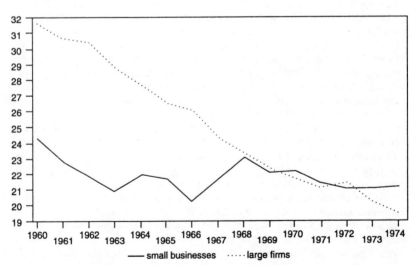

Sources: Bank of Japan, *Financial Statement of Small Business in Japan* for small businesses and *Financial Statement of Principal Enterprises in Japan* for large firms.

5.4 THE REALITY OF THE 'LOAN-CONCENTRATION' VIEW

As one proponent of the loan-concentration view described it,

> The loan-concentration mechanism is the financial mechanism which directs loans to the large firms sector, and as a result restricts the supply of loans to the small business sector (and the agricultural). Two types of study were carried out. One was the examination of the long-run structure of loan concentration, which showed a high ratio of loans to large firms as a per centage of total loans of all financial institutions, especially city banks . . . The second type studied the dynamic process of loan concentration over the course of trade cycles, . . . which showed a cyclical pattern of imposing strict restriction on small business loans in order to supply large firms' demand in tight-money periods and loosened small business loan restrictions only in slack-money periods. (Kawaguchi, 1965, p. 138)

Structural Concentration

Let me begin my critique with the first type of study, the degree of loan concentration. As the primary concern of Kawaguchi (1965) is the second type of study, I refer to Shinohara (1961) and Kawaguchi (1966) to examine the first. However, neither of these two studies offers evidence for a loan-concentration mechanism, nor do they show how the effects of selective lending vary from the situation which would obtain without selectivity. Therefore I take these studies as illustrative of the loan concentration view rather than as representative empirical studies.

The relevant section of Shinohara (1961, pp. 109–12) simply recounts the facts, beginning with loan concentration for equipment funds. Using 1956 data from *Conspectus of Listed Firms* (*Jojo Kaisha Soran*. Tokyo: Nihon Keizai Shimbun-sha, annual), he lists firms with total borrowing for equipment funds exceeding 200 million yen, and points out three facts: (1) 57 listed firms take about 80 per cent of the total borrowings for equipment funds of all listed firms, and 48.7 per cent of the national total; (2) electric power, shipping and steel firms are the dominant borrowers,[9] and the Japan Development Bank, Industrial Bank of Japan and Long-Term Credit Bank of Japan are the main lenders; (3) large firms capable of self-financing tend to depend on equity capital rather than borrowing.

Shinohara turns next to the working capital in the section entitled 'Loan *Keiretsu* of Banks' and points out four facts (p. 118): (1) the total borrowing of 344 firms with over 100 million yen in paid-in capital account for 51.1 per cent of the total borrowing of all corporate firms with more than 2 million yen in paid-in capital; (2) the concentration ratio of loans of each city bank to its ten largest borrowers is highest for Mitsui Bank at 11.9 per cent, and ranges between 8 and 9 per cent for the others; (3) this ratio is higher for the Japan Development Bank, Industrial Bank of Japan and Long-Term Credit Bank of Japan; (4) loans to large general trading companies (*sogo shosha*) are given top priority by large banks, and take large shares of their total loans. Shinohara concludes with the question: 'What type or degree of distortion has resulted from such loan concentration in the equipment and inventory investment behavior of large firms?', which leads to Kawaguchi's (1965) second type of study.

Turning to Kawaguchi (1966), we find a similar statement of the facts. Kawaguchi's section on the Reality of Loan Concentration begins by stating: 'The Japanese financial system has had a strong inclination to allocate funds to the large firm sector. In addition, the so-called "loan-concentration" function was strengthened in the postwar period by low interest rate policy strongly requested by the revived "Monopoly Capital", especially "Industrial Capital"' (p. 77). About borrowers Kawaguchi points out that: (1) large firms take a high proportion of total loans; (2) the ratio of increase in total capitalization to total sales is higher in large firms than in small businesses; (3) the ratio of total increase in equity and long-term debt to increase in long-term assets is higher in large firms than in small businesses. Stating, 'The indirect finance dominated by city banks was the core for such capital or loan concentration,' he asks, 'Why then do city banks realize such loan-concentration?' Focusing on bank behaviour, Kawaguchi points out that: (4) though the share of large firms' total borrowing does not change, a higher share of total loans of city banks and local banks goes to large firms than before;[10](5) the ratio of loans from *keiretsu* bank to each *keiretsu* borrower is calculated to illustrate close bank–borrower *keiretsu* connections; (6) even financial *keiretsu* banks loan to large firms outside their own *keiretsu*, including firms in competing *keiretsu* groups.[11] Kawaguchi proceeds to his next section on the 'Causes of Loan-Concentration', claiming that the strongest hypothesis for the formation of loan concentration, and therefore of financial *keiretsu*, is the 'One-Set-Ism' view of Professor Miyazaki.[12]

Loan Concentration during Trade Cycles

The primary goal of Kawaguchi (1965) was to investigate 'burden shifting' to small business during the tight-money period between the summer of 1961 and the end of 1962.[13] Kawaguchi argues that burden shifting to small business during the recent tight-money period was obviously as strong as that during the previous ones. Focusing on city banks, Kawaguchi points out that increases in city bank loans to small businesses were always smaller than those to large firms except in easy-money periods, and concludes that small businesses were forced to play the role of a cushion for large firms (p. 156).

Description of observations is Kawaguchi's main concern, but the 'hypothesis' that follows is more interesting for us, particularly for the examination of an adhesion relationship in the next section. He proposes a 'simple hypothesis' for the behaviour of city banks, after declaring that they are the core of the supply side in the loan-concentration mechanism. His 'hypothesis' is composed of seven parts (pp. 156–8): (1) a city bank has a close relationship, called an adhesion relationship (*yuchaku kankei*), with a group of large firms, and constantly supplies them with a larger amount of loans at lower interest rates than rational profit-maximizing behaviour would suggest optimal; (2) the low interest rate policy of the government stimulates large firms' demand for loans; (3) committed to heavy lending to large firms, city banks must severely restrict small business loans; (4) the low interest rate policy significantly lowers interest rates paid by large firms; (5) in order to survive and play the role, city banks have to make profits by lending also to small businesses, but with extremely high interest rates; (6) in tight-money periods, city banks continue to lend to large firms, in the process sacrificing potential profits by forgoing small business lending and borrowing at high cost from external sources; (7) as a result of their losses during tight-money periods, city banks try hard to recover in the ensuing period of easy credit, when large firms' borrowing demand is relatively weak, by increasing small business loans at the high loan rate prevalent in the previous tight-money period.[14] However, again I find here neither any hypothesis nor the evidence for the mechanism.

This representative literature is weakened by the absence of an explicit hypothesis accounting for deviation between the actual state of affairs and a hypothetical state without the alleged mechanism in evidence. No definition of burden shifting (*shiwayose*) or 'mechanism' is offered either, except for the one cited above. I find only repeated claims for the importance of an 'adhesion relationship' between large banks and groups of large firms.

5.5 THE REALITY OF THE ADHESION RELATIONSHIP

Let us examine the reality of the adhesion relationship more closely. The following questions are considered: What is the 'adhesion relationship', and what claims are made for it? Whose behaviour exhibits 'adhesion'? Whose interests are served by the relationship? What are those interests and how does the adhesion relationship satisfy them? Assuming the existence of adhesion relationships, do banks realize and maintain the alleged burden shifting to small business? The claims of Kawaguchi are again examined below.

What is the Adhesion Relationship?

In his 'hypothesis' mentioned in the previous section, Kawaguchi defines an adhesion relationship as a close relationship between a city bank and a group of large firms[15] whereby the former supplies the latter with loans constantly at lower interest rates in greater amount than rational profit-maximizing behavior would suggest optimal. Kawaguchi (1966, pp. 83–4) further suggests that the 'adhesion relationship' is a relationship between a bank and *keiretsu* firms in a *keiretsu* corporate group based on bank loans and stock cross-holdings:

> The formation through bank loans and stock cross-holdings of corporate groups called financial *keiretsu* is a result of loan concentration, or more

generally, capital concentration ... Once such concentration is established, it spurs further concentration, and especially in tight-money periods it prompts the preferential allocation of loans to *keiretsu* firms by restricting loans to non-*keiretsu* firms. The fortunes of the bank are thereby closely related to those of the *keiretsu* corporate group to which it lends so heavily.

As an explanation for the formation of the loan-concentration mechanism, Kawaguchi (1966, p. 87) points to the 'One-Set-Ism' view of Professor Miyazaki.[16]

Thus the 'adhesion relationship' is at the core of the loan-concentration view, means almost the same as '*keiretsu* relationship', and functions as part of the activities of 'corporate groups'. The logical next step is to define such terms as '*keiretsu* relationship' and 'corporate group'. However, readers of the next two chapters will find that we reach no clear definition of them either. As a result, neither a clear definition nor common understanding of the adhesion relationship exists, only vague images.[17]

Whose Interests are Served by the Adhesion Relationship?

According to the fifth part in Kawaguchi's above 'hypothesis', in order to survive and play the role, a city bank has to make profits by lending also to small business with extremely high interest rates. This raises five questions: (1) What is the target function of a city bank? (2) Does an individual city bank base its decisions upon its own interests or upon the interests of the firms in its *keiretsu*? Does the bank maximize with regard to individual or group objectives? (3) What constrains city bank decisions? (4) What is the 'role' of a city bank? Who decides it? (5) Which is more profitable for a city bank, loans to large firms or loans to small businesses?

The answer to the fifth question is obviously small business loans, because a city bank is alleged to supply large firms with loans at lower interest rates and in greater amounts than rational behaviour would suggest. Since this is the case, why do not banks attempt to maximize profits by shifting large firm loans to small business rather than vice versa, as the burden-shifting literature would suggest? Why do banks regard the opposite as their role? Who decides bank policy? No persuasive answer can be found in Kawaguchi's (1965) 'hypothesis' nor in the literature emphasizing the loan-concentration mechanism more generally.

The Adhesion Relationship and Burden Shifting

Suppose that each city bank has an adhesion relationship with a group of large firms and behaves as Kawaguchi's 'hypothesis' asserts. Will 'burden shifting' to small business appear and persist? Even a tight cartel among city banks to maintain adhesion relationships is subject to the threat of arbitrage[18] by other market participants attempting to exploit the profitable small business lending abandoned by the city banks.

The burden shifting view made possible by the adhesion relationship includes price discrimination in interest rates between small business and large firms. Lots of financial transactions and arbitrage opportunities exist in dealing among firms, including sales on credit between large firms and small businesses. Financial institutions other than city banks are another source of potential arbitrage. Moreover, the incentive to cheat on cartel agreements makes city banks the other potential source of arbitrage. Keep in mind that the number of city banks is not small enough to maintain a tight cartel, and the ratio of loans through the adhesion relationship to each borrower is not so high. Therefore, even on the supposition that each city bank has an adhesion relationship with a group of large firms, burden shifting will not appear, will not continue and cannot be presumed to exist.

Thus, our study of the 'adhesion relationship' which is the core of the loan-concentration view reaches a totally negative conclusion regarding the three questions above: (1) no clear definition of the 'adhesion relationship' exists; (2) no clear answer exists as to who chooses to establish and maintain the relationship; and (3) burden shifting cannot exist even if the adhesion relationship is accepted as genuine.

5.6   SMALL BUSINESS FUNDS SHORTAGE

Many readers may criticize the argument in previous sections as unrealistic, and assert, often with evidence, that small businesses have faced a severe funds shortage. In this section I examine the persuasiveness of the evidence for this view, and cite two tables as counter-evidence. Because all these figures suffer from the biases of the dual-structure view, special care must be taken over the underlying methodology and to the definitions of terms, especially 'small business funds shortage'.

The following view is widely acceptable as a benchmark for examination:

> Though the term small business funds shortage is so popular as to be immediately remembered with the term small business, it is not clear at all what it is. When *funds shortage* means simply that a firm cannot borrow the precise amount it wants, it is not peculiar to small business. In both Japan and the USA, even large firms face the same problem. Moreover, banks often refuse firm requests for additional loans, even at a higher interest rate. While total demand and supply in the financial markets balance mainly through changes in interest rates, factors other than the interest rate are taken into account in each loan transaction. The credit rating of the borrower, the ratio of compensating balance, the intended use of funds, collateral, the bank's current balance position, etc. are examples. (Yamashita, 1969, pp. 195–6)[19]

No quantitative critiques have succeeded in proving the existence of any deviation from this benchmark view.

Success Ratio of Small Business's Borrowing Proposals

One piece of evidence for small business funds shortage is the 'success ratio of small business's borrowing proposals', found in the SMEA's *Survey of Credit Conditions for Small Business (Chusho Kigyo Shinyo Jittai Chosa)*. Let me examine by way of reference the 1970 *Small Business White Paper*, from which Table 5.2 is adapted.[20] The *White Paper* points out that the funds shortage for small businesses in 1950 resulted mainly from the weak position in the financial markets, which was based on their low productivity and inadequate equipment. The low success rates listed in the table are offered as illustrations of the weak positions of small businesses.[21]

Table 5.2   Success ratio of small business's borrowing proposals (per cent)

	Manufacturing(*)	*Commerce(*)*
Full	9.9	8.7
More than half	12.8	7.3
Less than half	11.9	6.1
Nil	8.3	5.9
Never proposed	53.5	71.2
Total	100.0	100.0

(*) A small business is a firm with less than 200 employees in manufacturing and with less than 20 employees in Commerce.
Source: Adapted from 1970 *Small Business White Paper*, p. 87; originally from Small and Medium Enterprise Agency, *Chusho Kigyo Shinyo Jittai Chosa (Survey of the Financial Reality of Small Business)*, 1950.

No assertion based on these figures can be persuasive. Five points should be noted. First, when the financing difficulties of small businesses is indicated, no information on large firms is presented, and therefore no conclusions on the subject of discrimination can be drawn between large and small firms.

Second, these figures are significantly biased. Small business owners, particularly those who have faced the prospect of loans inadequate to meet desired investment levels (including most owners and directors of even large firms), have an interest in emphasizing this fact by giving a lower success ratio, especially when asked about the problem by the government agency in charge of small business. Small businesses propose amounts of borrowing to prospective lenders greater than their needs, for they expect that only a portion of the proposed amount will be lent. As a result of both smaller numerator and larger denominator, the success ratio is biased downwards. In addition, this questionnaire asks only for the amount of lending, and pays no attention to such other factors as the interest rate, collateral and guarantees by other means, such as by a third party, or loan terms, which tend to increase the bias. The 1952 *Survey* asks, 'Why couldn't you borrow?' Ranked by number of responses, the answers are, 'The amount proposed was too large', 'Because of the lender's funds shortage', 'The proposed term was too long', 'Lack of collateral', 'Because of the unstable future of our business', and so on.[22]

Third, the insufficient explanation of the figures gives rise to a greater difficulty in understanding. Only in response to a 'yes' answer to the question, 'Had you a need to borrow (including discounts of customers' bills) over the past six months?' are firms asked about their success rate. As shown in Table 5.2, since 53.5 per cent of manufacturers answered 'no' to the first question, 21.3 per cent of firms which needed loans could borrow the full amount $(9.9/(100.0 - 53.5) \times 100)$ and 48.8 per cent could borrow more than half.[23]

Fourth, most of the small businesses surveyed employ less than 30 employees. For instance, in the 1950 *Survey*, 36.6 per cent of the sample are small business with less than four employees, 47.4 per cent with four to 29, 14.0 per cent with 30–99, and 2.2 per cent with 100–199. Of the first group 82.4 per cent answered 'no' to the above first question, 'Had you a need to borrow over the past six months?' But 46.5 per cent of the second group, and only 21.4 per cent and 11.9 per cent of the third and the fourth groups, respectively, answered 'no' to the same question. The ratio of small business which could borrow more than half their proposed amount is 42.4 per cent for the first group, 55.5 per cent for the second, 71.6 per cent for the third and 84.4 per cent for the fourth (*Report of the Survey*, p. 18).

Fifth, the figures in Table 5.2 are but a snapshot. Figures for 1952 and 1953 are much higher,[24] and 'Between the depression in 1954 and the boom in 1956 . . . the success ratio has risen gradually' (Morita, 1960, p. 414).

Discrimination against Small Business Loans

Following the above citation, Yamashita (1969, p. 196) summarizes the financial difficulties peculiar to small business in three points: (1) extreme insufficiency of long-term funds, especially compared to large firms; (2) instability of small business loans; and (3) discrimination against loaning to small business.

On the topic of discrimination, Yamashita begins with a claim that no one will oppose:

> the discrimination . . . in small business finance is a case where the terms of loans for small businesses are unreasonably more severe than those for large firms even when borrowers are identical in terms of use of funds, loan term, credit risk, etc. Therefore, differences in interest rates alone do not imply discrimination. (p. 200)

After a short discussion, he concludes, 'It may sound too hasty to assert the existence of the discrimination against small business in the financial markets, but it is obvious from the reality of the Japanese economy' (Yamashito, 1969, p. 201). However, his only evidence is that during 1958–62 the gap in nominal interest rate on loans for small businesses and large firms was larger than the gap in the real rate. Evidence like this does not make the existence of discrimination 'obvious' at all.

Small Business Difficulty in Obtaining Long-term Loans

Yamashita (1969) mentions three pieces of evidence for small business difficulty in obtaining long-term loans.[25]

Ratios of Long- and Short-term Debt to Sales

In presenting ratios of long- and short-term debt to sales, Yamashita (1969, pp. 196–7) argues that they clearly illustrate small business difficulty in obtaining long-term finance:

> Though the short-term debt to sales ratio is higher for large firms than for small businesses, the gap is not so wide. However, the long-term debt to sales ratio for large firms is almost twice as high as that for small businesses. Thus the difference in the total debt to sales ratio between large firms and small businesses results from the long-term debt to sales ratio.

Without taking conditions on the demand side into consideration, however, who can draw useful conclusions about the difficulty of small business in obtaining long-term loans?[26]

Comparison of Achieved and Desired External Funding for Equipment Funds

Table 5.3 presents Yamashita's (1969) second piece of evidence. Originally presented to the Financial System Research Council (*Kin'yu Seido Chosa-kai*) meeting of 11 September 1968, the data come from the Ministry of Finance's 'Questionnaire on Corporate Finance'. Yamashita concludes that the table 'shows that the gap between desired and realized funding narrows with firm size . . . Thus . . . we can conclude that the long-term debt to sales ratios for each firm size group indicate the small business difficulty in finance' (p. 198). The figures for 'Achievement' are the answers to the question: 'Which was the biggest source of external funding for equipment during the past two years?' The figures for 'Desire' are responses to the question, 'What source do you most prefer for external funding of your equipment needs?' Who can draw useful information from the gap between the corresponding figures on the question of small business difficulty in long-term financing? For instance, suppose a firm desired in the past two years and also prefers now to finance 70 per cent of its equipment funds by long-term debt, and in fact financed 35 per cent by long-term debt, and 32.5 per cent each with short-term debt and with bonds. The answers to both questions in this case are both 'long-term debt'. Yamashita (1969) interprets the coincidence as indicating that this firm achieves its desires.[27] Who else can draw such useful information from these figures?

Table 5.3 Comparison of achieved and desired external funding, size in paid-in capital (per cent)

Method	A Ach(*)	A Des(*)	B Ach	B Des	C Ach	C Des	D Ach	D Des	E Ach	E Des	Total Ach	Total Des
Short term loans	7.3	7.8	23.1	16.9	25.1	16.5	27.7	14.8	33.7	20.2	21.4	14.4
Long term loans	73.7	73.0	61.0	67.8	55.0	64.1	47.7	64.8	35.4	53.9	57.7	66.4
Bonds	3.8	5.3	0.0	0.0	0.0	0.9	0.0	0.3	0.0	0.0	1.0	1.6
Equities	7.3	9.3	3.1	8.3	2.2	9.1	4.2	10.6	2.2	10.7	4.2	9.4
Mutual trading credits	2.8	1.8	3.6	1.8	3.9	3.5	8.4	3.6	12.9	3.9	5.5	2.7
No answer	5.3	3.0	9.1	5.2	13.9	6.1	11.9	5.8	15.7	11.2	10.2	5.6
Total	100.0	100.0	100.0	100.0	100.0	100.0	100.0	100.0	100.0	100.0	100.0	100.0

Notes
A: Enterprises with more than 1 billion yen in paid-in capital, B: 1 billion yen–100 million yen, C: 100–50 million yen, D: 50–10 million yen, E: less than 10 million yen.
(*) Ach = Achieved, Des = desired.
Source: Financial System Research Council (Kin'yu Seido Chsa-kai) (1970, p. 106).

Long-term Conformity Ratio
(= (Fixed Assets)/(Stockholders' Equity + Long-term Liabilities))

Though Yamashita (1969) refers to the ratio of fixed investment to long-term liabilities as his third piece of evidence, I use instead the long-term conformity ratio, defined as the reciprocal of:

(stockholders' equity + long term liabilities)/fixed assets

For instance, Miyazawa and Kato (1965, p. 49) point out that in 1956–62 the ratio of increase in stockholder equity and long-term liabilities to that in fixed assets, the reciprocal of long-term conformity ratio,[28] was 91 per cent for small business and 102 per cent for large firms, and concludes: '102 per cent for large firms means that they could finance sufficient long-term funds, but small businesses could only obtain 91 per cent of their needs'.[29]

Will the ratio be 100 per cent when there is no difficulty in long-term loans? How does deviation from 100 per cent indicate the severity of financing difficulties? The Financial System Research Council (1970, p. 106) includes an international table of long-term conformity ratios for manufacturers, showing that during 1956–67 the ratio was a stable 60 per cent in the USA, 65 per cent in the UK, 75 per cent in West Germany, and 90 per cent in Japan. If the overall ratio and its deviation from 100 per cent is to include information indicative of the seriousness of long-term small business financing difficulties, the ratio must consistently exceed 100 per cent across industries. However, the figures for individual industries are distributed widely on both sides. For instance, the 1963 Bank of Japan *Financial Statement of Small Business* shows a distribution of the reciprocals between a maximum of 116.8 per cent in pulp and paper products and a minimum of 78.1 per cent in rubber products.[30]

Does the ratio have its asserted meaning? Lev (1974, p. 4) asks:

> Why do academicians shy away from traditional financial statement analysis? The major reason seems to be the failure of financial analysis to keep pace with the developments in economics and finance . . . A large amount of data and numerous financial ratios are available, yet the usefulness of the traditional tools and techniques has not been established.[31]

In a section on long-term solvency ratios in Chapter 2, Lev does not discuss the long-term conformity ratios, but rather the debt to equity ratio and times interest earned (or interest coverage ratio). He concludes at the end of this chapter:

> Financial ratios are indicators of economic phenomena underlying the firm's operations. They rarely provide the analyst with final answers; more often they point to areas where further investigation may be rewarding. Ratio analysis should therefore be regarded as a preliminary stage in the process of investment decision making. (p. 30)

The Instability of Small Business Loans

Yamashita's phrase 'instability of small business loans' is equivalent to Kawaguchi's (1965) 'burden shifting', which I examined and rejected as unpersuasive in the previous two sections. To support my view, I cite two tables from the Financial System Research Council report (1969). Table 5.4 lists responses to the question: 'Has the loan attitude of your core bank changed since last September when the monetary policy turned restrictive?' The survey was conducted nine months after the policy change. The results show that, the smaller the firm size, the higher is the ratio of respondents answering 'Unchanged'. In general, note that the larger firms appear to have suffered more from the restrictive policy. Therefore I conclude that 'burden shifting' did not occur in this tight-money period.

Table 5.4   Change in loan attitude of core banks, size in paid-in capital (per cent)

Loan attitude	A	B	C	D	E	Total
(1) Loan rate increase	44.7	49.9	46.3	40.3	25.8	43.4
(2) Tightening of the amount	8.8	5.5	5.6	6.8	12.4	7.4
(3) (1) + (2)	27.7	20.3	16.9	11.9	11.8	19.0
(4) Unchanged	16.0	21.8	27.3	39.7	44.4	27.5
(5) No answer	2.8	2.6	3.9	1.3	5.6	2.9
Total	100.0	100.0	100.0	100.0	100.0	100.0

Note: For size of enterprise, see the notes for Table 5.3.
Source: Financial System Research Council (1969, p. 26).

Table 5.5 summarizes the answers to the question: 'Which of the following alternatives was the main reason for postponing or reducing equipment orders during the tight-money period, if your company did so? For firms without such an experience, please answer as if you did'. More than half of the effective answers chose 'Outlook for business and industry'. The smaller the firm size, the greater the number of firms choosing this response. Larger firms tended to select the response 'Tightening of the amount of loans' in greater numbers than small firms; indeed, 40 per cent of large firms with over 1 billion yen in paid-in capital chose this response. Thus it was large firms that the restrictive monetary policy was aimed at and which responded significantly to this policy change. This is the opposite of the loan-concentration view.

5.7   CONCLUDING REMARKS

The answers to my five questions listed in this chapter's introduction are obvious. (1) What in fact occurred is totally different from the alleged reality

Table 5.5   Reason for postponing equipment order, size in paid-in capital
(per cent)

Reason	A	B	C	D	E	Total
(1) Outlook for business and industry	37.0	43.4	49.4	52.9	54.5	45.9
(2) Policy against trade cycle	11.0	10.6	5.6	10.6	4.5	9.2
(3) Borrowing rate increase	1.0	1.0	4.3	2.6	2.8	2.1
(4) Tightening of the amount	40.0	30.1	25.1	14.8	15.7	27.1
(5) Difficulty in equity and bond issue	1.0	0.8	0.0	0.3	0.0	0.5
(6) Others	2.5	1.6	1.3	3.9	3.9	2.5
(7) No answer	7.5	12.5	14.3	14.8	18.5	12.6
Total	100.0	100.0	100.0	100.0	100.0	100.0

Note: For size of enterprise, see the notes for Table 5.3.
Source: Financial System Research Council (1969, p. 31).

behind the term. (2) The view has been logically inconsistent. (3) The existence of the loan-concentration mechanism has never been proved persuasively. (4) I find no answer to the question: Who created and maintained this mechanism and why? (5) The view does not take market forces into consideration. The non-existence of answers to questions (4) and (5) reflects the fact that the supporters of this view recognise Japan's economy as a world of exchange by coercion rather than by agreement. Therefore the main conclusion is simply that the 'loan-concentration view' is totally wrong: a *de facto* mechanism never existed in the Japanese financial sector that allotted loans to large firms rather than small businesses, thereby harming the financial interests of small business. This conclusion is consistent with and also a part of conclusion of Chapters 2 and 3: that the dual-structure view is wrong. The view that a close long-term relationship, called an 'adhesion relationship', functions as the loan-concentration mechanism between a large bank and a group of large firms is also wrong. This suggests that the conventional argument for main banks and corporate groups, which I examine in the next two chapters, is also wrong.

This conclusion is valid for the pre-1970 period, for which the dual-structure view is dominant even today. As everyone agrees that the loan-concentration mechanism was severer before 1970 than now, my conclusion implies that neither the loan-concentration mechanism nor 'adhesion relationships' ever existed. For the implications of this conclusion, simply read again the concluding remarks of Chapters 2 and 3.

6 Main Bank and its Functions

6.1 INTRODUCTION

Many of the premises underlying the study of postwar Japan's economic system, now thought of as appropriate common ground, are ill-defined and untested. They are thought to be so obvious that few notice the need for testing.[1] How the flow of funds within an economy influences its performance is one example.[2] Two untested views address this question: (1) that the government can control the economy and improve macroeconomic performance by intervention in the flow of funds; (2) that the existence of a stable pipe for finance – a pipe through which funds are supplied stably in any conditions – decisively influences the performance and growth of a firm.

The second view is reflected in the literature on corporate groups, financial *keiretsu*, *keiretsu* loans and the loan-concentration mechanism.[3] This premise must be assumed if we are to understand the content of prior studies and related controversies. One example is the study and controversy over the 'adhesion relationship', examined in the previous chapter. Another example is the 'One-Set-Ism' view proposed in the 1960s as a feature of corporate group behaviour.[4,5] Despite much criticism, this hypothesis acquired and maintained both academic and popular support, being a big issue which continually produced 'provocative new results'.[6] This general assumption also is the basis for the recently fashionable view that financial factors have contributed much to the industrial success of Japan.[7] This view has generated much new research on the formation of the financial system, at the core of which is research on 'main bank' or 'Mainbank'. Though the term 'main bank' became popular among academics only in the 1980s, it was a slangy word used by economic journalism in the 1970s. Other terms for the same phenomenon were more popular, like *keiretsu* loans, *keiretsu* relationship and 'adhesion relationship'. The term 'main bank relationship' derives directly from these.

Like earlier research, that on 'main bank' suffers from vague definition and untested propositions. But without investigation of reality as we see it and the factors which make the existence of 'main bank', or finance in general, so influential, we can be sure neither of the usefulness of the study based on 'main bank' models and its conclusions, nor of the reasons for constructing 'main bank' models.

In this chapter, I study three places where 'main banks' are thought to play a role and examine how frequently we observe their alleged behaviour. The period of study is the decade beginning in the mid-1970s.[8] In what follows I distinguish between 'main banks' and 'core banks' to avoid confusion. The former denotes the main bank of conventional literature, while the latter denotes a bank with the biggest share of loans to a given borrower. These categories are not mutually exclusive: main banks are quite often also core banks.

As mentioned in the previous chapter and in Section 1.5 of this book, the term 'main bank relationship' describes a large bank's relationship with a group of large firms, often called an 'adhesion relationship'. As such, our conclusions about the existence of adhesion relationships should already cast doubt on the validity of the main bank argument. Even when the 'main bank' argument is valid, it applies only to a small portion of the Japanese economy dominated by large firms.

In Section 6.2, I study the stability of the relationship between banks and large firms and show that they are less stable than expected. Section 6.3 reviews the use of the term 'main bank' and the functions considered to be representative of main banks. Sections 6.4 and 6.5 examine the behaviour of main banks towards firms experiencing financial trouble: Section 6.4 empirically studies the bank's function as a 'big pipe' in an emergency, and Section 6.5 examines the 'lender of last resort' function. In both sections I draw negative conclusions on the existence of these functions. Section 6.6 updates the chapter with my comments on recent studies. Section 6.7 is devoted to concluding remarks.

My conclusions, negative at each point, oppose the conventional view. I argue that hypothesized 'main bank behaviour' and hypothesized 'main bank relationships' do not exist. Note that not the existence itself of 'main banks' or 'main bank relationships' but the function of 'main banks' and their influence on macroeconomic performance of the Japanese economy are the issues of this chapter and that my conclusion does not preclude the existence of such relationships. I also argue that explicit contracts called 'main bank contracts' do not exist, and that the effectiveness of 'implicit contracts' can only be tested in the way used in this chapter.

6.2 THE STABILITY OF CORE BANK AND LARGE FIRM RELATIONS

Among firm–bank[9] relationships in Japan, stable long-term links between a large firm and a large bank are regarded as the most basic.[10] The first test of the 'main bank' argument is its stability. I focus on the extent to which the core bank, a bank with the biggest share of loans to a given borrower, of a large firm persisted as its core bank over time.

Table 6.1 shows the stability of the core bank between March 1973 and March 1983 for all 819 firms listed on First Section of Tokyo Stock Exchange (TSE) in July 1983, except banks, security firms and insurance companies. Firms with a single core bank during this time (S) are classified in six groups by core bank type. Firms which changed their core bank (US) are classified in nine groups by type of change. For example, US(6) represents change between city banks. Each group is further divided into six classes by average growth rate in sales. The aim is to discover whether core bank stability

Table 6.1 Sales growth rate and core bank stability, 1973–83 (number of firms)

Group name / Growth rate	Groups by sales growth rate (10 year average, per cent)						Total
	G(1) (~0.01)	G(2) (0–4.99)	G(3) (5.00–9.99)	G(4) (10.00–14.99)	G(5) (15.00–19.99)	G(6) (20.00~)	
A Total	4	65	306	331	90	23	819
B Unclassifiable[1]	1	5	15	38	14	3	76
C=A–B Classifiable	3	60	291	293	76	20	743
US Case where core bank changes	1	22	88	99	25	12	247
US(1) Change between city bank and trust bank within a group[2]	0	4	19	14	4	1	42
US(2) Change between city bank and trust bank across groups	1	3	4	9	2	1	20
US(3) Change between trust bank and LTCB[3]	0	0	3	7	1	1	12
US(4) Change between city bank and LTCB	0	2	18	19	5	5	49
US(5) Change between LTCBs	0	1	1	2	0	1	5
US(6) Change between city banks	0	3	3	8	3	0	17
US(7) Change between CCBAF[3] and other banks	0	2	15	12	1	1	31
US(8) Change of the number of core banks[4]	0	1	4	11	5	1	22
US(9) Others	0	6	21	17	4	1	49
S Case where core bank does not change	2	38	203	194	51	8	496
S(1) City bank is the core bank	0	22	118	134	25	7	306
S(2) Trust bank is the core bank	1	6	28	16	3	0	54
S(3) LTCB is the core bank	0	8	39	26	18	1	92
S(4) CCBAF is the core bank	0	1	6	4	1	0	12
S(5) Multiple core banks[4]	0	0	5	5	2	0	12
S(6) Others	1	1	7	9	2	0	20

Notes to Table 6.1

(1) Cases where outstanding borrowing at either point of time is zero, and cases unlisted in 1973 and data unavailable.

(2) Following Toyo Keizai Shinpo-sha, *Kigyo Keiretsu Soran*, banks in each parenthesis are in the same group: (*Mitsui Bank, Mitsui Trust Bank*), (*Mitsubishi Bank, Mitsubishi Trust Bank, Nippon Trust Bank*), (*Sumitomo Bank, Sumitomo Trust Bank*), (*Fuji Bank, Yasuda Trust Bank*), (*Sanwa Bank, Toyo Trust Bank*).

(3) Long-term Credit Bank and Central Cooperative Bank of Agriculture and Forestry.

(4) Cases where multiple banks share the core bank position are classified under S(5) where there is no change in the number and composition, and under US(8) otherwise.

Source: Adapted from Miwa (1990a, p. 145, Table 6.1).

---

depends on the growth rate of a borrower. The Japan Development Bank (JDB) and Export–Import Bank of Japan are not included, even when one or the other is the biggest lender to a given firm.[11] Data on growth rate are taken from Daiwa Research Institute, *1983 Analysts' Guide*; data on financing are from Toyo Keizai Shinpo-sha, *Kigyo Keiretsu Soran* (*Conspectus of Corporate Keiretsu*), 1973 and 1984.[12] The term 'financing' includes both long- and short-term borrowing but excludes bills discounted.

As indices of the 'stability' of the core bank relationship I use two ratios, NS/NT, NS(1)/NT, shown in Table 6.2. S is the group of firms with a stable core bank, S(1) those firms with a city bank as their stable core bank, and T the total set of firms. NS, NS(1) and NT are the number of firms in each set. Leaving the figures for G(1) and G(6) aside owing to the small sample size, this table shows that the stability of the core bank relationship does not depend on the borrower's growth rate.

Figures for the total (T) are 66.8 per cent for NS/NT and 41.2 per cent for NS(1)/NT. The interpretation of these figures is subject to controversy. However, those who support or hold deep interests in the conventional view of *keiretsu*, adhesion relationship, corporate groups and main banks, argue a special role of city banks, therefore, NS(1)/NT, and must be surprised that the ratio of 'stable core banks' is only 41.2 per cent. For those interested in the behaviour of six or seven gigantic city banks alone,[13] the critical figure must be even lower, perhaps about 30 per cent. Note that S also includes such financial institutions as trust banks, long-term credit banks, the Central Cooperative Bank of Agriculture & Forestry, regional banks, life insurance companies, and so on.

Table 6.2   Indices of core bank stability, 1973–83 (per cent)

	G(1)	G(2)	G(3)	G(4)	G(5)	G(6)	Total
NS/NT	66.7	63.3	69.8	66.2	67.1	40.0	66.8
NS(1)/NT	0	36.7	40.5	45.7	32.9	35.0	41.2

Note: See the notes for Table 6.1.
Source: Adapted from Miwa (1990a, p.145, Table 6.2).

· However one views these figures, 66.8 per cent and 41.2 per cent,[14] they obviously cast doubt on the plausibility of the dominant view of the Japanese economy, which can be summarized as follows. Close relationships with a large bank, especially a city bank, are indispensable if a large Japanese firm wishes to survive and flourish. No borrower voluntarily ends such a relationship, and it is prohibitively difficult to replace one bank relationship with another.[15] Note that these figures include firms which did not change core banks even though such potential existed. The fact that many firms did change banks suggests the number of firms potentially able to do so is large.

Corporate Groups and Stable Core Bank Relations

Supporters of the corporate-group view – those who insist that firms in a 'corporate group' behave as a unit and dominate Japan's economy – raise two objections to this argument. The first objection focuses on the definition of large firms. They assert that the First Section of the TSE contains many irrelevant firms, and that corporate groups contain only important firms, which are large, long-established and have high social status. Among these firms, they argue, the ratio must be much higher. The second objection concerns cooperative behaviour among banks. Since banks in a given corporate group (a city bank and a trust bank in the same group, for instance) cooperate, they argue, and since the above argument neglects this point, results will change greatly when such cases are dropped from the category US. However, the following rebuttal shows that there is no need for modifying the above conclusion.

Objection 1: Definition of Large Firm

The first objection to my conclusion is that stable relationships between large firms and large banks apply only to a limited group of firms, typically to those in corporate groups. It asserts that a nucleus exists where the stability prevails. Implicitly asserting that out of the nucleus stable relationship is rarer than the average, this criticism does not challenge our conclusion that on average the core bank relationship among large firms listed on the First Section of the TSE is not as stable as commonly believed, and that the core bank relationship does not dominate even the large firm sector. As we are interested in the importance of the core bank relationship for the whole economy, rather than simply the existence of an 'adhesion relationship' for individual firms, we need not modify the conclusion even if we find a nucleus. However, we do not.

Table 6.3 shows indices for the stability of core bank relationships within corporate groups. As is the custom, I track the 'six major corporate groups' – Mitsui, Mitsubishi, Sumitomo, Fuyo (or Fuji), Sanwa and Daiichi Kangyo Bank (DKB). Each group is determined as members of each presidents' meeting (*shacho-kai*; for the details, see the next chapter) at March 1983.

Table 6.3 Six major corporate groups and indices of core bank stability (1), 1973–83 (per cent)

	Mitsui H(1)	Mitsubishi H(2)	Sumitomo H(3)	Fuyo H(4)	Sanwa H(5)	DKB H(6)	Ex-zaibatsu type H(A)	bank type H(B)	all groups H(T)	Total
A Total	24	28	21	29	42	45	73	111(*)	184	819
C Classifiable	18	20	15	24	33	32	53	84(**)	137	743
NS/NT	72.2	75.0	53.3	75.0	75.7	62.5	67.9	71.4	70.1	66.8
NS(1)/NT	55.0	65.0	46.6	50.0	57.6	50.0	56.6	54.8	55.5	41.2

Notes: See the notes for Table 6.1.
(*) Four firms belong both to H(5) and H(6), one of which belongs also to H(4).
(**) Of 47 cases (184–137), 38 are financial institutions and unlisted firms, and nine are zero borrowings.
Source: Adapted from Miwa (1990a, p. 148, Table 6.3).

Financial Market

These are divided into two subgroups, 'ex-*zaibatsu*-type' and 'bank-type' groups. H(1) to H(6) correspond to each group, H(A) and H(B) to the total of ex-*zaibatsu* type groups and bank-type groups respectively, and H(T) to the total of all groups. On the right side I note the totals from Tables 6.1 and 6.2.

Though slight differences exist across the corporate groups,[16] the ratio NS/NT for H(T) (70.1 per cent) is almost the same as that for T (66.8 per cent). The ratio NS(1)/NT for H(T) (55.5 per cent) is much higher than that for T (41.2 per cent). Thus, when the scope of the term 'bank' is unlimited, the asserted nucleus does not show up; when limited to city banks, however, we do see a nucleus. That 55.5 per cent of large firms in corporate groups have stable core bank relationship with city banks – slightly over half of those firms – is far from the conventional view as stated in Kure and Shima (1984, p. 27): 'A city bank at the core of a corporate group is the 'main bank' of member firms'. Though 55.5 per cent is much higher than 41.2 per cent, I see no need to modify the previous conclusion.[17, 18]

Objection 2: Cooperative Relations among Banks within a Corporate Group

The essence of the second objection is that a firm's change of core bank between banks in the same corporate group, especially between a city bank and a trust bank, should not be counted as an unstable (US) relationship because of close cooperation among the banks. It is claimed that such shifts result from a shift in borrower's demand from short- to long-term debt or vice versa. Therefore it is claimed that the share of unstable cases will decrease drastically both among all large firms and among member firms of the six major corporate groups when those cases are shifted from the category US to the category S.

To see how this argument applies to all large firms in the sample, see Table 6.4, which shows (NUS(1)+NS)/NT instead of NS/NT alone, and (NUS(1)+NS(1)+NS(2))/NT instead of NS(1)/NT alone.[19] The figures for the whole sample are listed in the first column; those for corporate group members are found in the second to fourth columns. The first column shows that the share of total firms with stable core bank relationships rises by 5.6 per cent to 72.4 per cent. Again I leave readers to interpret the importance of this shift. My view is that 5.6 per cent is not a drastic change.[20]

Table 6.4   Six major corporate groups and indices of core bank stability (2), 1973–83 (per cent)

	T	H(A)	H(B)	H(T)
(NUS(1)+NS)/NT	72.4	86.8	72.6	78.1
(NUS(1)+NS(1)+NS(2))/NT	54.1	83.0	57.1	66.4

Note: see the notes for Table 6.3.
Source: adapted from Miwa (1990a, p. 149, Table 6.4).

The figures for corporate group members are worth greater attention, since cooperation among banks in a group is mainly for the benefit of other members. NUS(1)/NT for H(T) (8.0 per cent) is larger than that for the total sample, and (NUS(1)+NS)/NT for H(T) exceeds that for the total by 5.7 per cent. However, as a comparison with Table 6.3 shows, NUS(1)/NT is 18.9 per cent for H(A) and 1.2 per cent for H(B), indicating that most of the 8.0 per cent comes from H(A), ex-*zaibatsu*-type groups.[21] Also, NS(2)/NT is small for H(B), and figures in Table 6.4 for H(B) are almost the same as those for the whole sample. Therefore, even when cooperative behaviour exists in a corporate group, it operates only among ex-*zaibatsu*-type firms. The relative unimportance of these groups and the importance of the difference from the whole sample suggest no need for modification of my earlier conclusion.

Moreover, the basis of this general objection is unpersuasive on three counts: (1) As shown in Table 6.1, the number of firms in the category NUS(2), 20, is almost half of NUS(1), 42. Thus the exchange of core bank position between city and trust banks across groups occurs half as frequently as that within a corporate group. (2) NUS(4), 49, is larger than NUS(1), 42. Exchanges between a city bank and a long-term credit bank (LTCB) occur more often than intra-group exchanges between city and trust banks within a group. This is inconsistent with the assertion that the latter occurs as a result of borrower's demand shift between short- to long-term debt, since LTCBs specialize in long-term loans and belong to no group.[22] (3) In only 15 of 54 firms in the category S(2), those firms with a trust bank as their stable core bank, do city banks of the same group as the core bank take the second largest loan share. In only nine of the remaining 39 cases does the city bank of the same group take the largest share among city banks. The sum of these two subgroups amounts only to 24, 44.4 per cent of 54 cases.

6.3 MAIN BANKS AND CORE BANKS

In the following two sections, I examine the other side of the 'main bank' argument: the functions of main banks and their importance to the Japanese economy. First, I detail the conventional view. The term 'main bank' is typically used in laments like 'the tragedy of not having a main bank' and 'the tragedy of a firm too close to a main bank'.[23] The former usage clearly differentiates the term 'main bank' from 'core bank' since by definition every borrower has its core bank.

Like the term *keiretsu*, 'main bank' is a slangy term used by economic journalists with great frequency but with little agreement over its definition. Kure and Shima (1984, pp. 26–7) are a representative example:

[Main bank relationship] depends on an agreement between a bank and a firm. A firm borrows from and deposits to its main bank larger amounts than it does with other banks. In return, the main bank provides maximum

possible support to the firm in terms of loans, etc. when the firm falls into
distress and faces difficulty in raising funds . . . *Keiretsu* loans, which
connote a closer relationship than a main bank relationship, comprise a
loan to a firm whose stock the bank holds and sends directors to. Main
banks sometimes change, but *keiretsu* loan partners seldom change.

In the case of Kojin, mentioned above as an example of 'the tragedy of not
having a main bank', Daiichi Kangyo Bank (DKB), which had the largest
share of loans to Kojin among all of its banks, held 3.44 per cent of stocks
(the fourth largest share after three life insurance companies) and sent two
directors in October 1974, just before Kojin's bankruptcy. Daiichi Life
Insurance, which held the largest share of Kojin stock (8.38 per cent) and had
almost the same loan share as DKB, sent its president.[24] The popular
expression of that time for this case, 'the tragedy of not having a main bank',
suggests that neither DKB nor Daiichi Life, nor any of the four largest
shareholders was Kojin's main bank. However, Kure and Shima's definition
suggests that either (or both) were the main bank and that a *keiretsu* loan
relationship existed.

Kure and Shima emphasize that the main bank relationship 'depends on an
agreement between a bank and a firm', as well as on such observable features
as a bank's share of outstanding loans, share of stockholding, and the
number of executives dispatched from outside. However, because this
'agreement' is implicit and vague, neither side can verify its existence. The
importance attached to the relationship may differ between a lender and a
borrower, and the closeness of the relationship may differ between cases and
change greatly over time.[25]

Thus there is neither a clear definition of the term 'main bank' nor a
common understanding of the 'main bank' view. Below I examine two types
of main bank function, and observe the frequency of the alleged behaviour.
Both are expected when borrowers get into trouble. The first is the 'big pipe'
function, most clearly observed in tight-money periods and when borrowers
need a large quantity of funds. Second is the 'lender of last resort' function,
which obtains when a firm 'falls into distress', becomes a 'risky borrower', or
when rumours to this effect spread in the market.

My conclusion that neither function exists in practice is contrary to the
conventional view. Also, as noted above, the main bank relationship is
alleged to exist only between large firms and large banks but, as the data
show, these relationships account for only a small portion of the overall
economy. Therefore the emphasis put on the main bank relationship by the
conventional view is misguided.

6.4 THE MAIN BANK AS A BIG PIPE

Two aspects of the big pipe function can be distinguished. The first operates
to secure funds in tight-money periods,[26] suggesting that the main bank's

loan share increases in such periods relative to that of other banks. The implication is that large firms in main bank relationships have the advantage of a stable big pipe for fund raising and can commit to equipment and R&D investments for long-run growth. The second aspect of the big pipe function obtains when a firm needs a large quantity of additional funds. It is typically asserted that main banks first loan for a large share of the additional funds raising and persuade other banks to follow,[27] suggesting that the main bank's loan share increases relative to that of other banks when the firm borrowing increases dramatically. The implication is that large firms in main bank relationships enjoy a wider choice set than other firms in responding to a changing environment.

Let us examine the 'big pipe' function for large firms in three sectors – electric power companies, general trading companies and real estate companies – where: (1) large firms are representative large borrowers; (2) large firms have main banks; (3) bankruptcy of the firm is only a remote possibility. The first point is important if we wish to make claims about the importance of main banks to the Japanese economy as a whole. The second point allows us to see clearly the big pipe function in action. Condition three is mentioned because the examination of the function for 'risky borrowers' is the subject of the following section. I conclude that observation of lender–borrower relationships does not support the big pipe function view for any of these three sectors.

Electric Power Companies

I choose electric power companies for conditions (1) and (3), but not for (2). Nine power companies currently exist in Japan, each of which is a local monopoly. All are large borrowers,[28] and have expanded total borrowing rapidly. Observation does not support the big pipe function in this sector.

Relationships between each firm and their banks are characterized by three features: (1) the Industrial Bank of Japan (IBJ) takes the core bank position in all cases;[29] (2) while each firm diversifies its sources of funds tremendously, the share and rank of each lender has stayed stable; (3) several banks loan the same amount of money to a given firm. In sum, the relationships are stable and each firm can raise a large quantity of funds without a main bank relationship.

In the case of Tokyo Electric Power, for example, the IBJ (9.6 per cent)[30] takes the core bank position after the JDB (18.2 per cent). The Long Term Credit Bank of Japan ranks third, and five trust banks (TB) take the next positions in the order of Mitsui, Mitsubishi, Yasuda, Sumitomo and Toyo. However, two life insurance companies, Daiichi (3.2 per cent) and Nihon (2.8 per cent) and one city bank, Mitsui (2.5 per cent), have larger shares than Toyo Trust Bank. Apart from the Bank of Tokyo, the city banks can be divided into five groups, with stable loan shares divided evenly between them, from the highest to lowest: Mitsui; Mitsubishi, Fuji, DKB; Daiwa; Sumitomo, Sanwa, Kyowa; Tokai, Saitama, Takugin, Taiyo and Kobe.[31]

From this information we may conclude that no bank appears to have functioned as a big pipe for either electric power company. The above characteristics can be explained in either of two ways: (1) as a result of the borrower's choice among a wide set of alternatives,[32] or (2) as a result of collusive behaviour among banks (possibly led by a specific bank). Since many lenders are competing fiercely for a larger loan share, the possibility of the latter explanation being true is small. Therefore we may conclude that each firm has the opportunity to borrow from a wide variety of lenders, that is, each can borrow on an open market and need not seek out a big pipe relationship with a specific bank.

General Trading Companies (*Sogo Shosha*)

Large general trading companies are like the electric power companies in that they are large borrowers,[33] but they differ in that each is a core member of major corporate groups. Observation does not support the big pipe function in this sector either. Here I select one from each of the six major corporate groups, Mitsui & Co. (Bussan), Mitsubishi Corporation (Shoji), Sumitomo Corporation (Sumisho), Marubeni Corporation (Marubeni), Nissho Iwai Corporation (Nissho) and C. Itoh & Co. (Itochu).[34]

A dramatic decline in the main bank's loan share during the period under study holds true for each, which is a result of the introduction of the government restriction on big loans to a single borrower. This regulation was first introduced as informal regulation and then written into the Banking Act as Article 13.[35] The decline was especially dramatic over the year prior its implementation in March 1980.[36]

Two periods are noteworthy: from April 1979 to March 1980, a year prior to the enforcement of the above restriction on big loans outstanding (period I); and March 1972 to March 1976 (period II). In period I, loans to general trading companies both from main banks and other major lenders fell dramatically. The adjustment process to this environmental change revealed the workings of the system and the behaviouristic features of the participants, especially those in the main bank relationships. Period II can be conveniently divided into two sub-periods. The two years up to March 1974 were the last phase of the 'high-growth era': the economy was booming, and general trading companies actively invested in land, stocks and natural resources. The following two years, however, were characterized by economic downturn brought on by the 1973 oil crisis and the subsequent anti-inflationary tight-money policy.

In period I, I focus on five companies. Sumisho is excluded because of its small size and the consequent ineffectiveness of the size restriction upon its borrowing. In each case, the following conditions obtain:

1. Main bank loans decreased dramatically. The maximum decrease was 56 billion yen, from 145 billion yen to 89 billion yen, in the case of lending

by Mitsui Bank to Bussan. The minimum decrease was 17 billion yen to 72 billion yen, in the case of lending by Sanwa Bank to Nissho. The average decrease was 33 billion yen.

2. Loans from the second largest lender (in three cases, the Bank of Tokyo) also fell dramatically. The maximum decrease was 25 billion yen to 99 billion yen, in the case of lending by the Bank of Tokyo to Bussan. The minimum decrease was 4 billion yen to 62, in the case of lending by DKB to Nissho. The average decrease was 17 billion yen.

3. Most of loans from IBJ, the Long Term Credit Bank of Japan, and city banks other than the largest two increased.[37]

4. Almost the same applies to trust banks. Loans from the largest trust bank lender fell (except for the case of lending from Toyo Trust Bank to Nissho). The maximum decrease was 15 billion yen to 66 billion yen, in the case of lending by Mitsubishi Trust Bank to Shoji. The minimum decrease was 3 billion yen to 52 billion yen, in the case of Yasuda Trust Bank to Marubeni. The average decline for the four trust banks under consideration was 8 billion yen.[38] All loans from other trust banks increased.

5. Except for the Bank of Tokyo, there was almost no change among city banks in lender rankings. The same is true for the trust banks.

These features can also be explained by either of the views offered above for the case of the electric power companies. Many lenders were competing fiercely for a larger loan share in this sector as well, so the possibility of collusion among banks was small. Accordingly, though each general trading company had a main bank, it had an opportunity to borrow from a wide variety of lenders. Therefore we should not attach too much importance to a relationship with a main bank (or banks in a group).[39]

Turning now to period II, total borrowing of the six general trading companies as of 31 March 1972 was 2795 billion yen. The corresponding figure for 1974 was 4354 billion yen, 1.56 times larger than the 1972 amount,[40] and 5644 billion yen in 1976, 1.30 times the 1974 amount. Table 6.5 shows the loan share of each trading company's main bank. Comparison of the 1972 and 1974 figures reveals how a main bank relationship functions when borrowers need a large quantity of additional funds, and thereby serves as a test of the second type of big pipe function. The main bank loan share rises in three cases and declines in three cases. This observation does not support the conventional view that such loan shares should increase under conditions of added corporate financial need. Two points also support the conclusion: (1) the average increase in borrowing for 1972–4 of cases with rising loan shares (1.55) is smaller than that of cases with falling loan shares (1.63); and (2) in 1970–72, when the total borrowing of these general trading companies increased at an even faster rate, the main banks' share declined without exception.[41] Comparison of 1974 and 1976 allows us to test the big pipe function in tight-money periods. That the loan share of main banks declines in all cases implies that this assertion too is invalid.

Table 6.5   Main bank loan share (per cent)[*]: general trading companies

	1970	1972	1974	1976
General Trading Company (main bank)				
Mitsui & Co. (Mitsui Bank)	15.5	13.9	14.8	12.5
Mitsubishi Corporation (Mitsubishi Bank)	21.5	19.6	17.9	15.7
Sumitomo Corporation (Sumitomo Bank)	20.2	17.5	17.9	17.1
Marubeni Corporation (Fuji Bank)	20.6	19.9	15.0	12.9
Nissho Iwai Corporation (Sanwa Bank)	21.7	19.1	21.3	19.7
C. Itoh & Co. (DKB)	13.1	12.4	10.6	9.7

Note: (*) Borrowing from Export–Import Bank of Japan is subtracted from the denominator.
Source: Adapted from Miwa (1990a, p. 158, Table 6.5).

Real Estate Companies

The third sector I investigate is real estate companies, which I chose to examine for the same reasons I chose to examine general trading companies. Observation does not support the big pipe function in this sector either. I choose four presidents' meeting members, Mitsui Real Estate, Mitsubishi Estate, Sumitomo Realty & Development and Tokyo Tatemono, and one large non-member firm, Tokyu Land.[42] Table 6.6 shows the loan shares of the main banks (here, core bank shown in parentheses) at seven points in time.

Table 6.6   Main bank loan share (per cent)[*]: real estate companies

	1970	1972	1974	1976	1978	1980	1982(**)
Real Estate Company (main bank)							
Mitsui Real Estate (Mitsui Trust Bank)	19.0	16.3	13.9	12.4	13.1	11.7	10.2
Mitsubishi Estate (Mitsubishi Bank)	10.0	14.8	20.5	17.4	17.3	17.0	17.9
Sumitomo Realty and Dev. (Sumitomo Bank)	18.1	22.2	17.9	19.0	16.6	17.9	14.8
Tokyo Tatemono (Fuji Bank)	52.2	44.7	32.3	28.5	25.2	21.6	16.9
Tokyu Land (Mitsui Trust Bank)	27.9	23.3	20.2	18.6	18.9	18.8	17.2

Notes:
(*) A core bank is treated as a main bank.
(**) All figures are for the end of March each year, except Tokyo Tatemono for which figures for the end of December of the previous year are used.
Source: Adapted from Miwa (1990a, p. 159, Table 6.6).

Total borrowing by all five firms in 1974 was 1.47 times as large as that in 1972, and in only one case (Mitsubishi Estate) did the share of main bank lending rise. Thus, as for general trading companies, the second subtype of big pipe function was not valid for real estate companies. In 1970–72, when total borrowing rose even faster (the increase for 1970–72 was 1.83), the main bank loan shares rose only in two cases. Over the next two years of tight-money policy, total borrowing increased 1.30 times, but only in one case (Sumitomo Realty & Development) did main bank loan share rise.[43] Finally, in 1980–82, when firms other than Mitsubishi Estate increased borrowing (the four firms' average increase for 1980–82 was 1.28) after an interval of stable borrowing amount,[44] the main bank loan share did not rise for any firm except Mitsubishi Estate. We may therefore conclude that the first subtype of the big pipe function was not valid for real estate companies.

6.5 MAIN BANKS AS THE LENDER OF LAST RESORT

The Case of Eidai Industries

Eidai Industries illustrates the lender of last resort function held by advocates of the conventional main-bank view. Eidai was a manufacturer of prefabricated houses, listed on First Section of Tokyo Stock Exchange, which petitioned for aid under the Company Resuscitation Act as it went bankrupt on 20 February 1978. Eidai was known to be suffering from business depression since the end of 1974, and from the settling term ending in December 1975 it reported a large deficit and paid no dividend to stockholders. In the autumn of 1975, five banks agreed to lend cooperatively for reconstruction under the leadership of Eidai's 'main bank', Daiwa.[45] They agreed to make additional loans and to exempt Eidai from a semi-annual interest payment of 2 billion yen. Thus an economic journal commented on the case as 'the collapse of the "myth" that there is no bankruptcy among bank-managed firms'.[46] Table 6.7 shows the total loans to Eidai, the loan shares of five banks and the total of five banks' shares. By December 1974 when Eidai's business troubles became widely known, total loans had increased dramatically, clearly contrasting with the following period of stable growth.

Table 6.7 illustrates the claimed main bank last resort function in four ways:

1. Reflecting the agreement on cooperative loans for reconstruction, the five banks' shares increased dramatically, especially after 1975. Loans from other banks fell over 1974–6.
2. Among the five, the two city banks grew dominant, especially Daiwa, relative to the almost constant shares of the three other banks.
3. This process began a few years before 1975. Only after this process did major lenders ask Eidai for a reconstruction plan and negotiate for cooperative loans.[47]

Table 6.7 Total loans and loan share: the case of Eidai Industries

	1969	1971	1972	1973	1974	1975	1976	1977(*)
Total loans (billion yen)	3.8	19.4	39.5	57.2	70.4	73.1	81.3	90.0
Loan share (per cent)								
B(1) Daiwa Bank	28.1	18.0	10.6	12.4	18.0	21.9	27.8	33.8
B(2) Bank of Tokyo	2.6	2.6	7.3	8.6	11.1	11.8	16.5	21.4
B(3) Fuji Bank	—	1.0	5.6	8.0	7.7	7.7	7.6	8.7
B(4) DKB	18.4	6.7	6.6	5.9	6.4	6.8	7.3	7.9
B(5) Mitsubishi Trust Bank	21.1	10.3	10.4	10.1	12.6	12.0	12.2	11.9
B(T) Total of five banks' shares	65.8	38.7	40.5	45.1	55.8	60.2	71.3	83.7

Note: (*)Figures are for the end of December each year.
Source: Adapted from Miwa (1990a, p. 162, Table 6.7).

4. More than one bank functioned as the lender of the last resort. Those who decided or were forced to join the agreement were Eidai's major lenders at the beginning of the reconstruction process.[48] Other factors such as the term and size of past transactions seem indeterminate.[49]

The focus of inquiry is not on such questions as why Eidai went bankrupt when it did, who made the final bankruptcy decision, why its main bank or a group of banks maintained their cooperative commitment to Eidai, or what made such cooperative behaviour possible. Instead, the essential question is how frequently we observe the relations we see between Eidai, Daiwa Bank and the other four banks. My conclusion is that they are rather rare.[50]

Risky Borrowers

The problem of critical importance here is how to specify 'risky borrowers'.[51] I adopt the following schema: the onset of losses is the first warning signal. Three years of losses is the second stage of seriousness, for this signals structural rather than temporary problems. The third and last stage begins when borrowers ask for exemption from interest payments. At this stage, the total liabilities exceed total assets in most cases, and the borrower becomes a 'bank-managed firm'.[52]

Through careful monitoring of the borrower, each bank tries to recover as much of its loaned principal and accrued interests as possible before the third stage arrives. If, as is often argued, main banks have the most advantageous access to information on the borrower, main banks can use this information for their own gain. Other lenders are well aware of this and watch carefully for a decrease in main bank lending as an indicator that the main bank is attempting to cut its losses on the basis of inside information. On the other hand, the banks wish to exploit a decline in main bank lending to gain relative loan share. Because the success of the main bank in recovering loans depends totally upon the reaction of other lenders and the borrower, the relations between them as well as the eventual outcome are complex. Moreover, the period during which information on the lender of last resort function can be observed ends before the onset of the third stage. Therefore our task is to select firms at the second stage and examine the main bank's behaviour before and after this period. I therefore use a list of 'risky borrowers' taken from the 11 August 1984 issue of *Toyo Keizai*. This list assembles all listed firms which have continually reported losses on income before interest payment[53] for at least three years before March 1984, namely firms at the second stage of decline. Excluding banks and insurance companies, 134 of 1646 listed firms are on the *Toyo Keizai* list.[54] I classify them into three groups: firms with three years of losses (G(A)), firms with four years of losses (G(B)), and firms with more than five years of losses (G(C)). The number of firms in G(A), NG(A), is 70; NG(B) is 27; and NG(C) is 37.[55]

Stability of Relationship between Core Banks and Risky Borrowers

The nature of the relationship between core banks and risky borrowers is illustrated in Table 6.8, which corresponds to Table 6.2 and Table 6.4. No clear differences in the indices of stability of the bank/firm relationship appear either when I divide the sample into firms listed on First Section of Tokyo Stock Exchange (column 1; relatively large firms) and all others (column 2), or when divided into G(A), G(B) and G(C) (columns 3–5). We may therefore conclude that the indices for the group as a whole (G(T)) in column 6 represent all of its parts.

Comparison of each index in column 6 with a corresponding index for all firms listed on First Section of TSE in column 7 (from Tables 6.2 and 6.4) unambiguously shows that the former is lower than the latter, thereby indicating that the main bank relationship is more unstable for risky borrowers. The difference between the indices is largest for NS(1)/NT, that is, the difference is clearest for relationships between city banks and risky borrowers. In only a quarter of cases does the same city bank stay in the core bank position at two points in time.[56] The results suggested by Table 6.8 differ greatly from the conventional main-bank view. The bank with the largest share of loans, the core bank, appears not to support borrowers as strongly as do other banks, but instead draws back from business with firms that fall into distress. This behaviour is especially remarkable among city banks.[57]

Main Bank Loan Shares of Risky Borrowers (1)

The next question is whether main banks function as lenders of last resort for risky borrowers. To answer this question, I compare core banks' loan shares in 1973 and 1984. (As shown in Table 6.8, in more than 40 per cent of cases, the shares of different banks are compared.)[58] Of 134 firms, 123 comparisons are possible.[59] Table 6.9 shows the direction of change in the core bank's loan share. We observe no evidence for the lender of last resort argument in this table, either by examining all firms (G(T)) or in any of G(A), G(B) and G(C).

The same is true over a much shorter period. Table 6.10 shows that the corresponding figures for 1983–4 gives almost the same result, but now the number of cases where a core bank's share of loans declines exceeds the number where it rises.

Thus borrowers facing an emergency need for funds are not only unable to maintain stable relationships with their main banks but also unable to expect main banks to serve as lenders of last resort.[60]

Main Bank Loan Shares of Risky Borrowers (2)

To examine main bank behaviour in detail, let me divide risky borrowers into four subgroups by both borrowing volume and core bank loan share. Draw a

Table 6.8 Stability of relationship between core bank and risky borrower, 1973–84

	Firms listed on First Section of TSE	Firms listed on other stock exchanges	$G(A)$	$G(B)$	$G(C)$	Total of risky borrowers $G(T)$	Total
NS/NT(per cent)	60.3	56.5	54.9	70.8	50.0	58.3	66.8
NS(1)/NT (per cent)	25.9	24.2	25.8	25.0	23.5	25.0	41.2
(NUS(1)+NS)/NT (per cent)	70.7	66.1	67.7	70.8	64.7	68.3	72.4
(NUS(1)+NS(1)+NS(2))/NT (per cent)	48.3	45.2	45.2	50.0	47.1	46.7	54.1
NT (number of firms)	58	62	62	24	34	120	743

Source: Adapted from Miwa (1990a, p. 165, Table 6.8).

Table 6.9   Direction of change in main bank's loan share (number of firms): risky borrowers (1), 1973–84

	G(A)	G(B)	G(C)	G(T)
Up	33	11	17	61
Down	28	13	18	59
No change	1	1	1	3
Total	62	25	36	123

Source: Adapted from Miwa (1990a, p. 166, Table 6.9).

Table 6.10   Direction of change in main bank's loan share (number of firms): risky borrowers (2), 1983–4

	G(A)	G(B)	G(C)	G(T)
Up	33	11	13	57
Down	34	13	21	68
No change	2	2	2	6
Total	69	26	36	131

Source: Adapted from Miwa (1990a, p. 166, Table 6.10).

line between firms borrowing more than 10 billion yen in 1984 and those borrowing less. The former group contains 57 firms and is denoted as group B. The latter group contains 74 firms and is denoted as group S. Draw another line between firms whose core bank share in 1984 exceeded 20 per cent and the others. The former group contains 71 firms and is denoted as group H. The latter group contains 60 firms and is denoted as group L. The number of firms in each group, NG(i,j) is:

$$NG(i,j) = \begin{pmatrix} 14 & 57 \\ 43 & 17 \end{pmatrix} \quad \begin{array}{l} i = B, S \\ j = H, L \end{array}$$

NG(B,L)[61] and NG(S,H) dominate the others. Therefore, among risky borrowers, the larger a firm's total borrowing, the lower the main bank's loan share, and vice versa.[62,63]

Examine Table 6.11 for G(B,L) and Table 6.12 for G(S,H). Both correspond to Table 6.9. For G(B,L), the number of firms whose main bank loan share declines exceeds the number whose main bank's loan share rises. For G(S, H), the number of firms whose main bank's loan share rises is larger than the number of cases where it falls. This tendency grows clearer the longer a firm faces 'emergency' conditions.[64]

Table 6.11 Direction of change in main bank's loan share (number of firms): risky borrowers (3), 1973–84, G(B,L)

	G(A)	G(B)	G(C)	G(T)
Up	12	1	3	16
Down	7	8	8	23
No change	1	1	0	2
Total	20	10	11	41(*)

Note: (*) Data unavailable for two cases for 1973.
Source: Adapted from Miwa (1990a, p. 168, Table 6.11).

Table 6.12 Direction of change in main bank's loan share (number of firms): risky borrowers (4), 1973–84, G(S,H)

	G(A)	G(B)	G(C)	G(T)
Up	15	6	13	34
Down	9	4	5	18
No change	0	0	0	0
Total	24	10	18	52(*)

Note: (*) Data unavailable for 5 cases for 1973.
Source: Adapted from Miwa (1990a, p. 166, Table 6.12).

The first column of Table 6.11 shows that for G(A) – those in the red for three years – cases where the main bank's loan share rose during 1973–84 exceed those where it fell. However, the corresponding figures for 1983–4 are seven (up) and 13 (down), a movement in the opposite direction.[65]

Summary of Section 6-5: Main Banks as Lenders of Last Resort

A borrower facing financial emergency is both unable to maintain a stable relationship with its main bank and also unable to expect it to serve as a lender of last resort. This conclusion is stronger for borrowers whose main bank is a city bank. Moreover, main bank loan shares for firms facing financial emergency tend to decline for large borrowers and rise for small borrowers. This tendency appears before the onset of firm losses and becomes clearer as losses persist. Hence main banks act as lenders of last resort for small borrowers only, and large borrowers, who are expected to benefit from the lender of last resort function, do not. Therefore the evidence does not support the view that main banks serve as lenders of last resort.

6.6   BRIEF COMMENTS ON RECENT MAIN BANK LITERATURE

Since the 1980s, apart from the traditional literature on *keiretsu* loans and the loan-concentration mechanism, a new wave of theoretical interest and empirical research has developed around the formation and functioning of 'main banks'.[66] I will not review that literature here. In my view, this research, like that before it, assumes that financial factors have affected Japan's economic development. However, I believe this assumption is invalid.

Some, like Hoshi *et al.* (1990, 1991), focus on the workings of 'financial ties among group firms' (1991, p.38) and investigate their influence on the investment behaviour of individual borrowers. Declaring that the 'most important financial link is between group firms and the banks at the center of each of the six primary industrial groups' (p.38), Hoshi *et al.* chose '*Keiretsu no Kenkyu*'s classification scheme because it focuses on the strength of a firm's relationship to the financial institutions in the group' (p.40). With this choice, they adopted the conventional view of the Japanese economy. These relationships are the same as *keiretsu* loans or 'adhesion relationships' criticized as unpersuasive and concluded as non-existent in Chapter 5. Moreover, as shown above, financial ties – main bank relationships in this chapter – are neither so stable as usually argued nor do they function as alleged. On the basis of this choice, they contrast the behaviour of affiliated firms (firms in these groups) with that of unaffiliated.[67] They apply recent high-tech models to their targets, but such research can be likened to laser attacks on sand castles or mirages.

Yet for those who plan to study this new literature, please note the following five points on their theoretical explanations. Assuming the existence of financial ties between large banks and large firms, two explanations are given: the risk-sharing function of the ties and the main bank's monitoring function.

First, not only these financial transactions but also all organizations like 'firms' and all organizational transactions like long-term relationships other than a pure market or 'spot' transaction have a 'risk-sharing' character. Therefore 'risk sharing' is a right answer to the question, 'Why, instead of market transactions, are some given forms of organizational transactions adopted?' but only in that it is not wrong. This answer is not wrong almost everywhere.

Second, examine how risk is actually shared. Though there exists no common understanding, the main-bank view assumes that main banks lower loan rates and even exempt borrowers from paying them when they fall into distress. As shown in the text, however, such behaviours are rare: that is, only when the third stage of business downturn arrives and banks decide to let the borrower survive as a 'bank-managed firm'. Therefore, before accepting a 'risk-sharing' explanation, search the evidence for reduction and exemption of interest payments in the main bank literature. Moreover, other lenders will 'free ride' if a main bank reduces the interest payments required by distressed borrowers. When a main bank asks a borrower to pay *ex ante* a premium for risk sharing, a borrower in prosperity will refuse it. The potential for 'free-riding' on the back of a main bank's interest payment reductions to distressed borrowers may make borrowers unsure of the alleged main bank behaviour. If a borrower took it seriously, it would raise the main bank's loan share and reduce the number of lenders.

Third, be aware of the identity of the monitoring body, and the cost of monitoring, in studying the 'monitoring' explanation. Quite often a monitoring model is applied to such Japanese firms as Toyota, Hitachi, SONY, Mitsubishi Heavy Industries, Mitsubishi Corporation, the firms studied in Section 6.4, and most firms in the six major corporate groups. Who takes the trouble to monitor such firms? Who shares the main bank's monitoring costs? Making loans to such firms is a safe business, and the market mechanism must prevail here. Therefore banks compete for larger loan shares, and their shares are rather stable over time as in such homogeneous product industries as sugar, cement and steel. Before applying a main bank monitoring model to these firms, examine the necessity of monitoring and its cost bearing.

Fourth, in studying the literature applying a monitoring model to distressed firms, pay attention to the question: 'Why do other banks trust main banks to behave as their representative and reveal timely, accurate information about the borrower?' As shown above, in many cases main bank relationships are unstable and main banks do not function as lenders of last resort.

Fifth, the main bank monitoring explanation assumes that banks are in fact capable of monitoring firms satisfactorily. Given the scale economy of bank monitoring, it is argued that one or several banks monitor a borrower on behalf of other lenders. This is often called the 'signalling' or 'cowbell'. If they do so, however, how can we explain the tremendous number of bad loans Japanese banks made in the late 1980s?[68] An underlying assumption of main banks' magnificent monitoring capability is now dubious, which banks have known well. Why do other banks and borrowers put trust in main banks' capability?

Isn't the new literature preoccupied with the view that Japan is and must be peculiar and different from other economies? Note also that, as is usually the case elsewhere, only those interested in main banks write about them.[69]

6.7 CONCLUDING REMARKS

The conclusion of this chapter is consistent with those of the preceding chapters, especially that of Chapter 5. It is a natural consequence of them, too.[70] That conclusion, quite plainly, is that the main-bank view is totally wrong. Accordingly, such phenomena discussed with the term 'main bank' and related phrases, which are claimed to be the core financial factors which have contributed to Japan's industrial success, do not exist. Since there exists neither clear definition of the keywords nor common understanding of the arguments, proving that the main bank relationships do not exist is a bit like proving the non-existence of UFOs. Stable main bank relations between large firms and large banks, especially city banks, do not exist. Neither do the 'big-pipe' or the 'lender of last resort' functions exist.

The main-bank view was accepted as part of the dual-structure view. Even today many accept the dual-structure view and regard the main-bank view unquestioningly as the equivalent of the *keiretsu* loan view. Few have tried to clarify the main bank argument, operationalize a hypothesis and test that hypothesis empirically.

Japanese borrowers have a wider variety of lenders from which to borrow than is presumed by the main-bank view, and have access to an open financial market. Like the *keiretsu* loan view and the loan-concentration view, the main-bank view implicitly assumes that banks dominate loan transactions, but borrowers with multiple borrowing opportunities need not accept the follower position. In fact, the number of lenders is large and the core bank's share of each firm's loans is low.[71]

Though theoretical research on the formation and the function of main banks developed on the assumption that financial factors and their characteristics in Japan have been important to the industrial success of Japan, the phenomena to be explained have never existed and this assumption is invalid. Thus this research can be likened to the use of high-tech weapons to attack mirages.[72]

7 An Anatomy and Critique of the Corporate-Group View

7.1 INTRODUCTION

In this chapter focus is placed directly upon the Japanese corporate group view rather than upon corporate groups. The primary purpose is to anatomize the corporate group view by dividing it into parts, aspects or components in order to make a detailed examination. Based on this anatomy, studying corporate groups and the corporate-group view in an empirical manner is secondary.

Corporate groups, especially the 'six major corporate groups', such as Mitsui group and Mitsubishi group, are often called horizontal *keiretsu* and taken to be symbols of the 'peculiarity' of the Japanese economy and of its closed nature. Each corporate group member is thought to be gigantic, and the groups in aggregate are understood to dominate Japan's economy. For instance, Nakatani (1984, p. 227) begins his 'The Economic Role of Financial Corporate Grouping' with the statement:

> One of the most peculiar aspects of Japanese industrial structure is that the majority of Japanese firms belong to so-called inter-market business groups – *kigyo syudan* or *keiretsu affiliations* – within which firms are linked through reciprocal shareholdings, and lender–borrower and buyer–seller relations.[1]

In fact, however, each group member is not so large and small business dominates Japan's economy instead. As shown below, the corporate-group view is based on a specific view of financial markets, sharing much with the main-bank view, adhesion relationships in the loan-concentration view and the dual-structure view of the Japanese economy.

Those who have read the preceding chapters, especially Chapters 5 and 6, must have already realized both on theoretical and empirical grounds that the corporate-group view is wrong. The primary purpose of this chapter is to provide an anatomy of the corporate-group view, for those who wonder why such an entirely wrong view has been widely accepted and persisted even among academics, and for those who want to understand what the view is. The main questions here are anatomical and archaeological: What is the corporate-group view? What are the basic views of the economy underlying this view? When and how did it appear? Why was it accepted and has it been supported by both academics and the public?[2] What follows will satisfy the same kind of reader's interest in the views on main banks, adhesion relationships and the dual structure, which are all ill-defined but closely related to the corporate-group view.

Outlining the corporate-group view is made difficult by three points. (1) The wide variety of corporate-group views and their interpretations makes choosing only one to define that view a challenge. (2) Existing views and interpretations are not clear enough to be compared and tested. Different views often created controversy, which, however, was rarely productive and seldom contributed much to better understanding of the view. As a result, it is difficult to understand exactly what it is. (3) Since most views basically recognize economic phenomena as a result of exchange by coercion rather than by agreement and are not based on functional analysis, it is difficult to understand why and how 'analytical' conclusions can be drawn. Like the adhesion relationship of Section 5.5, 'corporate-group' views do not include a microeconomic statement of their rationale to answer questions like, 'Whose interests are served by the relationship?' or 'What are those interests and how does the adhesion relationship satisfy them?' To represent the various corporate group views, I choose Miyazaki (1976). Since Miyazaki (1962), Professor Yoshikazu Miyazaki has been the creator and most influential promotor of the corporate-group view, and Miyazaki (1976) is the compilation of his works.

Section 7.2 introduces the problem, by drawing readers' attention to the assumptions they make about the definition, existence and importance of corporate groups. The latter half of Section 7.2 briefly discusses the Six Major Corporate Groups. Sections 7.3 to 7.7 anatomize and discuss Miyazaki (1976). In Section 7.3, I introduce readers to the basic character of the corporate-group view, by examining his explanation of the basis for his tables for corporate groups (*kigyo shudan-hyo*). Section 7.4 critically reviews Miyazaki's aims and shows how and why they are unacceptable to most economists. Section 7.5 examines Miyazaki's uses of the corporate-group view to explain patterns of 'ownership and control'. Miyazaki makes a strong claim for the importance of a '*keiretsu-shihai* (control) mechanism', but neither defines nor offers evidence for this control. Sections 7.6 and 7.7 form the core of the chapter. Like the adhesion relationship, Miyazaki's corporate-group view is almost impossible to understand,[3] and needs reconstruction by interpretation. Section 7.6 dissects Miyazaki's view to show seven features. Section 7.7 rebuts Miyazaki with six questions. Each question is sufficient on its own to effectively reject the corporate-group view as an effective analytical concept for the study of Japan's firms, industries or economy. Section 7.8 adds three comments for those who still remain supporters of the corporate-group view. Section 7.9 offers concluding remarks.

This chapter is an anatomy and does not draw clear conclusions. The anatomy is carried out upon the conclusion of the preceding chapters that the corporate-group view is wrong. Naturally, the anatomy is consistent with and supports the previous conclusion.

7.2   DEFINING THE PROBLEM

Two Episodes Illustrating the Corporate-Group View

The Fair Trade Commission (FTC) once asked Toyota, 'Toyota belongs to Mitsui group. What is the ratio of intra-group trades to the total?' The manager who answered the inquiry later told me, 'Frankly, I was embarrassed. The main reason why Toyota is thought to be a member of Mitsui group is that it is a member of Mitsui's presidents' meeting (*shacho-kai*). We have never paid this question any heed and therefore cannot supply the requested data. Even if Toyota is a member of Mitsui group, where is the group's boundary?'[4] Indeed, Nippon Yusen, a shipping company and core member of the Mitsubishi group, carries the largest share of Toyota's exported cars. Mitsui O.S.K. Lines, the second largest shipping company in Japan and a member of the Mitsui group, does not.

At a meeting of a FTC study group on 'the closed nature of the Japanese economy', discussing 'intra-group trades' within corporate groups, I asked a former general trading company employee whose firm belongs to an ex-*zaibatsu* type group, 'Do corporate groups actually exist?' His immediate answer was, 'Of course; it's too obvious. We even have an association for alumni of all member firms and its annual meeting'.

But whether a group exists or whether it has an association for alumni of member firms (like whether a senior high school has an association for alumni) is not the critical question. Whether its existence can be proven, for instance, by its annual meeting and the association members' list updated every year is not critical either. The critical issue is whether 'corporate groups' have remarkable influence on the pattern of trade. This businessman is clearly not aware of the importance of the distinction: the influence of corporate groups appears obvious to him, so he grasps at phenomena consistent with his interest.

The importance of settling on a definition of corporate groups cannot be ignored. First, what are the 'corporate groups'? How is the set of 'groups', the object of the study, defined, and what are included in the set as its components? What else are in the set other than such components as the Mitsui group, the Mitsubishi group, and the Sumitomo group and where does the list end? Second, what is included in each corporate group? Where does each group members' list end, and how is its boundary determined? The most common answer to the first question is the 'six major corporate groups' and that for the second is presidents' meeting members. However, few think this definition adequate. Many have their own alternative, and several popular information sources based on different definitions of corporate groups have sold well. Toyo Keizai Shinpo-sha, *Kigyo Keiretsu Soran*, (annual), Nihon Keizai Chosa-kai, *Keiretsu no Kenkyu*, (annual), and Miyazaki (1976) are notable examples. Though alternatives tend to be either underspecified or vague, supporters of each alternative are seldom asked to clarify the definition, and therefore to examine its difference from others,[5] because of the common belief among supporters of the corporate-group view in the influence of corporate groups.

Because the list of corporate groups and the theory derived therefrom depend totally on the definition chosen for corporate groups, it is important that the criteria for that definition be both theoretically justifiable and empirically useful.[6] And 'whether corporate groups exist or not' is a futile question, since the answer depends fully on the definition both of 'corporate groups' and 'exist'. As shown below, Miyazaki's (1976) main concern seems to lie in making a list of corporate groups, called Tables of Corporate Groups (*kigyo shudan-hyo*), rather than in justifiability or utility.[7]

A Summary of the Presidents' Meeting (*Shacho-kai*) of the Six Major Corporate Groups

The following is an anatomy of the corporate-group view, carried out upon the previous conclusion that this view is wrong and that readers need a brief introduction to what that view is talking about. Table 7.1 and Table 7.2 summarize information on the presidents' meetings of the six major corporate groups. Table 7.1 summarizes information on each group. As mentioned in Section 6.2, the first three groups are called ex-*zaibatsu* type or of prewar *zaibatsu* origin,[8] and the second three are called bank-type or bank-centred. Some presidents' meetings began in the 1950s, but most started in the 1960s. Members, who number between 20 and 47, lunch once a month for two hours. The presidents' meeting cannot serve as the headquarter or central office of the corporate group, for as the FTC reports:

> At the meetings, outside lecturers present reports on internal and external economic conditions, and information is exchanged on the general economic situation. At the meetings of prewar *zaibatsu*-origin corporate groups, such matters as approval of usage of trade marks as well as donations made by the group in its entirety are reported.[9]

Items (7) to (9) of Table 7.1 show figures for intra-group relationships, that is, stockholding,[10] borrowing and transactions. I believe that most readers will be surprised at the low level of these figures. Note that the total number of employees of each ex-*zaibatsu* type corporate group's member firms is less than that of such firms as Volkswagen, General Electric or Philips, and the total sum of employees in all three groups is less than that of General Motors.[11] Also note that these figures have a meaning for such comparisons only when summing up can be justifiable, which, as shown below, can hardly be.

Table 7.2 shows the position of the six major corporate groups in the Japanese economy during 1970–90. Though the number of group members has grown steadily, the ratio of those firms in aggregate to all non-financial corporate firms, measured in terms of employment, total assets, sales and income before extraordinary items, has been declining slightly. I believe again

Table 7.1 Presidents' meeting (*Shacho-kai*) of six major corporate groups

	Mitsui	Mitsubishi	Sumitomo	Fuyo	Sanwa	DKB	Average of total
(1) Common name of group							
(2) Name of presidents' meeting	Nimoku-kai	Kinyo-kai	Hakusui-kai	Fuyo-kai	Sansui-kai	Sankin-kai	
(3) Year of establishment	1961	1954 or 55	1951	1966	1967	1978	
(4) Number of members	24	30	20	29	44	47	32
(5) Meeting held on	every first Thursday	every second Friday	once a month	once a month	once a month	once in three months, on the third Friday	
(6) Number of employees of all member firms (thousands)	240	242	155	330	390	464	264
(7) Ratio of intra-group stock holdings (per cent, 1989)	19.5	35.5	27.5	16.4	16.5	14.6	21.6
(8) Ratio of intra-group borrowings (per cent, 1989)	24.0	18.0	26.6	19.5	17.0	12.1	17.5
(9) Ratio of intra-group transactions of manufacturing members (per cent, 1989)							
Sales	18.8	25.6	38.1	12.7	6.3	11.9	16.4
To general trading companies	17.8	21.4	37.4	11.1	4.8	6.9	13.7
Purchases	12.0	15.0	16.4	4.0	5.2	8.2	9.0
From general trading companies	11.2	10.3	15.3	2.1	3.0	4.8	6.4

Notes:
(1)–(6) are from Toyo Keizai Shinpo-sha, *Kigyo Keiretsu Soran* (1991). Figures are for 1 October 1990. (7)–(9) are from FTC, *The Outline of the Report on the Actual Conditions of the Six Major Corporate Groups*, (February 1992). For example, the ratio of intra-group borrowings = borrowings from institutions within the same group/the total borrowings of member corporations of the same group.

Table 7.2   The six major corporate groups' position in the Japanese economy, excluding banks and insurance companies (per cent)

	1970	1975	1980	1985	1990
Number of members	130	131	155	164	164
Employees (share, per cent)	5.9	5.1	4.9	4.5	4.1
Total assets (share, per cent)	17.5	15.8	15.3	14.2	13.6
Sales (share, per cent)	15.0	14.9	15.6	16.0	15.2
Income before extraordinary items (share, per cent)	13.6	8.3	12.1	14.2	13.7

Source: Toyo Keizai Shinpo-sha, *Kigyo Keiretsu Soran*, annual.

that most readers will be surprised at the low level of these figures. Some may feel that figures in the table neglect subsidiaries and affiliates. The FTC reports, however, that in 1987 subsidiaries (firms with an equity stake of more than 50 per cent) of all non-financial member companies accounted for 4.2 per cent of total assets and 3.8 per cent of sales, and affiliates (firms with an equity stake of above 25 and below 50 per cent) accounted for 4.9 per cent of total assets and 3.3 per cent of sales. These numbers do not affect the picture substantially.[12]

Note also that, although many large firms are members of these corporate group presidents' meetings, others are not. Prominent non-members include all electric power companies, Nippon Telegraph and Telephone, Kajima Corporation, Nippon Oil, Bridgestone, Nippon Steel, Matsushita Electric, SONY, Honda, Mazda, Daiei, the Industrial Bank of Japan, Nomura Securities, Japan Air Line and Yamato Transport. Also note that within the same group are such fierce competitors as Hitachi, Iwasaki Electric, Sharp, Kyocera and Nitto Denko in the Sanwa group. Further, three firms belong to two different groups, and Hitachi belongs to three groups, as mentioned in Section 6.2.

7.3   MIYAZAKI'S TABLES OF CORPORATE GROUPS (*KIGYO SHUDAN-HYO*) (1976)

Since the publication of '*Kato kyoso no ronri to genjitsu: keiretsu shihai kikoh no kaimei* [The logic and the reality of excessive competition: a study of the *keiretsu* control mechanism]' in 1962, Professor Miyazaki has been the champion of the corporate-group view. The 1976 book is a compilation of Miyazaki's work on corporate groups. His main concern is to present some tables on corporate groups (hereafter, Tables) and to emphasize the importance of corporate groups. However, one of the criticisms of Miyazaki since 1962 is that it does not define basic concepts and therefore is not clearly understandable.[13] In his 1976 book, Miyazaki also presents his views without defining basic concepts. He simply calls his view '*sagyo kasetsu*' [literally, a working hypothesis].

Miyazaki argues that the Tables are based not on a 'subjective and intuitive' standard but on an 'objective' one (p. 66). In order to determine the strength of the relationship between each firm and a corporate group, Miyazaki uses an 'appropriate' combination of such indices as presidents' meeting membership, dispatched executives, stockholdings, loan amounts and corporate bond underwriting. Miyazaki's basic idea is most clearly revealed in his response to Futatsugi's (1977) critical comment on these allegedly 'objective' standards:

> For such works, it is essential to define corporate groups by accepting a combination of standards as working hypotheses, and to improve them step by step by comparing them with reality. Therefore, I cannot accept criticisms of my working hypothesis as 'subjective and intuitive'. [Futatsugi] might make this claim if he were going to deny the existence of corporate groups, but when he is sure of their existence, he must instead propose a better working hypothesis for their definition. He cannot just abandon his effort by emphasizing 'subjectiveness'. My book is just an essay to define corporate groups with objective standards which are as economically meaningful as possible. (Miyazaki, 1980, pp. 172–3)

In response to this comment, six questions arise: (1) How can one argue, without defining corporate groups, 'He might make . . . but when he is sure of the existence'? (2) Why is it essential 'to define corporate groups . . . and improve hypotheses', when he is sure of their existence? How can one be sure of their existence when the process of definition is essential and subsequent to the discovery of their existence? What is 'the reality'? How can one 'compare'? (3) What are 'objective standards which are as economically meaningful as possible'? What do 'economically' and 'meaningful' mean? (4) What does Miyazaki mean by 'just an essay'? Does he intend to say that he is just drawing a line to define members, which does not extend to an argument like the corporate groups' 'One-Set-Ism' view regarding equipment investment behaviour? (5) What is Miyazaki's 'working hypothesis'? What is it based on? How does he introduce it? (6) When he is sure of the existence of corporate groups, why does he continue to emphasize their definition instead of going on to other features such as the function of corporate groups and their relations with non-members?[14]

Here the first question is the most basic. The corporate-group view supporters seldom take it seriously, and Miyazaki (1976) neither examines nor explains this point. He states his assumptions early on:

> As in the USA, nobody denies the existence in Japan of interest groups which take a peculiar form of combination called 'corporate groups'. We need not talk much about prewar *zaibatsu* . . . Following the announcement of the completion of *zaibatsu* dissolution in July 1951, presidents' meetings began to form as organizations for communication among executive managers and for collective decision making, and 'corporate groups' peculiar to Japan came to public attention. Mitsubishi group's decision in August 1963 to merge three heavy industrial firms born

as a result of the deconcentration of Mitsubishi Heavy Industries[15] is the most striking event. Their collective action in a meeting with the then First Vice-Prime Minister of USSR in May 1964 and in the Mitsubishi Pavilion in EXPO'70 also displays their existence and power. The whole affair is brought to light now. (1976, p. v)

To summarize: nobody has ever denied the existence of corporate groups; they drew public attention again in postwar Japan when they formed presidents' meetings; a series of impressive events brought the whole affair to light. Try to answer these questions: Are the presidents' meetings decision-making organizations? If so, on what issues do they make decisions? How are compromises and decisions made given the diversity of interest and opinions among members? What is meant by the 'Mitsubishi group's decision'? I believe that most readers will be surprised and disappointed at the events which Miyazaki cited to display the existence, the power and 'the whole affair' of corporate groups.

7.4   MIYAZAKI'S AIMS

Miyazaki states at the outset:

Studies of capitalism in prewar Japan were based on issues of land ownership . . . In studies of the postwar Japanese economy, however, issues of joint-stock companies, focusing on the 'ownership and control' relationship, are of primary concern. Thus I study in this book Japanese firms in the postwar period, especially in the 'high-growth era'. (1976, p. iii)

However, these points have been criticized.[16] The use of the terms 'ownership' (*shoyu*) and 'control' without definition has also been criticized:

An organization as complex as a large contemporary firm involves a complex mechanism for distributing the surplus it generates. Irrespective of legal definitions of rights and responsibilities, ownership of the firm, in an economic sense, is not easily defined. 'Ownership' is not a black-and-white affair, but a 'grey' matter to varying degrees: who gets what share in the firm's profits, who is responsible for the losses, and who participates to what extent in its managerial decision-making process. 'Control' or 'manage' (*shihai*) is even more difficult. The Japanese word *shihai* expresses a number of nuances, and depending on context can be rendered into English as control, manage, govern, direct, rule, dominate or sway. Unless one's purpose is propaganda, it is best to avoid using the term at all in social-science discourse unless its meaning is clearly defined at the outset. (Komiya 1990, pp. 168–9)

Miyazaki never clearly defines 'ownership' and 'control'. Ignoring the problems instead, he devotes all his energy to 'defining corporate groups with objective standards which are as economically meaningful as possible'.[17]

Prewar studies of capitalism in Japan often emphasized land ownership, since most people regarded land as the most basic productive factor. Why and how did 'joint-stock companies' become the most basic factor of production in postwar Japan? The appropriateness of this judgement must be questioned and at the least we first require definition of 'ownership' and 'control'. Even when 'joint-stock companies' in postwar Japan decisively influence the distribution of economic surplus, the goals of research should be more than just the study of 'ownership and control' and the 'definition of corporate groups with objective standards'. The critical question should be: What is the most basic resource which makes 'joint-stock companies' the object of primary concern? Miyazaki (1976) takes 'funds' in such forms as shareholdings and loans as the most basic factor of production. Most academics, especially economists, do not agree with this view; this point is supported by the recent explosion of interest in economic organization, symbolized by the nexus of contract theory or contract theory view of a firm.[18]

7.5 CORPORATE DECISION MAKING AND OWNERSHIP

As shown, Miyazaki (1976) studies the 'ownership and control' relationship and defines corporate groups in his tables never defining the terms 'ownership' and 'control'. He applies his result to real phenomena, interprets them and proposes the 'One-Set-Ism' view of corporate group behaviour in equipment investment. For a better anatomy both of his corporate-group view and of 'One-Set-Ism', let me examine whether his causal argument is valid. The Miyazaki chain of causality is that: corporate groups → equipment investment behaviour of the 'One-Set-Ism' type → have tendencies towards 'excessive competition' and high growth. My primary concern here is whether deviation between the following hypothetical states is identifiable: (1) a state where corporate groups exist and have decisive influence over the investment behaviour of individual firms, and (2) a state where corporate groups do not exist or lack decisive influence. Miyazaki (1976) includes the core part of Miyazaki (1962) subtitled 'a study of the *keiretsu* control mechanism', but I find there neither a strong assertion for an effective '*keiretsu* control mechanism' nor its supporting evidence.

Miyazaki (1979) distinguishes 'control' from 'business leadership':

As R.A. Gordon points out, business leadership is 'the function of organizing and directing business enterprises, of making the decisions which determine the course of a firm's activities'.[19] Control is different from such active leadership. Control is the power to select and dismiss managers. In Japan, 'corporate control' implies that a parent company (companies) through shareholding holds the power to select and change managers. When the principal shareholders are stock companies instead, the power to select managers is in the hands of managers of parent companies. (p. 234)

As equipment investment decisions fall under 'business leadership', my prime concern is whether 'the power to select and dismiss managers' is actually in the hands of 'corporate groups', and, if so, whether it is used effectively.

In Chapter 5, 'Corporate Groups Before and After the War', Miyazaki compares the three major prewar *zaibatsu* with three major postwar ex-*zaibatsu* type corporate groups (Mitsui, Mitsubishi and Sumitomo).[20] Noting that the 'separation of ownership and management' was accelerated and the dominance of managers in presidents' meeting member firms was strengthened by the 'war crime purge' and the 1950 corporate law amendment, which permits non-stockholding directors (1976, p. 249), Miyazaki cites Noda (1963, p. 263):

> The power to control management in large firms in postwar Japan is in the hands of those who are independent of ownership. So long as the firm is run well, they have wide discretion in business matters (even in ex-*zaibatsu*-type firms). Thus the influence from the outside control group has been remarkably weakened.

He also comments that links created by dispatched executives have been tremendously weakened.[21] Therefore Miyazaki actually argues that, even in ex-*zaibatsu* type corporate groups, these groups or those who control the groups (indeed, who they are is the critical question, discussed below in Section 7.7 as the third question) neither hold the power to 'select and dismiss managers' in charge of 'business leadership' nor effectively use it. This conclusion also applies to other corporate groups. Thus Miyazaki (1976) observes that decisions on equipment investment are independent of 'corporate group' influence. Even when there exist tendencies toward 'excessive competition' in the Japanese economy, as at least the title of Miyazaki's 1962 paper suggests, this cannot be a direct result of 'corporate groups' or '*keiretsu* control'.[22]

This conclusion applies also to all other decisions under Miyazaki's term, 'business leadership'. Thus the answer to my primary concern here is clear: deviation between the two hypothetical states noted above is unidentifiable. Even when 'corporate groups' exist, they influence neither the behaviour of individual firms nor industrial performance. Therefore they cannot influence the industrial performance of the Japanese economy as a whole, and cannot be an important factor in its industrial success. 'Corporate groups' are not worth the attention of analysts seeking to understand the Japanese economy.

7.6   SEVEN FEATURES OF MIYAZAKI'S TABLES OF CORPORATE GROUPS

Though popular and widely supported, Miyazaki is, as shown, not clearly understandable.[23] Before analysing the argument in the next section, therefore, I try here to interpret it. Miyazaki offers 'an essay defining corporate groups with objective standards which are as economically meaningful as possible' (1976, p. 66). No explicit explanation for the term 'economically meaningful' is available, however, so I am left to guess at the meaning from his process of constructing the Tables and their explanations.[24] Miyazaki's corporate groups can be summarized in seven sometimes overlapping features.

First, Miyazaki claims that inter-firm connections can be represented by seven concrete indices for which data are available for four: fund-raising relations, shareholding relations, personnel relations such as dispatched executives, and historical relations. However, he declares that, 'The concrete standards for classification based on these four indices are enough to study corporate groups from the side of inter-firm connections and that of control relations by capital' (p. 60). His standards of classification are based on 'presidents' meeting membership, dispatched executives, shareholdings, loans and corporate bond underwriting' (p. 66), and therefore his index of 'historical relations' appear to correspond to presidents' meeting membership.

The second feature of Miyazaki's corporate group view is that 'parent firm–subsidiary' connections are principal, and the 'connections between subsidiaries' are supplementary. The 'parent firm–subsidiary connection includes connections with firms which were formerly departments of parent firms . . . and connections with firms in which parent firms hold the majority of stocks, and which cannot make independent decisions.[25] Apart from such firm-to-firm connections, in a corporate group many firms are connected to a parent through presidents' meeting, shareholdings, loans and dispatched executives, which comprise another kind of connection' (pp. 60–61).

Third, Miyazaki takes financial institutions as the core of a corporate group. This interpretation is drawn for two reasons. (1) As the first of three types of corporate groups, he talks about ones in which financial institutions are the core: 'As in ex-*zaibatsu* type . . . a financial group such as a bank, trust bank and insurance company is the core, or one bank is the core with *keiretsu* loans. Of these, some, like Mitsubishi, Mitsui, Sumitomo . . . form presidents' meetings which function as the central decision-making unit, but others do not.' He continues, 'financial institutions are not the core' in the second type, like the Toshiba group. 'In some of these, the core firm is a member of a corporate group of the first type' (p. 61). (2) Three of Miyazaki's five items in his classification standards – presidents' meeting, loans and corporate bond underwriting – are irrelevant to corporate groups in which 'financial institutions are not the core', implying that Miyazaki's corporate-group view is constructed mainly from corporate groups in which financial institutions are the core.

Fourth, Miyazaki considers that firms in 'parent firm–subsidiary connection or in a corporate group' are in a *keiretsu* and do not make independent decisions. This interpretation is drawn from the statement on *keiretsu-gai kigyo* (non-*keiretsu* firms): 'Of course, all large firms with over 5 billion yen in assets are not in a parent firm–subsidiary connection or a corporate group. Not a few are non-*keiretsu* firms which make independent decisions, to which the 'standard of classification' does not apply' (p. 61).

Fifth, Miyazaki regards presidents' meetings as of top importance, as suggested by his statement that 'the classification of firms into corporate groups needs parent subsidiary connection determination, presidents' meeting evaluation and financial group determination. . . Firms in an ex-*zaibatsu type keiretsu* have a meeting called the presidents meeting, which coordinates group policies, plans joint ventures among members and determines whether a new use of ex-*zaibatsu* name should be permitted' (p. 63).[26]

The sixth feature is that a 'financial group' plays a crucial role.

A group of financial institutions as in Mitsui, Mitsubishi and Sumitomo discuss decision making in their presidents' meeting and behave as if each were a single unit, which I call here financial group. In this study, I classify corporate groups by the sum of dispatched executives and loans from the financial institutions in a financial group rather than by individual financial institutions, which means that I treat the group of financial institutions in a group as an institution. (pp. 65–6)

Miyazaki's seventh feature of corporate groups is related to the relative weights attached to 'shareholding ratios' and 'loan amounts'. By his standard of corporate linkage, shareholding ratios of 20 to 40 per cent are equivalent to loans equalling to 50 to 100 per cent of a firm's equity value. The basic idea is worth attention. Miyazaki explains: 'The ratio of equity to total assets of firms in my study varies between 25 and 30 per cent . . . that is, the liability to equity ratio is about 2.5. Therefore loans equivalent to the total value of equity equal 40 per cent of liabilities . . . which thus is equivalent to 40 per cent of shareholdings' (1980, pp. 171–2). Despite the differing risk-bearing role of each, Miyazaki (1976) regards shareholding (or investment) and loans as functionally equivalent, 'funds'-supplying activities.[27]

To summarize, Miyazaki's corporate-group view consists of the following: a core financial group, which behaves as if it were a single unit; around the financial group are many firms linked through presidents' meetings, shareholdings, loans and dispatched executives; firms in parent–subsidiary connections or in a group (*keiretsu*) do not make independent decisions; some presidents' meetings function as the central decision making unit of a group; financial institutions occupy a dominant position because they 'control' the investment funds *keiretsu* firms need.

7.7 SIX QUESTIONS ON MIYAZAKI'S CORPORATE GROUP TABLES

In this section I ask six questions on Miyazaki's 'essay to define corporate groups with objective standards which are as economically meaningful as possible', and on the 'corporate groups' thus defined. My criticism takes the form of questions, because Miyazaki's ill-defined terms make effective analytical criticism impossible. Each of my six questions is such an effective rebuttal that, unless a reader regards all of them as ineffective, the corporate-group view must be abandoned as an effective analytical tool of Japan's economy, industry and firms.

What Aspects of 'Corporate Groups' Exist?

As mentioned in Section 7.3, Miyazaki (1976) assumes 'the existence of corporate groups'. But what does this mean? The existence of 'financial groups'? The existence of a group of firms which are connected to these financial groups and cannot make independent decisions? The existence of a presidents' meeting which functions as the central decision making unit of a corporate group? All of the above? What else is assumed? Does Miyazaki assert the existence of corporate groups on the basis of his observation of these phenomena, or does he implicitly assume the existence of something higher or superior instead – like UFOs or something transcendental – of which these phenomena are merely imperfect manifestations?[28]

Logical Consistency and the Validity of Factual Judgement

Does Miyazaki assert that the corporate-group view is valid? This question arises from four points. (1) Regarding presidents' meetings, Miyazaki comments:

> Recently, in any corporate group the president of a firm in heavy industries is stronger than that of a bank . . . Depending on the issue, different firms play the core role in the presidents' meeting. Banks may play this role for financial issues and a big manufacturer may dominate issues of new technology. Thus the presidents' meeting has a core, but relations between its members are not those of senior and junior. (1976, pp. 249–50)

This comment is inconsistent with three of the seven previously stated 'features': that the 'financial group' is the core of a group; that the 'funds' supply is the core of a group; or that firms connected with the financial group do not make independent decisions.

(2) For the first half of the 'high-growth era', Miyazaki comments:

> Like prewar *zaibatsu*, presidents' meetings in those days had and used the power to make decisions on new business and loans in an emergency. But they had no power to control personnel affairs, and they could not coordinate individual interests or make a collective decision. Thus we often observed struggles for larger market share among firms in the same group. (1976, p. 250)

This comment is inconsistent with the regard for presidents' meetings as of top importance in corporate groups.

(3) As already quoted in Section 7.5, Miyazaki comments: Even executives dispatched from banks serve mostly as accounting specialists . . . Human ties within postwar *keiretsu* corporate groups are incomparably weaker than

those in prewar *zaibatsu* (1976, p. 255). This comment is inconsistent with the first and second features that emphasize the importance of dispatched executives.

(4) Miyazaki's treatment of only the ex-*zaibatsu* type groups is inconsistent with his comment that 'wide variety exists among corporate groups, from associations for communication and friendship to central decision making units' (1976, p. 63), but his selective treatment cannot claim to deal with corporate groups comprehensively.

Who Makes Decisions?

Miyazaki gives no account of who makes decisions and the nature of the decisions made. If presidents' meetings play a crucial role as central decision making units of corporate groups, the following questions arise: Who actually participates in decision making? How can the presidents' meeting compromise and decide on anything given the diversity of interests and opinions held by its members? What is the target function of a participant's decision making? Apart from that target function, is there any common group standard which strongly affects member decisions, by restricting feasible sets or by subordinating individual interests? The same questions arise when I accept the assumption that a 'financial group' is the core of each group. The same applies also to a city bank which is regarded as the core of this financial group. Does the president or the board of directors of the bank make independent decisions? That is, are such decisions unaffected by such outside interests as 'corporate groups' (other than the stakeholders usually taken into consideration, such as shareholders, employees, depositors, borrowers, and so on)? No answer is given in Miyazaki (1976).[29]

Why are Financial Institutions so Important?

Why are financial institutions so important to Miyazaki? So long as 'funds' or 'capital' are tradable and the basic function of a financial institution is intermediation, it is unimaginable to attach so much importance to the 'control of funds', the role of financial institutions and the existence of a 'financial group'. How can 'funds' control the corporate group's will and decisions?[30]

Do Presidents' Meetings Play an Important Role?

As mentioned above, Miyazaki (1976, p. 63) claims that the presidents' meeting 'coordinates group policies, plans joint ventures among members and determines whether a new use of the ex-*zaibatsu* name will be permitted'. What else does the presidents' meeting do? What coordination role does it play? What is the list of such joint ventures? Is permission to use the group name so important?[31] Do presidents' meetings play an important role? Apart from the existence of the presidents' meeting itself, I find almost no statement and no explanation of its importance.[32]

Are Presidents' Meeting Members Controlled by the Financial Group?

Are presidents' meeting members controlled by their financial group? If so, why and how? As mentioned, Miyazaki (1976, 1979) distinguishes 'control' from 'business leadership'. Does the corporate group (or something transcendental) possess and use the power to appoint and dismiss managers of a firm which Miyazaki identifies as 'controlled' by the group? Does holding 40 per cent of corporate stock assure 'control' of the firm equivalent to loans equal to the equity value? Following the statement quoted in Section 7.5, Noda adds the following: 'Today most managers in large firms are specialists consistent with such requirements as knowledge, capability, and experience for corporate management and control' (1963, p. 264).

When a financial group (or T) acquires the power through its share-holdings to select managers, can the group use that power? Is the use of that power considered profitable? Under what conditions is it profitable to use the power? The definition of 'control' is unclear and an essay to determine whether a firm is 'controlled' is irrelevant if the group cannot use its control, that is, when it can rarely improve its profitability by using that control, or when 'ownership matters only in an emergency' (Imai, note 18 above). The relevant question here is, as in Section 7.4, what is the most basic production factor for both the postwar Japanese economy and for each large firm? The answer to what makes 'most managers in large firms . . . specialists' is the same: Today the essential task of a firm is not to carry out routine works steadily but to create information, to search for new business opportunities, and to develop an accumulation process for continual innovation through the interaction of agents (Imai, 1989, p. 141). Seldom today, therefore, do funds suppliers appear prominent or powerful in such interactions.

What will happen when suppliers of funds use their power to select and dismiss managers (acquired by their positions as either shareholders or creditors) against the will of management specialists (owners and suppliers of managerial resources)? Either of two consequences will follow: (1) firms will attempt to change their sources of funds, or (2) declines in managerial morale, performance and the quality of job applicants will occur, together with managerial attrition. Funds suppliers therefore realize that, even when they have the power to affect management, that power is hard to use profitably, and is used seriously only in an emergency.

The reality of 'control' by the corporate groups is thus far from what Miyazaki (1976) assumes for his Tables: that financial groups subordinate presidents' meeting members. The role of dispatched executives is not determined by such 'control' and counting the number of dispatched executives as an indicator of corporate group influence is therefore unreasonable. The group of owners and suppliers of managerial resources acquires the power to select and dismiss managers and also uses the power to decide on the source of their investment funds. It is this group, therefore, rather than a faceless corporate group, which decides on the type of executives to be invited from outside and whether particular executives proposed by large shareholders or lenders should be accepted.[33]

Illustrations of the Sixth Question

The relationship between Hitachi and Hitachi Metals is taken by Miyazaki (1976, pp. 60–1) as representative of a 'new subsidiary established by the separation of a department of a parent firm', with a comment that under a 'parent–subsidiary connection' the latter is 'a firm which cannot make independent decisions'.[34] According to Hitachi Metals' *Yuka Shoken Hokokusho* (*Security Reports*), published by the Ministry of Finance, for the term ending in March 1987, Hitachi held 52.8 per cent of Hitachi Metals' stock. In addition, 15 of 17 board members were former Hitachi employees. Two were originally employed by Hitachi Metals directly after their college graduation. Of the 15 from Hitachi, 12 (including all eight managing directors and above) moved to Hitachi Metals when it was established in 1956, and one moved in 1957. Of the remaining two members, one is the president of Hitachi and the other moved to Hitachi Metals in 1979 and was appointed a member in 1983.[35] Note, however, that at this moment already 30 years had passed since 1956. I cannot seriously accept these facts as evidence for Miyazaki's argument that 'the parent firm has the power to select and dismiss managers' (p. 232). Is it appropriate to judge from these facts that such a subsidiary as Hitachi Metals 'cannot make independent decisions'?

The relationship between Hitachi and Hitachi Cable is almost the same. As of March 1987, Hitachi held 50.84 per cent of Hitachi Cable's stock. Of 19 board members, 16 (including all 11 managing directors and above) moved from Hitachi in 1956 when Hitachi Cable was founded. Two of the remaining three were originally employed by Hitachi Cable directly after their college graduation. The last position is held by the president of Hitachi.[36]

The next case is the relationship between Toshiba and Toshiba Machine. Toshiba Machine gained notoriety in March 1987 for violating COCOM (the Coordinating Committee for Export to Communist Area) export restrictions. As Toshiba held 50.08 per cent of Toshiba Machine's stock, the public's primary concern was whether Toshiba knew about and committed the violation. My concern here, however, is merely how Toshiba's 'power to select and dismiss managers' was used in Toshiba Machine's general stockholder meeting of June 1987.[37] Of the 13 board members appointed at that time, four were new, three of them having been employed by Toshiba Machine directly after their college graduation. The last new member was appointed to the position of executive managing director from auditor at Toshiba. Besides him, only one member moved from Toshiba remained on Toshiba Machine's board. He moved to Toshiba Machine in 1983 and was appointed managing director in 1985. His career in Toshiba as a semiconductor specialist suggests that his appointment at Toshiba Machine was not for 'control' purposes but for his expertise. Among the five who disappeared from the board members' list was an executive managing director who had moved from Toshiba in 1979. Judging from the number and positions of shifted executives, therefore, no change occurred in the 'power' of Toshiba.[38] These observations can be explained not by Toshiba's control of Toshiba Machine but by assuming that Toshiba Machine was run by specialist managers who could make independent decisions and that Toshiba's intervention, if any, was marginal.

7.8 THREE ADDITIONAL COMMENTS

Assuming the existence of 'corporate groups', supporters of the corporate-group view talk about corporate groups without a clear definition and common understanding of this term. My job on the corporate-group view in this chapter therefore is analogous to examining the validity of the UFO existence view. I add three comments in this section for those who still support the corporate-group view.

Misunderstanding My Message

Because the existence of corporate groups depends totally upon the definition of the terms 'corporate group' and 'existence', the question 'whether corporate groups exist or not' is futile. As a result, I assert none of the following: no corporate groups exist; corporate groups must be judged non-existent regardless of the criteria used to define them; corporate groups have no *raison d'être*; corporate groups have no influence.

This chapter focuses on a type of 'corporate group' represented by the six major corporate groups. In addition to the argument of the previous chapters, I express strong doubt here about accepting as valid the assumption of the existence and critical role of such corporate groups for an understanding of Japan's economy. In particular, any argument about or explanation of corporate group behaviour based on the activities of either financial group or presidents' meeting is unacceptable and invalid. (Note, however, that I do not deny the validity of the argument for other types of groups or associations, for example Toyota's suppliers' cooperative association, as shown in Chapter 4.[39])

Danger and Invalidity of the Existence Assumption

Whether corporate groups exist or not is a futile question. But assuming the existence of corporate groups such as the Mitsui and Mitsubishi Groups in order to understand Japan's economy is invalid and dangerous, since the conventional arguments about such groups are far from the truth. Four points follow. (1) Statements such as: 'when one is sure of their existence' (Miyazaki, 1980, p. 172) are unacceptable.[40] (2) Materials based on this erroneous assumption are of no value to an understanding of Japan's economy, and indeed cause further misconceptions to arise. Representative materials include: Toyo Keizai Shinpo-sha's *Kigyo Keiretsu Soran* [*Conspectus of Corporate Keiretsu*], Nihon Keizai Chosa-kai's *Keiretsu no Kenkyu* [*Studies of Keiretsu*], Dodwell Marketing Consultants' *Industrial Groupings in Japan*, Fair Trade Commission's *The Outline of the Report on the Actual Conditions of the Six Major Corporate Groups* and Miyazaki (1976). (3) Previous studies on the causes of corporate group formation depend totally upon the existence assumption and are therefore of no value.[41] (4) Lots of empirical studies examine differences between corporate group members and non-members in the mean value and variance of profit rates and growth rates, but these too depend totally upon the existence assumption. Consequently, they lack theoretical justification and do not test a hypothesis and therefore cannot escape from the criticism, 'After all, what are they doing?'[42]

Be Careful not to Bark at a Voice

Much has been written about 'corporate groups' without clearly stated and justified assumptions. This literature simply amounts to a grotesque pile of vague assertions. Adding to this pile, even by contributing something new and definite, raises the risk of being lumped together with the large literature, which can be likened to joining much ado about nothing, or of becoming a dog barking at the voice of a dog barking at a shadow. Without careful identification of the difference of one's argument from others, nobody will distinguish it from those hundred others. The best way to avoid such a tragedy is to dispense with the term 'corporate groups' altogether.

Three points must be clarified if we are to define a corporate group: (1) The degree of exclusiveness of 'corporate groups'. Miyazaki's Tables simply assume that corporate groups are exclusive and closed to outsiders. Indeed, the corporate-group view and the term '*keiretsu* relationship' in general almost always assume this point. Readers must therefore take care to recognize the importance of long-term relationships without accepting assumptions of exclusiveness.[43] (2) The nature of the relationships among firms. The conventional view assumes a hierarchical, power-based 'parent–subsidiary connection' between core firms (typically a financial group, including a city bank) and a representative member. Readers must take care to separate such assumptions from their discussions of firm linkages and long-term relationships. (3) The importance of the boundary distinguishing group members from non-members. While the conventional corporate-group view recognizes diversity in the strength of relationships between core firms and other group members, it leaves unstated the critically important assumption of a rigid boundary distinguishing group insiders from outsiders. Readers who recognize the importance of long-term relationships to the formation of corporate groups must take care not to assume that the boundaries of the groups cannot be blurred and fluid.

7.9 CONCLUDING REMARKS

Michael Gerlach's recent book, *Alliance Capitalism*, is the best known current English-language study of the *keiretsu* or corporate groups. Gerlach argues, '[i]f the shacho-kai serves to define membership and express group interests, then flows of resources are the concrete manifestations of these interests in the ongoing life of each firm's interactions with its affiliated enterprises' (Gerlach, 1992, p. 113). He studies the structure of flows of loans from group financial institution, share cross-holdings, outside directorships and trade in intermediate products and finds 'clear indications of the significance of the keiretsu in organizing intercorporate exchange in Japan' (p. 113). He concludes that the alliance structure of Japanese industrial organization results, for instance, in 'a market structure with substantial barriers to entry to newcomers, especially in high value-added industrial sectors' (p. 247).

Gerlach's study follows directly from the conventional view, concluded as wrong in the preceding chapters and anatomized in this chapter. As with the adhesion relationship of Section 5.5 his argument does not include a microscopic statement of its rationale to answer questions such as, 'Whose interest are served by the relationship?' 'What are those interests and how does the adhesion relationship satisfy them?' Those who sympathize with his book should ask these questions, as we have done in this volume. Gerlach's book is a huge collection of all sorts of assertions and anecdotes for the conventional view. Readers of this part will find in his book how easy it is to collect many such stories and understand that still many are barking at the sound of a dog barking at a shadow of what nobody knows.

'"Administered prices" is a catchy phrase which promises everything, explains nothing, and thereby gets in the way of our learning something' (Adelman, 1963, p. 23). With this statement, Morris Adelman begins his testimony to the U.S. Senate Judicial Subcommittee on Antitrust and Monopoly. The quotation comes to my mind at the end of this anatomy and critique. Reading 'corporate groups', 'main banks', '*keiretsu*', or 'alliance capitalism' for 'administered prices' captures my present frank feeling well. No further remarks are necessary; I let Adelman (1963, p. 24) conclude:

What does administered prices supply in understanding either price formation or public policy? Less than nothing, because it is a waste of time, which is a valuable resource, and lulls us into a false satisfaction which becomes one more barrier to cross. By mouthing phrases we head off thinking ideas . . . To explain why a price and a pattern of output is what it is and not something else takes analysis of supply, demand, and market control; setting up models of competition, monopoly, collusion, imperfect collusion, etc., and seeing which best fits. All this labour is saved, and in addition one has the nice feeling of being profound and up to date by saying: 'Administered prices.'

Part III
Industrial Policy

8 Industrial Policy of Japan: A Beginner's Guide

8.1 INTRODUCTION

> It is well known that the Japanese government devised a complicated system of policies to promote industrial development and cooperated closely for this purpose with private firms. It is not generally well understood among non-Japanese, however, exactly through what process policy decisions were made and organized, what were the policy means, and what actually were the policies. Even in Japan, while a great number of fragmentary reports appeared at the time in newspapers and elsewhere, an overall picture of the system of industrial policy was seldom clearly presented to the public. Consequently, what is well known among insiders quite often is unknown to the public, including academics. Therefore it is a hard task to explain the system of Japanese industrial policy. (Komiya, 1975, pp. 307–8)

This statement, with which Ryutaro Komiya began a section on 'industrial policy', describes accurately the condition of common understanding of Japan's industrial policy both among academics and the public in the mid-1970s. I believe that until now there has been no fundamental change in this condition, even after the publication of Komiya et al. (1988).[1]

Not only the content of industrial policy but also the direction of academic interest changes over time. In reading historical documents and the related literature, therefore, it is hard to realize for what purpose, why and for whom such material was written, and what was the central issue of controversy. It is much harder to understand both from the minutes of a symposium on a related topic what was not discussed and from the government's document what the government officials did not want to mention. Most of the existing information on industrial policy is of such character, and thus intrinsically biased.[2] Therefore one needs an understanding of the actual situation in order to collect and survey the related literature, selecting the relevant information from a great number of fragmentary reports and sources. Such an understanding can rarely be acquired and accumulated directly through government documents, public statements of government officials and the published literature. Hints often come through informal conversations both with people involved in actual policy formation and implementation and with conference participants before and after formal discussions. Finding such information also requires some preliminary knowledge and skill.[3]

What follows in this chapter is a guide for this purpose, based on my own observations and interviews, press reports and the like. Though such accurate guides as Komiya (1988) and Tsuruta (1988) are already available, no sources can be perfect for all research interests. As mentioned in Section 1.6, the next two chapters discuss policies for coordination within industry, and therefore this chapter focuses on this type of policy among the list of industrial policies.

We observe two peaks of intensity of interest in Japan's industrial policy, as shown in Section 8.2. It is critical for the study to realize the difference of interests between two peak times both in the subject and in the direction. The term 'industrial policy' became popular in Japan later than the second half of the 1960s, but policies for industries have a much longer history. Section 8.3 introduces the term 'industrial policy' as an expression, discussing how and for what purpose this term was adopted for policies for industries. Section 8.4 discusses the substance of industrial policy. In this section, I examine the following issues with concrete examples of specific industrial policies: What were policies for industries? How were these policies implemented? Under what restrictions did industrial policies operate? What was the government's role and relationship with the business sector? In Section 8.5, the core of this chapter, I discuss the industrial policy formation process, the role of policy councils (*shingikai*) and the nature of information available to outsiders, such as policy council reports and their inherent bias. Section 8.6 discusses the difficulty in identifying the impact of industrial policies. Section 8.7 offers concluding remarks.

8.2   CHANGE IN INTEREST IN INDUSTRIAL POLICY

Both the direction and the intensity of interest in industrial policy have changed greatly over time. In the intensity we observe two peaks. One is in the second half of the 1960s, reaching its climax in 1970 with the merger of Yawata Steel and Fuji Steel into Nippon Steel (hereafter I refer to this period as Period I).[4] Interest in this topic returned in the 1980s when Japan's industrial policy gathered worldwide attention, mainly stimulated by the industrial success of the Japanese economy (hereafter I refer to this as Period II).

In Period I, the focus centred on the relationship between industrial policy and the Anti-monopoly Act[5] and related competition policies. There was a heated debate on the role of anti-monopoly (or anti-trust) policy, which was then a newcomer to the system of national economic policy. Industrial policy, or more accurately the policies of the Ministry of International Trade and Industry (MITI), conflicted with the emerging anti-monopoly policy as the representative of the traditional policies. The debate was mainly among those who were familiar with the process and the history of economic policy, the policy 'insiders'. The interest in this period was almost exclusively domestic. In Period II interest in Japan's industrial success and its industrial policy was initially international and then spread domestically. Also, rather than the insiders of Period I, the general public displayed strong interest in this latter period. The central questions were: What was the net contribution of industrial policy to Japan's industrial success? How did success occur and why in Japan? And, finally, what are the lessons for other countries, particularly for less-developed nations?

As shown in Section 1.2, for the study of Japan's industrial success the period before 1970 is of critical importance. Consequently, Period I must be of prime concern for those who are also interested in Period II. Thus an analysis of the government's policies both in Period I and Period II begins with those in the late 1960s. However, the current debate and the direction of academic interest are completely different from those at that time, causing difficulty and confusion. Another difference is that the questions in Period II are positive ones, such as 'What did the government do?' and 'What effects did the government have?' The central points of the debate in Period I, however, were normative, such as 'What should be the role of the government?' and 'What should be the ideal position of the anti-monopoly policy in the national economic policy system and its relationship with industrial policy?' Therefore in Period I there was a kind of theological debate which was broad and exuberant but abstract and difficult to follow.

As a result, for those interested in Period II, it is not easy to read and apply the materials written concerning the industrial policy of Period I during that time. The reason can be summarized by seven points: (1) detailed information on what the government did under the name of 'policy' is lacking; (2) no information exists on the effect of these policies; (3) few record exists on the *ex post* evaluation of whether some concrete policy was beneficial to the economy; (4) little information is available on the decision and implementation process of industrial policy, reflecting the 'theological' character of the debate; (5) most literature, typically the minutes of symposia among insiders, and other government documents are so polemical that it is difficult to fully understand the historical background and institutional arrangements of the period; (6) information on the details of concrete policies, their background, the environment and effects is mostly provided from one side of the debate, that is, from the policy supporters, which therefore are significantly biased;[6] (7) the debate has focused on the steel, oil refining, petrochemical and motor industries which are different from those industries of recent concern, such as electronics.[7]

Even today there is little literature concerning the policies in Period I along the direction of interests of Period II, particularly that written by those who know well both what actually occurred and the institutional environment of the time. One has to distinguish the author's interest from the factual material that does exist while searching for information which is accurate and appropriate to one's own interest.[8]

8.3 'INDUSTRIAL POLICY' AS AN EXPRESSION: CHARACTER AND BACKGROUND

'Industrial policy' has only recently become a frequently used term in Japan. People began to use it after the second half of the 1960s when Japan's GNP was catching up to and outgrowing that of other G7 countries, with the exception of the USA (see Table 1.1). They used the term mainly in relation to manufacturing industries and to the policies of The Ministry of International Trade and Industry (MITI).

In the 1960s, the Japanese public began to demand a more open economy and supported strongly the view emphasizing the free workings of the price mechanism and increased inter-firm competition. They also insisted that anti-monopoly (anti-trust or competition) policy play a larger role in ensuring competition. In response, the government, especially MITI, tried to justify their intervention in the business sector as a well-designed and rational economic policy. In this context the government began to refer to their actions as 'industrial policy'.[9] Therefore industrial policy was not a newly introduced policy with a clear concept but a newly adopted term. The often cited statement of Kaizuka (1973, p. 167) is instructive: 'industrial policy is the policies formulated and implemented by MITI'.[10]

The decade following the second half of the 1950s saw a series of liberalizations, such as the liberalization of import restrictions, foreign exchange controls and inward direct investment,[11] forcing the government to change its relationship with industry. Prior to the industrial policy debate was the new industrial order debate in the first half of the 1960s, where *jisyu-chosei* [coordination by themselves; hereafter, self-coordination] or *kanmin-kyocho* [literally, the government–business cooperation scheme; hereafter the *kanmin* system] became the symbolic slogan. 'The *kanmin* system was a resource allocation policy in which the government tried to guide private investment in line with its expectations of economic growth by intervening in the investment activities of the firms in an industry' (Tsuruta, 1988, p. 70). The government proposed the *kanmin* system to which industry was strongly opposed, preferring self-coordination. 'By self-coordination is meant the development of the new industrial order through the autonomous (or joint) activities of the firms in an industry. Lying behind this insistence . . . was the fear that the *kanmin* system would be a forerunner of direct government controls' (ibid., p. 69). Note, however, that the two systems confronted in the debate

> had the following elements in common: (1) the view that the organization of industry was distinguished by the presence of excess competition and insufficient scale, (2) the feeling that it was necessary in coping with international competition to merge firms and concentrate production so as to expand firm size, and (3) that the Anti-monopoly Act should be gutted so as to give freedom in principle to form cartels and to arrange mergers. (ibid., p. 69).

Consequently, the main difference was not about the goals but over which side was to take the leadership and what was the appropriate role of the government.[12]

The industrial policy debate in the second half of the 1960s, following the new industrial order debate, focused on the elements which were taken for granted in the previous debate. This debate has four characteristics. (1) Industry and the government, who were at odds in the previous debate, found themselves in agreement in the latter industrial policy debate. Therefore the conflict was between policy 'insiders' who had detailed information and the policy 'outsiders' who did not. This debate was largely abstract and theological. (2) As a result of the previous debate, industry and the government were in agreement both on the necessity of such policies and on placing reduced emphasis on the anti-monopoly policy. But there still remained conflict on how the policy should actually be implemented and what the role of the government should be. Partly because of the agreement and the remaining conflict, there is a lack of literature on the details of concrete policies of the period. (3) Focus centred on 'excessive competition'. However, hardly any participants in the debate have bothered to explain with any degree of clarity what they meant by this phrase. One of the few attempts made was that of Morozumi, a higher official of MITI (1966, p. 61): ' "excessive" competition is competition such that the losses to the national economy exceed the gains that arise from that competition'. But as Komiya (1988, p. 11) commented, 'the use of "excess" is tautological and the meaning of "loss" or "gain" to the "national economy" is vague, so it cannot be said that this definition has much content'. The debate was between those who took for granted the necessity of the policy preventing 'excessive competition' and those who emphasized the price mechanism and the role of the anti-monopoly policy. The debate continued without clear common understanding of the key concepts. While the debate went on for some time, it was only a repetition of prior arguments on a different plane.[13] (4) As the central goal of industrial policy was the prevention of 'excessive competition', the main policy measure, at least in the minds of the debate participants, was the reorganization of industry through mergers, output coordination and investment coordination.[14]

8.4 THE SUBSTANCE OF INDUSTRIAL POLICY

It was in the second half of the 1960s and after that the public began to use frequently the term 'industrial policy' and the industrial policy debate gathered wide attention. This does not imply that prior to that period there were no such polices as to be called 'industrial policy' by those who are along the research interest dominant in Period II. Many, especially those who appreciate its contribution to Japan's industrial success, call the 1960s the 'heyday of industrial policy'. Few challenge the view that the role of the government was larger, and its intervention in business was more frequent and forceful, in the first half than in the second half of the 1960s. Before this debate government programmes were called Industry Rationalization Policies, Industry Upgrading (*kodo-ka*) Policies, Industrial Structure Policies, Industry Reorganization Policies and so on.[15] Therefore, those along the research interest of Period II, when asking what was the net contribution of industrial policy to Japan's industrial success, have to go back at least to the first half of the 1960s and even further, to the second half of the 1950s, when the term 'industrial policy' was not in general use.

Let us see what industrial policies were, how and under what restrictions they were implemented, and what was the role of the government and their relationship with business. For illustrative purposes we will look to the list-price system (*koukai hanbai seido*, literally open [public] sale system) and investment coordination in the steel industry, and output coordination in petroleum refining.[16]

The steel list-price system began in June 1958 and was abolished in June of 1991. Despite its long existence it was until the end of 1962 that the list-price system was materially functioning in line with the initial objectives. This system was basically for a self-coordination on price and output, and the government supported the system but did not play a significant role. The so-called Sumikin (Sumitomo Metal Industries) Incident (see Section 9.2 and note 16 of Chapter 9) occurred in relation to output coordination in 1965, three years after the material collapse of this self-coordination system.

December 1959 marks the beginning of investment coordination in the steel industry when MITI requested that the industry members coordinate their implementation of the long-term capacity plans. Formally, the goal was for the industry to draw up a long-term investment plan for approval by the Industrial Finance Committee of the Industry Rationalization Council. Before any noticeable achievements were realized, however, the discussion among industry members called 'coordination' ended and, for example, in 1965–1967, each firm's plans were, in effect, approved in full.

Beginning in 1962 petroleum refining fell under the Petroleum Industry Act, which had the striking distinction of ensuring strong government intervention in output, pricing and investment of that industry. The Act was intended to allow 'to the minimum extent required coordination of the activities of firms in the industry, as with the liberalization of petroleum imports it is expected that the petroleum market will be in disarray'.[17] What is interesting is that the method of output coordination in the petroleum refining industry, even under this Act, is similar to that of the steel industry. MITI requested the cooperation of the Demand Specialists Committee of the Petroleum Association of Japan in January and February of each year, to draw upon industry-wide coordination plan, the Petroleum Supply and Demand Plan, which was to meet the Petroleum Supply Plan required under Section 3 of the Petroleum Industry Act. According to the Fair Trade Commission, 'the Petroleum Supply Plan . . . only indicates the planned volumes which MITI feels desirable for the country as a whole, and does not indicate production levels for each individual petroleum refiner'.[18] Output coordination under the Petroleum Industry Act began in the second half of FY 1962. However, in the second half of FY 1963, the so-called 'Idemitsu Incident' interrupted these attempts at output coordination.[19]

These examples illustrate the answers to the questions posed above. (1) The Petroleum Industry Act and the related institutional arrangements were established during and after a series of liberalizations. With these the government tried to maintain the existing government–industry relationship under the pretext of preventing market disarray after liberalization. Thereby neither new policy concepts nor new institutional arrangements were introduced, but only new terms and phrases.[20] (2) Around 1965, these newly introduced arrangements proved to be ineffective in achieving the initial objectives. This suggests that the basic character of the government–industry relationship was transformed with the liberalization of trade and capital movements. (3) During this period the new industrial order debate arose between those who intended to maintain the existing government–industry relationship and those who supported future change. This was a response to changes in the policy environment and institutional arrangements, but the debate was silenced as the process of change continued. The debate influenced neither policy implementation nor the direction of the change in the government–industry relationship. (4) The government played an important role both in the new industrial order debate and the industrial policy debate. Though the central issues and the players were different in the two debates, there was a common goal for the government, that is, to convince the public of the validity of market intervention. Consequently point (3) above on the new industrial order debate also applies to the industrial policy debate.[21,22]

8.5   INDUSTRIAL POLICY FORMATION AND INFORMATION AVAILABLE FOR OUTSIDERS

What actually was done in the way of policies for industries? How and for what purpose were those policies formed and implemented? What was the effect of these policies? Is information concerning these policies available to outsiders, that is, for those who neither were involved in policy formation nor had a direct economic interest in individual policy decisions? It appears that there is no well-organized information available. Judging from its volume, the most important source of information on Japan's industrial policy is a series of reports and related documents of policy councils (*shingikai*), in particular the Industrial Structure Council and its predecessor, the Industry Rationalization Council. As mentioned above, however, they are products of a politicized process and hardly needed to explain the policy to outsiders. As a result, those materials are strongly biased.[23] Before going into the details of the bias, let us see the policy formation process and its participants in the 1960s.

Industrial Policy Formation Process

The government and the related business firms viewed most policy actions as a part of the government's routine work which needed no formal policy formation process. As mentioned above, 'industrial policy' was a term attached to what the government had been doing all along, and only a portion of this required a formal process for policy formation and implementation. What follows concerns only the latter, a portion of the government actions that required a formal process.

'Through what process were decisions relating to industrial policy made in Japan? There are almost no empirical studies of this question based on questionnaire surveys or other data'. Komiya (1988, pp. 14–20)[24] beautifully illustrates the formation process, and I summarize here the essence of his argument on policies in the 1960s.

The Diet played almost no part in setting industrial policy. Those groups whose influence was substantial in the formation of industrial policy on the government side were the *genkyoku* – the bureaus, divisions and sections within ministries responsible for particular industries – and the bureaus and divisions that mediated between different parts of a ministry and different ministries. On the private side there were the industry associations and playing an intermediate role were the policy councils, the Industrial Structure Council being the representative, that are formally part of the government. In addition, two more groups perhaps had some influence, the *zaikai*, a group of corporate executives, and financial institutions that supplied funds to industry. It was quite unusual for only one of the above groups to have a predominant influence regarding any given decision. Thus industrial policy formation consisted of the above players trying to convince each other as to the proper policy position, to realign their respective goals, or even at times to strong-arm their opponents.

MITI is the single most important *genkyoku* ministry within the Japanese government. The Heavy Industries Bureau, for instance, was one of its five *genkyoku* bureaus, within which could be found, among other sections, *genkyoku* sections for iron and steel, industrial machinery, electronics and electrical machinery, automobiles, aircraft and rolling stock. Each *genkyoku* had the primary responsibility for developing and supervising policies for a given industry, and as a part of the responsibility it drew up policy relating to its industry or industries.[25]

Immediately after the war, the government took the leading role in the interaction of the *genkyoku* and the business associations. As time passed, however, the balance of power shifted towards the industry groups, so that the *genkyoku* ministry came to play more of a mediating role. Later the *genkyoku* took into consideration the express interests of the industry (or at least its leading firms), organizing these interests and interacting with other sections, bureaus and ministries on the industry's behalf.[26] Many of the industry associations consisted of nothing more than friendly gatherings, or forums for exchanging information with others in the industry. Therefore the majority of the business associations had relatively little influence on either outsiders (the government and politicians) or insiders (individual, especially dissident, firms).[27]

Policy councils (*shingikai*) are only a part, rather a minor part, of the policy formation process. Policy council members are formally nominated by the minister of MITI and therefore tend to include those individuals thought useful by MITI bureaucrats. The majority thus consist of industry leaders, *zaikai* members and former bureaucrats, with there being in addition a small number of scholars, journalists, and the like. It is not the case that only things desired by the ministry are reflected in the councils' reports. Industry representatives do speak out strongly on issues that directly affect their interests. In fact, on such issues, policy councils served as a forum in which parties could adjust proposals to reflect their joint interests.[28] Thus proposals that were passed through these councils, that is, that had been negotiated to reflect vested interests, could afterwards be implemented relatively smoothly, at least in terms of those industries represented on the relevant councils.[29,30]

Information Available for Outsiders and Its Bias

Because of the characteristics of the policy formation process and the role of policy councils in it, the council reports and related documents were strongly biased in favour of those interests who designed the policy. The most important point is that these reports were basically for insiders who participated in negotiating the policy. Since each party had almost no incentive to disclose conflicting information,[31] and reports were written under strict constraints necessary for agreement, only the minimum information necessary was included.

From this, ten points follow. (1) Part of an agreement which one party does not want to be publicly known is not included. (2) That which one party strongly wants to be documented, subject to the agreement of other parties, is included. (3) Reports also include policy declarations on what members agree to pursue and ask the support of the public, particularly when a new law subsidizing an industry is sought. (4) No information is usually available on each party's interests and the negotiation of those interests. Neither is information on what the government or some party proposed but could not reach an agreement upon. (5) No information is usually available on how their interests interacted with other sections, bureaus and ministries. (6) Points on which the *genkyoku* does not expect to reach an agreement are not on the policy council's agenda and therefore the subsequent reports do not include these issues. (7) The evaluation of past policies is not included unless indispensable, for example the revision or continuation of an earlier policy.[32] (8) Until very recently there has been little explanation of what was actually discussed in the policy councils.[33] (9) In the 1960s, these reports paid little attention to the Anti-monopoly Act, since its position was minor during this era of its 'hibernation'.[34] (10) There is no information on what was known to the parties or what some party did not want to make public. Reports do not indicate the 'joint interests' of parties or the alternatives rejected.

As a result it is difficult to understand the actual policy formation from these policy council reports and related documents. Likewise, discussion with these insiders on and after the release of council reports, and memoirs they publish later, share the same bias, often being manipulated. They therefore require much caution when reading. Note at least two points. First, a

statement made just after a report usually has a specific objective and
demands careful investigation, especially when it includes precious information. Second, every individual who takes part in the policy formation is a
representative of a party with vested interests and therefore has no incentive
to express an opinion contrary to the council report. This applies also to
retired government officials, both because of implicit organizational norms
and because of individual interests.[35]

As mentioned above, policy councils are only a part of the policy
formation mechanism. Moreover, many policy actions are recognized both
by the government and the industry as routine work which needs no formal
policy formation process. In addition to the fact that council reports do not
cover all industrial policies, five additional points follow. (1) Industrial policy
implementation typically takes the form of informal regulation (*gyosei
shido*).[36] Informal regulation is not an enforceable order with legal basis but
an undocumented, quite often oral, form of guidance or advice.[37] There exists
no detailed record of informal regulations. (2) Government official in direct
charge recognize informal regulation as a part of routine work and neither
keep detailed records nor perform *ex post* evaluation of such activities.[38] (3)
As mentioned above, no individual in the related parties, both in the
regulating and the regulated, has an incentive to express an opinion contrary
to informal regulation. (4) As a result of the undocumented nature of
informal regulation, only government officials in direct charge know the
details of policy application, and these officials change their position
regularly in a short time.[39] (5) Even journalists and scholars who took part
in policy formation, especially in policy councils, rarely had the same type of
interests as are common in Period II, and seldom collected and preserved
relevant information.

There is little to gain by asking government leaders about their policies,
what objectives they pursued, or the effectiveness of these policies. Officials in
responsible positions seldom tell us how effective they think government
policy has been. The most we can hope for are the opinions and
'explanations' of retired officials and members of various policy councils.
Although active officials are thought sometimes to express their opinions
through retired officials or through these councils, this information is
unreliable. Obviously, it is also biased, and it would be simplistic and
dangerous to carry out a policy study that relied too much on such
information.

With the high growth of Japan's economy and its industrial success, a lack
of careful attention to the bias of government reports, typically those of
policy councils and related documents, leads readers to conclude that
industrial policy has been effective.

8.6   EVALUATION OF INDUSTRIAL POLICY

What policies or policy actions should one take into consideration when
evaluating the effectiveness of industrial policy? The task of identifying and

evaluating the impact of a policy is seldom easy. Ideally, the task of identification can be accomplished by finding the deviations between the actual state of affairs and the hypothetical state without the policy actions. The difficulty lies, above all, in how to model such a state. In the case of industrial policy, it is clear neither what the policy function was, nor what policy actions were pursued. With little attention paid to the difficulty, most academic literature and government reports fail to clearly specify the boundaries to the term 'policy' and take a larger set of actions into consideration. Thus there is a tendency to overestimate the role of the government and the impact of government policy.[40]

The merger of Yawata Steel and Fuji Steel, which gave birth to Nippon Steel, is often used as a representative example of policies to promote mergers among large firms. If, however, this is seen as being the result of (industrial) policy, and it is claimed that this is representative of industrial policy, then it is necessary to make clear what the policy function was, in what way the policy operated and how the policy contributed to bringing about the merger. In my view,[41] what the policy contributed, if anything, was moral support for the directors of the firms in making the decision to challenge Section 15 of the Anti-monopoly Act.[42] This Act prohibits a merger whose effect 'may be substantially to restrain competition in any particular field of trade' and was regarded as being the biggest obstacle to this merger. The basic fact is twofold: the directors of two firms decided to merge with the support of shareholders, and the FTC examined the application and judged it legal. The industrial policy debate on the pros and cons of this merger arose, but that debate seems to have had no effect on the success of the merger.

Another example is the case of the steel list-price system.[43] First, if, as those involved at the time claimed, the use of depression cartels was to be avoided, even though they were permissible under the Anti-monopoly Act, the policy of output (and price) coordination through the list-price system was used as a substitute. This was merely a cosmetic change. Second, it is necessary to judge on the basis of specific facts what the influence of the government (that is, MITI) was on the output of individual firms under the list-price system. The content of policy cannot be understood simply from the fact that the list-price system was implemented, or that the government took the lead in having it implemented (although, in fact, that does not seem to have been the case). Furthermore, even if MITI indicated specific targets that it officially warned the industry association or individual firms to respect, it is still not possible to know the actual content of the policy.[44,45]

Note, however, that it may not be useful to ask too vigorously what the policy variables were and how the government controlled them,[46] since, 'while a great number of fragmentary reports appeared at the time in newspapers and elsewhere, an overall picture of the system of industrial policy was seldom clearly presented to the public' (Komiya, 1975, pp. 307–8). Further, as mentioned above, government reports almost never provide detailed information on the role of the government or the effectiveness of the policies. One has to take care over the definition of industrial policy, and clarify the set of industrial policies being evaluated.

8.7 CONCLUDING REMARKS

The most basic thing one has to do in the above study is to clarify what one
wants to know about 'Japan's Industrial Policy'. For those who are interested
in the industrial success of the Japanese economy and are investigating how
the government policy has contributed to it, my advice is to set aside the
phrase 'industrial policy' and focus on the secondary or side-effect of
industrial policy, that is, the function as a system for the exchange of
information on both new technologies and market environment.[47] Note that,
though almost every industry has a counterpart in government, called
genkyoku, which devotes all its efforts to protecting, encouraging and
supporting firms in that industry, the problem comes from the simple fact
that nobody can protect and subsidize everybody. Note also that in two
sectors with the strongest political backing, agriculture and small business,
the policies have not been very effective. Therefore investigation must begin
with the case studies of individual policies, not with such general questions as
why and how industrial policy contributed to Japan's industrial success.

Note two additional points, even when one could draw lessons from the
investigation of Japan's industrial policy and examine their applicability to
other economies. First, clarify what were the policy variables, under what
constraints they were operated and what was the relevant policy environment, for which the task of identification mentioned in the previous section is
critical. Second, the attitude of people in general to industrial association
activities and to the government–business relationship, which is influenced by
the tradition since the Meiji Restoration of a 'strong' central government and
the wide-ranging economic controls that were present during and immediately after the Second World War, may be a condition affecting the form and
effectiveness of Japan's industrial policy. The fact that these industrial
association activities and the close government–business relationships still
survive several decades after the end of the war implies the existence of wide
public support for them. Before the application of one country's policy
lessons to other economies, one has to study carefully the policy environment
there, not only institutional and political but also historical and cultural, and
examine whether conditions for successful policy application are satisfied.
For Japan's industrial policy, the public acceptance of those activities and
relationships is one such condition.[48] This issue certainly requires further
close study.

9 Economic Consequences of Investment Coordination in the Steel Industry

9.1 INTRODUCTION

> Perhaps one-fifth of United States national income originates in industries subject to some direct regulation, and yet economists know very little about how regulation affects the market performance of an industry. The preambles of regulatory statutes hardly provide a reliable guide. Neither does the intensity of the complaints of regulated businessmen. (Caves, 1964, p. 172)

With this statement Richard Caves begins a paper on 'Direct Regulation and Market Performance in the American Economy'. He argues that 'the right questions have not been asked about the effects of regulation, nor the right tests performed' (p. 172).[1] A big wave of interest in the effectiveness of direct government regulation began in the 1960s, with theoretical research being followed by empirical studies. During this period people were optimistic about policy effectiveness as the government's role in the economy expanded rapidly. In the 1970s, this optimism gradually faded as the age of deregulation began, becoming a worldwide trend in the 1980s.[2]

In Japan government regulation of and intervention in the private business sector, for example in industrial policy, extends over an area wider than in the USA. As emphasized in the previous chapter, little information on concrete industrial policy is available. Seldom has the government stated or explained the objective of a concrete policy. There is almost no *ex post* discussion on the effectiveness of the policy, either. Consequently, 'an overall picture of the system of industrial policy was seldom clearly presented to the public. Therefore, what is well known among insiders quite often is unknown to the public, including academics' (Komiya, 1975, pp. 307–8). The same is true of the impact of government policy. Much debate has centred on industrial policy, but most of this is based on strongly biased information as mentioned in the previous chapter. Putting aside the term 'industrial policy', what is necessary is case studies based on the careful collection and examination of detailed information identifying the impact of government policies.

'Investment coordination' is representative of one type of industrial policy by the Japanese government. This was adopted in many industries around

1960, including the steel industry. Here the term 'investment coordination' or 'equipment (investment) coordination' means the attempt to control individual firm equipment investment, based on market demand forecasts and capacity utilization rates. The objective was to 'avoid excess capacity and the price competition that results from it'.[3] This chapter is a case study identifying and evaluating the impact of an investment coordination program in the steel industry and related government policies. Focus centres on the period from just before 1960 to around 1970, the heyday of Japan's industrial policy in general and investment coordination in particular.

It is generally difficult to identify and evaluate the impact of government policy. The former is indispensable for the latter, and can be accomplished by finding the deviations between the actual state of affairs and the hypothetical state without the policy actions. The difficulty lies, above all, in how to model such a state. In the case of industrial policy, little is clear on what the government could do and actually did do, what was the role of government and business players, and what was the net contribution of the resulting policy. This applies to the case of the investment coordination programme in the steel industry. As will be shown below, investment coordination in this industry was basically not a government-led investment cartel but a collective action of major steel firms. This again was part of coordinating behaviour of firms in an oligopolistic market. Therefore drawing and then testing a theoretical hypothesis on the existence and the direction of the impact of investment coordination and the net contribution of related policies is difficult if not impossible.[4] Instead, I choose another way to draw a conclusion, by combining the result of two studies.

The investment coordination programme in the steel industry, and the related government policy, were ineffective in the sense that they had no definite impact, at least directly, on the investment behaviour of individual firms and the total investment of the industry. This conclusion comes from two studies, which are presented in Sections 9.3 and 9.4. The first study, in Section 9.3 considers the existence of government power to enforce its policies. When coordination is effective and the net contribution of policy impact definite, there must be strong enforcement powers (or incentives) to ensure the implementation of the coordination agreement. The second one in Section 9.4 is, looking closely at the coordination process and the result of each year's coordination, to investigate whether we observe such phenomena as should exist when the coordination is effective. By forming a negative judgement from these two studies, I draw the above conclusion.[5] Section 9.2 is an introductory section on the form and basic character of investment coordination in the steel industry, and the coordination process for fiscal year (FY) 1965 is briefly introduced as an example.

Note that this chapter is a case study, and does not consider the effectiveness of investment coordination in general. The extension of my analysis to other industries and policies is the goal of the next chapter. Note also that I distinguish the impact of the coordination programme from that of the related government policies, and that I conclude that neither of them had a definite impact.[6]

9.2 INTRODUCTION TO INVESTMENT COORDINATION IN THE STEEL INDUSTRY

The Form of the Steel Investment Coordination

Investment coordination in the steel industry was basically a *jisyu chosei* [hereafter self-coordination], where individual steel firms coordinated investment plans by themselves. The government and policy councils (*shingikai*), formally a part of the government, are thought to have affected the investment decision of individual firms by expressing their opinion on coordination efforts and by negotiating directly with individual firms. In the 1950s the coordination of individual firms' investment plans in the steel industry 'was directly guided by MITI with the control of industrial finance (including an issue of the government guarantee for the World Bank loans) and the Foreign Capital Act for technology import licences'.[7]

The beginning of 'investment coordination' which we study here was in December 1959, when MITI requested that the industry members[8] coordinated, through self-coordination, the implementation of their long-term capacity plans. Formally, the goal was for the industry to draw up a long-term investment plan for approval by the Industrial Finance Committee of MITI's Industry Rationalization Council. Each firm in principle was to discuss and report by the end of the fiscal year (the end of March) for the next fiscal year (FY) on the coordination of investment. This principally meant coordination in the construction of new blast furnaces; often this was not done until the FY had begun. This coordination programme continued in the same form until FY 1966.

With the interim report of the Basic Steel Issues Subcommittee of the Heavy Industries Division of the Industrial Structure Council (ISC)[9] in October 1966, the form of the coordination programme changed. The Steel Committee, newly established within ISC, was to play the central role: (1) to draw up both long-term and annual supply and demand forecasts;[10] (2) to draw up standards for investment coordination; (3) to estimate long run capacity necessary to meet the forecasted demand; and (4) to calculate the new capacity on which construction could be coordinated in each year. The allocation of investment among firms was to depend in the first instance on self-coordination efforts among themselves. Where agreement could not be obtained, decisions were to be made under the informal regulation or *gyosei shido*[11] of MITI, which again was backed by the decision of the Minister of MITI (*daijin saitei*) in case of necessity.[12] Beginning in FY 1967, the coordination programme continued in this form.[13]

The Character of Investment Coordination

In Japan, as in other countries, one of the primary concerns of individual steel manufacturer's management has been to form and maintain a coordination mechanism to stabilize prices and profitability. This is one of the industries which an economist looks to for a discussion on coordinating oligopoly and cartels. For instance, Scherer and Ross (1990, pp. 235–36) begin the chapter on 'Conditions Facilitating Oligopolistic Coordination' with a talk on the Gary dinners in 1907–11, and argue that 'until the late 1960s, for instance, American steel producers were fairly successful in abjuring price competition on standard products without resorting to formal collusion'. As in other countries, Japan's steel industry is oligopolistic and most markets for final steel products of manufacturers with blast furnaces are highly concentrated.[14] Fairly high barriers to entry for new firms and homogeneity of products facilitate industry coordination. On the other hand, to maintain stable coordination has hardly been easy. Demand for steel products fluctuates tremendously over time since most of them are derived demands and the biggest share of this demand comes from fixed capital investment in the private sector. An unexpected demand fluctuation causes violent price changes because of low price elasticity, which limits coordination efforts but at the same time is a strong incentive for manufacturers to coordinate.[15]

Investment coordination in the steel industry was a part of a larger coordination effort. In this rapidly growing industry, manufacturers had to coordinate not only price and output but also equipment investment for increasing capacity. As shown in Table 9.1 below, the production of steel (in raw steel base) grew from 23.2 million tons in 1960 to 92.4 million tons in 1970, a fourfold increase in ten years. From the start, industry members had to discuss how much capacity in total should be added and who should invest.

Even with successful coordination efforts there remains the issue of the distribution of profits. In the 1960s, there was fierce competition for market share among steel manufacturers.[16] If one could have had a precise forecast of future demand, coordination would have been smooth even in such a rapidly growing industry. The result would have been a stable allocation of output and investment shares. In the steel industry, however, the forecasts were almost always inaccurate, and individual firm's forecasts on which their own investment plans were based differed remarkably. Investment coordination was based both on government forecasts and that of the Japan Iron and Steel Federation. Although these forecasts were revised upward almost every year, their estimates had been lower than those of such firms as Yawata Steel and Fuji Steel which consistently underestimated the actual demand (see Table 9.1 below).[17] Consequently, to reach an agreement on the total amount of investment was difficult. Coordination meetings were an opportunity both for producing more accurate demand forecasts and for negotiating the total amount of investment and its allocation among industry members.

Unless the sum of the amount of individual firm's investment exceeds the agreed value, the profit of each firm is expected to increase with the amount of its own investment. When the sum exceeds the agreed value, negotiation for output reduction begins as a part of these coordination efforts. In this case, a firm's profit decreases with the amount of newly built capacity, since it was the custom to allocate the agreed amount in proportion to the actual output of each firm in the past, with only slight modification for new capacity.[18] Each firm has an incentive to discourage both the amount of other firms' planned investment and the total industry investment, making its own profit safe while increasing its market share. Therefore, firms with relatively weak future demand forecasts proposed investment plans that were larger than what they actually intended to undertake, underestimated future demand, insisted that investment coordination be strictly maintained and demanded that the amount of investment be in proportion to each firm's past output. Firms with relatively strong forecasts also exaggerated their investment plans, but overestimated future demand, were reluctant to participate in investment coordination itself and were strongly opposed to fixing the share of investment as a proportion of past output.[19]

As a result, the sum of the amount of investment plans almost always exceeded any strong demand forecast, and each firm's demand forecast varied greatly. There were conflicting claims that coordination was unnecessary or that stricter coordination was required.

The History of the FY 1965 Investment Coordination : An Illustration

In the history of investment coordination, that for FY 1965 was one of the most complicated. At the start of the coordination procedure MITI advised the steel industry to cease all new investment, calling for a one-year moratorium. The majority of firms, like Kawatetsu, however, insisted that a year was too long and that the period should be no more than six months. Opposition was strong, especially from Sumikin which was building its third blast furnace at its Wakayama steel mill (hereafter, Wakayama no. 3).[20] It planned to initiate the construction of Wakayama no. 4 in April just after the completion of no. 3, and did not agree to the half-year moratorium proposal. Sumikin strongly urged other firms, especially Yawata and Fuji, to oppose the moratorium. Coordination negotiations did not reach a conclusion until July, more than three months later than scheduled,[21] when industry members agreed to an output coordination of raw steel by MITI's informal regulation subsequent to the fall in steel prices.[22] The final conclusion was that for the fiscal years of 1965 and 1966 firms were free to initiate new construction of blast and converter furnaces, but no new rolling mills.[23] As a result, five major steel firms announced the initiation of new blast furnace construction: Wakayama no. 4 in August, Mizushima no. 1 of Kawatetsu in October, Tokai no. 2 of Fuji in January 1966, Sakai no. 2 of Yawata in April and Fukuyama no. 2 of Kokan in October.

Let me conclude this section with a comment from one observer of the FY 1967 coordination process, Mr Tokunaga,[24] which can be viewed as an evaluation of the entire history of investment coordination:

> The final outcome of the FY 1967 steel industry investment coordination, the result of roughly a half year's discussion, was that in effect each firm's plans would be approved in full, for both steel making and milling facilities. This was virtually the same outcome as that of the self-coordination which took place in FY 1965 and 1966, so that it can be seen

how difficult it was if only those involved tried to coordinate on their own to achieve what would be seen as desirable from the standpoint of the national economy. (Tokunaga, 1967, p. 58)

9.3 GOVERNMENT POWER TO ENFORCE POLICY

In the 1960s, investment coordination policies were adopted in many raw material processing industries such as steel, petroleum refining, synthetic textiles, paper and pulp. Machining and assembly manufacturing were largely excluded from this policy. As I will mention below, apart from the Petroleum Industry Act, there was no legal basis for this policy; having no such legal backing, such industrial policy was unofficial. The policy tool was informal regulation, and the central issue is whether this tool was in fact effective in affecting investment and whether there was anything that could ensure the effectiveness of government policy.[25] Therefore this section looks at the government's power to enforce its policies.

As shown above, the coordination of investment directly affects individual firms' profit, and therefore both to reach an agreement and to maintain the coordination effectively were hardly easy. When it was effective in affecting both the total investment of the industry and that of individual firms, there must have been some power (or incentive) to enforce the coordination efforts; that is, something that could ensure the effectiveness of policy efforts.[26] Limiting attention to the role of the government, I examine here whether it had the power to secure the investment coordination in the steel industry. First, I present examples of failed policies to show that the Japanese government often failed to achieve the policy objective. In the second part, I list and classify the various tools available to the government. I then search for the source of power in this industry and select four tools for closer examination: loans from the Japan Development Bank, the allocation of import licences of bunker coal, the preferential tax treatments and the decision of the Minister of MITI. In the third part, with closer examination of these four, I conclude that the government had almost no power to enforce coordination policies. This is one of the two bases for the final conclusion of this chapter.

Examples of Failed Policies

We observe many cases where the Japanese government failed to achieve its policy objective, which supports the validity of the argument in this section. What follows below has the same view. (1) The 1955 'People's Car' concept of MITI in the motor industry failed in spite of a wide variety of promotion policies including supplying low-interest rate loans through government financial institutions, granting subsidies, providing special depreciation allowances, exempting necessary equipment from import tariffs and approving essential foreign technology. One of the important reasons for the failure was that MITI had no power to control new entry and equipment investment which could serve to force the policy through (Tsuruta, 1977, p. 59).

(2) The 1961 'producer group' concept of MITI in the same industry also failed because it had no tools with which it could implement this policy (see Tsuruta, 1988, pp. 84–5, and US Department of Commerce, 1972, Chapter 2 of Part 2).

(3) The Act on Temporary Measures for the Structural Improvement of Specified Textile Industries of 1967 introduced the purchase-and-scrap programme to deal with 'excess capacity', which made use of government finances. Of the FY 1968 programme target to scrap one million looms, 620 thousand, rationed among individual firms and enforced by the government order, were scrapped, but almost none of those remaining for voluntary scrapping were (see Kurasawa, 1977, p. 39 and Yamazawa, 1988, pp. 404 and 409–10).

(4) To the contrary, many hold the view that the Foreign Capital Act functioned as the basis for the effectiveness of the investment coordination in the petrochemical industry (see Komiya, 1975, p. 315, Nakamura *et al.*, 1971, pp. 57 and 123 and Tsuruta, 1988, pp. 70–1). However, whether it succeeded in achieving the initial policy goal is another question (see Tsuruta, 1988, p. 73).

Moreover, as shown in Section 10.4, even when the government has the power (for instance, based on legislation, such as the Petroleum Industry Act) of enforcement, this power has not necessarily been used. As Yoshino (1968, p. 176) states, 'It is interesting to note that the MITI has been rather hesitant to resort to outright retaliatory actions against recalcitrants . . . even in those cases where the MITI is legally empowered to penalize violators, it takes formal action against them only on rare occasions'. Furthermore, as mentioned at the begining of this chapter, the government cannot (and sometimes will not) necessarily achieve the initial goal.[27]

Classification of Policy Enforcement Powers

The possible sources of power for policy enforcement in investment coordination can be classified into five groups: (1) industry acts or *gyo-ho*, such as, the Machine Industries Act (1956), the Electronics Industries Act (1957)[28] and the Petroleum Industry Act (1962); (2) non-industry-specific acts or *ippan-ho*, such as the Foreign Exchange and Foreign Trade Control Act and the Foreign Capital Act; (3) informal regulation; (4) the guidance of and coordination through the government institutions, such as the Industrial Finance Committee and the Steel Committee of the Industrial Structure Council; (5) the *Kanmin* Coordination Consultative Groups or the *kanmin kyocho kondankai*, such as the Chemical Fibres Consultative Group (established October 1964) and the Petrochemicals Consultative Group (established December 1964).[29]

Industry acts are again classified into three groups based on the method of intervention. First is the individual examination requirement. Under such acts as the Petroleum Industry Act, the Electric Utilities Act, the Gas Utilities Act, the Banking Act and the Security and Exchange Act,[30] the government controls new entries into the industry and investment by examining an application of each firm. A second form of industry act is that which established standards for new plants, such as minimum capacity.[31] Third is the informal regulation, backed by the power of the government endowed by law.[32]

The control of technology imports through licensing under the Foreign Capital Act is an example of the second group of enforcement mechanisms, non-industry specific acts. In the 1950s and 1960s, when the dependence on foreign technology was high, capacity expansion in industries where investment coordination was adopted quite often required a licence under the Act for technology imports. In issuing a licence, especially in the case of large scale expansion, the government often attached conditions on the size of new capacity and the timing of its utilization. The petrochemical industry is one such example. However, with the liberalization of technology imports,[33] the importance of the regulation of this type gradually decreased in the second half of the 1960s.

The final three groups of policy enforcement, groups (3) to (5), all include government intervention. Some informal regulation[34] is based on formal legal authority, for example the Petroleum Industry Act, but most is not. For instance, MITI, as a part of its routine work, sets standards for equipment investment and applies them to individual firms in some industries.[35] As shown in the previous chapter, both the membership and the role of policy councils differ greatly depending on the case. The Industrial Finance Committee of the Industrial Structure Council (ISC) is an institutional setting for investment coordination.[36] However, most industries on the agenda of this Committee have their own coordination arrangements, such as the Petrochemical Consultative Group. The Industrial Finance Committee was supposed to accept the conclusion of the Petrochemicals Consultative Group.[37] The fifth set of enforcement mechanisms, the *Kanmin* Coordination Consultative Groups, were established after the failure of the Specified Industries Act. Investment coordination was the main issue of the groups.[38]

Further examination is required for these three groups of policy enforcement to ascertain whether each mechanism, such as *Kanmin* groups enjoyed any enforcement powers.[39] For instance, we have to examine whether the Foreign Capital Act and loans from the Japan Development Bank could be effective as leverage for the coordination through the Petrochemical Consultative Group. The same applies to the role of the Petroleum Industry Act to the Petroleum Council. Tsuruta (1988, p. 73), however, concludes on the case of the petrochemical industry that 'The results obtained through *Kanmin* system . . . were the exact opposite of the goal of the original policy'.

The failed attempt to enact the Specified Industries Act with which MITI intended to recover its power to allocate import licences as leverage for the policy enforcement it had lost by the trade liberalization illustrates that the effectiveness of the coordination through policy councils without the power was strictly limited. Many groups strongly opposed the Act and killed it. As Yoshino [1968, p. 185] points out:

> It is extremely interesting to note that even in the drafting stage, both the Ministry of Finance and major city banks vigorously opposed the version of the Bill for the Promotion of Specific Industries proposed by MITI. Though not averse to the basic goals of the bill, the Ministry of Finance objected to it on the grounds that the formula would unduly commit it, and the financial institutions operating under its guidance, to the industrial policy of MITI, resulting in the loss of its independence and freedom.

If the coordination through councils had been effective, MITI would have neither tried to establish a new Act nor challenged strong opposition. The following opposing view on the *Kanmin* system plan under the Specified Industries Act from the industry revealed the basic character and the limit of the validity of the coordination programme through councils:

> The government argues that, under the new scheme, they participate in the coordination in a non-authoritative way. I wonder if it actually is possible. Even if they declare it at the start and try to maintain the position, the coordination will end in accepting the government's decision. Thus it is not substantially different from strict government control, and the result has the same evils as that of government control. (Kotoh, 1963, p. 116)

Policy Enforcement Power in the Steel Industry

Let us examine whether there existed sufficient government power to secure the effectiveness of the coordination policies in the steel industry. Note that effective enforcement powers were not necessarily limited to those directly related to investment coordination. As Tanaka [1980, p. 29] argued, to use power to seek revenge for some unrelated matter is the essence of informal regulation.[40]

There has never been an Industry Act for the steel industry.[41] Also, no non-industry-specific Act seems to have been effective for policy enforcement in this steel investment coordination of the 1960s. There are four possible coordination mechanisms: low interest rate loans, such as from the Japan Development Bank; the allocation of import licences for bunker coal; preferential tax treatments such as providing special depreciation allowances; and the decision of the minister of MITI in cases of rare necessity. I focus mainly on the first two alternatives.

One possible means of realizing investment coordination is to control the supply of low interest rate loans of government-affiliated financial institutions, such as the Japan Development Bank (JDB). These loans are not only a subsidy but are also supposed by many to function as a catalyst for private bank loans.[42] I conclude that this was not an effective enforcement mechanism. For some time after its inception, JDB concentrated on the electric power and sea transport industry, followed by coal mining, iron and steel, fertilizers and machinery, in that order. After the restrictive monetary policy of 1954–5, however, the bank specialized in only three industries–electric power, sea transport and coal mining–until 1960. The ratio of JDB loans to the steel industry to the total JDB loans decreased from 1957. It was with the implementation of the Second Rationalization Plan in 1956–60 that the production capacity of this industry began to expand rapidly. During the First Plan in 1951–5 the only newly built blast furnace was at the Chiba mill of Kawatetsu. By the end of FY 1960, however, 11 new furnaces were completed. Under the First Plan, 12 per cent of the total investment in the steel industry was financed by JDB loans, but this ratio declined to 1.5 per cent under the Second Plan.[43]

World Bank loans could also function as a source of government power, and again JDB functioned as an intermediary. The steel industry was one of Japan's largest beneficiaries of World Bank loans.[44] These loans were not effective for two reasons. First, the amount of World Bank loans to the steel industry was relatively large before 1960, but soon thereafter, the period under study, such funds were seldom available. Second, even before 1960, the biggest borrowers were Kawatetsu and Sumikin, which were relatively uncooperative with respect to government policies.[45]

The allocation of import licences for bunker coal is a second alternative source of policy enforcement power.[46] Though import of most items was liberalized in the first half of the 1960s, coal remained an exception. This was both to protect domestic production and to avoid the sudden collapse of the industry. The allocation of licences became famous because of the Sumikin Incident of 1965.[47] The vice-minister of MITI suggested restricting the allocation of import licences for bunker coal to Sumikin in order to force that company to accept the Ministry's informal regulation on output coordination. For two reasons I conclude that the effectiveness of licences allocations as leverage for policy enforcement was dubious even for output coordination, and was hardly effective for investment coordination. First, the MITI vice-minister's announcement of the use of such leverage provoked strong public criticism with most finding this to be an abuse of government authority. In addition, there were severe limitations on actually using such power.[48] What MITI suggested was to allocate import licences for bunker coal to that level of the output quota, but not to decrease the supply to Sumikin as a penalty.[49] Second, while almost every year investment coordination negotiations took a very long time, this form of leverage was never discussed. If the allocation of import licences for bunker coal could have been effective in policy enforcement, some industry members would have argued for asking MITI to use it on other occasions.[50]

Preferential tax treatment, such as special depreciation allowances, is the third possible source of enforcement power. I believe this mechanism also to have been ineffective. Though such tax policies influenced inter-industry allocation of resources, MITI could use them neither in influencing the allocation of investment within an industry nor as a discretionary means to obtain revenge for some unrelated matter. Therefore, though from 1951 the steel industry became eligible for tax breaks under the special depreciation allowance system and actually benefited from such allowances, they could not be an effective weapon for policy enforcement.[51]

The decision of the Minister of MITI (*daijin saitei*) in cases of rare necessity is the final possible enforcement mechanism. As mentioned in Section 9.2, when the Steel Committee was newly established within the Industrial Structure Council in 1967, the Minister's decision was introduced as the final weapon. The allocation of investment among firms was to depend in the first instance on self-coordination among industry members. When such coordination could not be obtained, decisions were to be made in conformity with MITI's informal regulation, which again was backed by the Minister's decision. In my judgement, however, this was ineffective for three reasons. First, this procedure was by itself an informal regulation lacking legal enforcement power. Second, this mechanism was never used even when coordination foundered. Finally, MITI reviewed the role of the Minister's decision in 1969 and abolished it in 1970.[52]

There was no source of government enforcement power and no strong incentive to ensure the effectiveness of investment coordination policies in the steel industry.[53] This is one of the grounds for the conclusion that the steel investment coordination programme and the related government policy in the 1960s were ineffective in the sense that they did not greatly affect the investment behaviour of individual firms or of the industry in general.

9.4   THE HISTORY OF INVESTMENT COORDINATION IN THE STEEL INDUSTRY

The Role of the Ministry of International Trade and Industry (MITI)

The investment coordination among steel manufacturers with blast furnaces began in 1959. MITI first indicated the amount of investment for new capacity construction, which was based both on long-term supply and demand forecasts and an 'appropriate' capacity utilization rate. The allocation of investment among firms was basically left to self-coordination, but in case it did not work well, informal regulation of each firm was adopted. (MITI, 1969, p. 47)

With this statement, MITI explains both the form of the steel investment coordination and its role within these policies. As it must explain that MITI's contribution to the investment coordination was the greatest,[54] the fact that the above statement is ineffective in explaining our observations implies that the contribution of MITI was not very impressive and that the coordination in general was ineffective. As will be shown below, long-term forecasts always underestimated actual demand, and firms did not accept the concept of an 'appropriate' capacity utilization rate.[55] Also, as shown in Section 9.2, the framework for the coordination programme set by MITI was not accepted by the industry members. Neither MITI nor any other participant had sufficient enforcement powers. In the case of FY 1965, the coordination negotiations ended in approving all the proposed plans.[56]

Table 9.1 shows the forecasts on which the coordination negotiations were based for the fiscal years during 1960–66, and the results for 1960–70 (all figures are in raw steel base). Table 9.2 shows the accuracy of these forecasts calculating the ratio of the actual amount of steel produced two years after each year's agreement to the forecast level of steel production for the corresponding year taken from Table 9.1. In FY 1960, for example, the forecast for FY 1962 was 21.5 million tons. Actual steel production, however, was 27.3 million tons. Thus the ratio of actual steel production to forecast production was 1.27, the market having been underestimated by more than 20 per cent. As shown in Table 9.2, the forecasts consistently underestimated steel production during the period.

Table 9.1 Steel production in the forecasts for each year's coordination and the results, FY1961–FY1966, in raw steel base (million tons)

Forecasts	60	61	62	63	64	65	66	67	68	69	70
1960	20.0		21.5 20.5(*)			26.0					38.8
1961		26.5	29.5	32.5	35.3	38.0					48.0
1962			31.4		36.5	39.0					
1963				29.0		36.4		43.1			
1964					36.0	38.5		44.5			
1965						43.0	45.4	47.7	50.0		
1966							43.6		51.9		60.0
Results	23.2	29.4	27.3	34.1	40.5	41.3	51.9	63.8	69.0	87.6	92.4

Note: (*) A figure in MITI's plan.
Source: Adapted from Kawasaki (1968, pp. 600 and 604); added figures for result in 1967–70.

Table 9.2 Ratio of the result of steel production to the forecast: performance in the third year (FY of coordination)

	1960	61	62	63	64	65	66
Ratio	1.27 1.33(*)	1.05	1.11	1.14	1.26	1.34	1.33

Note: (*) A figure denominated by MITI's forecast.
Source: See Table 9.1.

The forecasts continued to underestimate aggregate steel demand through the second half of the 1960s. Figure 9.1 illustrates the relationship between the forecast and the result for each year from 1965 to 1970. With this tendency to underestimate steel demand, except for periods of economic recession in FY 1963 and FY 1966, every year the forecasts had to be revised upwards. If these forecasts had actually been followed by those engaged in the coordination, Japan would have suffered from a serious shortage of steel, causing inflation and frustrating economic growth.[57] Fortunately, the coordination was ineffective.[58]

Figure 9.1   Forecasts and results of steel production, FY1965–FY1970, in raw steel base (million tons)

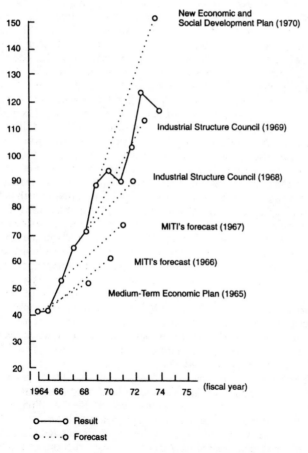

Source: Adapted from *Weekly Toyo Keizai*, 21 November 1970, p. 67.

The History of Each Year's Investment Coordination

To examine further the influence of the coordination programme on the investment decisions of individual firms and the government's contribution, I will present the history of each year's investment coordination. I focus on the coordination of the construction of blast furnaces which has been the basis for the determination of each firm's long-run market share. As mentioned above, the coordination scheme changed in 1967, and accordingly I divide the analysis into two periods.

Coordination before FY 1966

In the history of steel investment coordination, the two years in which the coordination failed most emphatically were FY 1960 and FY 1965. In the 1960 coordination, industry members discussed investment projects to be completed by FY 1962. MITI's demand forecast for FY 1962 was 20.46 million tons (in raw steel base) while the Japan Iron and Steel Federation (JISF) anticipated 21.52 million tons. In March 1960 the coordination programme approved the construction of three blast furnaces during FY 1960 and postponed the initiation of Kawatetsu's Chiba no. 4 furnace until the following year.[59] Actual production in 1960, however, greatly exceeded predictions and the long-term forecast had to be revised significantly upward.[60] As a result, the initiation of construction of three additional blast furnaces within FY 1960, including Kawatetsu, was approved in December. Thus the coordination programme approved all of the proposed blast furnace construction plans, with only a slight impact on the timing of construction. At the year-end meeting of the List Price Committee, the evaluation by Chairman Inayama of the General Affairs Subcommittee was that 'At the beginning of the fiscal year self-coordination failed miserably, for while somehow or other the appearance was maintained, the reality was exposed in that manufacturers did not in fact coordinate their efforts in the least'.[61]

Coordination efforts were not necessary for FY 1961's blast furnaces construction, and no blast furnace construction plans were proposed for FY 1962. When the recession began in 1962 some firms, anticipating a decrease in future demand, suspended or postponed the construction of new blast furnaces already approved.[62] The FY 1963 coordination programme began in this uncertain environment. Sumikin proposed to initiate the construction of the Wakayama no. 3 blast furnace in October, but postponed this project until the next year through the coordination negotiation. The FY 1964 coordination programme focused upon the construction of rolling mills in Kokan's Fukuyama plant. The construction of five blast furnaces was approved by the coordination programme without hard negotiations among industry members. As shown in Section 9.2, both the 1965 and 1966 coordination programmes resulted in the approval of all proposed plans.

As will be shown soon, the coordination programmes failed in setting a long-term rule for the allocation of blast furnace construction, and their focus always centred on the blast furnaces whose construction was planned to begin in the FY under consideration. As a result, the coordination tended to approve the initiation in the order of proposed plans, which was the reason why firms quite often planned to begin the construction in April.[63] Likewise, they stuck to the approval of the initiation within the FY both to restrain rivals' investment and to secure the priority for the construction in the next FY in case of disapproval in the current year. Moreover, as mentioned in the second part of Section 9.2, the meeting for coordination was also for negotiation and bargaining to determine the total amount of investment and its allocation. Thus it was rational for each firm to propose a plan with schedule earlier than was actually desired. Therefore, even when the coordination resulted in postponing commencement for several months on average, this does not necessarily imply that it effectively affected investment.[64]

Coordination after FY 1966

In the second half of the 1960s there appeared a *de facto* rule or an implicit understanding supposed to be observed among industry members for the ranking of blast furnace construction, and major steel manufacturers constructed blast furnaces at almost an equal pace. In the FY 1971 coordination programme, a part of this *de facto* rule was formalized.

We observe several attempts to form a long-term rule for the allocation of production capacity over the history of the steel industry's investment coordination programme. At least at the beginning, many proponents of the investment coordination took for granted the long-term rule for capacity allocation among firms. Kojima (1960, p. 42), for instance, argued, 'Needless to say, self-coordination is a control through cartel in the German style. Without the intervention of the government, steel manufacturers in the private sector discuss and coordinate by themselves their long-term investment plans, and rationalize the plan for the total capacity expansion.'[65] However, these efforts never succeeded in establishing a clear and effective rule.

At the outset of the first coordination programme of FY 1960, firms discussed a long-term rule for capacity investment. Mr Inayama, chairman of the meeting for self-coordination and then-president of Yawata, proposed that investment be coordinated on the basis of market shares held by the individual firms over the previous ten years. Kawasaki strongly opposed this proposal. They limited the coordination of blast furnaces to FY 1960, and approved all proposed construction projects. Attempts to establish a long-term rule returned with the coordination programme of FY 1965. Yawata's proposed market-share rule was opposed by Kawatetsu and Sumikin and the attempt failed once again.[66]

Following the interim report of the Basic Steel Issues Subcommittee of the Industrial Structure Council in October 1966, the coordination for FY 1967 began with a debate on the appropriate standards for investment coordination. However, there was sharp antagonism between two groups, with Yawata, Fuji and Kokan in one and Sumikin and Kawatetsu in the other.

Without reaching an agreement even for FY 1967, they asked non-steel industry members of the Industrial Structure Council, called 'neutral members', to mediate the conflict. The final result was to adopt a plan in which each of the five major steel manufacturers could initiate the construction of one blast furnace, without any agreement on the standards for investment allocation among industry members.[67]

The conflict continued into the FY 1968 coordination programme. Yawata insisted it could initiate the construction of the Kimitsu no. 2 blast furnace in April, before the completion of the Kimitsu no. 1. Sumikin responded by advancing by six months the time of initiation of Kashima no. 1 construction from April 1969, on the completion of Wakayama No. 5, to October 1968. Until that time, high construction costs prevented firms from initiating the construction of new blast furnaces while another project was not yet complete – the so-called 'parallel construction'. There were no cases of parallel construction in the history of the investment coordination programme. The confrontation revived the debate over the allocation rule, and Yawata's plan challenged the then established *de facto* rule prohibiting parallel construction projects. The final result confirmed the *de facto* rule. Yawata Steel's Kimitsu no. 2 blast furnace was to replace four blast furnaces, from no. 3 to no. 6, of Yawata's Azumada plant. Sumikin's Kashima No. 1 was not approved, however, this firm could construct a large scale blast furnace in Kokura to replace a smaller Kokura no. 2 blast furnace. At the same time, industry members debated alternative rules for the construction and replacement of blast furnaces. The resulting 'replacement rule' provided that the construction of a replacement blast furnace was free of the coordination requirement unless the net capacity increase exceeded 20 per cent or 500 square metres of output. This was the first occasion that the coordination programme formally adopted an allocation rule.[68]

The FY 1969 coordination programme authorized the construction of five blast furnaces for that year and two more for FY 1970.[69] This was the first occasion on which a policy coordination programme extended over more than one year.[70] In FY 1969 steel production grew much faster than forecast. Therefore the forecast demand of 150 to 170 million tons in raw steel base for FY 1975 of the New Economic and Social Development Plan for 1970 to 1975 was widely accepted.[71] As a result Kawatetsu and Sumikin proposed to initiate in FY 1970 the construction of Mizushima no. 4 and Kashima No. 2. However, in the spring of 1970, the market price of steel products began to decline, and there was increasing uncertainty concerning future steel demand. Nippon Steel, having already secured the right to initiate new capacity construction,[72] represented the weak demand forecast side, and Sumikin, planning to initiate Kashima no. 2 construction in February 1971 with the completion of Kashima no. 1 construction, represented the opposite side. The 1971 coordination negotiations continued at a slow pace and did not reach a conclusion until June.[73]

The FY 1971 coordination programme authorized the construction of four blast furnaces for FY 1971 and FY 1972, two postponed from FY 1970 – Mizushima No. 4 and Kashima no. 2 – and two newly adopted projects –

Kimitsu no. 4 for Nippon Steel and Fukuyama no. 5 for Kokan. Construction, however, carried certain conditions. With the introduction of a new furnace, a firm had to close an existing one of 2500 cubic metres for a certain period. The furnace could not come back on line before May 1974. Furthermore, industry members would follow the suggestion of MITI based on the demand–supply conditions for June 1974 to March 1975. These furnaces closed for the introduction of new ones would be free to operate after April 1975.[74]

It was only in the FY 1974 coordination programme that the construction plan of a new blast furnace was adopted.

In the history of the steel investment coordination there has been no long-term investment allocation rule among individual firms. However, in the second half of the 1960s, coordination activities took root in the industry and *de facto* rules for investment allocation appeared, such as the 'parallel construction rule' and 'replacement rule' discussed above. Also, the coordination programme became based on a demand–supply forecast covering a longer period of time. The convergence in individual firms' long-term demand forecasts was a cause of these results. Through the 1960s, demand forecasts consistently underestimated actual market demand and firms, particularly those with weak forecasts, had to drastically revise their estimates upwards. As a result, in the late 1960s firms had similar forecasts and each major steel manufacturer expanded capacity at a similar pace, generally one blast furnace in two years. Since investment coordination was a part of the overall coordination of the industry, it was closely related to the output coordination programmes. This is observed in the 1971 coordination programme which made new construction conditional on freezing existing capacity.[75]

In the first half of the 1960s investment coordination efforts slightly reduced the change in market share among steel manufacturers by delaying the capacity construction of relatively aggressive firms such as Kawatetsu and Sumikin. This effect was even greater in the late 1960s and early 1970s. This coordination policy's impact, however, should not be overstated. The new capacities were not always constructed as authorized through the coordination programme, which cancelled part of the policy impact. For instance, most firms completed those blast furnaces adopted in the FY 1971 coordination programme by FY 1973. Nippon Steel, however, postponed until FY 1973 the initiation of not only Kimitsu No. 4, authorized in FY 1971, but also Ohita no. 2, authorized in FY 1969.[76] Coordination efforts tended simply to adopt each firm's construction plans in full. Even when the coordination negotiations foundered, they ended in adopting each firm's plans in full or authorizing additional construction plans for firms on the weak forecasts side.[77] Firms on the strong forecasts side never gave up their construction plans. Neither each firm's capacity investment nor that of the industry in total was seriously affected by the coordination policy.

As shown above, the steel investment coordination programme of the early 1960s adopted each firm's plans in full. In the late 1960s each major firm constructed one blast furnace every two years, implying that new blast furnaces were almost always under construction. This fact, with their voluntary agreement not to adopt a 'parallel construction' plan, implies that each firm constructed new blast furnaces as it desired and at as fast a pace as possible. This, however, reduced the difference in market shares among major steel manufacturers. As shown in Table 9.3, each firm's relative market share among major steel manufacturers changed rather dramatically in the early 1960s, but was stable from the end of the 1960s onward, with the exception of Nippon Steel.[78]

Summary of the Historical Study

The history of the steel investment coordination can be summarized in six points, with which I conclude that the steel investment coordination programme and the related government policy in the 1960s were ineffective. This is the second ground for the conclusion of this chapter.

1. MITI's participation in the steel investment coordination programme failed to affect the behaviour of individual firms and actually had no definite impact on the steel industry. The role of MITI, if any, was to facilitate the continuation of coordination meetings and the formation of an agreement among industry members.[79]
2. Attempts at setting a long-term rule for investment allocation failed. With time there appeared a *de facto* rule for the ranking of blast furnace construction. This rule, however, did not significantly affect each firm's investment behaviour.
3. Thus investment coordination meetings were where industry members negotiated with each other to determine the total amount of investment and its allocation.
4. Steel investment coordination activities may have reduced the change in market shares of steel manufacturers. However, this change was slight, if any, and should not be overstated.
5. The investment coordination programme had no definite impact on the total investment of the industry.
6. Investment coordination was a part of the overall coordination of the industry, and closely related to the output coordination. Coordination attempts never broke down and the appearance of a *de facto* long-term rule for investment allocation must have supported the maintenance of the overall coordination programme.[80]

9.5 CONCLUDING REMARKS

The investment coordination programme and the related government policy in the steel industry in the 1960s were ineffective in the sense that they had no definite impact on the individual firm's investment behaviour and on the total investment of the industry.[81]

Table 9.3 Each firm's relative market share among major steel producers, in raw steel base (per cent)

	1960	1961	1962	1963	1964	1965	1966	1967	1970	1972	1974	1976	1978	1980	1982
Yawata(*)	32.3	30.1	29.1	27.5	26.3	25.8	25.5	24.6	45.4	44.1	40.9	41.1	41.3	41.3	41.4
Fuji(*)	22.8	23.2	23.0	23.0	22.6	23.8	23.3	22.5							
Kokan	14.5	15.6	15.2	14.1	15.0	14.1	14.9	15.1	17.5	17.6	17.7	17.6	17.5	17.5	17.5
Kawatetsu	12.8	13.1	12.3	13.7	14.6	14.4	14.6	15.2	14.9	15.5	16.4	16.0	15.9	15.9	15.9
Sumikin	8.3	8.9	10.9	12.5	13.4	13.8	14.4	15.4	15.2	15.0	16.1	16.0	15.9	15.9	15.8
Kobe	9.2	9.2	9.4	9.2	8.1	8.1	7.5	7.2	7.0	7.9	8.9	9.4	9.3	9.3	9.4
Major firms' share of the industry total(**)	69.7	71.0	70.9	70.3	72.6	73.0	73.8	75.5	78.6	77.8	79.1	77.2	73.7	71.5	67.9

Notes:
(*) Yawata and Fuji merged into Nippon Steel in March 1970, and the figures since 1970 are those for Nippon Steel.
(**) Sum of six majors until 1967, and five majors afterwards.
Source: Figures for 1960–7 are adapted from Ueno and Mutoh (1968, p. 136, Table 4) and others from FTC's report, The Reality of Four Major Oligopolistic Industries, October 1984.

Though we must be careful not to generalize the conclusion too much, three points should be noted. First, since the steel investment coordination was representative of similar programmes in many other industries, this suggests that the investment coordination in these industries had no definite impact either, unless some industry-specific factor played a definite role. Second, since the 1960s were the heyday of Japan's industrial policy, particularly in the form of coordination within industry, this conclusion suggests that the same type of policies in the 1970s and 1980s could not have any definite impact. Third, these two points also apply to the impact of related government policies.

10 Coordination within Industry: Output, Price and Investment

10.1 INTRODUCTION

Evaluating the impact of a specific policy is not easy, no matter what its form. In most cases, as with taxes, subsidies, low-interest rate financing and tariffs, the intended policy function and the instruments employed are generally clear. It is, however, extremely difficult to estimate the impact of a policy, to discern what would have resulted if the policy had not been undertaken, or if the policy had been different.

In the case of the focus of discussion in this chapter, coordination of output, price or investment within an industry (hereafter, intra-industry coordination or simply coordination),[1] it is clear neither what the policy function was, nor what was done in the name of policy. As an obvious consequence, there is almost no information available to evaluate the impact of such actions.[2,3] An accurate policy analysis presupposes an understanding of the significance of government actions. Because such policies varied across time and industry, one must be cautious about overgeneralizing the conclusions of this chapter. As mentioned in Chapter 8, because most of the studies publicized to date do not clearly specify the boundaries of what they mean by policy, there is a tendency to overestimate the role and impact of the government.

While there has been some recent change, intra-industry coordination has long been considered the core of industrial policy. Furthermore, the continual dispute over the suitability of specific coordination policies and the desirable relationship between such policies and anti-monopoly (anti-trust) policy has been one of the most prolific debates over postwar industrial policy.[4] It is also the case that the content of coordination as industrial policy varied quite substantially from era to era and industry to industry. Again, it is true that, 'while a great number of fragmentary reports appeared at the time in newspapers and elsewhere, an overall picture of the system of industrial policy was seldom clearly presented to the public, including academics' (Komiya, 1975, p. 308). Therefore it is necessary to work on developing a methodology which can lead to some general conclusions about the effectiveness of coordination as industrial policy.

In this chapter, keeping in mind the goal of deriving some general conclusions, the main focus of analysis will be the steel industry during the era of rapid growth. For purposes of comparison, we will also take up the petroleum refining industry during roughly the same period. The steel industry during this period is appropriate for six reasons.

1. During this period the steel industry was representative of other industries in which an intra-industry coordination were utilized.
2. In discussing the appropriateness of industrial policy, particularly from the standpoint of competition policy, the steel industry was consistently the focus of attention. Thus information can be obtained comparatively easily.
3. The steel industry was the main target of industrial policy throughout the postwar period and enjoyed favourable tax treatment and other benefits. The government, however, did not hold the same sort of strong powers over the industry as it did in other industries such as petroleum refining (detailed in Section 10.4) and petrochemicals. The steel industry is thus close to the archetypical case of industrial policy carried out by means of informal regulation or *gyosei shido*.
4. During this period of progressive trade liberalization, the government lost its hold over industry through the allocation of import licences. This was also the period when the Anti-monopoly Act was least influential. Because of these two elements, we can observe industrial policy carried out by means of informal regulation in its purest form.
5. In order for the government to be able to participate effectively in making intra-industry coordination function meaningfully, the industry must meet four criteria, the same criteria that make it possible to form a strong cartel. The steel industry met all of these: (a) the number of firms must be small; (b) the product must be undifferentiated; (c) production capacity must be readily expressed as a simple index, such as tons per month; and (d) the industry association must have a long tradition of carrying on a wide range of activities, with intra-industry coordination carried out either by the association or through the association by the government.
6. As stated in the opening paragraph of Section 10.4, the findings derived from analysing the steel industry prove useful in judging the situation in other industries.

Intra-industry coordination of output, pricing or investment has been consistently held to be an important part of industrial policy. However, in fact the government was almost never an active participant in the formulation or enforcement of this policy. Nor did the government have a clear, direct impact on the industry. Therefore government policy was ineffective.

Preliminary observations on the nature and role of informal regulation are made in Section 10.2, while Section 10.3 consists of case studies of the list-price system and investment coordination in the steel industry studied in the previous chapter. For the purpose of comparison, Section 10.4 takes up output coordination in the petroleum refining industry. Section 10.5 examines the secondary effects of intra-industry coordination and Section 10.6 presents the overall conclusions.

10.2 PRELIMINARY OBSERVATIONS ON THE NATURE OF INFORMAL REGULATION

The debate still continues today among specialists on administrative law as to when government interventions require a formal legal basis, and in which situations a legislative foundation is required for informal regulation.[5] Despite this legal debate, intra-industry coordination as industrial policy has almost always been carried out by means of informal regulation lacking a direct legal basis. For this reason, the 'regulation' proffered has not been made public, and only limited records remain. In most cases policy outsiders do not know the content of the informal regulation.[6]

The term 'informal regulation' is used as the translation of *gyosei shido* in this volume in preference to the standard translation of 'administrative guidance'. Like *keiretsu*, corporate groups and main banks, *gyosei shido* and 'administrative guidance' are ill-defined terms, and supporters of the 'strong government' and 'effective industrial policy' view expand the boundary of what they mean by *gyosei shido*, so that there is a tendency to overestimate the impact of the government policies. Moreover, since the term 'administrative guidance' is not used in any other country, its use here has a rhetorical effect which causes further misconceptions of the Japanese economy to arise, by making readers think that it must be peculiar to Japan, and that Japan must be different from other countries. But as Haley (1991) pointed out, administrative guidance is 'a Japanese species of informal enforcement . . . [and it] is not peculiar to Japan . . . Informal enforcement by official suggestion, advice, recommendation or pointed direction is not only common to all legal systems, it is indeed the most common form of law enforcement' (p. 162).[7] Quoting Kenneth Culp Davis's estimate in his well known *Administrative Law Treatise* that 'more than 90 per cent of all administrative action [in the United States] is informal', Haley commented that 'as in Japan most informal action in the United States escapes judicial review' (p. 227, note 97).

It is necessary to note that there are severe limits to the admissible range in which output, prices or the level of investment can fall when taken as policy targets in MITI's informal regulation for individual firms or an industry association.

When informal regulation is adhered to the targets chosen are within the range of alternatives acceptable to industry members so that government regulation and the actions of firms coincide. This indicates nothing more than that government officials avoid the situation in which those being regulated will refuse to follow government policy. In the normal case, there was indeed prior negotiation between the government and industry members on the permissible range of options and the particular targets that should be established within that range. When the government has 'power' because of, for example, its licensing authority, officials can negotiate for more stringent targets. Even in this case, however, there are severe limitations on using such power and the exercise of such leverage has generally been held as undesirable.[8]

Before undertaking a discussion of specific cases, we will look at an example of output coordination, representative of industry coordination in general. The main source of analysis is a collection of documents compiled by the Administrative Management Agency (Administrative Management Agency, 1981). The example taken up below consists of reports from both the government and industry in connection with supply/demand forecasts drawn up for output coordination in the synthetic fibre industry. The system is explained as 'a supply/demand forecasting method which is a method of output coordination wherein the government indicates a production target, and firms . . . each draw up their production plans with this target as a base, and then submit these to the government' (p. 105). The government in its report claimed:

> Looking at the actual results, the target given by the government and the plans drawn up by individual firms did not differ greatly, suggesting that this method was effective. This was because . . . at the stage of drawing up the supply/demand forecast, discussions were held with the Supply–Demand Council of the industry association and because firms themselves were also intent on reducing production, as excess production would lead to their own demise. (p. 105)

Such explanations are inadequate when, as here, the aim is to evaluate the effectiveness of government policy.

Assuming that the above explanation of the reason why government and industry plans did not differ greatly is correct, we cannot presume that there would have been much difference in the behaviour of firms or of the industry as a whole had the government not acted. Thus there is no reason to believe the above report's conclusion that 'this method was effective'. Regardless of whether there was in fact not much difference, it is above all necessary to clarify, on the basis of facts, what the role of the government was, how the government acted when the industry proposals conflicted with the desired targets, and the process by which conformity was maintained.

In the case of informal regulation, contact between the government (*genkyoku*)[9] and individual firms in an industry was normally carried out through the industry association.

> From the standpoint of the industry . . . the main function of the industry association was to convince the *genkyoku* . . . to adopt favourable policies. From the standpoint of the *genkyoku*, the function of the industry association and the firms of which it was comprised was to cooperate with the *genkyoku* in carrying out industrial policy, and to bring into line firms which were not well behaved or which voiced contrary opinions. (Komiya, 1975, p. 311).

The above government report states that 'the industry association played an extremely important role in carrying out the informal regulation of MITI' (Administrative Management Agency, 1981, p. 107).

The report does not offer a detailed explanation of the purpose of the output coordination programme and related policies. The government was not pursuing this policy programme with a clear goal of its own. Rather, the government was trying to prevent what it and many others thought was excess production and 'excessive competition'. It seems that both industry members and the government held such goals as axiomatic. The definition of these conditions, however, was not always made clear, and one cannot presume that consensus existed among the firms involved, or between industry members and government officials. Furthermore, there is no reason to presume that preventing excess production and 'excessive competition' had always to be the primary goal for all participants (see ibid., pp. 105 and 109).[10]

In the reporting of the government side, the first point raised in the evaluation of informal regulation was that 'it cannot be implemented when there is no agreement or acquiescence by the other party' (ibid., p. 110). The reporting of the industry side gave a frank view of the role of the government in output coordination, stating that the primary merit of informal regulation was that 'the government was effective as a fair and authoritative mediator' (ibid., p. 113). If one adds to this the statement by the government that the primary 'point about which administrators must take care . . . is to never cause balance to be lost in the overall situation' (ibid., p. 110), the following picture of the government role can be drawn.

A role for the government in an output coordination programme arises when there is a difference in intentions among firms, so that if matters are left to themselves the situation may result in excess production. Even in this case, there is no guarantee that the government will always be successful in fulfilling its role as a fair and authoritative mediator, convincing firms to agree to following policy targets. In order to be successful, a minimum condition is to never cause imbalance in the overall situation. The government does not have much of a free hand in carrying out the above role.

The report claims that firms acceded to informal regulation, and argues why that was the case, but one must note that this is only with 'regulation' of the kind depicted above.

10.3 THE COORDINATION IN THE STEEL INDUSTRY

The Coordination of Output and Price

The list-price system in the steel industry is held up as an archetype of 'output coordination' and 'price coordination'. Drawing upon a history of anti-monopoly policy, the outline of the system was as follows:[11]

(1) On the basis of government production targets, each firm reported monthly to MITI its expected sales for each product. (2) A manufacturer was to sell its steel products at the same time at a fixed location, agreeing

with wholesalers on the amounts to be purchased. Each firm was to carry out sales at the 'list price' that it had previously reported to MITI. (3) After reaching agreement with its wholesalers, each manufacturer was to report by product the quantity contracted with each wholesaler and to publish its aggregate sales, together with amounts left unsold. (4) Manufacturers were to have a designated wholesaler for each product and were to make sales only through that wholesaler. (5) If there were unsold products, then they were to be bought up by a sufficiently strong wholesaler at a predetermined price, and unsold amounts were to provide a basis for determining decreases in production for the following month. (6) MITI would take appropriate steps against manufacturers who went against MITI regulation as to production limits and appropriate pricing. (7) Each manufacturer was to deliver to MITI a written promise by the president of the company that it would abide by an 'Outline of Steel Market Measures', containing the above regulations. For monitoring purposes, a designated monitoring committee was also to be established.

This list-price system has been referred to as both a 'steel pricing system'[12] and an 'informal regulation cartel'.[13] For our purpose of taking up this industrial policy as an archetypical case and trying to evaluate the extent of its effectiveness, the above description is inadequate. It is necessary to weigh carefully what actual government action (here, the policies of the *genkyoku*, MITI) consisted of, and what the government's influence was. The above explanation gives the impression that MITI had a controlling voice or something close to it, and that it had a strong impact as a policy organ. This was actually not the case.

There are many items that need to be questioned to arrive at a clear understanding of the reality of the list-price system, but for our purposes the following two are particularly important: (1) Who determined the specific content of the production limits and appropriate prices to be administered by MITI and how were they determined? (2) What were the 'appropriate steps' MITI would take against manufacturers violating these limits? Were such steps ever actually employed?

Let us look at the first query. The period in which the list-price system was said to have functioned was rather brief, from June 1958 to December 1962.[14] However, even during this period the system was modified many times. On 25 July 1960, MITI revealed the 'Outline of Steel Market Measures', referred to in item (7) above, to the industry association (the Japan Iron and Steel Federation). According to the *de facto* leader of the list-price system, the Chairman of the General Affairs Subcommittee of the Public Sale ('list-price') Committee, Yoshihiro Inayama, 'if this system is adopted, then unlike the situation in the past, we can be confident that we can actually count on achieving stable steel prices' (Shin Nippon Seitetsu, 1970, p. 205).[15] Thus, with this, the list-price system would become a much stronger set of measures for output and price coordination.

The method was basically one of self-coordination where MITI would devise ceiling and floor prices and would use informal regulation when a firm went over the ceiling in its submitted price list and would similarly offer advice that if prices are less than the floor, it is permissible to coordinate output. The ceiling price was to be the price currently listed by manufacturers, while the floor price was to be that price less 2000 yen– 4000 yen per ton, but 'if the production cost has risen or fallen markedly, then the ceiling and floor prices are to be adjusted immediately'. Furthermore, 'when the list price was to be maintained, or the Subcommittee was to carry out an output coordination, then when the figures were filed with MITI, it would in turn transmit the output target to each firm. We would have to submit a written promise that we would in all cases adhere to the quantity' (ibid., pp. 206–207).

If in addition the following quotation is considered, then the answer to our first query should be clear. 'Until now output coordination has not been permitted, but this time it will be openly permitted, if the listed price falls below the floor price . . . We have thus been able to some extent to realize the measures for steel price maintenance which we had desired in the past' (ibid., p. 207).[16]

The output limits and appropriate prices to be administered by MITI were not in fact decided by MITI, but were determined by the manufacturers prior to any actual 'advice' incorporating floor price restrictions. At least from this standpoint, it cannot be held that MITI played any active policy role.

If MITI did play any policy role, it would have been to prevent manufacturers from violating output limits or target prices. From this standpoint we can now answer the second question presented above. The appropriate steps that MITI would take against manufacturers violating MITI regulation were made clear in 1962.

When looked at from the standpoint of output and price coordination, the real function of the list-price system would be called into play only when demand growth slowed or was expected to slow, so that excess capacity arose or was predicted to arise. The start of the list-price system coincided with the starting point of an unprecedently big boom, called the 'Iwato Boom' of June 1958. The economy continued to expand extremely rapidly until July 1961, when with an increase in the discount rate a period of tight monetary policy commenced. The phrase 'investment calling forth more investment' became the catch phrase of this growth period, and the rate of increase in demand for steel products far surpassed that foreseen even by optimists.[17]

Initially, the system was invented as an alternative to a depression cartel.[18] Helped by both expanding domestic demand and the steel strike in the United States, the system 'achieved its goals with great success' (ibid, p. 26).

The situation changed drastically, however, with the onset of the tight monetary policy. In mid-1961, in the market for sheet and coil, where there continued to be rapid expansion of capacity, prices fell substantially below list prices, giving rise to discontent among the steel industry. Furthermore, 'the steel market was facing its greatest crisis since the institution of the list-price system, and price for plates, which was the last to hold to the list price, fell below it in December, and from then on the situation became serious, with no hint of recovery' (ibid., p. 433, for 20 April 1962).

Between July and October of 1961, there were several attempts to revive the market. These attempts, however, had no discernible impact; the list-price system had effectively collapsed and industry members sought permission to form what had been avoided all along, a depression cartel. The functioning of the list-price system during this period deserves our attention. What is notable throughout is the continual complaints of steel manufacturers that measures promised were not being implemented. These complaints became obvious from the end of 1961, but the following is a particularly straightforward statement of the reasons why the series of market measures had failed.

Many points can be raised concerning the reason for failure of the market measures which have been drawn up with so much effort by the individual manufacturers. In fact . . . one of the most important reasons is that the measures which were supposed to be implemented were not put into effect as planned. (Ibid. p. 503)[19]

There is absolutely no indication that MITI made any active attempt to correct this situation.

Market conditions continued to deteriorate, on which Mr Inayama stated at the Public Sale ('list price') Committee meeting of 25 May 1962 that 'one should say that the list-price system . . . is not so much on the verge of falling apart as having already collapsed' (ibid., p. 445). A series of market measures were taken. The first of these was in the July–September quarter, when steel ingot production was to be reduced by 20 per cent from the third quarter of the previous year, with open hearth furnaces being sealed on 17 and 18 July. The second was that all the production of the manufacturers other than the ten blast furnace firms was to be bought up by wholesalers.[20] In addition to these two pillars of the policy, on-site inspectors were to be sent.

In the 24 April report of the List-Price Committee, there is the statement that 'MITI engaged in informal regulation to see, retroactive to January, that there was strict adherence to the targets for plates and medium shapes production, and the Output Reduction Monitoring Committee began to monitor the output of each factory' (ibid., p. 435). It was only in July, however, that it was reported that 'from the 23rd of this month on-site inspectors have been sent to each factory, to monitor the reduction of production of plates, medium shapes and wire rods' (ibid., p. 469). The judgement was voiced at the end of October that, owing to the market measures, 'it appeared at one time, from the end of June to the beginning of July, that the market was recovering, but thereafter the market failed to pick up at all, and efforts to undersell at very low prices became rampant' (ibid., p. 503).[21]

In all this the following two points should be noted. First, there is no indication that MITI was an active participant in the process of debating and implementing these market measures.[22] Second, as noted for the reduction in ingot production, 'there was the fear that, when it came to reducing ingot production, monitoring would be very easy, and with each manufacturer considering its own interests, nothing has to this date been done' (ibid., p. 448). This statement is symbolic of the nature of the list-price system, but what is important for our purposes is that even in this there is no evidence of MITI taking an active role. The list-price system was not applied to all products, and there were also outsiders who did not participate in this coordination programme. There is no evidence that MITI tried to change this situation. In other words, not only was there no effective policy for strengthening output and price coordination, there is no evidence that the government even attempted an active role in this direction.[23]

It was stated that MITI would take appropriate action against manufacturers violating the system. However, in spite of there having been a stream of violations, by all manufacturers in fact, there is no evidence that any action was ever taken, or even threatened.

As a result of the above review, we are led to the conclusion that the government did not play a role or have a substantial direct influence on output and price coordination within the framework of the list-price system. In evaluating intra-industry coordination as industrial policy, our conclusion must be that it was ineffective in the case of the list-price system in the steel industry.

The Coordination of Investment

The situation describing the role and effect of government action in the list-price system is similar to the case of investment coordination in the steel industry, which we studied in the previous chapter. Here, the government took no active role and the investment coordination programme and related government policies – there was nothing that could be called policy – did not have in any direct way a clear impact on the investment behaviour of the firms involved.

Since the beginning of investment coordination in December 1959, the two years where it failed most signally were FY 1960 and FY 1965. For our purposes, it is sufficient merely to quote again the view of Mr Tokunaga, who was involved in the 1965 coordination programme and observed the FY 1967 coordination process.[24]

The final outcome of the FY 1967 steel industry investment coordination, the result of roughly a half year's discussion, was that in effect each firm's plans would be approved in full, for both steel making and milling facilities. This was virtually the same outcome as that of the self coordination which took place in FY 1965 and 1966, so that it can be seen how difficult it was if only those involved tried to coordinate on their own to achieve that what would be seen as desirable from the standpoint of the national economy.[25]

10.4   OUTPUT COORDINATION IN PETROLEUM REFINING

As has been seen thus far, at least in the case of the steel industry during the rapid growth era, the government was not actively involved in, or had no notable influence on, intra-industry coordination, whether it was in the form of output, pricing or investment. The goal of this section is to attempt a generalization of our evaluation of intra-industry coordination as industrial policy, by examining other industries, with the case of the steel industry as a base for comparison.

The reasons for the steel industry during the rapid growth era being chosen as the main focus of analysis have already been set out in Section 10.1. Recalling the fifth reason in particular, for intra-industry coordination to be effective an industry had to meet four conditions, which the steel industry satisfied. If any one of the four conditions was not met, then coordination would be unlikely to be successful. In this case, the role that the government could play is limited, and it is inconceivable that government participation will be effective. Most industries would be thought to fall into this category.

The next point is to ask, when these four conditions have been met, what additional conditions must at the same time be fulfilled in order for coordination in other industries to be evaluated as having been different from that of the steel industry. While such conditions cannot be comprehensively examined, a likely candidate is that, for at least output, price and investment coordination, the government is expected to pursue coordination efforts and has the power to do so. Here we will take up petroleum refining under the Petroleum Industry Act as a typical case in which these conditions are met. With the steel industry as a basis for comparison, we will examine intra-industry coordination in the petroleum refining industry and the government's role in forming a coordination programme.

From 1962, petroleum refining fell under the Petroleum Industry Act, and the industry had the striking distinction that there was strong government intervention in output, pricing and investment. The course of enactment and implementation of the Act teaches us many things, as the Act was intended to allow 'to the minimum extent required coordination of the activities of firms in the industry, as with the liberalization of petroleum imports it is expected that the petroleum market will be in disarray' (Tanaka, 1980, pp. 19 and 28).

The first point to be noted is that, in the process of enacting the Petroleum Industry Act, there was strong criticism of the government's direct intervention. Initially, a draft bill, made public in December 1961, attracted such opposition that the Petroleum Industry Bill submitted to the Diet in March of the next year had been substantially revised.[26] In the debate in the Commerce and Industry Committee of the House of Representatives, director-general Kawade of the MITI Mining Bureau testified concerning the formation of petroleum supply plans under Section 3 of the Bill: 'The petroleum supply plan will be a guide for the activity of firms, but it is possible that the sum of individual firm production plans will substantially exceed the overall plan target. However, we are not thinking of automatically notifying each firm of the excess and asking them to reduce output accordingly.'[27]

Concerning Section 15 of the Bill, director-general Kawade also testified that the notification of standard prices 'will be done to appeal to the social responsibility of firms as a psychological measure, and will not be legally binding' (ibid., p. 23). Finally, on the permit for new facilities of Section 7, which in the implementation of the Act would later be used as the strongest lever for achieving compliance with MITI's intentions, he testified that 'they will be licensed in accordance with the Act, and we are saying that we will issue a licence whenever these three basic conditions are met. We think it is unfair to use this as a means to obtain revenge for some unrelated matter' (ibid., p. 29).[28] This last sentence is famous as a government's defensive reaction to a popular understanding of the essence of informal regulation.

The actual implementation of the Act differed from the above explanation of the bill. This testimony, however, provides a frank indication of the strong criticism that government intervention faced. This gives us an understanding of the limitation placed on MITI policy.[29]

The second point is that, at least formally, the method of output coordination in the industry, even under the Petroleum Industry Act, did not differ greatly from that of the steel industry. MITI requested the cooperation of the Demand Specialists Committee of the Petroleum Association of Japan in January and February of each year, to draw up the Demand Forecast. This forecast formed the basis for the Petroleum Supply and Demand Plan, which in turn underlay the Petroleum Supply Plan required under Section 3 of the Petroleum Industry Act (Fair Trade Commission, 1983, p. 205).[30] According to the Fair Trade Commission, 'the Petroleum Supply Plan . . . only indicates the planned volumes which MITI feels desirable for the country as a whole, and does not indicate production levels for each individual petroleum refiner' (ibid., p. 210).

For example, for the publication of the Petroleum Supply Plan for the second half of FY 1962, the first plan under the Petroleum Industry Act, MITI had each firm submit its plans to the Petroleum Association of Japan as a way of anticipating the direction the industry was taking. This was done prior to the registration of production plans by the refiners, which was required by the same Act. The total amount of crude oil required, however, was 25 per cent more than that of the Supply Plan. After consulting the Petroleum Council, formally a part of MITI, MITI informed the Petroleum Association of Japan that the industry should engage in output coordination (see ibid., p. 212).

The third item to be noted is that under the industry Act government participation in the petroleum refining industry differed from that in other industries when its requests to the industry association for output coordination failed. In the case of the petroleum refining industry, 'in order to obtain "voluntary" cooperation through "self-coordinating" discussion among industry members, MITI in fact had to use forceful guidance or direct intervention. Such informal regulation functioned successfully because in the background MITI held power to license investment and to issue a formal request for a change in production plans' (ibid., p. 211). At the time of the above coordination for the second half of FY 1962, 'there was disagreement among those in the industry on the standard for coordination, and developing it was not easy. At that point MITI through informal regulation pushed for self-coordination, obtained the approval of the Petroleum Association of Japan for a standard, and pressed for output coordination on this basis' (ibid., p. 211).[31] It is doubtful that this could have been done without the power described above.

For the second half of FY 1963 the previous standard was maintained. 'Idemitsu Kosan and Daikyo Oil, which had expressed displeasure with output coordination from the start, opposed carrying it out, but under strong guidance from MITI the Petroleum Association of Japan . . . decided upon output coordination.' In response, Idemitsu Kosan

> was unhappy because it would not be able to adequately utilize its newly completed facilities, and so it did not go along with output coordination and instead went ahead with its own production plans. It did not respond to the efforts of the Petroleum Association to persuade it to conform, and on 12 November gave notice that it was quitting the Petroleum Association. (Ibid., pp. 213–14)

This is the so-called Idemitsu Incident. MITI officials and the Chairman of the Petroleum Council tried to persuade Idemitsu to cooperate in output coordination. Idemitsu, however, refused. In January, 'Idemitsu finally began to move when MITI indicated that it had decided to issue a formal warning as provided for by the Petroleum Industry Act.' In a meeting on 25 January between the Minister of MITI, the Chairman of the Petroleum Council and the President of Idemitsu, a compromise plan emerged. This agreement took into account some of Idemitsu's demands, for example future output coordination would cease,[32] and for January to September 1964 a new standard would be adopted allowing for greater output by Idemitsu.

The fourth point we wish to note is that, as can be seen above, even when the government had 'power', it was not a simple matter to make output coordination function effectively or to maintain the system.

The fifth item is that output coordination took place with 'strong guidance and direct intervention' by MITI while, at the same time, even though standard prices were posted 'in order to improve the market for petroleum products,' these efforts were successful neither in improving nor in maintaining market conditions.[33] A straightforward description of the situation at this time comes from an interview – itself unusual – on 1 April 1964 with Minister Hajime Fukuda of MITI:

> The most regrettable thing is that, even though for example output coordination is being carried out under informal regulation as part of the implementation of the Petroleum Industry Act, there has been much haggling and posturing among the firms, and there is a lack of any semblance of cooperation in seeking stability for the petroleum industry as

a whole. This has led to delays in and violations of output coordination, and I believe has resulted in the loss of the anticipated benefits. At this time I am strongly demanding a change of heart by each member of the industry, to cooperate as one in eliminating the excessive competition which stems from an excessive concern with market share. I am calling for renewed resolve in adhering strictly to output coordination and posted prices, so that the petroleum industry will carry out its social responsibilities in full. (Ibid., p. 216)

Let us now summarize in five points the information relevant for reaching our initial evaluation of intra-industry coordination in general. (1) Whether it related to output, prices, or investment, there was severe criticism of government intervention in the activities of individual firms. (2) Even when the government enjoyed sufficient powers, self-coordination was normally chosen as the basic approach. (3) Only when self-coordination did not function well did government participation commence. In order for such participation to be influential, some sort of power was needed for leverage. Furthermore, there had to be a consensus that the use of such power was proper. (4) In order for government participation to achieve its goals, active cooperation by the relevant firms was essential. Thus it was necessary to set out the principles underlying the government's actions and obtain the agreement of industry members. In this sense, the room for discretion by the government in its use of power was not wide. (5) Even when the government used its power to participate in coordination, it was not easy to actually attain its goals.

In considering jointly the conclusions of our above discussion on output coordination in the petroleum refining industry, the results of the discussion of the steel industry in the preceding section and the conclusion drawn at the beginning of this section, that in most industries the government was neither an active participant in coordination nor had great influence, we are led to the following generalization about intra-industry coordination in its various forms. Intra-industry coordination in the form of coordination of output, pricing or investment has been consistently held to be an important part of industrial policy. However, in fact the government was not an active participant in this policy programme, or it failed to have a clear, direct impact on industry.

10.5 SECONDARY EFFECTS

While the above conclusion rejects any direct effect of government industrial policy, there may be secondary effects. When pursuing output, price or investment coordination, there are regular meetings and the exchange of all sorts of information with the government and among rival firms. This is likely to influence the behaviour of industry members. If the evaluation of the coordination programme and related government policy encompass such influences, then the impact of government activities may not be small. The government can perhaps be regarded as an active participant in that its presence gave rise to the coordination meetings.[34] This influence takes many forms, but one suspects that in almost no case was this foreseen by even the responsible government officials. The two main points to be noted are as follows.

First, many firms opposed the government's policy of intra-industry coordination.[35] When, however, there is a history of industry association activity, where 'coordination' has served as a forum for meetings over time with rival firms along with the government, an individual firm opposing the policy would face severe criticism by rival firms and government officials. One might presume that the actions of each firm would be heavily influenced by coordination. The extent of such influence would appear to increase with the period of coordination and the degree to which policy measures had taken root.[36] When rival firms confer regularly on the direction in which markets are currently moving, future demand expectations and future capacity, and discuss the necessary responses, then one need hardly stress again that this will influence the behaviour of each firm, and hence influence the industry as a whole.

Second, when rival firms confer with each other or with the government on a regular basis, the information exchanged is not limited specifically to intra-industry coordination. One can thus find the following favourable evaluation:

> The issues with which industry is currently faced are jointly examined, and information is exchanged on new technologies and domestic and foreign markets . . . so that it cannot be denied that these fora have been an extremely effective measure for collecting and exchanging and transmitting information about industry . . . In sum if one thinks of this as a system for the exchange of information, then . . . it may well have been one important cause underlying the high growth rate of postwar Japanese industry. (Komiya, 1975, p. 324)

The above effects or influences should perhaps be treated as by-products or side-effects. However, a difference of opinion is likely regarding the evaluation of intra-industry coordination.[37]

The attitude of people in general to this sort of industry association activity and to the relationship between the government and business stems in large part from the tradition, since the Meiji Restoration, of a 'strong' central government and from the influence of the wide-ranging economic controls present during and immediately following the Second World War.[38] Accordingly, even if intra-industry coordination as industrial policy had taken a different form or not occurred at all, there must have been the above mentioned effects. It is for this reason that such effects are not taken up as positive features of intra-industry coordination as industrial policy in this chapter.

10.6 POLICY EVALUATION AND RELATED POINTS

It is claimed that intra-industry coordination as industrial policy was used in many industries. In almost all cases, however, government participation had almost no discernible impact. Basically, our overall evaluation is that the intra-industry coordination policy was ineffective.

There are two important observations related to this. First, the exceptional case of the petroleum refining industry, where the government was given strong powers, supports the conclusion that in such a case it is significantly more feasible to carry out intra-industry coordination as industrial policy. However, while in the petroleum refining case intra-industry coordination was not always effective, the *de facto* policy guidelines, subsequent to the Petroleum Industry Act, 'were added to the effect that there should be consideration given to small private firms independent of foreign capital, which expressed in a direct way the exceptional nature of the industry law . . . so that claims for consistency as industrial policy are extremely dubious'.[39]

Second, what should we learn from the lively debate that developed over the appropriateness of the goals of industrial policy, and in particular intra-industry coordination? The elimination of 'excessive competition', the strengthening of 'international competitiveness', the promotion of exports, the improvement of the balance of payments, the 'development and modernization of the domestic industrial structure', obtaining a stable supply of basic natural resources and other extremely generalized slogans were all stressed as goals or justifications of industrial policy. However, the nature of these was such that 'for each industry and *genkyoku*, what was important was that, in short, favourable measures be provided to the industry. If something was useful in persuading the relevant parties, it would be used as needed with the addition as appropriate of any reason or excuse' (Komiya, 1975, p. 322). If attention is paid to this, then it can readily be understood why there was no resolution of the debate over the appropriateness of goals, and why the same debate was repeated time and again. As the 'goal' was to 'persuade the relevant parties', then it need not be presumed that there was any consensus among firms or an industry and the *genkyoku*. It is possible that there was not even any coordination of actual opinions as to the goals.

Part IV

Intra-firm Organization and Inter-firm Relationships

11 Corporate Governance in Japanese Firms: The Body of Employees as the Controlling Group and Friendly Shareholders

11.1 INTRODUCTION

In the preceding chapters I assumed a neoclassical firm as the basic decision-making unit. This real-world neoclassical firm is controlled by shareholders with the board of directors as the agent of those shareholders. This firm purchases factors of production other than 'capital' in the market. The firm's objective is to maximize profit under given constraints, such as the production function and demand conditions. Also I assume zero transaction costs, unless otherwise stated. Transaction costs are not zero, however, and institutions do matter. If we are interested in the formation and functioning of firms, inter-firm relationships and the market, we must closely examine the validity of the above assumptions. Such an analysis is essential for understanding Japan's intra-firm organization and inter-firm relationships.

As shown in Section 11.2, the predominance of small businesses and the slimness of large firms are the two basic characteristics of the Japanese economy. One possible source of Japan's industrial success is the effective use of the inter-firm division of labour. In order to understand this inter-firm division of labour, several questions must be answered. Who coordinates this division among individual agents and how is it accomplished? Are there any specific institutional arrangements which make this coordination easy? Why have these arrangements functioned particularly well in Japan?

Debate surrounding the Japanese economy is full of stylized facts, many of which are due to fundamental misunderstandings or are based on shaky ground. There is a strong temptation to rely on these misleading facts when explaining Japan's industrial success, which often leads us to the Japan-is-different view. Each of these conventional views and models of the Japanese economy, such as the dual-structure view, the *keiretsu* loan model, the main bank model and the corporate group model, is based on such stylized facts. Each of them also has its own specific view of the coordinating agent and related institutional arrangements. As shown above, these views are incorrect on both theoretical and empirical grounds. Some may argue that 'the market' alone can explain the coordination. The 'market' explanation is correct; however, it is almost always unsatisfactory and we want to proceed beyond this answer. As I mention in Section 11.2, economists do not have a highly

195

developed theory of either the firm or the market. Therefore it is sometimes misleading to analyse these issues with established standard economic models. However, I will approach these issues with theories that incorporate a firm's real-world features, even though such theories are still rudimentary. This will give us a much better understanding of the organizational issues concerning the Japanese economy than was the conventional view alone. In return this will contribute to the study of the firm and the market in general.

Part IV focuses on two specific aspects of Japanese firms: corporate governance and inter-firm relationships. However, first we need to define what is a firm. This chapter begins by asking three related fundamental questions. First, what are the boundaries of a firm? Second, who decides these boundaries and the internal organization of a firm? Finally, how are these boundaries related to the legal definition of a firm? Underlying these three questions is the basic puzzle of Coase (1937): why a firm emerges at all in a specialized exchange economy.

My argument in this chapter is basically the nexus of contract theory associated with Jensen and Mechling (1976). The central dilemma for most organizational issues is, using Simon's (1976) words, who is 'the controlling group', in other words, who 'has the power to set the terms of membership for all the participants' (p. 119). With the importance of employees' investment in organization-specific human capital formation, the body of employees takes this key position, and selects directors to be its representatives. Other stakeholders, such as friendly shareholders and friendly lenders, rationally agree with the controlling group. Since a firm in the real world is just a legal fiction, the legal boundary of any given firm usually does not coincide with the boundary used by the controlling group in their decision making. A firm, for Coase in particular and economic analysis in general, is a set of activities and/or agents within the boundaries, given by the controlling group, which hereafter will be referred to as the effective boundary. Therefore the firm described in Coase (1937) is different from firms in both the real world and in economic statistics.

The basic factor which determines an organization's controlling group is not capital ownership (shareholdings) or corporate financing (loans, bonds and so on) or its representative directors. Rather it is the organization-specific human capital accumulated in the body of employees which will be examined in detail in this chapter. Once we realize this, many economic phenomena related to the organization must be re-examined, such as the predominance of small business and the slimness of large firms in the Japanese economy. For this controlling group the legal boundary is only one of many constraints in the decision-making process, and may not significantly affect the intra-firm organization or inter-firm relationships. The inside–outside characterization of a firm, as described by Coase, depends on transaction costs. Here again the legal definition does not necessarily affect the economic definition of a firm. In this view, even for a firm owner–manager it is in their interest to be friendly to the body of employees. Therefore the question of whether the management is separated from control is irrelevant.

In this chapter I study Japanese firms alone, but I do not argue that they are different in any sense from firms in other countries. Firms in Japan, America or any other country are never badly managed to any extreme. The reason is straightforward: most poorly managed firms either fire their managers, improve management performance or go out of business. 'Elementary notions of comparative advantage suggest that some firms in any country will *always* be uncompetitive compared to firms in the same industry elsewhere' (Ramseyer, 1993, p. 2020). The nature of the basic logic underlying the discussion in this chapter – that the fundamental factor which determines the form, character and workings of organizations is organization-specific human capital found in the body of employees – is technological and therefore not peculiar to any one country. Therefore, when a crucial difference is observed between economies, it must be caused not by some difference in the underlying basic mechanism but by environmental factors, such as the legal system, history or culture. As I mention in the last section, in countries other than Japan we find almost identical observations and arguments on both the corporate governance of firms and the nature of economic organizations.

Section 11.2 describes the two basic facts about the Japanese economy; the predominance of small businesses and the slimness of large firms. Next, I briefly examine the concepts of organization and their relation to actual firms. In Section 11.3, using large firms in the transport equipment industry as representative of Japanese firms, I illustrate key characteristics of directors and friendly shareholders. Section 11.4 discusses why the body of employees becomes the controlling group of a firm, and Section 11.5 explains why a friendly shareholder will tend to stay friendly. In Section 11.6, I first explore the role of shareholders and banks, and then the irrelevance of the classical 'separation of management from control' issue. Section 11.7 returns to the issue of why the body of employees is the controlling group, since it is futile to ask who 'controls' the firm as it is a matter of definition in a world of exchange by agreement. Section 11.8 describes how the discussion of this chapter is related to the study of inter-firm relationships, the subject of Chapter 12. In the final section, Section 11.9, I conclude with two points. First, the basic logic underlying the argument in this chapter is technological and applies to other economies. Second, though the argument explains how the theory of comparative advantage works, it is not effective in explaining Japan's industrial success.

11.2 TWO BASIC FACTS ABOUT THE JAPANESE ECONOMY AND DEFINITION OF THE PROBLEM

The Predominance of Small Businesses and the Slimness of Large Firms

In discussing Japanese firms and Japan's industrial organization, most have in mind such firms as Toyota, Nissan and Honda in the motor industry and NEC, Hitachi and Sony in the electronics industry. Some may believe that

Toyota's unique '*kanban*-system' is common throughout the Japanese economy. On the contrary; most Japanese firms are small, most Japanese workers are employed by small firms, and more than half of Japan's value added is produced by small firms. The dominance of Japan's small firms has a long history and their importance in the domestic economy has not changed significantly for the past 30 to 40 years.

In 1991, the total number of establishments in Japan's private sector, excluding the agriculture and fishery sectors, was 6.5 million, and 99.1 per cent of these establishments were small business. There were 55 million employees in the same private sector, 79.2 per cent of whom were employed by small businesses. Limiting our attention to the manufacturing sector, we find almost the same picture. In 1991, 99.4 per cent of the 857 000 establishments were small businesses, and of the 14.1 million employees in the manufacturing sector 73.8 per cent were employed in small businesses. The corresponding figures in the manufacturing sector in 1957 were 99.6 per cent and 72.3 per cent, respectively. This suggests stable predominance of small business. Throughout these 30 to 40 years, more than 55 per cent of Japan's value added has been produced in the small business sector, and less than 45 per cent by the large firm sector – in manufacturing, this sector includes those firms with 300 or more employees.[1]

A comparison of large firms in Japan, America and Europe reveals that Japanese firms are rather slim and have far fewer employees in relation to their sales. Table 1.7 of Chapter 1 gives some examples. For instance, although Toyota's annual sales are about one half those of General Motors and about 1.3 times those of Volkswagen, Toyota (72 000) employs less than one tenth the number of GM workers (751 000) and less than one third the number of Volkswagen workers (266 000).

In Japan, large firms occupy a rather small part of the economy. These firms are relatively slim and depend greatly on their transactions with outside suppliers. Some readers familiar with the literature on the Japanese economy may comment that the majority of small businesses are so heavily dependent on certain large firms that they cannot make independent decisions, and that many large firms form corporate groups, behave collectively and therefore dominate the Japanese economy. Furthermore a few large banks act as main banks and appear to dominate Japan's financial markets, which allows them to control their client firms. As shown in Parts I and II, however, these conventional views are incorrect. For instance, the belief that large firms dominate the economy through group activity is false since both the strength of the group's unity and the group's total size as the sum of 'member' firm's sizes are overemphasized, despite the definition of 'corporate groups'. These two basic facts are a result of independent choices of many firms, most of which are small businesses.

The Definition of the Problem: Organizations and Firms

Before studying intra-firm organization and inter-firm relationships we must first give a definition of the 'firm'. Three questions related to the definition are critical. First, where are the firm's boundaries? Second, who decides the boundaries and internal organization of the firm? Third, how are the boundaries related to the legal definition of the firm? Underlying these three questions is Coase's (1937) basic question of why a firm emerges at all in a specialized exchange economy.

What we observe in the real world, and adopted in the previous discussion, as 'firm' is a legal entity based on corporate law. This implies that we have assumed a consistency between an actual firm and a relevant unit of economic analysis. What happens if an actual firm differs from this model, particularly when analysing inter-firm relationships and intra-firm organization? If the leading player who decides the boundary and internal organization of a firm is different from the one corporate law assumes, namely the body of shareholders, the relevant boundary may be different from the legal boundary, and the latter might be regarded only as one of many constraints on decision making.

The firm in economic theory . . . is a 'shadowy figure' (Coase, 1988, p. 5). As Oliver Hart (1989, p. 1957) notes, little could be further from the truth than to think that economists have a highly developed theory of the firm. Most formal models of the firm are extremely rudimentary and bear little relation to the complex organizations we see in the world today. Theories that attempt to incorporate real-world features of firms often lack precision and rigour, and therefore fail to be accepted by the theoretical mainstream. Neoclassical theory, the staple diet of modern economists, views the firm as a set of feasible production plans. Hart (1989, p. 1958) states:

> It does not explain how production is organized within a firm, how conflicts of interest between the firm's various constituencies–its owners, managers, workers, and consumers–are resolved, or more generally, how the goal of profit-maximization is achieved. More subtly, neoclassical theory begs the question of what defines a given firm or what determines its boundaries.

The above mentioned two basic facts of Japanese firms and industrial organization, namely the predominance of small businesses and slimness of large firms, must be interrelated and should be explained in a manner that incorporates Coase's question. As the basic issue applies to 'organization' in general, let us begin with a discussion of organization.

> The term *organization* refers to the complex pattern of communication and relationships in a group of human beings. This pattern provides to each member of the group much of the information and many of the assumptions, goals, and attitudes that enter into his decisions, and provides him also with a set of stable and comprehensible expectations as to what the other members of the group are doing and how they will react to what he says and does. The sociologist calls this pattern a 'role system'; to most of us it is known as an 'organization'. (Simon, 1976, p. xvii of Introduction)

Various types of organizations exist and the 'firm' is only one of them. Therefore it is not appropriate to begin the study of organizations with firms. The economic system consists of a network of people and organizations, with lower-level organizations linked together through higher-level organizations. A key characteristic of the actual firm is its independent legal identity, enabling it to enter into binding contracts and seek court enforcement of those contracts.

The nexus of contract theory, on which my argument depends, is often associated with Jensen and Mechling (1976). They argue:

> it is important to recognize that most organizations are simply *legal fictions which serve as a nexus for a set of contracting relationships among individuals* . . . The private corporation or firm is simply one form of *legal fiction*[2] *which serves as a nexus for contracting relationships* . . . *The firm is not an individual.* It is a legal fiction which serves as a focus for a complex process in which the conflicting objectives of individuals . . . are brought into equilibrium within a framework of contractual relations. In this sense the 'behavior' of the firm is like the behavior of a market; i.e., the outcome of a complex equilibrium process. (pp. 310–11)

As Milgrom and Roberts (1992, p. 20) point out, a full description of the organizational architecture involves many more elements: the pattern of resource and information flows, the authority and control relationship, the distribution of effective power, and the allocation of responsibilities and decision rights. They argue that, once our focus turns to the elements of organizational architecture, defining an organization as a legal entity may become inappropriate because it can easily misidentify the effective boundaries of the organization.

The effective boundary of the organization does not always coincide with the actual boundary of the organization as a legal entity. If there exists a discrepancy between these two boundaries, it makes little or no sense to distinguish the 'inside' of the actual firm from the 'outside', particularly for understanding the workings of organizations. The central issue is 'who decides the effective boundary'. Thus, as March and Simon (1958) noted,

> The distinction between units in a production–distribution process that are 'in' the organization and those that are 'out' of the organization typically follows the legal definition of the boundaries of a particular firm. We find it fruitful to use a more functional criterion that includes both the suppliers and the distributors of the manufacturing core of the organization . . . Thus, in the automobile industry it is useful to consider the automobile dealers as component parts of an automobile manufacturing organization. (pp. 89–90)

They listed the following five classes as the chief participants of most business organizations: employees, investors, suppliers, distributors and consumers.

In the next chapter I show that the effective boundary of the firm as a decision-making unit is different from that of a firm as a legal entity and the in-and-out distinction based on this legal definition is irrelevant. These points are directly related to inter-firm relationships. In the following sections I investigate corporate governance in Japanese firms.

11.3 ACTUAL FIGURES OF DIRECTORS AND FRIENDLY SHAREHOLDERS

The view one takes of firms and organizations is apt to depend on one's assumption of how investors, employees and other players come to be associated in a common venture. In what follows I take the view of Easterbrook and Fischel (1990, p. 185):

> The corporation and its securities are products to as great an extent as the sewing machines . . . the firm makes. Just as the founders of a firm have incentives to make the kinds of sewing machines people want to buy, they have incentives to create the kind of firm, governance structure, and securities people value. The founders of the firm will find it profitable to establish the governance structure that is most beneficial to investors, net of the costs of maintaining the structure. People who seek resources to control will have to deliver more returns to investors. Those who promise the highest returns. . . will obtain the largest investments.

Managers who control such resources do their best to take advantage of investors, but they find that the dynamics of the market drive them to act as if they had investors' interests at heart. It is almost as if there were an invisible hand.

The basic issues are who are the founders of the corporation and who take their position when the firm grows larger. The fundamental question is, in Simon's (1976) words, who makes up 'the controlling group'? By the term 'controlling group' he means 'the group that has the power to set the terms of membership for all the participants', and selects for the organization 'the basic value criteria that will be employed in making decisions and choices among alternatives in an organization' (p. 119).[3] Here I do not intend to develop a general theory. Instead, following Dore (1992), I focus on the controlling group of large Japanese firms and the role of shareholders in corporate management. As mentioned later, the same argument applies to small businesses.

The essence of Dore's argument is found in the following statement.

> In the conception of the firms—or at least of the large corporation–. . . the one stakeholder whose stake is seen to be of paramount importance is the body of employees. The primary definition of the firm is a community of people, rather than a property of the shareholders, and this conception shapes business practice . . . The economic behaviour encouraged by these

underlying conceptions is more conducive to business efficiency . . . than behaviour based on the assumptions embodied in American – or for that matter Japanese – corporation law. (p. 18)[4]

Employees are the most important stakeholders in most large Japanese firms, which means that the controlling group is the body of employees. In such firms, the directors and managers are selected from among employees, and are almost always able to expect strong support from the majority of employees, as long as their decision making is generally consistent with employees' interests.[5]

Friendly Shareholders (*Antei-Kabunushi*)

The question is why and how the body of employees, as the controlling group, can secure their interests and defend themselves from other stakeholders, especially shareholders. The most basic and important reason for this is that such attacks generally do not benefit other stakeholders. An additional reason[6] is the role played by *antei-kabunushi*, those stable shareholders friendly to the existing management (hereafter, friendly shareholders). This is important for the defence of management's position against hostile shareholders, especially during takeover bids. Dore (1992, p. 20) states, '[a] large part of a firm's equity is in the hands of friendly, corporate stockholders: the suppliers, banks, insurers, trading companies, dealers it does business with'.

Let me begin the discussion by examining certain characteristics of large firms' shareholdings. To illustrate my point, I use data on large firms in the transport equipment industry listed on the Tokyo Stock Exchange, such as cars, car parts, shipbuilding, railway vehicles, and so on.[7] From this data two points immediately become clear. First, for most large Japanese firms, a large part of the equity is in the hands of a small number of shareholders. The average concentration ratio of the ten largest shareholders of 11 firms with over 10 000 employees in 1990 (Group A) was 35.03 per cent in 1980 and 36.49 per cent in 1990. This figure ranges from 26.20 per cent (Mitsubishi Heavy Industries) to 59.50 per cent (Isuzu) in 1990. The corresponding figures for 29 firms with employees between 2 000 and 10 000 in 1990 (Group B) were 55.70 per cent in 1980 and 54.53 per cent in 1990.[8]

Second, the largest shareholders are corporations, mainly financial institutions and trade partners. In 1990, for every firm in Group A, the ten largest shareholders were corporate shareholders. Of these 11 firms in Group A, financial institutions were the ten largest shareholders in two cases, nine in eight cases, and eight only in one case. Non-corporate shareholders, including employees' shareholding associations, appeared on the ten largest shareholder's list in only three of 29 Group B cases in 1990. In the same year the average number of financial institutions in the list was 7.6.

At the end of March 1990, the ten largest shareholders of Nissan and Honda were all financial institutions. In many cases, the largest shareholder was a non-financial corporation and the others were financial institutions, such as Mazda (Ford held 24 per cent), Daihatsu (Toyota, 14.19 per cent), Fuji Heavy Industries (Nissan, 4.24 per cent), Aichi Machine (Nissan, 32.10 per cent) and Yamaha Motor (Yamaha, 33.42 per cent). Of the ten largest shareholders of Toyota, nine were financial institutions. Toyoda Automatic Loom, from which Toyota originally spun off, was the fourth largest shareholder with 4.35 per cent of Toyota's total equity.

The term *antei-kabunushi* is widely used, but ill-defined. *Antei* [literally, stable] here has a dual meaning, one for their stable position as shareholders and the other for their contribution to the stable position of the existing directors. Emphasizing the importance of the latter, I choose 'friendly shareholders' as its English translation. The position of large shareholders remained stable for a long time. Of the ten largest shareholders in 1990 of the 11 Group A firms, on average seven to eight were also on the top ten list in 1980. Most large shareholders new to the list in 1990 were financial institutions which in 1980 were listed in the top 11 to 20 shareholders. There were only two non-financial institutions new to the top ten list in these 11 Group A firms, Ford as the largest shareholder of Mazda with 2 per cent per cent and GM as the third largest of Suzuki with 3.6 per cent.

The stability of large shareholders is symbolized in the case of Koito, a car-parts manufacturer. In 1989 to 1991, Koito was the target of a take over attempt by Boone Pickens, a well-known corporate raider from the USA. Pickens was Koito's largest shareholder, owning 26.43 per cent of the total issued share at the end of March 1990. While the share price had stayed at around 500 yen per share, prices rose dramatically to 5,470 yen on 31 March 1989. However, what is most striking is the stable behaviour of large shareholders. Between March 1980 and March 1990, only three dropped out of the list of the 20 largest shareholders. None of the remaining 17 shareholders decreased their shareholdings and 14 actually increased their ownership. Of the three which disappeared from the list in 1990, not one was a top ten shareholder in 1980 and the combined holding of the three shareholders was only 3.24 per cent of the total shares issued in 1980. Apart from the Boone company, both of the two new large shareholders appearing on the top 20 list in 1990 were mutual life insurance companies, whose combined holding was only 2.17 per cent of ownership. In 1980, the ten largest shareholders had 50.78 per cent ownership and the 20 largest had 61.71 per cent ownership.

In most large Japanese firms, the controlling group is the body of employees. In such firms, the directors and managers are selected from among the firm's employees and are almost always able to expect strong support from the majority of employees, as long as their actions are generally consistent with the interests of these employees. Large shareholders remain as such and faithfully support existing management. They maintain the right as large shareholders under the present corporate law and legal system to deprive the existing management of their leadership in the firm. However, we are in a world of exchange by agreement rather than by coercion, therefore these shareholders have no incentive to unite for this purpose: otherwise, nothing prevents them from uniting in order to realize the benefits. If such a situation were to occur, the positions of directors and managers would not be stable. Thus they are friendly to the existing management and called friendly shareholders (*antei-kabunushi*).

In the large Japanese firms most members of the board of directors are selected from among employees. For instance, all 55 directors of Toyota in June 1993 were former employees. The same was true for 31 of 33 directors of Honda in March 1993. Of the two remaining seats, one was occupied by a former high official of the Ministry of Foreign Affairs and the other by an interlocking directorate of the chairman of Mitsubishi Bank. All 35 directors except one of Nihon Denso in December 1993 (with 41 996 employees), of which Toyota owned 23.07 per cent of the equity and Toyoda Automatic Loom 7.28 per cent, were former employees. The only exception involved an interlocking directorate of the chairman of Toyota. Almost the same was true for Aisin Seiki (employees: 10 935), 21.67 per cent of whose equity was owned by Toyota in March 1993. Here 25 of 28 directors were former employees and the remaining three were all from Toyota, one of them with an interlocking directorate serving as a Toyota vice-president.

The same picture applies to smaller firms. In March 1993 all 24 directors of NOK, a car-parts manufacturer with 3790 employees, were former employees. Of NOK's entire equity, 22.55 per cent was owned by Freutenberg of Germany and 4.04 per cent by Toyota, the fourth largest shareholder. Of the 21 directors of Kayaba, another car-parts manufacturer with 4480 employees, 19 were former employees in March 1993. The largest shareholder of Kayaba was Toyota, with 9.12 per cent, followed by Nissan, with 8.73 per cent. The remaining two directors were both former managers of Fuji Bank, the third largest shareholder. Finally, there is Koito. In March 1990, 16 of Koito's 20 directors were former employees. Of the remaining seats three were held by former managers of Toyota and one involved an interlocking directorate, a vice-president of Matsushita, the third largest shareholder.

On average, an employee/manager is elected to be a director in his or her early fifties, and stays on the board for six to seven years. For instance, in 1993, most directors of Toyota had first become members when they were between 50 and 53 years old.[9] Unless they resigned, on average these new directors were promoted four years later to a higher position, such as managing director, executive managing director, vice-president or president. Of Toyota's 55 directors, 23 held a higher position and ten were newly selected at the general meeting of shareholders in September 1993. Three facts are important. First, every year new directors are selected from among the employees to fill the seats of resigning board members. Second, directors chosen from the body of employees continuously dominate the board. Finally, the large shareholders, individually and as a group, continuously support, with the selection of board members from among company employees, the resulting employee-dominated board itself.

The case of Koito illustrates the stability of the board's constitution and the position of each member even when the constitution of large shareholders changes drastically. Boone Company's appearance as the largest shareholder had no observable impact on the board of directors presented for election at the June 1991 meeting of shareholders. Both the constitution of large shareholders and that of Koito's board of directors have remained stable for 20 years since a drastic change in 1971–2. In September 1971, the largest shareholder was Matsushita, and neither Toyota nor Nissan was on the list of the ten largest shareholders. Eight of the ten directors were former employees. Of the other directors, one was the founder of the firm and the other involved an interlocking directorate of a vice-president of Matsushita. By September 1972, Toyota was the largest shareholder with 21.81 per cent ownership and Nissan was second with 8.89 per cent ownership. Matsushita remained as the third largest. The board changed at the general meeting of shareholders in June 1972 in three respects. First, the number of directors increased from ten to 14. Second, while all of the previous directors remained on the board, two new directors came from Toyota, both as managing directors. The other two new members were selected from among employees. Third, the president and one vice-president (no. 1 and no. 2 position) were occupied by two former vice-presidents who occupied the no. 3 and no. 4 positions.[10] No other change occurred and the interlocking directorate of Matsushita's vice-president remained. The two directors from Toyota stayed as directors for more than 20 years, and were the president and a vice-president when Boone Company appeared as the largest shareholder.[11] The point is that even such a drastic change in large shareholders was not accompanied by a noticeable impact on the board's constitution.

11.4 THE BODY OF EMPLOYEES AS THE CONTROLLING GROUP

Why is the body of employees the controlling group and why do large shareholders accept and support this group? 'Today the essential task for a firm is not to carry out routine work steadily but through interaction of agents to create information, to search for new business opportunities, and to develop an accumulation process for continual innovation' (Imai, 1989, p. 141). To survive and grow, a firm has to accumulate a stock of human capital with which it establishes an organization suitable for its task. This accumulation process takes a long time and the guarantee that in the foreseeable future nothing will drastically devalue the accumulated human capital. This requires friendly shareholders.

This process, when effective, has four characteristics. First, it requires each participant's long-term investment in his or her own human capital. Second, the required investment is more or less specific to the particular organization; that is, the skill is organization-specific. Third, it is used in the team production process described by Alchian and Demsetz (1972, pp. 782–83), in that the product is not a sum of the separable outputs of each cooperating resource, and that not all the resources used in the team production belong to any one person. Fourth, with long-term investment each participant acquires the right to be a member of the organization, but can recover the investment cost and receive its reward not by selling the right but by staying with the organization. Quitting the organization will devalue the skill gained since it is organization-specific. When the stability of the organizational structure is uncertain–when there remains the possibility of change in the incentive system, such as economic rewards and promotion, and in the basic corporate strategy–participants hesitate to invest in the formation of the required skill. This results in the firm's low performance, discouraging talented young candidates from joining the firm. When only some participants are confident in the organization's stability, the value of a confident worker's skill will be lower than otherwise because of the lower skill of less confident workers. Thus, by making the stability of the organization certain, the body of employees can make the best use of their resources.

Besides securing large, stable shareholders supportive of the existing management, the selection of employees as directors and top managers is an indication of the organization's stability. A director who was a former employee, say for 30 years, has already made a long-term organization-specific investment which allows him to understand the firm's core assets and the firm's business nature. This director also understands the importance of the organization's stability to its prosperity. Moreover, once a *de facto* rule of selecting directors from the employees is established, every participant is confident in the organization's stability since directors unfamiliar with or hostile to the existing nature and structure of the firm are generally avoided or can be easily removed.

The economic organization through which resource owners cooperate will make better use of their comparative advantages to the extent that this facilitates the payment of rewards based on productivity. This applies to every resource owner. Investors, for instance, part with their money willingly, putting it in equities rather than other investment alternatives because they believe the returns of equities are relatively more attractive. The same analysis is true in determining investment alternatives in the case of firms. Once owning the equity of a firm, the investor realizes the importance of the organization's stability and wants to be a friendly, but profitable, shareholder. An investor can recover the investment and receive his reward by selling the equity. He can also decrease the risk of investment by diversifying his or her portfolio. Neither option is feasible, however, for an employee investing in organization-specific skill.

Note two points. First, as this observation is a result in a world of exchange by agreement rather than by coercion, who 'controls' the firm is a matter of definition, so any attempt to answer such a question in general is futile. Therefore my argument that the body of employees is the controlling group is a judgement based both on the theoretical model and observations as shown above and will be discussed again in Section 11.7.[12] Second, one may agree with the literature regarding the 'discretionary' power held by managers of large firms and apply them to firms where the controlling group is employees. How does it happen that shareholders willingly allow directors to act contrary to their interests, since the rewards for their investment largely depend on the performance of the directors?[13]

11.5 WHY DOES A FRIENDLY SHAREHOLDER REMAIN FRIENDLY?

In a world of exchange by agreement, a shareholder agrees to be friendly and stays friendly because the expected rewards from being friendly are higher than would otherwise be the case. The controlling group of a firm has to deliver rewards large enough to attract suppliers of other resources. In order to induce a large shareholder to be friendly and remain friendly, the controlling group has to offer additional incentives beyond those available to an ordinary shareholder. Otherwise, those who hold rather pessimistic expectations of the firm's future prospects relative to the market will cease to be friendly.

Three types of incentives are popular. First, cross-holding equity ensures the stability of both organizations, functioning as mutual hostages between friendly shareholders. Second, trade partners often benefit from other organizations' stability and are willing to pay a premium for this benefit. Since stability is the basis of the firm's prosperity, contributions to its stability increase the seller's profits and enable it to provide better products at lower prices to a buyer. It also serves the buyer as a guarantee that the supply of products will not cease either at the supplier's will or as the result of an invasion, such as a take-over, by a buyer's rival. In this case, the seller's skill also becomes relation-specific. Third, a firm can offer additional incentives through allocating profitable business opportunities.

Mutual life insurance companies, some of which are the largest shareholders in Japan, are typical of the third type of beneficiary. Since they are not corporations but mutual companies, cross-holding is not possible. Usually they are neither big purchasers of the manufacturing firms they own nor do they have much interest in the stability of the manufacturing firm's organization. We observe, however, both loan transactions and insurer–customer relationships between life insurance companies and their shareholding firms. Almost the same picture applies to other financial institutions, such as banks and trust banks. However, in the case of these financial institutions cross-holding does prevail. For instance, of the ten largest shareholders of Toyota in June 1993, nine were financial institutions including two mutual life insurance companies. The largest three shareholders, each with 4.9 per cent ownership, were banks. Toyota was a large shareholder in all three banks: the largest shareholder of Tokai Bank and the fifth largest shareholder of both Sakura Bank and Sanwa Bank.[14] The same thing happens with smaller firms. Kayaba, for example, owned many shares of Fuji Bank and Yasuda Trust Bank which in turn owned 5.0 per cent and 4.3 per cent, respectively, of Kayaba's equity in March 1993.[15]

Cross-holding of equity also prevails between trade partners. For instance, Toyota cross-holds equity not only with so-called 'Toyota Group' firms such as Nihon Denso and Aishin Seiki, and other *Kyoho-kai* (Toyota's suppliers association) members such as Kayaba, Koito[16] and Asahi Glass, but also with material suppliers like Nippon Steel. The case of Akebono Brake, the largest brake supplier in Japan, demonstrates this fact. Of Akebono Brake's ten largest shareholders in March 1993, five were car assemblers, Nissan (no. 1 with 15.66 per cent), Toyota (no. 2 with 15.49 per cent), Isuzu (no. 4 with 5.12 per cent), Hino (no. 6 with 2.30 per cent) and Mitsubishi (no. 9 with 1.50 per cent). Akebono cross-holds equity with all these firms as well, though in each case the market value of Akebono's ownership is around 10 per cent of that cross-held by the car assemblers.

Unless a shareholder enjoys some of the additional incentives listed above, it may not become or remain a friendly shareholder. Therefore individuals seldom appear on the list of friendly shareholders except when the individual belongs to the controlling group, for example as one of the founders or directors of the firm. A corporation without additional incentives may not intend to remain friendly, and will likely sell the stock when that is profitable, but usually with prior notification to the firm.[17,18]

Though friendly shareholders enjoy rewards higher than ordinary shareholders, on some occasions this premium is not high enough to induce them to stay friendly. When the share price of Koito rose to the level of over 5000 yen, almost ten times higher than the previously stable level, the expected capital loss of Koito's shareholders over the next few years would exceed its premium. Even under such circumstances, the friendly shareholders did not sell their shares. This can be explained as follows. The stability of the organization, which is the controlling group's objective in asking a group of shareholders to be friendly, is a result of friendly shareholders' team action, and the effectiveness of an individual shareholder's action depends on other shareholders. Therefore both the firm and friendly shareholders as a group will oppose any individual shareholder's action which endangers the organization's stability. In particular, trade partners may face serious damage themselves. Once it sells the shares of a firm to which it is supposed to be friendly this firm loses the trust of other friendly shareholders, both of other shareholders and of its cross-holding partners. This will in kind endanger the stability of its own organization by threatening the position of friendly shareholders. The stability must be viewed by employees as long-lasting. This requires trust on the part of each shareholder, to respect the team's character and to act in the team's interest. It is expensive for a corporation to recover this trust once it has been lost.[19]

When the body of employees establishes its controlling group position within a firm and is supported by friendly shareholders, it is costly for large shareholders to unite in order to deprive the existing management of their leadership in the firm. Management is strongly supported by the body of employees. New management, whether invited from outside or selected from inside among employees, intent on changing the nature of the organization or corporate policy will face strong resistance from the body of employees since its accumulated human capital is organization-specific. Moreover, as a result of the prevalence of such firms, the external market for managers is not well developed. It is difficult to find a new body of management capable of improving the firm's performance for shareholders. When a bank with a large share of a firm's equity appoints its manager as the president of the firm, there is unlikely to be any significant change in the firm. Unless accepted by the body of employees as its representative, the director cannot change corporate policy. Hence appointing a leading director from outside is rarely effective in improving the firm's performance.

11.6 RELATED ISSUES: THE ROLE OF OTHER STAKEHOLDERS AND AGENCY COSTS

The Role of Shareholders, Banks and Directors

The basic reason why the body of employees is able to secure its stability and defend itself from attacks from other stakeholders is that such attacks generally do not benefit other stakeholders. An additional reason is the role played by friendly shareholders. With the understanding that the controlling group is the body of employees and that it has the implied power to select the friendly shareholders and to choose the sources of corporate funds, we can draw three logical conclusions all of which are contrary to the conventional view of the Japanese economy.

First, the friendly shareholders are selected because they are *supposed* to be friendly to the present directors and managers. When once friendly large shareholders threaten the present management, the directors change their selection of the friendly shareholders. Cross-holdings or group holdings (for example, among 'corporate group' firms) are the result of such voluntary selection. Accordingly, the shareholding patterns and the names of large shareholders give us limited information: In other words, identifying the friendly shareholders seldom reveals the true distribution of power.[20]

Second, sources of corporate funds, including banks, are selected on the basis of the lender's support of the present body of directors. Therefore, when once friendly large lenders, such as the main bank(s) or lead bank(s), become hostile to the present management, the directors change their source of funding. The phenomenon that the largest lender often has a large share of the borrower's stock is only one result of such voluntary selection.[21,22]

Third, members of the board of directors and top managers are selected on the basis of their support of the present directors and employees. Even directors who are supposed to represent the interests of other stakeholders are friendly to the present body of directors, and they remain in such a position unless they become troublesome. The structure of the board of directors is a result of this voluntary selection. Accordingly, the number of directors who formerly represented other stakeholders, such as banks and trade partners, within the corporate structure gives us little information about the distribution of power.[23]

The Separation of Ownership and Management, and Agency Costs

The directors of such [joint-stock] companies, however, being the managers rather of other people's money than of their own, it cannot well be expected, that they should watch over it with the same anxious vigilance with which the partners in a private copartnery frequently watch over their own . . . Negligence and profusion . . . must always prevail, more or less, in the management of affairs of such a company. (Smith, 1776, p. 233)

Since the time of Adam Smith, the separation of ownership and management, or the separation of management from control, within a large modern corporation has gathered wide attention. Berle and Means (1932) further provoked public interest in the firm's form of social control.[24] In postwar Japan the same argument has prevailed, and many have insisted that the separation was even more clearly realized in Japan than in the USA.[25]

My above argument presents a different view of this ownership–management separation. The classical view states that each shareholder is so small that the cost of uniting is prohibitive, limiting the effective control of management. In Japan, however, a small number of large shareholders own the dominant portion of equity, for whom the cost of uniting is not high. They support the existing management as friendly shareholders, since it is more profitable for them to do so than to manage the firm by themselves or to replace the management. Here, the separation of ownership and management, and that of management from control, is not a serious social problem.

The same is true for the argument about non-zero agency costs. As Jensen and Mechling (1976, p. 328) pointed out, these costs (monitoring and bonding costs and 'residual loss') are an unavoidable result of the agency relationship. To conclude that the agency relationship is non-optimal is what Demsetz (1969) characterizes as the 'Nirvana' form of analysis. Friendly shareholders choose to accept these costs instead of avoiding them by managing the firm by themselves.

Thus far I have focused on only large firms listed on the Tokyo Stock Exchange. The same logic also applies to large unlisted firms, and even to small unlisted firms. What would happen if an owner of a large unlisted firm, where the body of employees is the controlling group, made a decision against the interests of this group, for instance suggesting selling the organization to some other firm in ten years? Such a firm can neither attract young talent nor induce employees to invest in organization-specific skill formation, resulting in the firm's poor performance. Thus an owner–manager chooses to be friendly to the body of employees, and the non-separation, or non-dispersion, of ownership does not affect the firm's basic decisions. The same holds true for small businesses. In order to survive and grow, even an owner–manager of a small business has to follow the same path.

11.7 THE BODY OF EMPLOYEES AS THE CONTROLLING GROUP, REVISITED

In a world of exchange by agreement, who 'controls' the firm is a matter of definition.[26] It is difficult to identify the controlling group which holds the power to set the terms of membership for all participants and to select the basic value criteria that will be employed in the organization's decision-making process.[27] However, with two observations concerning the distribution of surplus within firms, I conclude that the body of employees is the controlling group. Other stakeholders, such as shareholders, trade partners and banks, when they join the organization, accept their leader's position and stay friendly unless circumstances change.

First, large firms usually do not increase dividend payment even when there are large profits. Instead, firms expand retained earnings and reinvest this profit into the organization mainly for the employees' benefit. Over a long periods of boom and depression, other stakeholders have stayed friendly unless circumstances change. For instance, with stable dividend payment of only 5 yen a year per share, many shareholders remain friendly. Banks which are sure to recover their loan principal and promised interest payments will continue to support existing management. Once-prosperous firms, such as Toyobo, Toray, Mitsubishi Heavy Industries and Nippon Steel, are the notable examples. For instance, Toray earned large profits in the 1960s when it enjoyed a monopoly in nylon production and was one of the pioneering suppliers of polyester. However, Toray's dividends increased slowly, reaching their peak at 8 yen per share per annum in FY 1969. Dividends soon decreased to around 5 yen per year.[28]

Second, large firms spend large sums of money on their employees in preparation for periods of hardship, such as a business depression. Many large firms begin to diversify in their heyday when they spend retained profits. Mergers and acquisitions (M&As) are not popular for this objective,[29] since the purpose is not profit itself through efficient use of internal funds but the creation of an expanded workplace for employees. As a result, diversification attempts on average have not been very successful, and thus financial statements tend to show weak profits. Besides investments for diversification, large firms often pay extra money to employees working outside the firm, called *shukko*. For instance, recently Japanese steel firms have suffered a serious slump, and many workers continue as employees, but work outside the firm. The reward is lower because their organization-specific skill is almost worthless outside the home company, which must pay extra to compensate for the difference in salary. In the case of Nippon Steel, the largest steel maker, the number of employees working outside the firm was more than 15 000 in 1993 (this number had been over 10 000 since 1989), about 30 per cent of Nippon Steel's total employment. The firm is said to pay compensation until these employees reach the retirement age of 60. This firm still pays the shareholders' annual dividend of 2.5 yen per share even though the business is seriously in the red. Other major steel makers have ceased paying dividends, but even those firms also continue to pay extra payments to those employees working outside the firm.[30] In a world of exchange by agreement, at any moment each agent can re-evaluate the future prospects. The last case demonstrates that shareholders cannot force the directors to refrain from decreasing dividends to zero, instead of continuing the extra payments.[31]

One may argue that friendly shareholders are not homogeneous and that conflicts of interest arise among friendly shareholders. Also many argue that, unless the firm is willing to pay the required minimum dividend, shareholders are allowed to voice their concerns to the management. The above case suggests, however, that there may exist potential conflicts of interest among shareholders, and that each shareholder may have a chance to voice concerns only for the common interest of a stable dividend payment, which is not always realized or observed.

11.8   ORGANIZATION AS A DECISION UNIT AND FIRM AS A LEGAL FICTION

The view of organizations underlying the above discussion does not depend on the legal definition of a firm. As Tirole (1988, p. 16) points out, the economist's contractual view of a long-run arrangement of its units 'has relatively little to do with the legal definition of a firm'. The controlling group, the body of employees and the existing directors supported by them, recognize in their decision making that the legal boundary of a firm is only one of many constraints. But this legal boundary is not necessarily critically binding.[32] Once our focus turns to the elements of organizational architecture chosen by the controlling group, defining a formal organization by using the legal definition becomes inappropriate as it can easily misidentify 'the effective boundaries of the organization' (Milgrom and Roberts, 1992, p. 20). Thus, unless the issue depends on the actual boundary of the firm as a legal entity, it makes little or no sense to distinguish the 'inside' of the firm from the 'outside'.

In terms of firms as legal entities, large Japanese firms are relatively small. The size of the actual organization may differ greatly from the legal size. The same applies also to the predominance of small businesses. It is the effective boundaries of the organization that are crucial to understanding the working mechanism of the economy. In the next chapter, I will focus on how 'the effective boundaries' are relevant and important to the decision making of the controlling group.

The controlling group is often a union of several groups, each of which does not necessarily exercise equal bargaining power. Employees are a collection of different groups of workers, and one group of workers or a collection of groups of workers form the controlling group. Thus the preceding discussion does not imply that employees in a firm are strongly united and form the controlling group as a whole. Other groups of workers outside the controlling group may be in a relatively weak position. As a result, in a R&D-oriented firm, for instance, the body of personnel in the R&D field often forms a part of the controlling group, and its representatives are selected as board members. This functions as a guarantee for a high return on investment in organization-specific R&D skill formation.

This view also suggests that the legal boundary of the firm is much larger than the actual boundary for the controlling group's decision-making process.

In some cases a firm can be better understood as a collection of independent decision making units, each of which has its own controlling group that forms a part of the firm's controlling group. Thus the firm's controlling group can be thought of as the union of each individual decision-making unit's controlling group. Each individual group is not necessarily exclusive to any one union. Some of the individual groups stay within the firm while others cross the firm's boundary and are part of other firms' boundaries. The tie between groups is strong in some while relatively weak in others.[33]

Therefore, not only an inside–outside distinction with the legal definition of a firm makes little or no sense, but also the marking of effective boundaries, whatever the definition, does not necessarily make sense. Any effective boundary cannot be the only one which affects the behaviour of a controlling group or a body of particular resource owners joining the group. Two points follow from this observation. First, an activity or a decision unit is often both inside the boundary with one definition and outside with another, but the controlling group remains the same. Second, that an activity or a decision unit is inside the boundary of an organization whose controlling group is X does not imply that it is outside the boundary of another organization whose controlling group is not X.[34] For instance, Toyota and Nissan are arch-rivals, but both have maintained long-term close relationships with the same suppliers. Thus these suppliers can be regarded as inside the boundaries of these two organizations, often called *keiretsu*.[35] I call these relationships 'long-term relationships with non-exclusiveness' and will study them closely in the next chapter, since their prevalence is one of the most striking peculiarities of Japanese industrial organization.

I now turn to those issues concerning the factors which determine an organization's effective boundaries, relations between those boundaries, and their working mechanism. The two basic facts of Japanese firms and industrial organization, namely, the predominance of small businesses and the slimness of large firms, and the intra-firm organizational structure and inter-firm relationships in general are interrelated and should be explained in the manner discussed above. The nature of the basic logic underlying the above argument is technological in character, which means it must be common everywhere and is not peculiar to Japan. Environmental factors, such as the legal system, history as culture condition both the skill formation process and the shape and function of the organization.

As Hart (1989, pp. 1958–9) states, 'neoclassical theory begs the question of what defines a given firm or what determines its boundaries. . . . [m]ost formal models of the firm are extremely rudimentary, capable only of portraying hypothetical firms that bear little relation to the complex organizations we see in the world'. I do not intend to present a new formal model, nor do I have a persuasive answer to the above issues. The study of inter-firm relationships in the next chapter has two justifications. First, the Japanese economy by itself is worthy of close study, particularly because of its rapid growth and size, in which the form and working of inter-firm relationships are strikingly unique. Second, the Japanese economy is a rich source of material for studying general issues related to organizations.

The basic logic used in this chapter is exactly the same as that used in Chapter 4. Therefore all the inter-firm relationships closely organized by assemblers such as Toyota and Nissan should be considered as organizations. Each bundle of inter-firm relationships is organized by the controlling group formed as a union of the controlling groups in each unit, which is long-term but non-exclusive. The common objective which governs the behaviour of all the units in a group and the relationships among these units is the formation and maintenance of both the organization- and relation-specific human capital.[36] The controlling group of the whole system is the assembler, which has the power to set the terms of membership of this system, and selects the basic value criteria for the system.

Beyond this, however, I do not have persuasive answers to such subtler questions as follow. (1) Why is Toyota so slim and why does it buy a large portion, about 70 per cent, of its car parts from outside? (2) What affects the assembler's make-or-buy decisions? For instance, the items that Toyota makes 'in-house' are different from Nissan's. (3) Why did Toyota establish Hosei Brake in 1968 as a joint venture with Akebono Brake, the largest brake maker in Japan, besides buying brakes from Akebono and how does it coordinate the relationships with these two suppliers? Most other Japanese car assemblers purchase brakes from Akebono, but none has such a joint venture. To answer these questions, we need at least a rough picture of what supports these relationships, and a rough estimate of the cost of forming and maintaining these relationships. Other readers may be concerned with the exclusivity concerning newcomers and the harmful effects this has on competition and efficiency of the market. These points are discussed in the next chapter.

11.9   CONCLUDING REMARKS

In Japan, organization-specific human capital is the fundamental factor governing the structure and function of organizations, such as firms, and inter-firm relationships. Those organizations are organized so as to induce core employees to invest in the development of organization-specific skills through the establishment of a stable organizational structure. As a result, the body of employees is the controlling group, and most directors are selected from among employees. Friendly shareholders, and friendly funds suppliers like banks, support the existing directors, including directors selected from outside the firm. The slimness of Japanese large firms and the predominance of small businesses in the Japanese economy, with long-term but non-exclusive relationships, should be analysed in a manner which recognizes the nature of Japanese organizations. Other characteristics of the Japanese case, such as the absence of hostile takeovers and the low number of mergers between well-managed firms should also be viewed with these factors in mind.

Two points should be noted. First, the basic logic underlying the above argument on the formation and maintenance of organization-specific human capital and its importance is technological, which means it can be applied everywhere, including Japan and the USA. Therefore this chapter's argument concerning Japanese organization must also be applied to organizations outside Japan. Some environmental factors may cause peculiarities, but the basic mechanism is the same. Thus Alchian and Demsetz (1972, p. 789) comment on American firms that '[i]nstead of thinking of shareholders as joint owners, we can think of them as investors, like bondholders, except that the stockholders are more optimistic than bondholders about the enterprise prospects'.[37] I do not argue in this chapter that Japan is unique. Whether the above form of organization is more prevalent in Japan than in other economies, such as in the USA, Germany and Italy, is another question. When there is something peculiar to Japanese organizations, such as intra-firm organizational structure or inter-firm relationships, it is due not to the role played by organization-specific human capital but to environmental factors that affect the formation and maintenance of this human capital.

Second, each individual resource owner makes the best use of his or her own resource under given constraints. When a group of human capital investors establishes an organization and takes the controlling group position in many organizations, its prevalence constitutes a constraint binding each individual agent's choice. Under these constraints, individuals, organizations and industries make decisions and compete. This results in the existing industrial structure of the economy and international division of labour. The above argument may explain part of the success of Japan's machinery industry. However, it is not necessarily useful in explaining the success of the Japanese economy in general. As shown in the next chapter, extensive division of labour has hindered the coordination among participants in many industries, such as the distribution and textile industries, resulting in high costs, low quality of products and low market responsiveness. In these industries we observe the same characteristics as those found in the car industry, such as the extensive division of labour, long-term close relationships with non-exclusive characteristics, directors selected from the body of employees, friendly shareholders and friendly creditors.

The above argument suggests that the assumption of a profit maximizing firm may be invalid. This is a logical consequence of the contract view of a firm. The existing firm is a legal fiction which may not represent the actual unit of decision making. Also the controlling group is not the body of shareholders whose target in the neoclassical view of a firm is to maximize profits. Even when the controlling group maximizes the joint extra income (the sum of income which is greater than that obtainable in an outside opportunity) of all participants including shareholders, say, 'profit in a wider sense', this is different from the term 'profit' in the classical sense and from the figures in financial statements.

How then to justify the previous arguments which depend on the profit maximizing assumption? Frankly, there is no other choice but to use the profit-maximizing assumption. However, this does not seriously affect the prior arguments, for three reasons. First, although a 'firm' is not profit-maximizing, each resource owner makes the best use of his or her resources.

Competition is fierce in Japan, not only in product markets for final goods, intermediate goods and materials, but also in markets for capital, labour, land and so on. When fierce competition prevails everywhere, the behaviour of such an organization cannot help but resemble that of a profit-maximizing firm. Second, deviations from profit-maximizing behaviour exist everywhere, irrespective of the firm size, and there is no reason to assume that they are greater, for instance, in larger firms. In addition, I used profit rate data in Part I not in absolute value but in relative value. Third, arguments other than the comparison of profit rate are invulnerable to the deviation from the profit-maximizing assumption. I referred to the number of new entrants without specifying who made the decision to enter, therefore the argument can be reinterpreted as that of a 'non-profit-maximizing firm'. The same is also true for the examination of whether small businesses are seriously handicapped under the dual structure. In general, the departure from the profit-maximizing assumption of a firm will not greatly affect the arguments in the first three parts of this volume, except for that in Chapter 7 on corporate groups, where the role of shareholders is crucial.

12 Inter-firm Relationships

12.1 INTRODUCTION

The predominance of small businesses and the slimness of large firms are the two basic facts of the Japanese economy. As shown in the previous chapter, however, a firm is a legal fiction and its boundary is usually different from the effective boundary of the decision-making unit, hereafter referred to as an *organization*. Therefore these two basic facts do not necessarily imply that the effective boundary of the Japanese organization is small and that the Japanese economy is idiosyncratically decentralized. In this chapter we consider how organizations and inter-organizational relationships are formed and function, how the economic activities within each firm are coordinated and who assumes the leadership in designing the system for this coordination.

In discussing Japan, the recent trend is to use such terms as *keiretsu* and networks, particularly when trying to explain the 'secret' of Japan's industrial success. But these terms are ill-defined and even misleading. As shown, *keiretsu* is too vague to be an analytical concept. Of three commonly discussed subgroups of *keiretsu* – horizontal *keiretsu* (corporate groups), vertical *keiretsu* (supplier–assembler relationships), and distribution *keiretsu* – in Chapter 7 the first was shown to be materially non-existent, and in Chapter 4 the second was found to be inappropriate for accurate analysis and should be replaced by other terms, for example the term 'supplier–assembler relationships'. In Section 12.2, I discuss the third, distribution *keiretsu*, but only as an illustration of what happens within closely related organizations, for which the term *keiretsu* is again a source of misunderstanding.

The term '*network*' has become the vogue in describing contemporary organizations. One of the major reasons of this increased interest is the emergence of what Best (1990) labelled 'the New Competition', the competitive rise of small entrepreneurial firms, of regional districts and of new industries, whose characteristic model of organization is a network of lateral and horizontal linkages within and among firms. Coupling the conventional image of the Japanese economy with *keiretsu* trading, the predominance of corporate groups and cooperative behaviour of firms, we see that there is now tremendous interest in 'network organizations' in Japan. The two basic facts mentioned above may stimulate this interest further. However, I do not use this in the study of inter-firm relationships for two reasons. First, as shown above, the conventional image is totally false. Second, as Nohria (1992, p. 12) points out, from 'a network perspective, all organizations can be characterized as networks and indeed are properly understood only in these terms. So to say an organization has a network form is a tautology'.

217

As mentioned in the previous chapter, economists do not have a highly developed theory either of the firm or of the market. The established formal model does not provide any rigorously persuasive answers to the following questions: How are inter-firm relationships formed and maintained? How do they function? Are they long-term and stable? Are they exclusive for rivals and closed for new entrants? Underlying these questions is the basic question of Coase (1937): 'Why does a firm emerge at all in a specialized exchange economy?'

Most of this chapter is a series of case studies on inter-firm relationships viewed from three points: (1) whether 'transaction costs', particularly for large Japanese firms, are lower than elsewhere; (2) whether inter-firm relationships fail to respond to changes in the market environment, such as demand and technology; and (3) whether new entry to some Japanese markets is made difficult, and even impossible in some cases, because of these relationships. I choose these three points for two reasons. First, the questions listed above are too general to answer directly. Second, these issues concerning Japanese inter-firm relationships attract wide attention both from critics who see them as a cause of the 'closed' nature of the Japanese economy and from those supporters who see them as a source of Japan's industrial success.

Neither Japanese nor American firms (nor firms in other countries) are particularly badly managed, and the mechanism of comparative advantage works in all countries. Inter-firm relationships upon which the production system is organized may be one reason for Japan's success in the machinery industries, including the motor industry. However, we observe similar relationships in comparatively disadvantaged industries, like the textile industry. Focus in this chapter centres not on the contribution of inter-firm relationships to productivity increases and economic growth, but on their functions themselves.

Beginning with Section 12.4, I present five case studies from three industries. The first is the supplier–assembler relationship in the motor industry. The other four cases are from industries which have been regarded as not so successful: one from the distribution sector and three from the textile industry. The basic objective of these case studies is to investigate Japanese inter-firm relationships in action, applying to them now developing theories of the firm. In this manner we can reach an understanding of the organizational issues far better than with conventional theories. In return this will contribute to the study of both the firm and the market. Japanese firms and their inter-firm relationships are a rich source of material for further research along this line.

At least four observations follow from these case studies. (1) An extensive division of labour with long-term relationships prevails throughout Japan. (2) These relationships are formed and maintained as a result of voluntary agreement of rational participants. A new entrant offering a profitable business opportunity in this manner develops such relationships with its trade partners. (3) 'Transaction costs' through these relationships are not particularly low for large firms in comparatively advantaged industries.

(4) Firms within these relationships often fail to adapt to environmental changes partly because of these relationships. This can also be explained as a rational choice of related parties not to adapt. The last point is observed not only in rather comparatively disadvantaged industries but in advantaged industries as well.[1]

Section 12.2 offers an illustration of inter-firm relationships. I briefly discuss distribution *keiretsu* and make six general comments on their alleged exclusivity. Section 12.3 defines issues for the case studies that follow. Beginning with Section 12.4 I present five cases on inter-firm relationships in the light of the three points mentioned above. Section 12.4 concerns the motor industry. Section 12.5 discusses the success story of Seven-Eleven Japan in the distribution sector. The next three sections are case studies from the textile industry: synthetic fibre, silk dyeing in *kohaba-yuzen*, and men's wool suits. In Section 12.9 I discuss one most striking peculiarity of Japan's industrial organization, namely, the predominance of stable, long-term inter-firm relationships with a non-exclusive characteristic. Section 12.10 presents concluding remarks.

12.2 AN ILLUSTRATION OF INTER-FIRM RELATIONSHIPS: DISTRIBUTION *KEIRETSU*

Closely coordinated inter-firm relationships abound in the fields of distribution and marketing, which the term 'marketing channel' symbolically reveals. Manufacturers, wholesalers, retailers and the like are found within channel arrangements. They share the workload for various production functions or product flows, such as physical possession, ownership, promotion, negotiation, financing, risking, ordering and payment.

As Stern and El-Ansary (1988, p. 14) argued, 'the basic economic rationale for the emergence of channel intermediaries and institutional arrangements can be understood in terms of the need for exchange and exchange efficiency, minimization of assortment discrepancies, routinization, and the facilitation of search procedures'. Like the car production system based on closely coordinated supplier–assembler relationships studied in Chapter 4, a marketing channel is organized and functions so as to minimize the costs for providing goods and services, where the activities of each decision unit are coordinated by a channel leader. The channel leader's power is the result of the specific characteristics, experience or history of the firm and its management, and in addition to its accumulated human capital. Alternatively, the power source may reflect particular characteristics of those environmental forces affecting the channel and the channel member's ability to capitalize on these forces. Thus the basic logic underlying the formation and maintenance of organization-specific human capital and its importance as seen in the previous chapter also applies to these marketing channels. Therefore an inside–outside distinction of a firm both as a legal definition and as an effective organizational boundary does not necessarily make sense.

The Japanese distribution system has quite often been criticized, particularly in the recent US–Japan Structural Impediments Initiatives, as causing the closed nature of the domestic market.[2] Critics argue that Japanese distributors, such as wholesalers and retailers, are members of distribution *keiretsu* controlled by a leader, typically a manufacturer, which makes it difficult for new rivals, particularly those from abroad, to establish distributors. This argument is too ill-defined for a close examination. With illustrations of inter-firm relationships I make six general comments on this argument, and in later sections I investigate the exclusiveness and closed nature of inter-firm relationships using case studies.

(1) Firms in almost every industry always assert that they suffer from 'excessive competition'. Coupled with Japan's industrial success, this fact is inconsistent with the argument that Japanese markets are closed to new entrants. Therefore, even if some markets are closed, their importance to the whole economy must be small.

(2) In every developed economy, members of a distribution–marketing channel are closely connected and their activities well coordinated when this is efficient. Thus whether there is something essential which distinguishes the Japanese distribution system as *keiretsu* from those of other economies deserves close examination.

(3) In a world of exchange by agreement, long-term relationships are not merely the result of choices in the past but must be based on its future prospects. Therefore the observed long-term stability does not imply its further continuation. As will be exemplified in the case studies, entrants which provided profitable business opportunities could find able trade partners even in markets where long-term relationships had prevailed.

(4) People often mistakenly believe that in Japan long-term relationships are maintained almost always with only one party at least for one side, and are therefore exclusive. At least in Japan, however, this is not the case. Like supplier–assembler relationships in the motor industry studied in Chapter 4, retailers in almost every alleged distribution *keiretsu* industry actually trade with multiple suppliers. Motor industry distribution is a noted exception, while other industries such as home electronics, cosmetics and groceries are not exclusive.

(5) A distribution–marketing channel is organized so as to minimize the costs of providing goods and services. If what consumers demand differs between economies, distribution–marketing organizations may also differ. One reason why members in the Japanese motor distribution channels are closely connected is that, with highly differentiated products, supply costs increase tremendously in the absence of such relationships. For instance, in one month in the spring of 1990, Toyota provided about 3 000 types of Mark II (a mid-size sedan called the Cressida in the US market). They produced on average only 7.8 cars for each type, and only one car for more than half of all types. Toyota sells cars in Japan through 312 dealers (about 4 500 shops each with about ten sales personnel), and it is rare for a dealer to sell more than two cars of the same type in one month. They can provide custom-made cars within two weeks.[3]

(6) The workload is shared among members of a marketing channel, according to the organizational design. As a result, the role of a retailer (for instance, a department store in apparel goods) in Japan is different from that in some other economies. This may function as an entry barrier or cause misunderstanding. For instance, a Japanese department store sells mostly on consignment, and it is the wholesalers who perform the merchandising function and bear the risk of unsold stock. One foreign apparel manufacturer proposed a direct trade with a department store but was advised to go to a Japanese wholesaler (an apparel maker). This foreign importer claimed this was an abuse of power by the distribution *keiretsu*.

Akebono Brake's recent success in the US market is another example. Like Japanese manufacturers in other machinery product markets, including car parts, Akebono, the largest manufacturer of car brakes in Japan, has supplied custom-made products to each assembler in a series of long-term relationships. Typically, a Japanese assembler requests a supplier to present a rough design of a customized part four years before the purchase of the product. Akebono proposed the same transaction to such US car assemblers as Ford and GM. These firms, accustomed to purchasing standardized products from US car parts manufacturers, welcomed the proposal. If a US car parts manufacturer proposes a transaction to Japanese assemblers with standardized products, buyers will likely request some customization without a high additional charge, as they do with Japanese suppliers. This usually prevents the parties from reaching an agreement. This is a result of differences in both the supplier's responsiveness to market demands and in social attitude toward customization.

12.3 ARE TRANSACTION COSTS LOWER FOR LARGE JAPANESE FIRMS?

Despite the two basic facts of the Japanese economy discussed above, many people may still argue that large Japanese firms play a predominant role in the economy because they subordinate and control small businesses. The conventional view of small businesses is symbolized by the term 'dual structure', which suggests that large firms in the modernized industrial sector subordinate, control and exploit small businesses in the traditional sector. This implicitly assumes that large firms can and do exercise significant power in exploiting small businesses, whose freedom of choice is restricted. What is the cause of this power? What is its origin and the limits to the 'area of acceptance' (Simon, 1976, p. 133), within which the subordinate is willing to accept the decisions made by large firms? These questions lead us to an understanding of Dore's (1983, p. 463) statement:

> Transaction costs for large Japanese firms may well be lower than elsewhere. 'Opportunism' may be a lesser danger in Japan because of the explicit encouragement, and actual trading relationship of mutual good-

will. The stability of the relationship is the key. Both sides recognize an obligation to try to maintain it.

Large Japanese firms do not necessarily enjoy a free lunch in these relationships with small firms. We must investigate how the stability of the relationship is maintained, and the related costs.

As shown in Part I, we should not interpret the prevalence of inter-firm long-term relationships among small businesses and between small and large firms as a direct result of the subordination of small businesses to large firms in the 'dual structure' situation. Like large firms, small businesses enjoy wide freedom of choice in a world of exchange by agreement, and we should regard these choices as mutual, voluntary agreements. Large firms also need to offer incentives to induce small firms to establish and maintain these long-term relationships.

Therefore, to validate Dore's statement, we have to ask why large firms can offer incentives at a cost lower in Japan than elsewhere. The prevalence of 'moralized trading relationships of mutual goodwill' and the strong tendency of most Japanese to 'feel more comfortable in high-trust relations of friendly give-and-take' (Dore 1983, pp. 463 and 472) may be persuasive for some; however, we must also ask why, how, and even whether it is true. 'Trust' is a charming and inviting term that, without a clear definition and understanding, creates confusion. As Granovetter (1992, p. 40) rightly noted, 'even [t]o say . . . that such devices produce "trust" seems . . . to stretch the word too far, where it applies to all situations where individuals are willing to enter a transaction'. I analyse below five cases of inter-firm relationships in three industries to see how they are maintained. I also examine whether transaction costs are indeed lower in Japan than elsewhere, and whether long-term relationships function as an entry barrier.

When we accept as valid Dore's (1983) argument that transaction costs for large Japanese firms may well be lower in Japan than elsewhere, the conclusion that the legal boundary of a firm is different from the actual one leads us immediately to the following questions. Why, then, do large firms exist? Does Dore's argument apply only to large firms? If so, then why is it possible, and what ensures that large firms enjoy such privileges? Transactions are thought to be brought within the firm when doing so would reduce costs. Therefore we need some explanation of why in Japan the costs for carrying out transactions within the firm are lower than the costs in the market. As Tirole (1988, p. 20) pointed out when commenting on the technological view, which defines the size of a firm, it is not clear why economies of scale should necessarily be exploited within the firm, when they could, *a priori*, also be obtained through contracting between legally separate entities. Inter-firm relationships should be seen as the result of voluntary agreements between firms, even when they involve large firms and small firms.

The following questions are related to what Dore refers to as 'moralized trading relationships of mutual goodwill . . . [whose] stability . . . is the key'

(p. 463), and the term 'trust'. Why have these relationships and trust emerged, and how have they been maintained and reinforced? How have they affected the behaviour of the firms, their trade patterns and both inter-firm and intra-firm relationships? What are their working mechanisms? What are the costs of their creation and maintenance? If there are differences in such relationships among industrial sectors, how and why they appear? To what degree should we blame the peculiarities of Japanese inter-firm relationships on 'environmental factors', such as culture and history? Arrow (1974, p. 23) observed that trust 'is an important lubricant of a social system. It is extremely efficient; it saves a lot of trouble to have a fair degree of reliance on other people's word'. However, we should be careful not 'to stretch the word too far', as Granovetter (1992, pp. 40–1) rightly cautioned. For him trust 'refer[s] to circumstances where one enters a transaction believing that transaction partners will behave properly for reasons that transcend pure self-interest'. Too much emphasis on such factors leads us to an 'over-socialized conception of man in modern sociology' (Granovetter ibid., p. 28)[4] as well as creating several myths concerning the Japanese economy. Conversely, too little emphasis leads to an 'undersocialized conception'.[5] In the following case studies we explore the development of trust as well as the creation, maintenance and reinforcement of commercial relationships. Japanese firms attain their efficiency 'in spite of relational contracting' (Dore, 1983, p. 473), which assures relatively stable trade relations.

In presenting the basic premises underlying the network perspective on organizations, Nohria (1992, p. 4) noted that '[n]etworks contain actions, and in turn are shaped by them'. However, it is not clear to what degree 'environmental factors' determine the peculiarities of inter-firm relationships in Japan. Here I only refer to phenomena that suggest the importance of Nohria's premise.

Trevor (1988) reported the development and changing process of inter-firm relations between Toshiba Consumer Products in Plymouth and its suppliers. This process began in 1981, just after the withdrawal of the joint venture partner, Rank Radio International. Trevor explained that by '[r]ealizing that management could not go on in the same old way, it committed itself to a new structure and style of work organization, employee participation and, last but not least, relations with suppliers' (p. 5). 'The absence in Britain and other Western countries of a well developed network of reliable suppliers with whom they can cultivate long-term business relations is seen as a serious disadvantage by Japanese companies' (p. 141). Toshiba requested its British suppliers to adopt the business practices of Japanese suppliers, and has succeeded in developing the relationships similar to those found in Japan. Many Japanese managers complain that one difficulty they face with their foreign subsidiaries is the custom of 'job hopping'. It makes their intensive on-the-job training and human capital investment unprofitable and unattractive. However, other managers say that it is not so difficult to overcome 'job hopping' by offering employees a chance to participate and receive further training, and thus benefit from higher rewards.

12.4   A CASE FROM THE MOTOR INDUSTRY

Next I present five case studies. The first one is of the supplier–assembler relationships in the motor industry, considered to symbolize Japan's industrial success. As mentioned in the Introduction, firms in Japan, the USA, or other countries are not particularly poorly managed. Likewise, neither car nor textile manufacturers (or firms in other industries such as distribution) in Japan are particularly badly managed. However, the notions of comparative advantage suggest that there will *always* be some firms in any country which are relatively uncompetitive compared to firms in the same industry. Later cases show that the inter-firm relationships among uncompetitive firms have the same characteristics as those among competitive firms.

A widely held misconception is that because of the closely connected network of inter-firm relationships, called *keiretsu*, competitive markets exist in a strictly limited area in Japan. I, and most other economists, disagree with Dore's (1983, p. 467) statement: 'Competition between Japanese firms is intense, but only in markets which are (a) consumer markets and (b) expanding . . . What does concern us here are markets in producers' goods, in intermediates. And for many such commodities markets can hardly be said to exist.' Contrary to this view, the following cases will show that competition is intense even in non-expanding, non-consumer markets.

The total number of cars made by Japanese car manufacturers was only 20 000 in 1955, when Toyota began their full-scale car production with the Crown. In ten years the number grew to 696 000 and in 20 years, 4 568 000, of which 40 per cent were exported. At the beginning of this explosive growth, there was no history of a comparable mass-production industry in Japan. Manufacturers had to improve the low quality of production material and sometimes defective equipment while raising the low level of product technology. For example, in 1958, Toyota successfully bid for a contract to supply vehicles through the US Army Procurement Agency (APA). However, Toyota had to make serious efforts to pass the APA's strict quality inspection (see Chapter 4). No suppliers could make car parts of sufficient quality. This suggests that the situation of car manufacturers at that time was similar to that of the above mentioned Toshiba Consumer Products in 1981.

Car manufacturers had to persuade suppliers to invest in the development of human capital, accumulate technical know-how of sufficient quality to improve the plant and equipment. Moreover, these manufacturers had to build their own production network along with their suppliers. This was not an easy task. Car manufacturers had to create complicated production systems on a large scale at great risk. Few viewed the future of the Japanese motor industry with much optimism. Finally, with an uncertain future, the financial situation of car manufacturers was a further difficulty.

Even after successfully establishing efficient production networks with suppliers, car manufacturers had to make continuous efforts to maintain this system. They had to induce suppliers to make additional commitments: to keep up with constantly changing consumer demands and rapid technical advances in production. Moreover, car manufacturers had to give technical assistance and advice to suppliers and, in supervising the total system, maintain product consistency and uniformly upgrade technical capabilities. The costs of such efforts, part of 'transaction costs' of such a production network, have been tremendous, as shown in detail in Chapter 4. One difficulty that Mitsubishi Motors at Mizushima confronted in establishing mass-production was to dispel the distrust of suppliers caused by their actions in 1958 and 1959, when demand for three-wheel trucks, their main product at that time, sharply declined (see Chapter 4). This case shows how difficult it is to acquire and maintain the trust of suppliers.

Impressed by the prevalence of long-term relations within Japan's car production networks, we may wonder what is the source of such efficiency improvements and product innovations. For example, it is said that Toyota has never broken off relations with any one of its near 200 suppliers. The answer to this puzzle is rather simple. Instead of the type of competition in spot markets, motor manufacturers try to induce suppliers to continuously improve both efficiency and product quality. For example, they usually adopt a double 'sourcing' policy, and use supplier rivalry to stimulate competition. Each supplier usually makes two or more parts, and a supplier with a good performance record can expect an increase in total sales for the next period. By supervising the suppliers' production process, constant meetings and joint R&D, car manufacturers often have the ability to provide accurate and detailed advice on improving a supplier's efficiency.[6]

Three points about this relationship deserve attention. (1) As pointed out in Chapter 4, each relationship has externality effects, namely, it affects other relationships in the whole production system, and therefore an assembler's freedom of choice is not so wide as it would be in the spot market. This is a cost of having a long-term relationship. (2) A purchaser's double 'sourcing' policy incurs costs as well. Toyota established Hosei Brake in 1968 as a joint venture with Akebono Brake, the largest brake maker in Japan. Toyota purchases brakes from both Akebono and Hosei. Akebono enjoys the top position in the brake market because of its production know-how and economies of scale. Therefore Toyota continuously incurs greater costs for this choice. (3) Because of the long-term characteristics of relationships, it is not easy to begin supplying Japanese assemblers. Once begun, these relationships continue because of the external effect faced by an assembler when terminating a contract even with an unqualified partner. But this point seems to be overemphasized in much of the literature. The decision to form a long-term relationship is forward looking and, as mentioned in Chapter 4, Toyota actually increased the number of suppliers over time.

12.5 THE DISTRIBUTION INDUSTRY: THE CASE OF SEVEN-ELEVEN JAPAN

The next case is from distribution, the success story of Seven-Eleven Japan. This is the largest convenience store franchise and the pioneer of this form of business in Japan. The average store area is 100m², where about 3000 items are displayed. The basic concept of a convenience store and the know-how for its operation were imported from the USA. However, both the actual layout of Japanese stores and their method of operation are different from those found in the USA.

Seven-Eleven Japan (hereafter, SEJ) has achieved remarkable successes in the Japanese distribution field. The first store appeared in 1974. By the end of February 1992, the number of franchise stores was 4752 and the number of SEJ employees was 1814. The equity value of SEJ at the end of March 1992 amounted to 38 per cent of that of Toyota with 72 000 employees and 150 per cent of that of Nissan with 56 000 employees. Convenience chains like SEJ have greatly changed Japanese daily life.

This success could only have been accomplished with active commitments of both franchisees and supporting wholesalers. Like Toyota in the 1950s (see Chapter 4), SEJ had to persuade the related parties to commit themselves to the creation of a well-functioning network of inter-firm relationships. Though SEJ was established as a subsidiary of Ito-Yoka-Do, one of Japan's most successful general merchandise store chains, in cooperation with South Land of the USA the prospects for the future of convenience chain store business at that time appeared to be just as bleak as that faced by Toyota in the mid-1950s. SEJ was not a large firm and almost nobody thought it would grow as rapidly as it did.

The Japanese distribution sector has been notorious for its under-development and inefficiency. In the industry the catchword of government policies during the past several decades has been 'modernization'. A stable network of long-term inter-firm relationships, often criticized as distribution *keiretsu*, can be found in almost every field of distribution. SEJ had to challenge these relationships and the sense of stability prevalent among related parties.

Three points about the success of SEJ deserve attention. (1) Despite the prevalence of distribution networks with long-term inter-firm relationships, traditional distribution channels were inefficient and not responsive to environmental factors for SEJ to complete successfully. This implies that the 'transaction costs' were high for established large firms, such as manufacturers and distributors of processed foods and daily products. Because of the coordination costs and the externality of each choice (recall the 'safety devices' mentioned in Chapter 4), leaders in the traditional channels were not responsive to environmental changes, such as demands and technological innovations.

(2) Confronted by established long-term inter-firm relationships, SEJ succeeded by cooperating with suppliers and franchisees, most of which were members of the traditional channels. This was possible not only because those relationships were not exclusive, but also because established relationships were a result of rational choices and some distributors changed their business to become more profitable. This, in return, suggests that at least some long-term relationships are maintained simply because related parties

do not find a more profitable business alternative. Coca-Cola's entry into the Japanese market is another famous success story. Facing the traditional distribution networks and anticipating the coming age of the automatic vending machine, in the 1950s Coca-Cola introduced into Japan a new type of distribution system called a 'route sales system' that bypassed the traditional channels. In this case, most partners were found from outside the traditional channels.

(3) The position of established large firms with long-term relationships is often implicitly assumed to be advantageous. This so-called 'first-mover' advantage, however, does not always hold true. On the contrary, in many situations the second-mover advantage may be greater. These relationships require the commitment of related parties, but commitment restrict one's own set of future possible choices or actions. It involves credible warranties that some future choices are destroyed. Thus an assembler's freedom of choice is limited in the motor industry. This also applies to home electronics makers who have well established long-term relationships with retailers, which, once the source of its prosperity, now results in high transaction costs. Because of past success and the existing externality among retailers, makers cannot appropriately adapt the distribution system to the changing environment by selecting new retailers.

12.6 THE SYNTHETIC FIBRE TEXTILE INDUSTRY

The next three cases are from the textile industry, the first involving synthetic fibre textile production, mainly that of nylon and polyester. The mass-production-type machinery industries, such as car and electronics products, are for most the symbol of Japan's industrial success. Inter-firm relationships and division of labour among firms in these industries, particularly those in the motor industry, have drawn much attention. As theories of comparative advantage suggest, however, firms in other industries are not particularly badly managed and also contributed to Japan's industrial success. The textile industry is a representative of those industries, which were once export industries but have lost their international comparative advantage.[7] Relative to the other two cases in the silk dyeing and wool textile industries, inter-firm relationships in synthetic fibre textile production is the most recent. The organizer's initial difficulties were similar to those faced by car manufacturers and Seven-Eleven Japan.

Synthetic fibre production began in Japan with two rayon producers, nylon by Toray in 1955 and polyester by Toray and Teijin in 1958. These two were not the most prosperous in the textile industry of that time. They faced two challenges: the creation of product markets and the organization of the production system. Here we focus on the latter. Although their primary concern was fibre production, they had to persuade firms to use these new fibres. Weavers, dye-works, garment manufacturers and retailers were all potential fibre users and members of the production system. Fibre producers were large firms, large enough to be the licensees of Du Pont and ICI patents. Neither the future prospects for the new business nor the stability of these two firms appeared promising. Like suppliers in the motor industry, related parties had to make commitments to the new technologies.

The synthetic fibre manufacturers chose to base production in a local area, called *sanchi* [literally, a local production area], in Fukui and Ishikawa Prefectures in the Hokuriku District. In this area, many textile firms and related manufacturing had formed a large specialized area for rayon textile production and had prospered for the preceding several decades upon the long tradition of silk textile production. Synthetic fibre makers organized their own production system called a 'production team' in this area. Inter-firm relationships within these teams were called *keiretsu* and differed in three respects from the traditional relationships in the textile industry. First, a fibre maker was the team leader, playing an active role in the team's technological development and providing technical guidance to other members. Second, a fibre maker bore an incomparably large portion of the risk in this new business, while other members finished products as piecework. Third, the degree of exclusiveness of inter-firm relationships was rather high, that is, members usually belonged to one production team only.

At the start large firms had to bear the costs of creating both the product markets and the production system. As in the case of car production, these costs continued since they required continuous effort to maintain and upgrade the system. However, such costs were not due to the then existing inter-firm relationships. Their challenge was made easier by the depression of 1957–8, the most serious of the postwar period. This forced rayon textile weavers of established inter-firm networks to search for other business opportunities (see Tanaka, 1965, pp. 349–53).

Around 1970 fibre makers changed their policy and persuaded other members to become more independent and began to trade with firms outside their team or *keiretsu*. A manager of a fibre maker explained that such an exclusive relationship implied an assurance that business would remain stable even during periods of severe depressions. Fibre makers judged that such high risk-bearing relationships were no longer profitable. Thus transaction costs for these large Japanese firms were tremendous from the start, so that the basic character of inter-firm relationships was transformed.

Another point which deserves attention in this case is the recent success story of *Shin-gosen*, a series of new polyester fibre materials and their related products. These new fibres created a new expanded market for polyester around 1990. Many industry people comment that, without close cooperation among firms in the industry, such a wide variety of products with high-quality characteristics could not have been created successively in such a brief period.[8] Seven to eight fibre makers compete with each other in these new markets, and only a few firms in dye-works and the finishing stage have the capability to meet the requirements of fibre makers. The non-exclusive character of inter-firm relationships promoted since the 1970s contributed greatly to this story.[9]

12.7 A CASE FROM THE SILK DYEING INDUSTRY

The next case is from the silk dyeing industry, a traditional industry with a long history in Japan. Here also we observe complicated, but highly cooperative inter-firm relationships. Producers form an extremely developed division of labour within each of several local areas, called *sanchi*.[10] Dye-works and the finishing stage of *kohaba* silk textile (silk cloth of single breadth), especially that of *kohaba-yuzen*, is a typical Japanese traditional industry. Even today, the work for *kohaba* silk textile processing depends on the technology and techniques inherited from the pre-capitalistic era. The inter-firm relationships and organizations among related firms reflect its long history.

Nakamura (1979) compares four *sanchi* famous for *kohaba* dye-works; three traditional urban locations found in Kyoto, Tokyo and Kanazawa, and one newly developed location in the rural area of Tokamachi. The production systems of the three traditional *sanchi* are organized around the historically inherited, widely-spread social division of labour. Though modern technologies have been adopted, the basic character of this production system has not changed. The division of labour in each *sanchi* is strongly affected by its size. In 1978, the Kyoto *sanchi* had a total of about 30 000 employees and was far larger than the other two which had fewer than 1 000 employees each. The Kyoto production system was characterized by a more extensive division of labour. These firms are typically small, specializing in one specific stage of production. There is a wide variety of techniques and production technology available in Kyoto, resulting in a greater variety of products.

Three points deserve attention. (1) Tokamachi *sanchi* was newly established in the rural area far from well developed traditional areas. This *sanchi* is characterized by a highly vertically integrated production system. Dye-works in Tokamachi began in 1963, in response to the increased demand for a standardized, less expensive *kimono* which could be manufactured with simple technology and unskilled workers under a mass-production system. The most profitable period for Tokamachi firms was the second half of the 1960s. The number of employees decreased dramatically from more than 8 000 in 1971 to fewer than 4 000 in 1977. The *kohaba* dyeing industry was a collection of at least two separate sectors, though closely substitutable in both demand and technology. Various products were supplied by different firms with different technology, and the long-term inter-firm relationships in the traditional *sanchi* did not function as a critical obstacle to the development of Tokamachi *sanchi*.

(2) The production system and division of labour, even in Kyoto *sanchi*, is poorly organized and needs government support to realize improvement. One policy presented by MITI emphasizes the creation of a 'linkage production unit' (see K. Nakamura, 1993). The extensive division of labour within the long-term inter-firm relationships and the present system has not been flexible enough to reorganize and restructure. Compelled by an incentive to improve their efficiency, firms introduced many new technologies and

adjusted to the changing markets. However, inflexibility remained and 'transaction costs' for firms in inter-firm relationships proved expensive.

(3) Firms in this industry tend to be small. However, we observe here almost the same characteristics as the three preceding cases with large firms. This implies that transaction costs do not depend on the size of the firm. Therefore, if transaction costs for large firms are lower in Japan than elsewhere, those for small Japanese firms must be also lower.

12.8   THE WOOL TEXTILE INDUSTRY: THE CASE OF MEN'S SUITS

In this section we observe the production and distribution of men's wool suits.[11] The Japanese have a special preference for wool products. Most men's suits are made of wool, and the largest market for wool textiles is men's suits. More than 10 million men's suits are produced and sold in Japan every year. In the USA and UK, only 38 per cent and 56 per cent, respectively, of men's suits are made of wool, in contrast to 79 per cent in Japan in 1988.[12] Most textile firms and related manufacturing have formed a large *sanchi* in the northern part of Aichi Prefecture, at the centre of which is the city of Ichinomiya. The demand for men's suits is highly differentiated and delivery requires a long lead time. Therefore supplying men's suits is considered a risky business.

For example, trade negotiations between textile producers and buyers (typically, in Japan, makers of clothing) for the spring–summer season in 1994 were carried out in April of 1993 on a sample basis. Retail orders for products, for the same season, were taken in September and October. Therefore, for the production of sample garments, textiles had to be supplied to clothes makers in June and July. To show sample textiles in April, weavers must gather information and decide on their production strategies by the end of 1992 or the beginning of 1993, 15 months before the market opens.

Most firms in *sanchi* are small, each firm specializing in one specific work stage. They form a well-organized production system with a widely spread division of labour. This area has a history of cotton textile production, but it was only around the turn of the century that firms in this area began wool textile production. Therefore the present production system should be regarded as a result of rational and free choices by firms rather than a product of historical traditions or a result of constrained choices.

In textile production there are two groups of relatively large firms. One group is at the finishing stage, dominated by the large firm of Tsuyakin Co. This dominance is due to economies of scale. Products of most weavers are finished by those firms as piecework. The other group of large firms consists of vertically integrated textile makers, such as Miyuki, Daido and Chodai. They have their own weaving factories located not in *sanchi* but in a neighbouring area. Each also forms a tight inter-firm relationship with independent weavers, most of whom depend solely on piecework from one of these textile firms.

Four points about the relationships in this industry deserve attention. (1) The relative share of vertically integrated firms has been quite stable, although there has been a significant change in the character of demand for their products. These changes include demand for standardized products by mass-production technology and demand shift to differentiated products of high quality.

(2) The division of labour in the production system has not changed greatly. This is despite the fact that the leadership within the production–distribution channels for wool products has shifted from weavers and wholesalers in *sanchi* to clothing makers, such as Kashiyama and D'urban, because of the shifting demand characteristics and the changing technological environment.

(3) Another consideration is the division of risk among members within the production–distribution channels. One example is the large department store, the traditionally dominant distribution channel for men's suits. Trade between department stores and clothing makers is on consignment, and the risk of unsold stock is borne by the clothing maker. Clothing makers purchase textiles from weavers on the condition that they will not cancel their orders made in advance and are allowed to return the products only when they are defective. When this rule is observed by all, the risk is borne by the clothing maker. However, because of highly differentiated demand and a long lead time, not all makers strictly observe this rule. Many orders are cancelled and the textiles are returned to weavers. In many cases, the returned products amount to up to 30–40 per cent of the total volume. In spite of this high ratio of cancelled orders, relationships between clothing makers and weavers, and the total supplying system in *sanchi*, are generally stable and long term. In such a 'high network density situation, there is more efficient information spread about what members . . . are doing, and . . . better ability to shape that behaviour' (Granovetter, 1992, p. 35). All weavers know and can accurately forecast the likely cancelling ratio of each clothing maker, and makers take this situation into consideration when trading.

(4) A revolutionary change has occurred, mainly at the distribution stage over the past ten years. There has been explosive growth in a new type of retail chain store for men's suits, which now occupies nearly 50 per cent of the market in volume. Aoyama and Aoki are examples of such retail stores. A typical store is located on the main road in the suburbs and has a floor area of 400–500m², displaying 1000 to 1500 sets of suits. The store has five or six salesmen, including the manager. The number of stores of the biggest chain, Aoyama, increased from 73 in March 1986 to 362 in March 1992 (Miwa, 1994, pp. 37–41). Although the change occurred mainly in the retail sector and the leaders were retail chain stores, such revolutionary changes inevitably required fundamental adjustment by manufacturing firms and wholesalers. Such changes could have occurred in spite of stable, long-term relations and, moreover, do not necessarily cause confusion within the industry.

12.9 LONG-TERM RELATIONSHIPS WITH NON-EXCLUSIVENESS

One of the most striking characteristics of Japanese industrial organization is the predominance of stable, long-term inter-firm relationships which are non-exclusive. People often mistakenly believe that long-term relationships exist only between two partners, and are therefore exclusive. In Japan, however, these long-term relationships are not necessarily exclusive and may involve multiple parties. Much has been said of the 'closed' nature of the Japanese economy and the exclusiveness of Japanese long-term inter-firm relationships. Many people argue that the Japanese market is closed in spite of its efficiency, and they insist that today it is necessary to accept some efficiency loss to survive in such a 'globally open economy'. However, the substantial current-account imbalance between Japan and the USA is a macroeconomic problem involving gross national product and gross expenditure as well as gross savings and gross investment. Therefore this section is related to the closed nature rather than the Japan–US trade balance debate.[13]

Toyota has adhered to a double 'sourcing' policy in the supply of car parts. It maintains a close relationship with at least two firms, sometimes including other divisions of Toyota itself, which develop and supply specific components. Toyota has advised suppliers, even firms of which Toyota is the largest shareholder, to do business with other manufacturers, even if it is a Toyota rival. As mentioned in Chapter 4, Toyota adopted this policy at the beginning of its explosive growth. As a result of such policies, many members of Toyota's suppliers' association (*Kyoho-kai*) also belong to an association of other car manufacturers, such as Nissan, Mazda and Mitsubishi. This is one factor which allowed new firms, such as Honda, Mazda and Mitsubishi, to successfully enter the car market in the early 1960s. The allegedly tight 'production *keiretsu*' in car production is not as closed and exclusive as is usually believed. This is one reason why Japanese car manufacturers could attain such large economies of scale and increased efficiency, despite the existence of stable long-term relationships in that industry.

It is easy to find other examples of similar inter-firm relationships in Japan. In the semiconductor manufacturing equipment sector, the market for testers is dominated by two firms. Fujitsu holds more than 20 per cent of the equity of Advantest, and NEC holds 50 per cent of Ando. Other semiconductor giants, such as Hitachi, Toshiba, Mitsubishi and Matsushita, are not disadvantaged by these allegedly 'exclusive' relationships. The market for lithography equipment has been dominated by Nikon. Although Nikon is a core member of the 'Mitsubishi group', it maintains long-term relationships with firms outside this group. In the semiconductor industry some intermediary goods, for example silicon wafers and ceramic packages, are produced by only a few firms. However, this has not caused problems for semiconductor manufacturers.

On the contrary, it is rather difficult to find a case in the car manufacturing or electronics sector in which a manufacturer does not sell its intermediary products and manufacturing equipment, even when there exists a large outside demand. For example, Matsushita, the largest consumer electronics products and robotics manufacturer in Japan, sells its component-inserting machine to its rivals, contributing to their high productivity. Key components for VCRs and microwave ovens are produced by only a few firms but are supplied openly, allowing many firms to easily enter the market as assemblers. The same mechanism applies to photocopiers, where there are more than ten Japanese manufacturers, and numerical control (NC) machines. The market for two core components in the NC market, numerical controllers and direct current motors, are dominated by Fanuc, which supplies to any NC machine manufacturer.[14]

Such inter-firm relationships are not limited to the machinery industry. There are only a few large advertising agents in Japan, and Dentsu dominates the market. Firms often maintain a close relationship with the same advertising agent. This has not prevented advertising agents from attracting clients who are rivals in the same industry, nor have these firms experienced any problems in this industry. When asked if trade secrets do not leak out to rivals, most companies reply that there is no history of such trouble.

In many cases, firms do not worry about rivals discovering the effects of their assistance and cooperative activities with partners. This seems to contribute to the efficient diffusion of technology and technical know-how and the improvement of product quality and economic efficiency of the industry. Often comments on the possibility of leakage were similar. For example, one executive said: 'We don't care too much about such a possibility. We trust each other, and our partners have business with us as their top priority. Moreover, rivals will do the same for us'. Sociologists may argue that the central question turns upon this sense of trust. I have not much to say about trust. However, what draws observers' attention seems to be the broad 'area of acceptance' (Simon, 1976, p. 133), the behaviour of firms in such inter-firm relationships and the willingness to accept the decisions of a trading partner. A firm trusts that the partner will make the relationship its top priority and that it will keep the firm's trade secrets and know-how confidential even if the relationship ends suddenly.

The prevalence in Japan of such stable long-term inter-firm relationships with non-exclusive characteristics gives Japanese firms and industrial organization three peculiarities. First, it is not difficult to enter a market, at least in production. Therefore the number of competitors in each market is often large and market competition fierce. Most business people and bureaucrats call such market situations *kato kyoso*, or 'excessive competition'. Second, the large number of competitors and fierce competition among them are the result of roughly similar levels of production technology and product quality among rival firms, which again is the result of the non-exclusive nature of business relationships. Third, through such non-exclusive relationships, economies of scale and economies of specialization, both in production and R&D, are realized. With such a non-exclusive character, firms can ensure that a partner will not abuse its monopolistic power created through long-term relationships.

12.10   CONCLUDING REMARKS

Is the Japanese economy different from other economies? Are Japanese firms and their inter-firm relationships different from those in other economies? Are there any important peculiarities in Japanese organizations and networks? Will studies of Japanese inter-firm relationships and organizations provide something instructive for restructuring organizations? The answers are, of course, both yes and no.

Many researchers have commented on the importance of the discrepancy between the behaviour of US corporate directors and the assumptions embodied in US corporate law. Dore (1983, p. 459), for example, declares that relational contracting, which is predominant in Japanese business, is 'in fact more common in Western economies than textbooks usually recognize'. Those who emphasize the importance of 'the explicit encouragement, and actual prevalence, in the Japanese economy of . . . moralized trading relationships of mutual goodwill' (Dore, 1983, p. 463) should remember the following conclusion of an American lawyer:

> [O]ne can conclude that (1) many business exchanges reflect a high degree of planning about the four categories–description, contingencies, defective performances and legal sanction–but (2) many, if not most, exchanges reflect no planning, or only a minimal amount of it, especially concerning legal sanctions and the effect of defective performances. As a result, the opportunity for good faith disputes during the life of the exchange relationship often is present. (Macaulay, 1963, p. 60)

Each firm and each group of firms has its own peculiarities, and therefore can survive in a market economy. Rather than merely identifying the differences in the Japanese inter-firm relationships, we should consider whether such differences cause anything remarkable and important. If the answer is yes, we should consider to what extent and how. Given Japan's industrial success, many people are interested in what underlies this growth and how it was attained. When coupled with the traditionally dominant views of the Japanese economy – symbolically encapsulated as Japan Inc. – the belief of a strong central government with an effective 'industrial policy', *keiretsu* trading, predominance of corporate groups and cooperative behaviours of firms (probably strongly backed up by exotism), there has been a strong tendency to identify unique terms and immediately view them as the main engines for Japan's economic growth. The dual structure and cheap labour, 'social dumping', protectionism and industrial policy are past examples. More recent attention has focused on Japan's industrial organization and such characteristics as *keiretsu* trading, corporate groups, main banks and stable but flexible inter-firm relationships.

We should not hastily select the causes of Japan's rapid growth and the 'flexibility' of its economy. Until recently, most viewed Japanese inter-firm relationships as 'backward', a fossil from the long era of feudalism. (This view still prevails in the distribution sector.) The situation was suddenly reversed in the 1980s, when people began to regard these relationships as the secret of Japan's industrial success. In my view, this reversal occurred, not through careful studies and ample evidence, but rather as a reaction to the impressive rapid growth and industrial success of the Japanese economy. Therefore we should keep in mind the possibility that the view will change dramatically when other sectors are carefully studied or when the speed of Japan's economic growth slows.

Debate on the nature of Japanese firms and the inter-firm relationships continues. The network concept has become fashionable, and we now witness a flood of articles and books on Japanese networks and organizations. This phenomenon has been amplified by the industrial success not only of Asian economies, such as Japan, but also of Italy. We are now searching for a set of anecdotes, instead of important real-world phenomena to apply recent theoretical research on organizations and networks (see Ramseyer, 1993, pp. 2012–13). Japanese firms and industrial organization, especially inter-firm relationships, are exciting and charming research targets, but also quite dangerous ones. Therefore we should not draw hasty conclusions.

Economists do not have a highly developed theory of the firm or the market, and we are still at the beginning of the study of actual organizations and markets. I agree with Simon's (1991) cynical comment:

A mythical visitor from Mars, not having been apprised of the centrality of markets and contracts, might find the new institutional economics rather astonishing. Suppose that it . . . approaches the Earth from space, equipped with a telescope that reveals social structures. The firms reveal themselves . . . as solid green areas with faint interior contours making out divisions and departments. Market transactions show as red lines connecting firms, forming a network in the spaces between them. Within firms (and perhaps even between them) the approaching visitor also sees pale blue lines, the lines of authority connecting bosses with various levels of workers. As our visitor looked more carefully at the scene beneath, it might see one of the green masses divide, as a firm divested itself of one of its divisions. Or it might see one green object gobble up another. At this distance, the departing golden parachutes would not be visible . . . [T]he greater part of the space below it would be within the green areas, for almost all of the inhabitants would be employees, hence inside the firm boundaries. Organizations would be the dominant feature of the landscape. A message sent back home, describing the scene, would speak of 'large green areas interconnected by red lines'. It would not likely speak of 'a network of red lines connecting green spots'. (p. 27)

The discussion of Japanese inter-firm relationships in this chapter, coupled with that of intra-firm organizations in the previous chapter, contributes to the study of both the firm and the market. Japanese firms and their inter-firm relationships are a rich source of materials for further research along this line.

Conclusion

To the degree that this book's analysis of Japan's economic phenomena and the basic view of the Japanese economy as a whole is correct, the conventional view of Japan and the basic doctrine underlying this view require correction. As matters stand, this conventional view forms and defines the common grounds for both academic research and policy debate, pulling them in the wrong direction and producing a pattern of results in the absence of an accurate understanding of economic phenomena and policy coherence. This situation is not inevitable; it flows from a small number of intellectual errors that can be corrected. The only cure for a bad theory is better theory.

Two decades ago, Patrick and Rosovsky pointed out that, despite all its economic success, Japan was not yet seen as a 'fully accredited member of the major-power club'. They argued that among the Japanese people this caused disillusionment with the past 20 years and fear for the future. Western criticism seemed to be directed at the one country in Asia that had succeeded in industrializing. Japanese exports encountered particular resistance in those Western countries, and protectionist talk had gained popularity, often associated with sinister descriptions of 'Japan, Inc.,' that mythical, all-powerful instrument of the national will (see Patrick and Rosovsky, 1976, p. 915). No fundamental change has occurred among Japanese people concerning this disillusionment and fear over the past 20 years, and the factors causing these feelings persist.

In my view, the factors which have caused this disillusionment and fear to persist are to be found both in Japan and abroad, particularly in the West. As Krugman (1991, pp. 2–3) argues, 'a few still hold the view of a monolithic 'Japan, Inc.' More common, however, is a conventional wisdom that runs something like this: despite its relative absence of legal barriers to trade, the Japanese market is de facto protected because it is not competitive in the same way as those of other countries. Collusive behaviour involving both firms and a highly cartelized distribution sector effectively shut out many foreign products, even when the imports would be cheaper and/or of higher quality than the Japanese version.' The basis of this conventional wisdom rests on anecdotal evidence – on the stories of businessmen who claim that they could not sell demonstrably superior goods in Japan. The dependence on such anecdotal evidence is again rooted in the conventional view of Japan, namely the 'Japan-is-different' view. A New York firm's claim, for instance, that it could not sell superior goods in California or London cannot be accepted as effective evidence of closed local markets. In addition, like the focus on a new movie star or a successful new entrant in the market, much of the debate on Japan represents a mixture of fascination and envy:

'Fascination, because of Japan's remarkable rise from relative backwardness and crushing military defeat to an extraordinary position of financial and increasingly technological leadership. Envy, because this rise stands in sharp contrast to the gradual decline of U.S. preeminence, which has been accompanied by stagnation or even decline in the living standards of large numbers of American residents' (ibid., p. 1). This tends to accelerate the acceptance of the conventional wisdom. As Krugman asserts, 'to economists, however, this is not enough' (ibid., p. 3). It is also not enough for the readers of this book.

In Japan, because of both historical experience, including the above-mentioned Western criticism of Japan and resistance to Japanese exports, and the long dominance in Japan of the dreadfully dogmatic Germanic theory – with which people recognize economic phenomena as a result of exchange by coercion rather than by agreement – most Japanese tend to believe that Japan is different from other countries, particularly relative to Western countries. It is these Japanese factors that have only poured oil on the fire. As shown in this book, the conventional view of the Japanese economy is totally wrong, and so is its underlying doctrine. Owing to the large volume of Japanese studies based on this incorrect view, and their translation into Western languages, the 'Japan-is-different' view has gained acceptance both abroad and at home.

The problem is that, while the debate over US–Japanese trade and investment relations has generated a remarkable amount of attention, actual facts and serious analysis are still in short supply. Now is the time for serious analysis. The basic question is not 'In what way does the Japanese economic system differ from those of other industrial countries?' (ibid., p. 2). Every country has its own peculiarities; so does every firm or each group of firms. Hence, each can survive in a market economy. This 'basic question' is quite often preoccupied with the Japan-is-different view. But, as shown in this book, this view is based on many stylized facts concerning the Japanese economy, most of which are vague and ill-defined, supported with little firm empirical basis. The most serious risk of depending on this incorrect doctrine is its indirect effect on the quality of economic discussion and policy making. If academics are committed to this incorrect doctrine, only incorrect questions will be asked. If top government officials are committed as well, their commitment inevitably sets the incorrect tone for policy making on all issues, even those which may seem to have nothing to do with that doctrine. If an economic doctrine and the basic view of the economy based on this doctrine are flatly, completely and demonstrably wrong, the insistence that discussion adhere to that doctrine inevitably blurs the focus and diminishes the quality of the resulting policy discussion across a broad range of issues, including some that are far from trade policy per se. Therefore, before asking this 'basic question'. serious analysis of Japan's economy must be supplied. Such is the objective of this book.

As I demonstrate above, the standard principles of economics explain the dominant patterns of Japanese economic phenomena. The principles are not those anyone invented to explain Japan, nor were they invented to explain any one particular society. Nowhere in this book do I argue that Japan is different from other countries. My argument needs no jargon, including *keiretsu*, corporate groups, main banks and industrial policy, invented for and frequently used to emphasize the peculiarities of Japan's economy. This conclusion implies that Japan's economy is not different from that of other countries, at least in the sense stated above. Any potential difference is that of environmental factors such as history and culture rather than fundamental mechanisms. On this basis serious analysis of Japan's economy should be carried out and the right questions can be asked about Japan's economy.

Patrick and Rosovsky (1976) ended their *Asia's New Giant* with the following statement:

> Since World War II, the United States has been the leader in nearly the entire economic sphere and experience elsewhere has seemed of small interest. Compared to the Japanese, we have become rather insular, secure in the belief that our own practices are the best, or at any rate uniquely suited to our own situation. This posture may well turn out to be a poor one for the last quarter of this century . . . [T]he capacity to learn from others, which the Japanese have so strikingly demonstrated, will be especially useful for Americans – indeed, for all people (pp. 922–3).

I am not sure whether the Japanese truly have the 'capacity to learn from others', when they misunderstood their own economy and have not learned from their own experience. But we should not limit our studies to the American and Japanese economies alone. We have lessons to learn from a critical analysis of every national economy.

I have dealt only with Japan in this book, with the basic contours of firm behaviour and function of markets. That I consider challenge enough. Japanese firms and industrial organization deserve greater attention, not because of Japan's *international competitiveness*, but because of the huge size of its economy and its history of development. Firms have, as ever-developing institutions, played a central role in the growth and prosperity of the world economy, and innovations in firm organization have enhanced welfare greatly. Therefore it would be of vast benefit to mankind to understand the underlying forces behind such institutional dynamics. It is my hope that others provide comparable analysis on other economies. This will enable us to carry out comparative studies of firms and industrial organizations for a deeper understanding of organizations and actual markets. This will also further develop theories of the firm and the market. The Japanese economy deserves close investigation and provides a rich source of materials for economic analysis; so do other economies.

Now is the time for a new generation of scholars, and the door is open for their study of both Japan's firms and industrial organization and the firm and the market in general. The conventional view of the Japanese economy must be displayed in museums, entitled 'A Tale, Full of Sound and Fury', with a warning: But Remember, To Err Is Human.

Notes

Preface and Acknowledgements

1. Chapters 2, 3 and 4 in Part I are a revised version of Chapters 1, 2 and 4 of Miwa (1990a), originally published in 1988, 1989 and 1989 respectively. Chapters 5, 6 and 7 in Part II are revised versions of Chapters 5, 6 and 7 of Miwa (1990a), originally published in 1989, 1985 and 1990, respectively. Chapters 8, 9 and 10 in Part III are a revised version of Chapters 11, 9 and 10 of Miwa (1990a), originally published in 1984, 1977 and 1984, respectively.

1 Introduction and Summary

1. Older scholars, probably over 40 years old, will remember the dual labour market models of people like Lewis and Ranis. People might study this dual sector development economics model, but they recognized the world as a result of exchange by coercion and could only borrow the expression.
2. Level of GDP per capita in 1987 at 1980 prices was 47 per cent higher than that in 1973, while it was 32 per cent higher in Italy, the second fastest-growing country among G7 members. See, for example, Maddison (1991).
3. See, for instance, Maddison (1991).
4. Hence the government's *Economic White Paper* in 1956 declared, 'No longer are we in the postwar age'. as mentioned at the beginning of this chapter.
5. Shipbuilding is another. Soon after the industry was freed from the restriction of reparations policy, exports increased explosively. Since 1956, Japanese shipbuilders have held the largest share in the world market, and in 1956 more than 70 per cent of completed tonnage was exported. See Miwa (1993b, pp. 143–4).
6. For the details of this industry, see Chapter 4.
7. For instance, see Komiya (1990, p. 174).
8. This was recognized widely, for instance, by Patrick and Rohlen (1987, p. 331): 'All too frequently big business has dominated popular perceptions of the Japanese economy. Large firms are deemed to have powered Japan's growth through their successes in generating output, raising productivity, absorbing and creating innovations through large-scale R&D, and creating and developing the "Japanese management system" of industrial relations, internal decision making, and close intragroup affiliations . . . [However,] small enterprise is the economic, political, and social heart and backbone of Japan. In particular, small-scale family enterprises have long been and continue to be a large and dynamic element in the political economy of Japan'.
9. For details, see the tables in the appendix of *Chusho Kigyo Hakusho (White Paper on Small and Medium Enterprises*, annual; hereafter, *Small Business White Paper*). Here I use the 1965 and 1993 editions. These figures are originally drawn from '*Census of Establishments*' and '*Census of Manufacturers*'. The standard definition of small business in Japan derives from Article 2 of the Small and Medium Enterprise Basic Act enacted in 1963, and depends on the type of

industry. In manufacturing, mining, and so on it includes enterprises with 100 million yen or less in paid-in capital, or 300 or fewer employees. Figures are establishment-based, not company-based (for example a company with a head office and five factories is counted as six in establishment-based statistics, but one in company-based statistics). The total number of large firms in the manufacturing sector in 1986 was 3 739 in the establishment base and 3 263 in the company base. Also the number of firms with more than 1 000 employees was 679 in the establishment base and 673 in the company base. Do not allow these small differences between the corresponding figures to trivialize the distinction between establishment- and company-based data.

10. Data from Fair Trade Commission (1986). A comparable figure was available from 1967. The corresponding data for capital stock show that the downward trend began at least in 1963 and that the concentration ratio in 1953 was at the same level as that in 1971.

11. In the USA the percentage was higher and there has been an upward trend, as shown in Scherer and Ross (1990, p. 63, Figure 3.1). An upward trend is clearer in the UK: see Hannah (1983, p. 92, Figure 7.1), with figures calculated from net output data.

12. On the definition of 'corporate group', see the first part of Section 7.2.

13. Bank of Japan, *Economic Statistics Annual*, 1963. Assets of security companies and post offices are not included in the denominator. The phrases 'city bank' and 'regional bank' are colloquial, not legal, terms. Both city and regional banks are established under the same provisions of Banking Act, and both have the same legal status and are usually called 'ordinary banks'. All six banks associated with the six corporate groups are city banks. Their average size is larger than that of regional banks, though the largest regional bank is larger than the smallest city bank.

14. Figures in 1990 are 15.5 per cent in the USA, 22.6 per cent in France, 15.2 per cent in Germany, 19.1 per cent in the U.K., and 7.9 per cent in Japan. See Table 1 of Pempel and Muramatsu (1993, p. 43) whose source is the OECD report, *Public Management Development, Annex*, 1991, p. 74.

15. The authors continue: 'At the same time, there has been a substantial devolution of activities to local government levels. The number of local civil servants increased from about 2.94 million in 1975 to 3.22 million in 1990' (Pempel and Muramatsu, 1993, p. 21).

16. OECD, *Public Management*, 1993, p. 352. US figures are from 1989.

17. Japan was admitted as a contracting party of GATT in 1955. Around 1960, the major West European countries re-established their currency convertibility and became IMF Article 8 (which forbids a member state from restricting payments and transfers for international transactions on current account) and GATT Article 11 members (such states are forbidden to use quantitative restrictions on imports for balance-of-payments reasons). Lagging only a few years behind, Japan embarked on a liberalization of import restrictions and foreign exchange controls, and became a GATT Article 11 member in 1963 and an IMF Article 8 member in 1964. Also in 1964, Japan acceded to OECD, which requested Japan to liberalize inward direct investment (the 'capital liberalization'). For details, see Komiya (1990), Chapter 1, esp. pp. 8–17.

18. The law is officially titled the Act on Extraordinary Measures for the Promotion of Specified Manufacturing Industries. For the debate and this Act, see Tsuruta (1988, pp. 63–70). For historical background, see Chapter 8 of this volume.

19. See, for instance, the fifth comment in Section 6.6 and Chapter 6, note 68.

20. Some of these firms are listed in the last part of Chapter 4.

21. Note the view in 'Now's the time to buy German', *Financial Times*, 9 November 1993:

> The key to opening successful negotiations is to understand the mentality of the seller . . . [T]his is likely to be very different from that of the typical buyer, an Anglo-American manager working for a stock-market listed company. The most important thing to know is that money is not everything for the owner of a German private company . . . [I]t can be an insult to try to persuade him to talk by promising an excellent price . . . Loyalty to the company he has built up over decades, to the community in which it is based and in which he lives and to the workforce, are likely to be more important. Any proposal with an opportunistic, asset-stripping flavour is likely to be given short shrift . . . [T]he owner will feel the company is likely to be destroyed, with disastrous consequences for his standing in the local community.

22. For example, see Lawrence (1991a, 1991b). The term *keiretsu* is used in English to refer to a variety of organizations or economic phenomena with various Japanese names, making the analysis of corporate groups all the more confusing. The use of the term in English corresponds to a wider range of phenomena than the same Japanese term.

23. Readers will realize that such conflation leads easily to the 'Japan, Inc.' view, a generalization from perceptions of *zaibatsu* interests and operations.

24. These figures are the three years average (Bank of Japan, *Financial Statements of Small Business in Japan*, annual) and small businesses here are firms with 50–299 employees. Corresponding figures for large firms are 66.4 per cent and 10.3 per cent (Bank of Japan, *Financial Statement of Principal Enterprises in Japan*, annual). However, for large firms 'city banks' include long-term credit banks and trust banks, whereas small business figures do not.

25. In Japan, for instance, farmers, small businesses and retailers have had strong political powers and used them to get policies favourable to them.

26. See, for instance, Komiya (1988, p. 13) and Tsuruta (1988, p. 82).

27. Tsuruta's (1988, p. 80) evaluation of industrial policy in the 'high-growth era', for instance, is basically the same: 'The goal of government policy was to bring about a concentration of production and the formation of an industrial structure of specialized manufacturers. This was done with the aim of improving international competitiveness in advance of the opening of the economy, but one cannot say that the policy was successful'. Krugman (1994b, p. 142), for instance, expresses an opposing view by stating, 'There is no question that before the early 1970s the Japanese system was heavily directed from the top, with MITI and the Ministry of Finance influencing the allocation of credit and foreign exchange in an effort to push the economy where they liked'.

28. The committee 'stressed the benefits of the activities of combinations and were impressed by the need for large-scale organization to meet German and American competition'. See Hannah (1983, p. 43). The Japanese government expressed just the same view in the 1960s.

2 Monopoly, Corporate Profits and the Dual Structure

1. For instance, it was in 1971 that the number of exported Japanese cars exceeded one million and that the Japanese yen began to appreciate against the US dollar from the previously fixed rate of 360:1.

242

2. In Japanese, the suffix '*ka*' attached to nouns means 'to make or put into' and corresponds to the English suffixes '-ize' or '-ification'. Therefore the term 'group-*ka*' corresponds to 'grouping' and '*keiretsu-ka*' to 'put into *keiretsu*'.

3. Quite often in this volume I use this term and 'view' instead of 'concept' and 'model' since, as shown below, nearly all popular phrases are too ill-defined to use as analytical concepts and models.

4. For the details of policies for small business, see the next chapter.

5. For a brief introduction to the debate, see Miwa (1990a, pp. 5–7).

6. Komiya (1962, p. 219).

7. See Miwa (1990a, pp. 9–10).

8. See, for example, Shinohara (1959, 1961). For the details of the 'loan-concentration mechanism' see Chapter 5 of this volume, and for *keiretsu* loans and corporate groups Chapters 6 and 7.

9. Kawaguchi (1962, p. 83) asserts under the title of 'function as the cushion for employment fluctuation' (that is, burden-shifting in the labour market): 'In depressions large firms evade wage reduction and dismissal of their workers by making suppliers (subcontractors) reduce the wage of their workers and dismiss them through reducing the volume of orders to them. Sometimes large firms dismiss their workers and push them into the pool of potentially unemployed in rural areas and at the bottom of the social ladder in cities. Recently they actively exploit their advantage in the labor market under dual structure . . .' This quotation illustrates the logic that view (2) depends on. Chapter 5 shows burden-shifting in the capital market, but not in the labour market. Kawaguchi's claim is neither logically persuasive nor empirically supportable.

10. This definition is used in this volume, unless otherwise stated, for example, in Chapter 1.

11. See, Miwa (1990a, pp. 10–11).

12. Even in the 1980s there remained strong support, both actual and potential, for the dual-structure view, and we observed a revival of this view when the Japanese economy suffered from depression after the second oil crisis. See, for example, Takahashi (1982).

13. In 1960 and 1970, the numbers of corporations with over 100 million yen in paid-in capital were 2 541 and 7 201, and firms with over 1 billion yen were 415 and 1 185. The number of firms in the former category is too big to be lumped together with the smaller number of large firms.

14. The size of paid-in capital of a firm with the same number of employees has changed dramatically in the process of rapid economic growth. Judging from matrix tables in Bank of Japan, *Chusho kigyo keiei bunseki* (*Financial statements of small business in Japan*, annual), which show the correspondence between the number of employees of a firm and its paid-in capital, the average amount of paid-in capital of a firm with 100–199 employees was 5 million yen in 1956, 10 million yen in 1962 and over 20 million yen in 1968.

15. For example, the survivor rate of small business is lower than that of large firms and data are compiled from figures collected from surviving firms.

16. Readers may ask why the big difference in profit rate narrowed or disappeared in the 1980s, but I have no clear answer. As I will argue in the next chapter, however, the deterioration of the relative profitability of small business in 1980s corresponds to a falling small business start-up rate (the ratio of new small business in a given year to all small business) and the net rate of business increase in 1980s. See note 16 of Chapter 3.

17. This is done for small business policy in Chapter 3.

3 The Image and Reality of Small Business and Small Business Policies

1. The yen/dollar exchange rate appreciated gradually from 263 yen (against US$1) in February 1985 to 242 yen just before enactment of the Accord, then jumped to 210 yen by the end of September, and rose further to 160 yen in May 1986.

2. History shows that the Japanese economy soon went into a big boom, later termed the 'bubble economy', and the depression caused by the yen's appreciation was not serious.

3. More on this term can be found in Chapter 4.

4. By then, 'small and medium-sized enterprise' had already replaced 'small workshop' in public discussion.

5. In reviewing the long history of small business studies, Takizawa (1985a, p. 2) positively and highly valued the accumulation of results. He argued, 'Small business research in Japan has a real history of more than a half century and accumulated a wide variety of rich and good results. Thus, it is not too much to say that Japan belongs to the group of developed countries in small business studies'.

6. Takizawa (1985b, p. 3) suggested that there were many answers to the question of 'what small business were' and thus no clear agreement on the definition of small business: To answer the question of 'what small business are' is regarded as both the beginning and the final end of small business studies.

7. For the reason for this choice, see Miwa (1990a, p. 26, fn. 7).

8. I should frankly confess that Nakayama (1948) is so full of ill-defined phrases and logical gaps that I cannot catch the exact meaning of his statement. It is the representative literature of its time, however, and, even now, is supported by the majority of small business specialists as the classic statement of its time.

9. For an overview of the controversy, see Miwa (1990a, p. 30, fn. 11). On the extreme side of the controversy was a large group of Marxian economists and politicized scholars who insisted that the dual structure was 'structural' and that policy could not be effective. Note that Marxian economics was the predominant strain of the discipline at that time in Japan.

10. As I mentioned in Chapter 1, Japan's standard definition of small business derived from Article 2 of the Basic Act and varies by industry. For manufacturing, mining and so on small businesses are defined today as enterprises with 100 million yen or less in paid-in capital, or 300 or fewer employees. The capitalization criterion has changed over time.

11. Nakamura (1964) symbolizes this shift by naming a group of successful small businesses 'chu*ken* kigyo', or medium-sized *vital* enterprises.

12. For the dual-structure transformation view, see Kiyonari (1973) and Sato (1974). See also Miwa (1990a, p. 31, fn. 14).

13. Kiyonari (1973, pp. 9–11). Kiyonari does not insist that small business with the Nakayama 'problem' entirely disappeared. See Kiyonari (1973, p. 11) or Miwa (1990a, p. 33, fn. 15).

14. Kiyonari (1973) claims that small business could not 'get permission to drop away', thereby suggesting that small business could not freely exit, and that the required conditions are not satisfied. However, I do not agree with him, for two reasons. First, I cannot find any persuasive reason for restricted exit. Second, large firms can not fill their growing demands for small business products when his conditions obtain, for under such conditions no small business expanded production capacities and no new firms entered. See also the third point below.

15. See Section 2.3, especially Table 2.1 and Figure 2.1.

16. See, for example, Table 2.70 of 1992 *Small Business White Paper*, which shows that the business start-up rate exceeded 6 per cent before 1981 for all industrial sectors. The rate for manufacturing sectors alone, however, fell from 6 per cent for the 1966–9 period to under 4 per cent for 1976–8 before stabilizing.

17. See Miwa (1990a, p. 36, fn. 18). For example, Kiyonari (1973, p. 4) argues that the 'dual structure' was supported by such socially institutionalized mechanism as that in the financial sector. Sato (1974, p. 9) insists there has been no fundamental change in the 'financial dual structure', which is regarded as the basic mechanism which supported the 'dual structure of the economy'.

18. On this point, Calder (1988, p. 318) noted: 'As Hugh Patrick ('Cyclical Instability and Fiscal-Monetary Policy in Postwar Japan', in William W. Lockwood (ed.). *The State and Economic Enterprise in Japan*, 1965) points out, credit restraint was the primary tool employed by the financial authorities in dealing with balance of payments deficits and inflationary pressures during the high-growth period; this restraint fell disproportionately on small firms lacking close ties with the commercial banks'.

19. Two other inconsistencies with the exploitation thesis can be added: (5) as mentioned in Section 3.3, a large number of active small business emerged and gained public's attention; and (6) as shown in Chapter 1, the total share of large firms in the economy, measured by total assets of the 100 largest companies, has fallen steadily.

20. This also implies that Itoh's (1985) 'unexpected development' mentioned in Section 3.2 does not refer to the real position of small business. Therefore, he frankly confesses that most small business specialists did not realize and anticipate correctly the efficiency-improving function of the subcontracting system.

21. Sumiya (1970, p. 61) states at the beginning of his study on petty enterprises that 'Japanese small business studies have been sceptical about quantitative analysis and do not clearly show their definition of small business'. This is a result of the history of small business studies that they began by focusing on the seriousness of the 'problem' of small business with the 'problem'. Recall Nakayama (1948) cited above. Also see Miwa (1990a, p. 38, fn. 24).

22. When based on statistics, the definitions of small business tend to converge. However, only scholars refer to such statistics or regard manufacturing firms with 300 employees or 100 million yen in paid-in capital as a small business. See Miwa (1990a, p. 38, fn.23).

23. Suppose, as is often emphasized, that wages in small business are much lower than those in large firms, and that this is accepted as a proof of 'exploitation'. Observed higher profitability of small business implies that small business owners exploit their labour, not that large firms exploit the small. This explanation, however, is inconsistent with the free entry–exit assumption. For the details of the 'dual structure' in the labour market, see Nakamura (1981, Chapter 5, Sections 1 and 2).

24. *Nihon keizai shimbun (Japan economic journal)*, 12 January 1975.

25. For the details of 'industrial policy', see Part III.

26. This Act was enacted on the basis of the Small and Medium-sized Enterprise Basic Act of 1963 and in order to modernize small business in each industry. The number of industries designated to benefit from the Act in the five years ending in fiscal year 1967 was 137. By 1975 the number had increased to 232. For a brief explanation, see Miwa (1990a, p. 45, fn. 34).

27. Yokokura (1988, p. 524) commented:

If . . . one compares the amount and content of the budget for small business policies with that of agriculture and fisheries, the other sector that along with small business has been labelled 'pre-modern', the following differential can be observed. Subsidies for agriculture, forestry and fisheries in the 1980 General Budget came to 1.9 trillion yen (including funds for land improvement and other activities to improve the infrastructure), while 1980 Fiscal Investment and Loan Programme (FILP) investments in agriculture, etc. came to 890 billion yen. In contrast, 1980 General Budget subsidies for small business policies came to 61 billion yen, while 1980 FILP investments for small business came to 3.4 trillion yen. In contrast to huge subsidies expended on agriculture, those for small business are small, and the small business dependence on FILP investments is high.

28. For example, the ruling Liberal Democratic Party (LDP) increased the amount of government budget for small business after the 1971 general election in recognition of the fact that the progress of the Japan Communist Party (JCP), especially in urban areas, and the defeat of LDP were the result of the success of the People's Association of Commerce and Industry (*Minshu Shokokai*, or *Minsho*), an organization for small business affiliated (informally) with JCP. See Yoshitani (1975, p. 343) and Patrick and Rohlen (1987, pp. 368–9).

29. This also explains why slogans and reports (that is, reports of government advisory committees and ministerial annual reports) often contain ambiguous statements and do not precisely reflect small business policy in action. This point applies not only to small business policy but also to other policies for industry. On this point, see also Chapter 8 below.

30. Yokokura (1988, p. 531) states:

There is some tendency for the indiscriminate application of policy to be found in areas other than small business policy, but it is especially evident in the case of small business policy because of the following mechanism. Specifically, because of the number of small businesses and their dominant weight in employment, together with the situation that small businesses have come to be viewed as 'weaklings', it has always been necessary for almost all of the political parties to proclaim the expansion of small business policy as one of their key policies. On the other hand, the arms of the government (the ministries and agencies) that draw up policy have responded by actively drafting small business measures (which can be expected to meet the approval of all political parties) because they generally have a favorable impact in increasing the drafters' budgets and authority.

For 'indiscriminate application of policy to be found in areas other than small business policy', see Part III below.

31. See Miwa (1990a, p. 40, fn. 27).

32. This Section depends entirely upon Miwa (1993c).

33. See, for example, Yokokura (1988) and Calder (1988, p. 318).

34. The PFC and SBFC differ only in the identity of their main customers. The PFC specializes in loans to smaller firms than does the SBFC, but both provide only long-term loans. The CCBCI is not very different from a typical private bank and functions like a bank. The government, however, provides 70 per cent of its capital (200 billion yen) and allows it to issue financial bonds in the market to raise funds.

35. See Noguchi (1993) for more information on FILP.
36. Under the special loan system, the SBFC provides special low-interest loans for particular purposes, such as for improving the industrial structure, preventing pollution, saving energy, and so on. But readers should keep in mind that these loans constituted less than 20 per cent of all loans by this institution and that the 'special low interest rate' is not as 'low' as might be expected, except for unusual cases. The share of special loans rose in the mid-1980s, in connection with the depression caused by the yen appreciation after the 1985 Plaza Accord, and to smooth the introduction of the consumption tax. As of December 1992, there were four types of special low interest rates. The highest is 0.05 per cent lower than the base loan rate (5.5 per cent), the second highest is 0.1 per cent lower, and the third highest is 0.45 per cent lower. The lowest rate applies only in very rare cases, such as special loans to the textile industry at 4.85 per cent and to small retailers at 4.6 per cent.
37. See Yokokura (1988, p. 523, Table II). Calculated on the basis of loan balances, the figures were 8.7 per cent in 1960, 8.8 per cent in 1970, 12.8 per cent in 1975 and 12.6 per cent in 1980. For those who believe that there were significant quantitative constraints on loans available for small business, to begin with, note that small business policy loans expanded the funds available to small business by only 10 per cent. Much of the gain from this increase, moreover, would have been passed through to other sectors via the capital market.
38. Even lending at 2 or 3 per cent below market rate lowers the average rates by only 0.2 or 0.3 per cent, which cannot be considered effective either.
39. Small business financial policies are widely held to have strong signalling or 'cowbell' effects in attracting private bank loans to selected borrowers. It is often asserted, in most cases orally, that the effects of small business policy loans therefore have far exceeded their actual size. If true, this refutes my evaluation. However, I cannot agree with this view. First, as explained above, most of the policy loans are provided indeterminately under the general loan system, whose doors are open to any small business. Therefore there is no room for intensive screening to provide 'signals'. Second, even if government selects firms in accordance with a particular set of standards, why and how can firms attract private bank loans? The underlying tautology is that in Japan the government always has the ability to beat the market. But this assumption is still open to careful investigation. Strangely, we see the same type of assertion in other areas of study of the Japanese economy, such as in regard to main banks and industrial policy, which will be discussed in Chapter 6 and Part III.
40. For the details of small business policies, see Miwa (1993c).
41. Nakamura (1985) continues: 'After two oil-shocks and with the further improvement in international competitiveness of Japanese industry, support for this view began to waver and the evaluation of the role of small business has gradually changed'. In contrast, I think this judgement too optimistic and instead believe that we are just at the beginning of this change. I have stronger sympathy with Kiyonari's (1982, p. 16) statement, a reaction to the revival of the dual-structure view:

> Why have Japanese intellectuals such a strong sense of closeness to the dual-structure view? Small businesses are always condemned as 'pre-modern' in exchange for deep sympathy. People will begin to talk about the future of the dual structure even with the slightest worsening of the labour market conditions. However, they are not eager to, and therefore they do not, understand exactly the reality of small business.

42. The business start-up rate among small businesses (the ratio of new small businesses in a given year to all small businesses), of over 7 per cent in 1970 has steadily declined. The business failure rate has stabilized at around 4 per cent, and the net rate of business increase has fallen below 1 per cent since 1981. Because small businesses are regarded as a major factor behind Japan's rapid economic growth, the declining business start-up rate has gathered wide attention. See the 1992 *Small Business White Paper* and Miwa (1993c). The most important point for our discussion is that this has happened even under given small business policies, which suggests that they are not effective. Such a low start-up rate in recent years is consistent with the low profitability of small business shown in Table 2.1 and Figure 2.1.

43. The literature on the Japanese economy and especially that on industry unconsciously accepts this framework of analysis, value judgements, and intrusion of anachronistic views with the adoption of such keywords. I agree with Komiya's (1970, p. 13) explanation:

> Especially in Japan, Marxism, Marxian Economics, Marx–Leninism, or ideology started from Karl Marx still has tremendous influence on the controversy over issues related to modern capitalism . . . This applies not only to the supporters of the position which basically depends on Marxism but more or less also to critics of Marxism.

In my view, up to the present there has been no notable change in this point.

4 Supplier–Assembler Relationships in the Motor Industry

1. For a critical review of past studies, see Miwa (1990a, Chapter 3), which appears in translation in *Japanese Economic Studies*, 20:2 (Winter 1991–2).

2. In the SMEA's *Basic Survey*, small businesses and large firms are divided by their number of employees, with small businesses employing less than 300 workers. *Shitauke* is defined as, on requests of a firm with larger amount of paid-in capital or more employees (called 'parent firm') than the firm under study, (1) to produce goods, parts, accessories, materials, and so on or (2) to engage in manufacturing and repairing the production facilities, equipments, tools and so on. By definition large firms are not engaged in *shitauke*, and the questions regarding *shitauke* are addressed only to small business. Note that orders from smaller business to small business are excluded from the survey.

   In addition, the dual-structure view that strong large firms subordinate weak small businesses influences the *Survey* and, therefore the resulting figures. Regarding the definition of *shitauke*, for example, three questions arise: (1) When orders are received from smaller firms, why are they not counted as *shitauke*? (2) How does *shitauke* differ from other transactions? In most cases, manufacturers produce according to their own estimates of market demand or orders from distributors based on their own estimates. Does this not mean that almost all manufactures are engaged in *shitauke* with distributors? (3) Let us consider a charter ship that transports cars of one manufacturer exclusively. Of the following – car users, car dealers, car manufacturers, shipping firm, shipbuilder and steel firms – which are subcontractors and under what conditions? More generally, when we note that all production activities are ultimately for consumers' demands, should not the large firms which produce, for example, large-scale computers, semiconductors, steel, cement, ethylene, plate glass and so forth be classified as *shitauke* manufacturers? In the overall scheme of things, the large firms are producing components, and other firms produce the final goods. Ignoring the definitional size restriction, if we accept the logic of this hypothetical situation we should also question the analytical efficacy of *shitauke*.

3. The same view is reflected in a survey of the Research Department of the Central Cooperative Bank of Commerce and Industry (1983, p. 71), which asked the following: 'How do you evaluate your firm's technological level relative to that of the parent firm: (1) above the parent firm; (2) roughly the same; (3) below the parent firm; (4) unknown?' The survey reported the following: '8.1 per cent of all respondents answered (1) and 43.4 per cent (2). Thus 51.5 per cent consider that their own technological level equivalent or superior to the parent firms'. This indicates rapid improvement in technological levels and self-confidence of *shitauke* small business'. Cf. Watanabe (1985, p. 400). Both the above question and the interpretation of the responses are based on the dual-structure view and consider gaps in technological levels as obstacles to the formation of equal business relationships. Note, however, that division of labour usually depends on economies of specialization which assume resource differences among participants. On this point, see Miwa (1990a, p. 59).

4. Strong interest in small business resulted in detailed but conceptually misguided studies. In the postwar period, the car industry was of special concern, and some of the field surveys and questionnaires, when interpreted with care, remain quite valuable.

5. The following statement of Donald Dore (1983, p. 463) seems to depend on the dual-structure view:

> Transaction costs for large Japanese firms may well be lower than elsewhere. 'Opportunism' may be a lesser danger in Japan because of the explicit encouragement, and actual trade relationship of mutual goodwill. The stability of the relationship is the key. Both sides recognize an obligation to try to maintain it.

An economists's intuition, when free from this view, leads us to the simple fact that there is no heaven even for large firms and to examine more closely how the stability of the relationship is maintained and its maintenance costs. This is the direction taken in this chapter. I will come back to Dore's statement in Part IV.

6. Since we are interested in the inter-firm relationship for division of labour, this point has critical importance.

7. The situation of this industry around 1950 is 'symbolized by the statement of Ichimanda, the Chairman of the Bank of Japan, which has come to be known as "No passenger car industry argument": "It is useless to develop the car industry in Japan. Now is the time of international division of labour, and we can buy from the USA" . . . The number of cars imported from Europe and USA in 1951–3 was 30 463, 64 per cent of the Japanese market. Furthermore, Japanese car manufacturers clearly recognized the seriousness of the huge gap between imported and Japanese cars in performance, styling, and price' (Miwa, 1976, pp. 348–9).

8. 'The industrial success of the Japanese motor industry' does not imply that every car manufacturer has enjoyed great success. Among the five firms which began car production in the first half of the 1950s, for example, only two have had remarkable success. Of the remaining three, one was only a modest success, another left the market, and one was merged with one of the successful firms.

9. 'Because it was rational' is an unsatisfactory answer, just as it is not easy to explain why choosing a Toyota-type supplier–assembler relationship was not rational for other assemblers in Japan and elsewhere.

10. 'Some purchased parts need additional machining and preparatory assembly before assembly. Of the machining works for products made from raw materials, and machining works and preparatory assembly for purchased parts, an assembler orders from machining firms with simple technology and relatively small- scale machinery where possible' (Takeshita, 1967, p. 282). The ratios of the value of materials, parts from vendors and payment for machining to total value of all assembler purchases are roughly 10, 60 and 30 per cent respectively (*Japanese Association of the Automobile Parts Industry 1984 Yearbook*, p. 106; hereafter *API Yearbook*). Vendors also maintain long-term trade relations with many machining firms, much like those between an assembler and machining firms. Therefore the weight of machining within the whole car production process exceeds 30 per cent. Of course, in many cases, the relationship between an assembler and a vendor has the same character.

11. This applies more clearly to the late-established assemblers, which can purchase from the vendors supplying existing assemblers.

12. However, a famous anecdote from a few years later states that an exported car immediately broke down on a US freeway. See Wada (1991, p. 36).

13. For a brief industry history, see Toyota Motor Corporation, *Toyota: A History of the First 50 Years* (Toyota City: Toyota Motor Corporation, 1989), and Wada (1991).

14. In June 1960 the government decided on a 'Trade and Exchange Liberalization Plan', and in October 1965 car imports were liberalized. The tariff rate on small cars, 40 per cent in 1965, decreased to 36 per cent in 1969, and then to 20 per cent in 1970, 10 per cent in 1971 and finally to zero in 1978. See Nakakita (1993, p. 353, Table 13.6).

15. The ratio of car production in 1968 to that in 1954 is 8.5 in Italy, 2.4 in the UK, 4.1 in France, 5.1 in West Germany, and 1.6 in the USA.

16. Even Toyota, which symbolizes the success of Japan's motor industry, had to make special efforts to pass the APA's (US Army Procurement Agency in Japan) inspection in 1958, for the APA quality requirements were quite strict. APA requested that Toyota press a quality control system on its suppliers, so in 1959 Toyota drew up a plan and implemented the programme. It faced great difficulty, however, because there was formidable disparity among suppliers in their understanding of quality control and its implementation. As will be discussed later, Toyota's Quality Control Committee began such activity just after the SMEA's '*keiretsu* diagnosis' in 1952–3, but the above fact suggests that it did not work well. See Wada (1991).

17. Basically, this was because of a chronic foreign currency shortage in Japan. At the beginning of the reinforced foreign currency quota period, 'the amount of quota for the import of car parts increased. This was for the increase of assembled part imports caused by the technical tie-ups between Nissan and Austin (December 1952), Isuzu and Rootes (March 1953), Hino and Renault (March 1953), and Shin-Mitsubishi and Willyz Jeep (September 1953). It ended with the increase of domestic production' (Ueno and Mutoh, 1973, p. 127).

18. *Aichi Economic Monthly Review*, December 1960.

19. In an assembly-type industry like the motor industry, meeting the scheduled date of delivery makes smooth production and considerable inventory cost reduction possible. However, it is not easy. Let me take the case of Mitsubishi Motors. Mitsubishi's Mizushima plant, built in 1943 for aircraft production, was

destroyed at the end of the war. After the war it was converted to car production, beginning with three-wheel trucks, and moving to 360cc car production in 1960, 800cc cars in 1965 and 1000cc cars in 1967. Isobe (1964, p. 25) reports that Mitsubishi reduced remarkably the overtime irregularity of its orders to machining firms. The lead time for delivery was between 20 days and one month or one month and two months. Delays were frequent. 20 out of 25 local firms regarded these delays as a serious problem. About 70 per cent of the 52 firms surveyed experienced delays, unrelated to firm size. This case illustrates that even machining firms with sufficient production capacity could not easily meet delivery dates and needed improved management.

The actual meaning of 'meeting the scheduled date of delivery' objective has continuously changed. The history of the Japanese motor industry is one of increasing numbers of product items and accessories, and the fight against the production–inventory costs they cause. The increasing importance of on-time delivery resulted in greatly increased accuracy requirements. All suppliers had to achieve this objective at the same time and at low cost. Keeping to scheduled delivery dates therefore also demanded improvements in productivity, quality, performance, price and product development. To do so at low cost is a significant achievement.

20. The assembly-type production process consists of a long sequence of machining and assembly stages. Total production cost depends heavily on how work is divided among participants. In the motor industry, many components are pre-assembled before delivery to the final assembler; otherwise the length and complexity of the assembly line would raise the distribution costs and make inspection difficult. See Tomiyama (1978, pp. 94–7).

21. Also see Wada (1991, p. 25, notes 4 and 5).

22. For instance, Mr Masaoka, Mazda's managing director in charge of purchasing, made this point in an interview:

> The biggest problem confronting us now is the development of effective use, especially of tools and dies. We are trying to reduce costs by learning to change them quickly . . . On this point, there is a tremendous gap between Toyota's suppliers and those of its rivals. Toyota's suppliers make efforts every day for efficient use of production facilities and reduction of fixed costs' (*1985 API Yearbook*, p. 79).

In addition, Mr Endo, senior managing director of Nissan, stated at a *Takara-kai* meeting (see Section 4.4): 'Members of Toyota's *Kyoho-kai* apparently make much greater efforts at rationalization . . . To us *Takara-kai* members, I would say that it has been a matter of indifference. The biggest problem for *Takara-kai* members is in reducing the number of production steps' (*1986 API Yearbook*, p. 88).

23. This Section depends entirely on Wada (1984, 1991).

24. An assembler could reduce these difficulties neither by manufacturing those parts 'in-house' nor by relocating its plant to the developed area, as was proved clearly by the assembler's choices.

25. As Wada (1991, p. 29) states, suppliers in *Tokyo* and *Kansai Kyoho-kai* were relatively large-scale. They generally supplied specialized parts, and their dependence on Toyota was low. Most of the suppliers in *Tokai Kyoho-kai* were medium and small machine factories, mostly engaged in stamping and machining work, and highly dependent on Toyota. *Tokai Kyoho-kai* members supplied no more than 20 per cent in value of Toyota's total parts purchases in 1966, but this amounted to 80 per cent in terms of the number of types of item.

26. The SMEA had extended its management diagnosis from individual enterprises (particularly manufacturing plants) to industrial groups, among which it included '*keiretsu* diagnosis', or 'diagnosis of groups affiliated with large enterprises'. Wada (1991, p. 30) argues that this event 'marked a turning point in relations between Toyota and its suppliers'.

27. Besides gathering information on sales, costs and so on, the investigating group assessed each factory in seven categories, scoring each on a scale of 10 000 points, and added short comments and advice on factory improvement. The categories and points for each were: management (3000), production (2500), labour(800), marketing and purchasing (1500), finance (600), accounting (1200) and research (400).

28. For the other seven proposals and Table for Conspectus of *Keiretsu* Diagnosis for Each Enterprise, see Wada (1991, pp. 31–3).

29. Wada (1991, p. 35) emphasizes the importance for the revitalization of the *Kyoho-kai* of interfirm competition among members in response to their rankings in the *Summary*, and to a lesser degree in response to Toyota's insistence.

30. The marks were based on seven headings: statistical QC (20 pts) and organization related to QC (15 pts); internal planning (15 pts); equipment control (10 pts); control on the manufacturing process (15 pts); quality guarantees (15 pts); storage education (10 pts).

31. They surveyed each supplier's management indices, debt– equity ratio, sales ratio to Toyota, labour conditions, labour cost, cost structure, content analysis of value added, equipment–labour ratio and its relation to sales, production volume and so on, and investigated their correlations. Wada (1991, pp. 39– 40) asserts that this large-scale touring study session was epoch-making for the *Kyoho-kai*'s changing role.

32. Tokai Rika Co. realized no-inspection-on-delivery of all parts (59 items) for Toyota's Koromo factory in May 1965. See Wada (1984, p. 90, fn. 74).

33. See Wada (1991, pp. 41–2).

34. In 1966 Toyota and its seven affiliates organized *Shacyo-kai* (presidents' meeting) and began to meet periodically to show Toyota's production plan, coordinate with others' long-run plans, and to discuss other problems. Also, in February 1966 the 'Eight Firms' QC Connection Group' was organized, composed of a 'QC Managers' Committee' and 'QC Section Chiefs' Meeting'. Subordinate to these groups were the 'Toyota VA (Value Analysis) Connection Group', 'All Toyota Statistical QC Study Group', and each type of occupation's 'QC Circle Interchange Group'. The QC Connection Group began work in 1967. See Wada (1984, pp. 92–3). Here let me comment on such expressions as Toyota Group, Affiliates, Subsidiaries, *Kyoho-kai*, and so on, each of which is loosely defined and causes confusion. Toyota uses the term 'Toyota Group' for the following 14 firms: Toyoda Automatic Loom Works, Aichi Steel Works, Toyoda Machine Works, Toyota Auto Body, Toyoda Tsusho, Aishin Seiki, Toyoda Spinning & Weaving, Kanto Auto Works, Towa Real Estate, Toyota Central Research & Development Laboratories, Toyoda Gosei, Hino Motors, Daihatsu Motor and Nihon Denso. Of these 14 firms, only ten deal directly with Toyota, and seven firms for parts and body manufacturing, the first four and Aishin, Kanto and Nihon Denso, belonged to the above mentioned QC Connection Group. Each Japanese carmaker organizes a cooperative association (*kyoryoku-kai*) composed of its first-tier suppliers. (About *kyoryoku-kai*, see Section 4.4.) *Kyoho-kai* is the name of Toyota's *Kyoryoku-kai*, to which 190 firms belonged in 1963 (112 in Tokai, 57 in Kanto and 21 in Kansai) and 223 belonged in 1984 (136 in Tokai, 62 in Kanto and 25 in Kansai; 171 when double counting omitted). Though Toyota

Group is united in terms of both funding and personnel, only 25 firms (when ten from Toyota Group are excluded) out of 171 *Kyoho-kai* members can be classified as united in terms of financial and personnel ties (Shiomi,1985, pp. 85–6).

35. As Wada (1991, pp. 44–5) points out, in 1966 Toyota set up the Purchasing Control Department to spread TQC know-how to the first-tier suppliers, because the first-tier suppliers themselves increased the use of outside suppliers in 1966–7 as a result of Toyota's policy neither to deal directly with those second-tier suppliers nor to exercise direct control over them. This implies that Toyota maintained a policy not to increase the first-tier suppliers. The company's historians state that 1970 was the year when the 'fundamental ideas and diverse methods' in the 'Toyota production system' had become systematized.

36. Recall the last part of Section 4.2 regarding the basic problem: the importance of the incentive and communication system between a Japanese carmaker and its suppliers.

37. Recall point (1) on logical consistency in Section 3.4.

38. Of 58 respondents, 11 are from firms of over 2 000 employees, 11 from firms of 1 000–1 999, seven of 800–999, 13 of 500–799, seven of 300–499, and 9 of less than 300. Therefore note that the size of the majority of surveyed suppliers exceeded the legal definition of small business. Also note that answers to Yes-or-No questioning are sensitive to the form of the questions, and that the term 'cooperation' is used instead of 'support', 'subsidy', 'guidance', or 'control'. I think that the use of one of the latter terms might lower the number of 'Yes' answers further. This study put the same question to suppliers of sewing machine, bicycle and camera makers, and got results with a similar tendency but lower numbers of 'Yes' answers.

39. See Mitsubishi Economic Research Institute (1965, p. 53). For their own production expansion, assemblers strongly required suppliers to synchronize production schedules. Toyota called this the 'super-market' method and Nissan called it 'just-in-time' or 'action plate' method. In order to deliver the precise amount of parts at the appointed time, suppliers had to modernize and rationalize management (Sei *et al.*, 1975, p. 80). Toyota applied the just-in-time precise-amount delivery requirement with the super-market method. Inside Toyota itself, the application to the production process began in 1952 and was completed in 1956. The method's application to suppliers began after that, however, and was limited at the start to bulky parts requiring lengthy transport time and to expensive key components. Only 30 of 120 *Kyoho-kai* members delivered some of their parts using this method in November 1959, and all the parts have been delivered under this method only since 1961, when Toyota's monthly production volume exceeded 20 000 (Japan Long-Term Credit Bank, *Monthly Research Report*, November 1963, p. 15). Mitsubishi Economic Research Institute (1965) listed the means of rationalization for each of machine and equipment, production methods and scientific management methods, and asked the year of introduction of each. The answers illustrate the voluntary character of suppliers' decisions. For instance, 36 firms out of 58 answered 'by 1960', and 50 answered 'by 1963' to 'the introduction of special purpose machinery to the core production process'. This result is independent of firm size. On the assumption that the adoption of a scientific management method is indispensable for rationalization and production expansion, Mitsubishi asked the year of adoption of schedule management, production control, quality control, materials management, personnel management and the suggestion system. By 1958, 38 out of 44 firms had adopted schedule management, 29 out of 46 had

adopted production control, 29 out of 49 had adopted quality control, 24 out of 39 had adopted materials management, 24 out of 38 had adopted personnel management, and 30 out of 48 had adopted the suggestion system. There was no variation by firm size here either. See Mitsubishi Economic Research Institute (1965, p. 49).

40. We can also easily find cases which suggest that suppliers voluntarily made important decisions. For instance, in 1959–62, in response to Toyota's plans for a monthly output of 30 000 vehicles, 'two collective industrial areas were established in Toyota City, a big one composed of plants of firms from outside Toyota City and a small one formed by the collective removal of local ironworkers. In neither case did Toyota formally request such collective action . . . As in neither case did Toyota make direct requests for collective decision, the relationship between Toyota and firms in these areas is not such characterized by subordination as that between "parent and child", but is an equal relationship like that between "man and wife"' (*Nihon Keizai Shimbun*, 6 August 1963).

41. These two firms accounted for 74.9 per cent of the domestic car production in 1963, and 70.4 per cent in 1964.

42. In the spring of 1991, the *Takara-kai* and *Shoho-kai* were reorganized into a single *Nissho-kai*.

43. *Nihon Keizai Shimbun*, 25 March 1963. At this time, the number of *Takara-kai* members was 107, with the average amount of paid-in capital about 50 million yen. See also *1967 API Yearbook*, pp. 320–21.

44. The *Shoho-kai* began the activity in 1966 to facilitate managers' communication among member firms (*1968 API Yearbook*, p. 281).

45. Even in 1991 Honda had no organization called a *kyoryoku- kai*, but, following *API Yearbook*, I use the list of 300 firms as a proxy.

46. In Japan, many cooperative associations of suppliers exist outside the motor industry, but those in the motor industry are the most famous and the most active. Thus, even though associations have worked for Toyota, they do not work well for all firms.

47. Here, the cooperative association includes the *Kyoho-kai*, the *Seiho-kai* (for tool and die suppliers) and *Eiho-kai* (for constructors and construction machine suppliers). Asanuma (1989, p. 5) reports that Nissan buys 10 per cent of its parts from cooperative association non-members.

48. Shiomi (1985, p. 97).

49. Odagiri (1992, p. 163) made an apparent mistake in saying that, 'though some suppliers joined up to six associations (apart from Toyota's), only three belonged to either of Nissan's two associations. It must be that Toyota is particularly nervous of information leaking to Nissan, its arch-rival, through the suppliers'.

50. *1987 API Yearbook*. Also Aishin Seiki, in which Toyota holds 21 per cent equity, belong to the cooperative of Toyota, Mitsubishi, Honda and others, and Toyoda Gosei, of which Toyota holds 46.2 per cent, belongs additionally to Mazda's cooperative.

51. In 1976, Toyota's *Kanto Kyoho-kai* organized a Cost Reduction Study Group to study Toyota's production system and exchange information with *Tokai Kyoho-kai* members, with remarkable success (*Ten Years of Kanto Kyoho-kai: 1976–86*, p. 11). Though, as mentioned above, *Kanto Kyoho-kai* members are able large-scale businesses, they could not have learned by that time from the results of *Kyoho-kai* activities developed mainly by *Tokai Kyoho-kai* members. This suggests that even between Toyota's two cooperative associations it was not

easy to establish good communications, in order to facilitate mutual understanding, knowledge transfer and exchange of intention, even though several
firms joined both.

52 For this distinction, or the degree of asset-specificity, see Tirole (1988, p. 25).

53. Such a supplier is attractive for other assemblers even when it maintains close
relationships with an original assembler. As shown in Section 4.4, the relationship
between an assembler and a supplier is not always exclusive. It is typical even for
a small-scale machining firm with high ability not to depend upon one assembler
for 100 per cent of its orders. For instance, in the above mentioned collective
industrial areas of Toyota city, 'Toyota requested the suppliers not to depend on
Toyota for 100 per cent of orders, and to reduce its dependence on Toyota to the
level of 60 to 70 per cent by finding outside markets through specialization. Thus,
the majority of firms receive orders from other assemblers, even though they are
known as Toyota's collective industrial area' (*Nihon Keizai Shimbun*, 6 August
1963). However, the SMEA's *Basic Survey* shows that, in the transport
machinery industry as a whole, the ratio of small businesses depending upon
one purchaser for 100 per cent of 'subcontracting' work is 88.4 per cent in 1976
and 90.4 per cent in 1981. Note, however, that only 86.2 per cent and 43.9 per
cent, respectively, of all small businesses were engaged in subcontracting work.
See note 2 above for this *Survey*.

54. For example, it takes a longer time to find alternative purchasers when suppliers
(and assemblers), as in the case of Toyota, locate plants outside well-developed
industrial areas like Tokyo district. Also, the higher the dependence ratio on the
assembler, the longer the time for new purchasers.

55. The higher the assembler's purchase ratio of some specific part from a supplier,
the larger is its potential loss from that supplier's departure.

56. Even in 1960, Toyota's prospects were not so promising. A Toyota manager who
has spent his entire career in Toyota since his graduation from Kyoto University,
one of the most prestigious universities in Japan, once told me, 'When I decided
to get a job in Toyota, all of my friends and relatives and my supervisor asked
why and advised me to choose other promising firms'.

57. It was not easy for an assembler to acquire and maintain the trust of suppliers.
For instance, the biggest problem for Mitsubishi's Mizushima plant in
establishing a mass-production line was to recover the trust of suppliers lost by
Mitsubishi's burden-shifting action in 1958–9 when three-wheeled truck
production, their main production item at that time, decreased drastically. See
Takizawa (1966, pp. 16–17).

58. Even though less than that of a vendor, know-how accumulated by a machining
firm should not be undervalued. As Mr Masaoka, Mazda's managing director in
charge of purchasing, remarked: 'Japanese machining firms have marveleous
manufacturing know-how, technology and know-how sufficient to arrange dies
and tools efficiently, and can maintain product quality without expensive and
handsome machines. Even making a car door needs lots of know-how, and
nobody can do it only with a drawing' (*1985 API Yearbook*, p. 76).

59. Die compensation (*kata-hosho*) is an example. An assembler pays a huge amount
of money to suppliers to compensate their costs in changing and reproducing dies
required by unexpected changes in assembler drawings. The compensation often
amounts to several hundred million yen per year. For Nissan's case, see *1986 API
Yearbook*, p. 98.

60. When an assembler opportunistically exploits one supplier, other suppliers will
alter their expectations and devalue the prospects of relationship with the
assembler. The assembler has to take such supplier reaction into consideration. In

an extreme case, the whole production system is taken hostage in Williamson's (1983) sense, and the assembler risks losing everything by taking action against only one supplier. See also the discussion of reputation and the reputation-bearer view of a firm by Kreps (1990).

61. Even if one of the four factors was assigned to a specific commitment (for example, factor (1)), it was a part of this basic safety device.

62. The benefits accruing to small business being placed in such a monopolistic position were hinted at by a successful small business owner at a 1988 conference discussing subordination and exploitation of small business in *keiretsu* relationships: 'Do any of you know that almost every small business owner wishes to be put into a *keiretsu*, and why?'

63. The answer is essentially the same as to the question regarding an 'organization', 'organizational transaction', or a 'firm as an organization'. See Part IV of this volume.

64. For instance, Isobe (1964, p. 22) reports the case of Mitsubishi's Mizushima plant: of 25 local subcontractors, eight are firms for plate work, eight for machining, three for plate work and machining, one for accessory and plate work, three for casting and forging, one for rubber parts, one for wooden parts, and one for window frames.

65. For the details of Toyota's 'two-vendor policy', see Matsui (1985). As Asanuma (1989, p. 4) states, this policy has been adopted in combination with the 'practice of non-switching'. At the level of such broad groups of parts as headlamps, brakes and steering columns, each assembler 'seeks to secure more than one – typically two to three – suppliers for each kind and hold them in parallel. One of these is in some cases an in-house parts manufacturing plant' of the assembler itself.

66. Assemblers can reduce the costs of increasing the number of supplier firms by pressing its own employees to establish a new firm or by starting trade with firms founded by former employees of a supplier. However, increasing the number of suppliers may raise total production cost and, as Wada (1991, p. 40) points out, Toyota increased its parts purchasing without increasing the number of suppliers in its expansion process in the 1960s.

67. For instance, Isobe (1964, p. 27) surveys the calculation method in Mitsubishi's Mizushima plant of man hour indication for suppliers' unit cost of production:

> They calculate a man-hour as the necessary time for a standard man in the factory at the standard load, including the time for transport within the production process. The man-hour indication for each supplier is calculated by adding a room which suits by its capacity and equipment this standard man-hour. They use the standard time strictly in determining the machining fee, but admit margins in calculating the load.

68. For instance, as mentioned in Section 4.3, the *keiretsu* diagnosis by SMEA in 1952–3 was a wonderful opportunity for Toyota to learn how to make a factory diagnosis of suppliers. From that time, suppliers began to attach control chart or inspection materials at delivery time. The large-scale touring study session since 1961 was in the same manner epoch-making for *Kyoho-kai*.

69. At a Nissan *Takara-kai* meeting, Mr Endo, Nissan's executive managing director, discusses supplier use of robots:

> I visited your factories over these three months. Though a few of you are making exceptionally active use of robots, almost none of you are using robots in the way we expected, and I was deeply disappointed. For instance, a robot

with welding gun used for welding is still a welding machine . . . To use it effectively, you have to make its hand by yourself, and make the most of the play-back feature for your parts manufacturing. Effective use of robots has to be made to replace workers in the transfer of parts, and in the assembly of components like the engine, we believe. Looking from such a standpoint, I could find almost nothing. (*1986 API Yearbook*, p. 91)

Endo also states that Nissan manufactures 100 of its annual increase of 300 robots itself and asks the *Takara-kai* members when they cannot make better use of robots to come to learn at Nissan's Electronic Training Centre where it educates its own maintenance personnel.

70. Ohshima (1987, pp. 81–2) states:

The strong international competitiveness of Japanese cars depends not only on the good design and performance, but also on 'production technology' of a level to provide reliable cars at a low price with a wide variety of options. High production technology can be achieved not by the introduction of many robots but by the active commitment of workers to pursue better efficiency and fewer rejected articles. In the motor industry, most firms produce, or at least design, machinery for their own use on the basis of the know-how accumulated within factories . . . In this industry, the competitiveness of each firm is embodied in its production technology and depends on the ability to develop better production technology for the production system, production line design and machine tool development.

71. Professor Wada of the University of Tokyo once told me, referring to an interview with the president of a Toyota supplier, that Toyota's *Kyoho-kai* members are divided into three *de facto* groups, usually dubbed simply A, B and C, and some information at early stages of development is shared only with group A firms.

72. The sensitivity of safety devices (Section 4.5) therefore varies by supplier ranking. Suppliers know their own ranking and understand the logic behind the ranking system. The safety devices impose costs on an assembler when it takes action against this common understanding.

73. See Robert Solow's comparison of the modern employment relation to a marriage rather than a one-night stand (Solow, 1980, p. 9).

74. Though my focus is on the trade relationship between an assembler and each supplier alone, a dense network of trade relationships among suppliers, as among Toyota's *Kyoho-kai* members, is also common. I owe this point also to Professor Wada.

75. In recent years, a shortened product life cycle means that development is quite often carried out through joint ventures among multiple firms in long-term relationships. Here, too, a firm's skill in communicating with its partners is critical to long-run profitability. Though not an instance from the motor industry, a president of a medium-size firm in the Kawasaki District once suggested Canon as a representative of a firm with good skill, and Nikon as an opposite.

76. Recall that Section 4.3 shows that Toyota did not clearly realize what was necessary from the beginning, but learned by doing.

77. Recall that by 1970 Toyota had systematized the fundamental ideas and diverse methods in the Toyota production system. This proves the difficulty in establishing good communication among firms for knowledge transfer, exchange of intention and the coordination of interests. See note 35 above.

78. Mr Taniguchi, managing director of Mitsubishi Motors in charge of purchasing, suggests that the book cost of fabricating parts for completed drawings with detailed specifications is determined by the current quotation among vendors (*1985 API Yearbook*, p. 93). Consequently, assemblers need suppliers' advice before drawings for cost reduction.

79. Mr Masaoka, director of Mazda in charge of purchasing, talks about the cooperative association:

> We recognized that vendors' participation from the early stages of new model development was indispensable for high-quality and low-price car manufacturing, but it took six months just to visit each vendor. Reducing this length of time was the reason for the cooperative formation . . . But making the cooperative work effectively was not easy. In the past, some vendors participated in new model development from the fairly early stage, and advised Mazda to reduce cost by earlier participation. This, they said, no assembler had ever tried. One reason for not trying was to keep assembler secrets. (*1981 API Yearbook*, pp. 81, 83)

Mr Endo, Nissan's executive managing director, also suggested this in a speech at *Takara-kai* meeting:

> We decided to ask you to come to our technical centre at an earlier stage of development than before, much earlier than the public announcement, and to talk more actively with you about the forms and necessary Industrial Engineering conditions. We sought your ideas and advice for improvement in better quality, easy making, low cost, and good looks . . . We expected you to provide us with your know-how, and our designers intended to reflect this in their drawings. But some of you misunderstood and mistook our intentions, I am afraid, believing this was just an opportunity for information collection, especially of forthcoming new product models. (*1986 API Yearbook*, p. 99)

The *de facto* grouping of Toyota's *Kyoho-kai* members, mentioned in note 71, is one measure of the problem.

5 Economic Analysis of the Loan-concentration Mechanism

1. Committee on the Review of Small Business Studies, *Small Business Studies in Japan* (1985, Chapter 11). Yamashita reflects the traditional, dominant view.

2. Indirect financing, where financial institutions intermediate the flow of personal savings to the corporate business sector, rather than direct financing, where funds are raised directly on the securities market, is often considered one of the characteristics of the Japanese financial structure. Bank of Japan, *Money and Banking in Japan* (1964, p. 29).

3. Reading the literature reminds me of Shinohara's (1968, p. 17) comment on the '*keiretsu-ka* dispute' between Keizo Fujita and Yoshio Kobayashi and its 'multiplier effect': 'these writings suggest to us that historical development is fluid and variable, while the concepts or terms to explain it are rigid or inflexible'.

4. Yamashita (1985, pp. 232, 233) declares, 'Hiroshi Kawaguchi pointed out the financial dual structure', and notes, 'backed up with wide and detailed knowledge, Kawaguchi's argument is full of suggestions and persuasive, . . . and also regarded as theoretically and empirically excellent'. See also Sato (1974) and Takada (1980). Reflecting the vagueness of the argument, however, no agreement exists on its originator. Kawaguchi (1965, p. 138) states, 'The "capital-" or "loan-concentration view" related to finance in a narrow sense,

presented by Professor Miyohei Shinohara as one of the necessary conditions for the formation and long-run maintenance of the dual-structure, emphasizes the vital contribution of Japanese financial sector to the maintenance of dual structure'. Shinohara (1968, p. 55) asserts that Tsuneyuki Okinaka's *Finance* (1957) first pointed out the cyclical instability of small business loans.

5. Sato (1974, p. 9) insists, 'No basic change has occurred to the "financial dual-structure" which was the basic mechanism of the "dual structure"'. Further, Takada (1980, pp. 189–90) asserts, 'Some argue that burden-shifting to small business under the dual structure has disappeared, but they are wrong . . . It is unrealistic to expect that burden-shifting of large banks, whose principal borrowers are large firms, will disappear, and the basic reality of small business will change'.

6. These figures are defined in Section 1.5, note 24.

7. Note that the low equity/total capitalization ratio was one of the characteristics of Japanese corporations, especially large ones. See Wallich and Wallich (1976, pp. 284–5).

8. The three year average of small business in 1963–5 was 21.4 per cent, and that for large firms was 27.6 per cent. For small businesses with 50–99 employees, the number was 20.8 per cent, for those with 100– 199, 21.2 per cent and those with 200–299 workers showed 22.9 per cent (Bank of Japan, *Financial Statements of Small Business in Japan*, annual).

9. Ten electric power and gas firms take 59.4 per cent of the total borrowing of the entire 57, and 17 shipping firms take another 18.9 per cent. Thus more than three quarters of total borrowing is done by these two groups of firms.

10. Because Kawaguchi defines a large firm as one with more than 10 million yen in paid-in capital, he includes much smaller firms than the normal definition would.

11. For details, see Miwa (1990a, pp. 109–11).

12. This view is recounted in Chapter 7.

13. Also see Shinohara (1961, Chapter 9), which Kawaguchi (1965, p. 139) praises as 'the sharpest' view. For the details of Shinohara's view, see Miwa (1990a, pp. 112–13).

14. Additional details and my critique can be found in Miwa (1990a, pp. 113–17).

15. Kawaguchi (1966, p. 83) also substitutes '*keiretsu* relationship' for 'adhesion relationship'. See Miwa (1990a, p. 119, fn. 37).

16. See Miwa (1990a, p. 119, fn. 37).

17. Sugioka (1965, p. 53) states in commenting on Miyazaki (1962), '*Keiretsu* is a slangy word used since 1952 in economic journalism, and is not a well-defined economic term . . . Therefore, it is indispensable to redefine clearly this word in order to adopt it as a basic term for economic analysis. Mr Miyazaki has not followed this process'.

18. See Tirole (1988, pp. 134–5).

19. Yamashita (1985, pp. 235–6), who refers to this article as a compact summary of the small business funds shortage literature, states that the funds shortage 'results basically from discrimination in the financial market . . . However, few have studied how and in what form the shortage is actually realized.'

20. Table 5.2 is from the first Section of Part II in the 1970 *Small Business White Paper* (p. 87), entitled 'Small Business and the Dual Structure Problems'. The *White paper* is subtitled 'The Transformation of the Dual Structure and the Increasing Variety of Small Business Problems'.

21. Kurasono (1960) and Morita (1960) also adopt these figures as evidence. However, the figures cited in Table 5.2 are from 1949, and the success ratio for 1950 is higher.

22. See Miwa (1990a, p. 126, fn. 52). The 1953 *Survey* (p. 108) reaches almost the same result.

23. Note that the total of the first four figures in Table 5.2 is 42.9, which is larger than 46.5 (100.0 – 53.5). When we use 42.9 per cent as the denominator, the corresponding figures for full and more-than-half borrowers are 23.1 and 52.9. Also note that some small businesses chose not to borrow from financial institutions. The 1952 *Survey* puts the question about successful borrowing only to firms answering '1' to: 'Where did you propose to borrow?: 1. financial institutions; 2. others'. Those borrowing elsewhere (17.0 per cent, versus 78.4 per cent borrowing from financial institutions) were asked, 'Why didn't you go to financial institutions?' Of the following choices – 1. I could borrow from others; 2. I thought they would not lend us; 3. There was annoying red tape; 4. It took too long; 5. Other – Only 22.2 per cent chose answer number 2. See Miwa (1990a, p. 127, fn. 54).

24. See Miwa (1990a, p. 127, fn. 55). The ratio of small business which could borrow the full amount in 1953 was 61.3 per cent.

25. The literature on loan concentration mentioned in Section 5.4 emphasizes long-term funds.

26. Yamashita's figures are from the Bank of Japan's 1967 *Financial Statements of Small Business*. They show a long-term debt to sales ratio for small business of 9.9 per cent, and one for large firms of 18.9 per cent. Corresponding figures for small business in individual industries differ widely, from a maximum of 16.3 per cent in glass and ceramics to a minimum of 5.0 per cent in textiles.

27. Teranishi (1975, p. 78) cites this table and states: 'This table shows that the achieved ratio of long-term debt to equipment funds is lower than the desired level for every firm size group. The smaller the firm size, the wider the gap. Note that even large firms with more than 100 million yen in paid-in capital suffer from huge unfilled demands'. Teranishi (1982, p. 510) includes the same table and statement.

28. Strictly speaking, this is a marginal ratio. However, I neglect the distinction of the marginal and the average, since the ratio is quite stable.

29. The source of these figures is the Ministry of Finance *Financial Statement of Incorporated Business*, as cited in the 1963 *Small Business White Paper*. 'Large firms' refers to those with 50 million yen in paid-in capital. The same view is expressed in the 1964 *Small Business White Paper*, Kawaguchi (1966, p. 11) and Teranishi (1982, p. 509). The corresponding figure for principal enterprises (340 large firms) for 1960–61 is 86.6 per cent (Bank of Japan, *Financial Statement of Small Business*), smaller than the small businesses' 88.7 per cent. Separating small business groups by size, we see figures of 91.6 per cent for small businesses with 50–99 employees, 85.6 for small business with 100–199 and 90.1 for small businesses with 200–299 workers.

30. The figures for principal enterprises (335 large firms) is 85.4 per cent, and that for small business is 93.0 per cent.

31. Lev attaches here a footnote from Horrigan (1968, p. 294):

> From a negative viewpoint, the most striking aspect of ratio analysis is the absence of an explicit theoretical structure. Under the dominant approach of 'pragmatic empiricism'. the user of ratios is required to rely upon the authority of an author's experience. As a result, the subject of ratio analysis is replete with untested assertions about which ratios should be used and what their proper levels should be.

6 Main Bank and its Functions

1. As a result, few have proposed research questions or even reviewed prior studies for this purpose. Kosai and Ogino (1980, pp. 167–8) is an exception.
2. Another example is the assertion or belief that Japan's government can realize sectoral development objectives and even individual firm development. The view that 'Industrial Policy' was the main engine for Japan's rapid economic growth reflects this presumption. As shown in Part III, however, this view is far from obviously valid.
3. Political activity in the 1950s reflects the first view: the Bill for Funds Committee (*Shikin Iinkai*) in 1955, which passed the House of Representatives but was shelved in the House of Councillors; Japan Socialist Party's Bill for the Amendment of Banking Act; the Financial Institution Council, established under Ministry of Finance by cabinet decision in 1956; and the Funds Coordination Committee, organized under the Federation of Bankers Association in 1957. For details, see Miwa (1993a, pp. 228–30).
4. As Goto (1975, p. 235) describes, 'In the conventional view, the characteristics of Japan's financial system and the prewar *zaibatsu* explain the formation of corporate groups'.
5. The *locus classicus* is Miyazaki (1962, 1976). Also see the next chapter.
6. For reviews, see Shinohara (1976), Kobayashi (1980) and Goto (1983).
7. For instance, Suzuki (1983, p. 190) argues: 'The basic discipline of financial institutions under the predominance of indirect finance, being based on 'long-term customer relationships', is to actively support small businesses with big growth potential. Therefore, protection of private financial institutions from competition by interest rate regulation has promoted rapid economic growth'. However, I do not agree with this view. Simply put, everybody from competing financial institutions, investors and business firms to entrepreneurs and even employees wants to find such small businesses. Why have financial institutions alone succeeded?
8. People tend to talk about the influence of 'main banks' and related topics during times of economic downturn. The periods around 1965 and 1975 are representative, and I choose to examine the latter.
9. In what follows, the term 'bank' represents all financial institutions.
10. Popular terminology is one indication of this – *keiretsu* loans, loan *keiretsu*, adhesion relationships, core banks and main banks.
11. For example, though Nippon Yusen borrowed 136.8 billion yen of its total borrowings of 221.1 billion yen from JDB (as of 31 March 1973), its core bank for our purpose is Mitsubishi Bank, from which it borrowed 16 billion yen.
12 Almost the same data set is now available in English from Dodwell Marketing Consultants, Tokyo, with the title *Industrial Groupings in Japan*. The tenth edition (1992/93) was published in June 1992.
13. The number six is the crucial number associated with the corporate group argument. The statement by Kazuaki Kajiwara, an economic journalist, is a classic example: 'The number of banks capable of being a 'main bank' in the Japanese sense is at most six or seven' (*Shukan Diyamond*, 24 March 1984, p. 75).
14. The stability suggested by these figures is similar to that of our relationships with barbers or dentists. The first reaction of most Japanese academics interested in these phenomena were, 'Indeed, it's surprisingly low'.
15. In this view, a firm is like a fish in a pond controlled by a bank, and leaving the pond or moving to another is life-threatening. Note that according to the dual-

structure view, such firms are envied by the majority of other firms, who do not enjoy the privilege of being in any pond.

16. It is interesting and ironic to find that the figures for Sumitomo Group are the lowest, since Sumitomo is noted for its cohesiveness and internal strength.

17. In Fiscal Year 1989 (from April 1989 to March 1990), excluding banks and insurance companies, there were approximately two million firms in Japan (Ministry of Finance, *Hojin Kigyo Tokei Nenpo*). Of these, 164 belong to one of six corporate groups. They together account for 4.2 per cent of employment in Japan's two million firms, 13.5 per cent of the total assets of those firms and 14.9 per cent of the total sales in 1985–9 (Toyo Keizai Shinpo-sha, *1989 Kigyo Keiretsu Soran*, p. 29).

	FY1970	*FY1975*	*FY1983*
No. of group firms	130	131	161
Employment (per cent)	5.9	5.1	4.9
Assets (per cent)	17.5	15.8	15.3
Sales (per cent)	15.0	14.9	16.1

(Toyo Keizai Shinpo-sha, *1985 Kigyo Keiretsu Soran*). Also, see Table 7.2.

18. The category S includes such exceptional cases as Tobu Railway, a member of Fuyo Group's presidents' meeting with a stable core bank relationship with Mitsui Trust Bank.

19. I examine only cooperative behaviour between city and trust banks, since insurance companies seldom take a core bank position.

20. The figure for (NUS(1) + NS(1) + NS(2))/NT (54.1 per cent) is 12.9 per cent higher than that for NS(1)/NT. This comes, however, from adding NS(2)/NT (8.3 per cent) rather than via NUS(1)/NT (4.6 per cent).

21. In H(3), Sumitomo Group, NUS(1) is 6 and NS(2) is 1, whose sum is equal to NS(1).

22. Almost the same is true for member firms of the six major corporate groups, since NUS(1) = 11, NUS(2) = 2, and NUS(4) = 16. The picture changes when divided into H(A) and H(B). The corresponding figures for H(A) are 10, 0, and 3, and for H(B) are 1, 2, and 13, and thus the assumption appears to be valid for ex-*zaibatsu*-type groups. However, note that, as mentioned in the previous note, NUS(1) for Sumitomo is 6, which dominates the picture.

23. The former quote describes Kojin (*Toyo Keizai*, 6 September 1975, p. 28) and Ohsawa Shokai (*Nikkei Business*, 16 April 1984, p. 72). The latter describes Eidai Industries (*Ekonomisuto*, 4 April 1978, p. 19).

24 Yuichi Nishiyama, Kojin's president, was sent to Kojin for strengthening its management in 1961 by Daiichi Life Insurance, where he had been an executive managing director. He has been the president since then (*Toyo Keizai*, 6 September 1975, p. 27).

25. Many also support a view said to be a statement by a famous manager who enjoyed great success in rebuilding firms after bankruptcy: 'The *main bank* is a financial institution which holds an umbrella over a firm on sunny days but closes it when it rains'.

26. The most popular phrases which this function reminds us of is 'cutting mutually loans to other banks' main-bank borrowers'. In a tight-money period, main banks allegedly decrease or deny loans to firms in a main bank relationship with other banks, since they should have its own big pipe already. Kure and Shima

(1984, p. 69) assert that in tight-money periods banks tend to put higher priority on loans to firms with close relationships with themselves, but Mr Kajiwara expresses an opposite view: 'Under tight-money conditions, banks can begin trade with new customers. They therefore decrease loans to their best clients, and seek out new ones' (*Shukan Diyamondo*, 24 March 1984, p. 72).

27. Representative cases are the role of Daiichi Bank for Kawasaki Steel in the construction of a new steel mill in Chiba, and that of Mitsui Bank for Toray in the introduction of nylon technology. What we are interested in here is the frequency of such events.

28 Outstanding loans for the smallest among them, Hokuriku Electric Power, totalled 249 billion yen as of 31 March 1983. Those for the largest, Tokyo Electric Power, totalled 3,644 billion yen. Corresponding figures were 294 billion yen for Nissan (0 yen for Toyota), 273 billion yen for Hitachi and 1015 billion yen for Mitsubishi Heavy Industries.

29 But here again I do not count the Japan Development Bank as a core bank.

30. The figure in parentheses is the average share of loans from each bank for 1973 and 1983. As before, data on financing are from Toyo Keizai Shinpo-sha, *Kigyo Keiretsu Soran* (*Conspectus of Corporate Keiretsu*), 1973 and 1984.

31. In the case of Chugoku Electric Power, nine city banks have almost the same share each.

32. One of these alternatives is to borrow from large regional banks in the firm's operating area. This was done by Chugoku Electric with Hiroshima Bank, and by Shikoku Electric with Hyakujushi Bank.

33. The smallest, Sumisho, had borrowed 709 billion yen on 31 March 1983, and the largest, Bussan, had 1868 billion yen in outstanding loans at that time. Data are from Toyo Keizai Shinpo-sha, *Kigyo Keiretsu Soran*, 1984.

34. On the basis of presidents' meeting (*shacho-kai*) membership, Nissho belongs to two corporate groups, and DKB group contains two general trading companies. See Toyo Keizai Shinpo-sha, *Kigyo Keiretsu Soran*, 1984. Note that, though Itochu belongs to DKB group, DKB's loans to Itochu have exceeded those from Sumitomo Bank only since March 1978.

35. Article 13, 'credit facilities granted to one person', prohibits loans to one person in excess of 20 per cent of the sum total of the bank's capital and reserves.

36. At the time of enforcement, only one bank was not in compliance (Mitsui Bank in the case of Bussan).

37. However, the third largest lenders in three cases are exceptions: Fuji Bank to Bussan, DKB to Shoji, and the Bank of Tokyo to Itochu. In the first case, loan fell by 36 billion yen to 90 billion yen.

38. However, the largest trust bank lender to Itochu was Sumitomo Trust Bank.

39. Note that corporate group trust banks do not behave as suggested in Section 6.2. Trust banks also decreased their loans, instead of compensating for the decrease in main bank loans. Several of the largest lenders did not behave as a group. The decrease in loans from the largest lenders was compensated for by banks in lower ranks of firm loan share percentage.

40. The corresponding increase for 1970–72 is 1.69, indicating that the period 1972–4 is not exceptional.

41. As mentioned above, DKB's loans to Itochu were smaller than those of Sumitomo Bank before March 1977. The latter's loan share was 14.0 per cent in 1970, 15.0 per cent in 1972 and 13.2 per cent in 1974.

42. Compared with the others, Tokyo Tatemono is relatively small. The largest, Mitsui Real Estate, borrowed 389 billion yen as of 31 March 1983. The fourth

largest, Sumitomo Reality & Development, borrowed 218 billion yen, but Tokyo Tatemono borrowed just 45 billion yen at the time.

43. The rate increase in Mitsubishi Estate's borrowing for 1972–4 was 20 per cent, and that for 1974–6 was 42 per cent. The corresponding figures for Sumitomo Realty & Development were 11 and 27 per cent. Both cases show behaviour, difering from the average, unfavourable to the conventional view, that is, the main bank's loan share declined in the period of relatively rapid increases in borrowing: in 1974–6 for Mitsubishi and 1972–4 for Sumitomo.

44. Total borrowing in 1980 was 1.01 times as large as that in 1976.

45. 'Though the Bank of Tokyo and DKB were Eidai's previous main banks, Daiwa Bank attacked their position in the 1960s by increasing its stockholding and loans, and acquired main bank status in the second half of the 1960s' (Suzuki 1978, p. 14).

46. *Ekonomisuto*, 4 April 1978, p. 16.

47. In March 1976, Daiwa Bank sent Mr Kiuchi, then president of Eguchi Investment Trust Management Company, to Eidai as president. In February 1977, Daiwa replaced Kiuchi with Mr Kawakami, then the competent executive managing director of Daiwa Bank. See *Ekonomisuto*, 4 April 1978, p. 18.

48. Note that the best choice for each lender at this moment is to recover its loans and end the relationship, if possible.

49. For instance, loans from Fuji Bank was 0 yen in 1969, and only 0.15 billion yen in 1971, and it ranked as the sixteenth largest in 1971.

50. The case of Kojin was treated differently in the media, but it is not easy to understand the difference from their appearance. Kojin began to suffer from business depression at almost the same time as Eidai, and went bankrupt by applying the Company Resuscitation Act on 28 August 1975. Also listed on First Section of Tokyo Stock Exchange, it was the 'biggest bankruptcy since the War' and described as 'a tragedy of not having a main bank'. It first reported a deficit in April 1975 at the end of the settling term; both income before taxes and extraordinary items and net income were positive in the previous term, ending October 1974. In the spring of 1975, DKB, Mitsubishi Trust Bank and Mitsui Trust Bank sent personnel and it became a 'bank-managed firm'. See *Toyo Keizai*, 6 September 1975, p. 26ff.

51. I do not collect cases of failing firms for study. They can hardly form an unbiased sample set, since some firms are merged before bankruptcy (Ataka Sangyo is the most prominent example) and others succeed in reconstruction.

52. See *Toyo Keizai*, 11 March 1978, p. 32ff.

53. Income before interest payment is used rather than income before taxes and extraordinary items to exclude 'noise' from income from selling stock and real estate.

54. As no information on whether interest payments are exempted is available, the list also includes some firms at the third stage of business decline. Moreover, in some cases, such as Kojin, the third stage arrives before the second.

55. Riccar and Aiden, two firms which went bankrupt by the end of 1984, belong to G(A). Two firms removed from the Stock Exchange, Yutani Heavy Industries and Nittoh Metal, belong to G(B) and G(C) respectively. The list does not cover all risky borrowers. For instance, Tokyo Ryowa Automobile went bankrupt, but is not listed.

56. I examine here stability over 11 years rather than the 10 years measured in the preceding tables, for the list is based on figures for March 1984. Figures for the decade before March 1983 do not affect this conclusion. Those figures,

corresponding to column 1 and G(T) are (56.9, 22.8, 67.5, 44.7) and (55.9, 23.7, 69.5, 49.2).

57. Note, however, that the denominator is not the number of borrowers whose core bank in 1973 was a city bank. When, for instance, a city bank can avoid being the core bank for firms which become risky borrowers ten years later, my claim will be an overstatement.

58. When we compare the core bank's loan share in 1973 with that of the same bank in 1984 which, for 40 per cent of cases, is lower than the loan share of the 1984 core bank, my conclusion overstates the main bank's loan behaviour.

59. Figures are unavailable for eight cases in 1973 and for three cases in 1984.

60. For instance, in the case of Eidai Industries, Daiwa Bank's loan share in 1977 exceeds that in 1971 and 1976. Its share in 1974 just after it became known that Eidai was suffering from business depression, is higher than that in 1972 and 1973, but lower than that in 1969. In the case of Kojin, the share of the core bank in October 1974 (Mitsubishi Trust Bank) is higher than that in April 1970 and April 1973 (Mitsui Trust Bank), but lower than that of April 1974 (Mitsui Trust Bank). In the case of Riccar, a company said to have no main bank, Mitsui Bank took the core bank position in 1973, 1983 and 1984, and its loan share rises both in 1973–4 (9.8 per cent to 12.4 per cent) and in 1983–4 (10.7 per cent to 12.4 per cent). However, the share in 1984 is lower than that in 1981 (12.7 per cent) and in 1982 (14.0 per cent).

61. NG(B,L) is the number of firms which belong to G(B,L), that is, all firms with total borrowing exceeding 10 billion yen and a main bank loan share under 20 per cent.

62. This conclusion is almost the same in 1983, one year earlier.

$$NG(i,j) = \begin{pmatrix} 14 & 60 \\ 44 & 16 \end{pmatrix} \qquad \begin{matrix} i = B, S \\ j = H, L \end{matrix}$$

63. Some readers may view this as a result of lenders' risk diversifying behaviour. Note that IBJ was both core bank and lent more than 2 billion yen in 1984 (20 per cent of 10 billion yen) to 94 firms. The average corresponding number for large city banks is 55. Toyo Keizai Shinpo-sha, *Kigyo Keiretsu Soran*, 1984.

64. Kojin and Riccar belong to G(B,L) just before their bankruptcy. Eidai belongs to G(B,L) for 1974 and to G(B,H) thereafter.

65. The change in total borrowing in 1983–4 shows that lenders as a whole are not drawing back from the business with them. There is no difference among G(A), G(B), and G(C), and total borrowing increases in 75 cases, decreases in 48 and there is no change in 8.

66. Examples include Horiuchi (1989), Sheard (1989), Aoki (1990) and Hoshi, *et al.* (1990, 1991). Sceptical views include Miwa (1991) and Ramseyer (1991, 1993).

67. Hoshi *et al.* justify this choice by referring to Nakatani (1984) and stating:

> There are a number of important differences between borrowing from a group bank and borrowing from other banks. First, group banks are likely to hold more debt in these firms than other banks and hence have stronger incentives to monitor them . . . In addition, group banks also tend to hold more equity in their client firms; this too gives them more powerful incentives to monitor. Moreover, group banks have in the past been active at helping member firms in financial distress; other banks often defer to the group banks, expecting them to take the lead in organizing financial workouts for distressed firms. Finally, former bank executives are often placed in top managerial positions at

these firms. This may facilitate the flow of information between the bank and its client firms. (1990, pp. 111–12)

Compare this with Kure and Shima's statement cited above in Section 6.3. See Chapter 7 of this volume for the details of 'corporate groups', and Section 7.8 for *Keiretsu no Kenkyu (Studies of Keiretsu)*. For the roles of stockholdings and dispatched executives, see also Chapter 11.

68. Recall the argument of Suzuki (1983) mentioned in note 7 above. In Japan and among Japanologists this argument is quite popular. Another example concerns industrial policy, and argues that the government selects a promising industry for the government support and functions as a 'cowbell' (see Part III of this volume). Likewise, government-affiliated financial institutions are said to select promising small businesses for lending, resulting in increased private bank loans to them (see Miwa, 1993c, fn. 37). For a recent account of bad loans, see Miwa (1993a, p. 188). Underlying all these views is the assumption that, in Japan, government can always beat the market. This is almost equivalent to the view that economic centralization works well and improves efficiency, and is close to the 'Japan Inc. view', which remains a view still open to careful investigation.

69. Indeed, the continued demand for the new literature backed up by the dual-structure view continually creates its supply.

70. To those who reply that every borrower and lender emphasizes the importance of the main bank relationship, consider the following. Every buyer and seller emphasizes the importance of mutual 'trust' of some kind. Every wife and husband emphasizes the importance of love, and answers, 'Yes, I love my partner' whenever asked and so long as they want to maintain the status quo. Answering this way is both cheap and at least non-damaging.

71. Thus borrowers are not like fish in a pond controlled by a bank, since they may leave or move to another pond without risk. See note 15 above. Given inter-bank competition, banks that demand too much of a firm's information drive away their borrowers. See, for instance, *Ekonomisuto*, 4 April 1978, p. 18.

72. See Ramseyer (1993, pp. 2011–13).

7 An Anatomy and Critique of the Corporate-Group View

1. Hoshi *et al.* (1990, 1991) follow Nakatani in using his refinement of *Keiretsu no Kenkyu*'s classification scheme, and reveal their acceptance of the conventional corporate-group view by stating:

   In many ways, the relationship between a group firm and its bank resembles the relationship between a division of a large firm and the central office: banks, like the central office, provide capital and managerial support, in exchange for which they get an ownership interest in the firm and some say in how it is run. (1991, p. 40)

2. How and why so many people have continually supported the view is not the question here. See Section 1.8 on this point.

3. The loan-concentration view, while based on a scheme, at least tells what occurs and insists on an interpretation of observed phenomena. By contrast, however, the corporate-group view is merely a scheme. As shown below, the corporate-group view does not tell what occurs at all.

4. FTC surveys the six major corporate groups and reports the result every four years. The most recent one was published in July 1994.

5. Those who think the criteria clear by which to judge membership in, say, the Mitsubishi group, choose one or a few from the following alternatives: (1) firms including 'Mitsubishi' in their name; (2) Mitsubishi's presidents' meeting members; (3) borrowers from Mitsubishi Bank; (4) firms whose core bank is Mitsubishi Bank; (5) firm whose loan share from Mitsubishi Bank exceeds 40 per cent; (6) firms in which Mitsubishi Bank holds over 3 per cent stock; (7) firms which have at least one director originally from Mitsubishi Bank; (8) borrowers from Mitsubishi's 'financial group' (Mitsubishi Bank, Mitsubishi Trust Bank, Meiji Mutual Life Insurance and Tokyo Marine & Fire Insurance); (9) borrowers from Mitsubishi Corporation; (10) firms whose largest dealer is Mitsubishi Corporation; (11) firms which took part in Mitsubishi's Pavilion for the Future in EXPO'70 in Osaka; (12) firms with a majority of elevators made by Mitsubishi Electric at their head office; (13) firms owning more than five 'Debonair' cars of Mitsubishi Motors.

6. The above first episode needs to ask, 'Is the criterion to include Toyota in the Mitsui group justifiable?' and 'Is the adoption of that criterion more effective in understanding Toyota's purchasing behaviour, for instance, than the other criteria or neglecting the group?' The second needs asking what can be newly explained by assuming the existence of corporate groups symbolized by an association for alumni.

7. The 'One-Set-Ism' view regarding equipment investment is one example of Miyazaki's way of thinking. As shown in Section 7.5, however, upon closer examination, it is hard to understand the content of his view.

8. Dissolution of the prewar *zaibatsu* took place as a part of deconcentration policies in occupied Japan under the force and supervision of the Allied Powers. For a brief history and policy evaluation, see Miwa (1993b). The conventional view exaggerates the policy's effects.

9. Fair Trade Commission, *The Outline of the Report on the Actual Conditions of the Six Major Corporate Groups*, February, 1992, p. 15.

10. The corresponding figures for Mitsubishi and Sumitomo are 20.2 and 21.2 in 1955, 20.8 and 29.2 in 1960, 23.7 and 28.0 in 1965, 26.8 and 28.9 in 1970, and 30.3 and 29.6 in 1975. Cf. note 12 below.

11. Recall Table 1.7 above.

12. Figures are from the Japanese version of the Fair Trade Commission report released in May 1989.

13. See Sugioka's comment cited in Chapter 5, note 17. I have to confess that after all I cannot understand Miyazaki (1976) clearly, as shown in Section 7.5.

14. Recall the second anecdote and related comments in Section 7.2. Note again that the existence question is futile.

15. On this deconcentration case, see Miwa (1993b, pp. 143–4).

16. Nakamura (1975, p. 44) criticizes the 'manager–control–collapse' view of Miyazaki (1972):

Why does Professor Miyazaki dare to deny managerial control? He maintains that the ownership–control linkage has been the basic evil of capitalism. As it changes form today to corporate ownership–control linkage, he must deny the importance of managerial control, which is relatively independent of stock ownership. But the traditional Marxist view of private ownership as the basic evil is inappropriate to the investigation of modern capitalism.

17. On the topic of managerial control, Miyazaki (1980, p. 184) declares that his 'argument depends basically on the traditional definition since Berle-Means' and

responds to Nakamura (1975) and Nishiyama (1979) as follows: 'The views of Nishiyama and Nakamura require a change in the definition of "managerial control", and are hard to accept immediately. Therefore, I have no choice other than to accept the Berle-Means definition already established among academics.' Thus, rather than rebutting his critics, Miyazaki asserts only that he applies the Berle–Means argument to Japan and that it is already established among Japanese academics. Recall the dogs metaphor mentioned in Section 1.8.

18. In short, 'organizations are composed of and therefore responsible to multiple stakeholders' (Kochan and Useem, 1992, p. 5). For the details of recent literature on organizations, see Chapter 11 of this volume. The statement from Imai (1989, pp. 141–2) exemplifies the new wave:

> Today the essential task for a firm is not to carry out routine works steadily but through interaction of agents to create information, to search for new business opportunities, and to develop an accumulation process for continual innovation. Seldom do capital owners (shareholders) appear in such interaction with power of critical importance. Even in a firm where shareholdings are not dispersed and shareholders keep decisive control over personnel affairs, they usually make use of it only in an emergency . . . They rarely intervene to influence the interaction. . . Thus, in corporate group relationships, the importance of holding more than the majority of stocks . . . has declined. Thus ownership matters only in an emergency. Otherwise, managers do not need the power delegated from owners for work coordination, and ownership expands the boundary neither of a firm nor of a corporate group.

19. Gordon (1945, p. 5)
20. While Miyazaki (1976, pp. 63–4) comments that 'corporate groups' are not the same and the 'authority and function' of their presidents' meetings differ greatly, in the three groups the 'authority and function' of the presidents' meetings are thought to be the greatest.
21. 'Human ties are weak even in Mitsui, Mitsubishi and Sumitomo. This is mainly because their holding companies were dissolved. Further, because of Section 13 of the Anti-monopoly Act which restricts interlocking directorates, a dispatched executive in most cases belongs exclusively to one firm . . . Even an executive from a bank is mostly dispatched as a specialist in charge of accounting . . . Therefore, human ties within postwar *keiretsu* corporate groups are incomparably weaker than those in prewar *zaibatsu*' (Miyazaki, 1976, p. 255). However, Section 13 is effective only when 'such interlocking directorates may be substantially to restrain competition in any particular field of trade', and his explanation is not persuasive.
22. Readers may then ask what the 'One-Set-Ism' view of equipment investment behaviour actually is, since even when corporate groups exist, they do not influence firm investment behaviour, and are therefore not as meaningful as an association of high school alumni. Noda (1963, p. 269) states, in commenting on Miyazaki (1962): 'We observed investment behaviour that can be summarized as "one group, one set". It was not bank managers but managers in each individual firm that took the initiative. The former played a role only to back up such active investment behaviour.' Moreover, the 'One-Set-Ism' phenomenon is observed only in such classical industries as banking, life insurance, trading, construction, chemicals, cement and shipbuilding. Corporate groups do not have one firm each in steel (blast furnaces), cars, home electronics, machinery or precision

equipment, sectors at the forefront of Japan's industrial success. 'One-Set-Ism' supporters, focusing particularly on equipment investment behaviour, appear to talk only about petrochemicals.

23. In addition, there are potential inconsistencies in Miyazaki's analysis. Though the 1976 book includes the core of his 1962 work, the preface states: 'The power of the presidents' meetings has been much strengthened since the recession of 1965, and they now hold the power to influence the selection of executives, especially the presidents, of individual firms' (p. v). Putting aside the question of whether this declaration is valid, the statement implies that Miyazaki thought presidents' meeting power to be weaker in 1962 when he published his study of the '*keiretsu* control mechanism' and Tables. The majority of the 'corporate-group view' supporters has the opposite view on this point, I believe.

24. The principal reference is 'Determination of Standards for Corporate Group Classification' (pp. 59ff).

25. Miyazaki also declares that 'so-called *shitauke* (subcontracting) are the same type of connection', a claim with which I cannot agree. See Chapters 3 and 4.

26. Issues of presidents' meeting definition have not been settled. See the last part of Section 7.3.

27. Such a view is unintelligible and unacceptable to most readers, I believe. Even when using a similar method, Nishiyama (1975, p. 25) attaches relatively much lower weights to loan amounts in calculating corporate linkage.

28. See the third question below, and especially note 29. Also recall the quotation from Miyazaki (1976, p. v) at the end of Section 7.3: 'The whole affair is brought to light now'.

29. A natural conjecture seems to be that Miyazaki assumes something transcendental (T), which controls and subordinates all decisions of bank managers, and those of financial and corporate groups. However, there is no way to prove that this is the case. The 'will' in the following statement suggests the existence of such a T: 'The high ratio of stocks held by all member firms of a group to the total reveals a strong will for exclusive control over the interior of the corporate group, by defending from invasion from outside'(Miyazaki 1979, p. 238). By contrast, note Komiya's (1990, p. 167) comment on 'Who owns the large firm?':

> When one nets out these interlocking shareholdings, insurance companies emerge as the leading holders of large companies' stocks. . . only four of the twenty insurance companies in Japan are stock companies, and they are relatively small. The other sixteen . . . are all mutual companies, which legally are owned by their *sha-in* or 'company members'. In the life insurance mutual company, the term *sha-in* . . . signifies those who subscribe to life insurance plans offered by the company . . . after all the interlocking shareholdings are cancelled out, and assuming that those left are the true owners, we find that the core big business in Japan is owned, at least legally, by perhaps the forty or fifty million subscribers to private life insurance plans.

Also as Nishiyama (1975, pp. 12–14) indicates, only large city banks and long-term credit banks, which are perfectly controlled by managers, have a strong influence on large firms, and 'each large shareholder has only 1 to 5 per cent of total stocks'. See Miwa (1990a, pp. 202–3, fn. 45) for more details. Regarding 'interlocking shareholdings', 'cross-shareholdings', or '*mochiai* of stocks', see the discussion in Chapter 11 below.

30. Recall the negative conclusions in Chapter 5 on the 'adhesion relationship' and in Chapter 6 on the 'main bank' relationship. In my view, this comes directly from

the traditionally dominant dogmatic Germanic theory, mentioned in Section 1.1, that recognizes economic phenomena as a result of exchange by coercion rather than by agreement (frequent use of terms such as 'monopoly capital' and 'finance capital' symbolizes this tradition).

31. Miyazaki (1976, p. 63) takes the name change of Nagahama Plastics to Mitsubishi Plastics and that of Iwaki Cement to Sumitomo Cement as examples. Mitsubishi and Sumitomo have some brand value, and stakeholders have common interest in its preservation, which in turn necessitates collective action. The problem is why this is so important. Note that some presidents' meeting members do not include the ex-*zaibatsu* names in their own names. Examples include Mitsukoshi, Toray, Nippon Yusen, Tokio Marine & Fire Insurance, Meiji Mutual Life Insurance, Asahi Glass, NEC and Nippon Sheet Glass. A recent notable case is the name change of Taiyo Kobe Mitsui Bank to Sakura Bank in April 1992.

32. Again recall the questions in the last paragraph of Section 7.3. Also recall the explanation of presidents meetings in the FTC report mentioned in Section 7.2. However, opposition among the 'corporate-group' view supporters remains. See, for example, Tanida (1980, p. 252).

33. For the details of this view, see Chapter 11 below.

34. Nishiyama (1975, p. 145) also takes this case as 'a representative case of the dependence-type'.

35. The situation is almost the same for the term ending in March 1977, ten years earlier: Hitachi held 54.17 per cent of Hitachi Metals' stocks; 15 of 16 board members came from Hitachi in 1956; the remaining member was the president of Hitachi.

36. The case of Hitachi Chemical in March 1987 is almost the same: Hitachi held 55.98 per cent of its stock; 13 of 17 board members (including seven of eight managing directors and higher) moved from Hitachi in 1963 when Hitachi Chemical was established; of the remaining four directors, three came from Hitachi, in 1965, 1968 and 1983, the last of whom was from the Head of Hitachi Production Technology Research Institute and was appointed managing director in 1987; the last position is held by the president of Hitachi. Thus a chair in all three firms for the president of Hitachi appears to be only a matter of form. He must be busy with his work in Hitachi; another should be appointed if Hitachi wanted to control its 'subsidiaries'.

37. No basic differences separate Japanese and American corporate law. See Yanagida *et al.* (1994). The violations by Toshiba Machine resulted in the resignations of Toshiba's two top executives and the appointment of a third-ranked vice-president as Toshiba's president. The president of Toshiba Machine also resigned and was replaced not by an executive from Toshiba but by a former executive managing director who had been a member of Toshiba Machine from the start.

38. Some may comment that this small change in board membership at the meeting in June 1987 was made because of the short interval (three months) after Toshiba Machine's COCOM export restriction violations became public, but no change in board membership occurred at the meeting in June 1988 either.

39. Even in this case, many traditional studies mistakenly presume that such ties as funds and dispatched executives imply some form of 'control' and call these corporate groups *keiretsu*. The *raison d'être* of these groups is essentially the same as the answer to Coase's (1937) question 'why a firm emerges at all in a specialized exchange economy'. For further discussion on this point, see Chapter 11.

40. Those who insist that 'there is something essential which should be called corporate groups', bear the burden of identifying that essential quality and making clear why it should denote corporate groups. My advice is to dispense with the term 'corporate groups' altogether because of its vagueness.

41. For a brief review of this literature, see Goto (1983), Odagiri (1992, pp. 188ff), and Uekusa (1982, pp. 286ff). As pointed out above, in note 39, a study of the cause of 'corporate group' formation must be a case of economic organization studies *à la* Coase.

42. For instance, see Caves and Uekusa (1976), Uekusa (1982, pp. 280ff), Nakatani (1984), Hoshi *et al.* (1990, 1991) and Odagiri (1992, pp. 188ff). As Komiya pointed out in commenting on Nakatani, 'There exists no way for other corporate group members to subsidize a member who has got into trouble in order to raise its profit rates' (1988, p. 62, fn. 17).

43. On this non-exclusive characteristic of long-term relationships, see Section 12.9 below.

8 Industrial Policy of Japan: A Beginner's Guide

1. Originally published in 1984 in Japanese, this volume is the result of a two-year joint research project. Frankly, I was often surprised and shocked at the debate and discussion among the conference participants which reflected their poor understanding of industrial policy.

2. Exceptions include Komiya (1975), Kosai (1981), Tsuruta (1982), Komiya *et al.* (1988) and Miwa (1990a).

3. Two opposite views on the statement of US government officials on the USA–Japan trade dialogue existed in the discussion following the above mentioned conference. 'They are too naive in reading the government documents', was one comment, and 'It is only a strategy. They know the reality very well', was another.

4. I will return to this merger in Section 8.6.

5. This Act corresponds to anti-trust laws in the USA.

6. As a result, detailed information on failed attempts is seldom provided. For instance, MITI tried to adopt two important policies in the process of moving towards liberalization in the motor industry, the 1955 'People's Car' concept and the 1961 'producer group' concept. Neither of these two plans saw the light of day, however. Though there still remains the problem of definition and identification, only a rough image of these concepts is observable and policy 'insiders' seldom speak on these topics. On these concepts, see Mutoh (1988, p. 316).

7. Instead, such industries as energy, transport, telecommunication, textiles and financial industries will be selected as ones where the government intervention has been the strongest, and agriculture and coal mining as ones where the amount of the government subsidy has been the greatest.

8. An academic who had participated in the debate informally commented on the original version of papers adopted in the next two chapters, 'After all it was like a war, and we had to win . . .'

9. Morozumi (1966) is representative of the literature.

10. This first appeared in 1968.

11. See Chapter 1, note 17.

12. For the details of this debate, see Tsuruta (1988, pp. 63–70). Though 'excessive competition' was the key concept for the new industrial order, both sides took for

granted the necessity of policy to prevent such competition. Neither a clear definition of 'excessive competition', the policy goal, nor extensive discussion on it is available even today, and the government literature has a strong proclivity to emphasize the importance of its role and leadership. Note that the symbolic event in the debate was the government's failed attempt to enact the Act on Extraordinary Measures for the Promotion of Specified Manufacturing Industries (the Specified Industries Act), which implies that the government was the loser in this debate. On this point, see also Tsuruta, ibid.

13. When economics textbooks began to talk about 'market failures' at the last stage of, or after, the debate, the proponents of the policy immediately adopted this phrase: industrial policy is a response to market failures. Today everybody knows that the government almost always fails and such an adoption of the phrase was too naive, however, the debate was theological and therefore this point is not critical. Recall the statement of Stigler (1975) quoted in Section 1.6.

14. Recall note 28 of Chapter 1 on the British industrial policy in the 1910s which stressed the economic benefits of combinations and the need for large-scale organizations to meet German and American competition.

15. 'A system of using policy councils (*shingikai*) on major policy matters has gradually come into use in postwar Japan. These are consultative bodies whose deliberations are referred to in the process of policy formation, and whose principal members are private individuals, including former bureaucrats' (Komiya, 1988, p. 18). The Industrial Structure Council, which advises the Minister of International Trade and Industry on industrial policy in general, was established in May 1964. This was a reorganization of two consultative bodies, the Industry Rationalization Council born in 1949 and the Industrial Structure Committee born in 1961.

16. All these examples are from Chapters 9 and 10 below.

17. Tanaka (1980, pp. 19 and 28). Komiya (1988, p. 6) refers to this Act 'with its presumption of pervasive direct government controls for the purpose of "providing for a stable and inexpensive supply of oil" as an example of prewar and wartime economic thinking'. He comments that it 'reflected the strong influence of wartime government materials planning, though another contribution was the memory of oil embargo placed on Japan by the United States and other countries'.

18. Fair Trade Commission (1983, p. 210).

19. For the details of the Incident, see Section 10.4.

20. 'During the period right after the war policy makers possessed a fair amount of leverage over industries and private firms through their power of approval of import licences, foreign capital inflows, and technology import licences . . . During the rapid growth era the leverage of the government disappeared bit by bit, or at least its importance declined drastically, with the liberalization of trade and capital movements' (Komiya, 1988, p. 9).

21. Note that before this period the government hardly needed to persuade the public of the validity of intervention because of both the traditions since the Meiji era and the institutional arrangements inherited from the prewar and wartime economy.

22. In emphasizing the importance of the conflicts between the Anti-monopoly Act and industrial policy, Iyori (1986, p. 71), a former high official of FTC, states that 'whether Japan's remarkably high rate of economic growth . . . can be attributed to the maintenance of competition by means of anti-monopoly policy or to skilful control and guidance through the use of industrial policy is subject to unending debate'. This picture has been widely accepted as persuasive. However, as I wrote

in a book review (Miwa, 1990b, p. 95), 'he overestimates the importance of the role of the government. Today many Japanese economists think that the contribution, if any, of the government in attaining economic growth is indirect and rather minor'.

23. A paper heavily relying on such policy councils' reports was presented at the above-mentioned conference on Industrial Policy. Participants familiar with the policy formation process unanimously criticized it as too naive. One compared policy councils to a school arts festival or a school open day. What outsiders observe has almost no relation as everyday education, and it requires a tremendous amount of skill and prior information to learn from observations something essential on the school and education. However, to counter Patrick's statement quoted in Section 1.8, Johnson (1982, p. 9) offers a view expressed by Shigeru Sahashi, former vice-minister of MITI and a leader in the government's failed attempt to enact the Specified Industries Act, to assert that 'many Japanese would certainly dispute Patrick's conclusion that the government provided nothing more than the environment for economic growth'.

24. For more details, see Komiya (1975, pp. 307–18).

25. Thus, as now, each industry had one associated *genkyoku*. As Kyogoku (1983, p. 347) points out in Japan 'the basic unit of bureaucracy in allocating responsibility is the division in the main ministry with jurisdiction [over the industry; *genkyoku* Section] . . . For matters within a given jurisdiction, each division of the ministry by itself personifies the Japanese government'.

26. The central question here is for what the government took the leading role before the shift of the balance of power. Though it is still an open question, it seems too simplistic to say that it was only for consumers' interest and that the character of the policy changed with the shift. Note that from the start each *genkyoku* had to compete with others for the interest of its associated industry.

27. As shown in the next two chapters, none of these groups, including industry associations, had a strong influence on dissident firms.

28. For instance, the 1961 'producer group' concept mentioned in note 6 above 'was made public in May 1961 by the Industrial Finance Committee of the Industrial Rationalization Council. The concept envisioned producers being divided into groups of two to three firms each, with one group for "mass production" vehicles . . . a second group for specialty vehicles . . . and a final group for minicars' (Mutoh, 1988, p. 316). In the end this plan never saw the light of day, since it could not pass the Council. Therefore we still have Honda, Mitsubishi and Mazda.

29. 'The Industrial System Committee of the Industrial Structure Advisory Committee was . . . exceptional in its drawing up of the Specified Industries Act. Its seven members included former bureaucrats, but no one who was at that time involved in private industry . . . Industry . . . was against the Specified Industries Act, and the ruling Liberal Democratic Party was reluctant to pass the bill, while the opposition parties took the stand that the proposed Act was an evil that would render the Anti-monopoly Act an empty shell. With opposition from beginning to end, debate was halted and the bill killed' (Tsuruta, 1988, pp. 69–70).

30. I do not assert that these policy councils were useless. As Komiya (1988, pp. 18–19) argues, 'one point that needs to be emphasized regarding such councils is their role in the exchange of information and obtaining consensus on policy matters . . . forums such as these have been a very effective means for the collection, exchange, and dissemination of information on industry and as such have contributed greatly to postwar growth'. See also Komiya (1975, p. 324) and Section 10.5 below.

31. As is usual, disclosure of information increases the possibility of intervention by outsiders.
32. Even in cases such as textile, coal mining and agriculture, where the government continually intervened, informative policy evaluation is seldom included.
33. From the 1970s these reports began to include a short introductory Section discussing the benefits for the economy; this, however, has essentially almost always been the same and has had little relevance to the actual situation.
34. It was after the flood of cartels during the period of the first oil crisis and its accompanying inflation in 1973–4 that Japan really recognized the importance of this Act. See Miwa (1993b, pp. 144–5).
35. Note that the bias increases when a reader solely depends on materials available in English. We must pay attention to the question of for whom and for what purpose it is published in English.
36. I use the term 'informal regulation' as the translation of *gyosei shido* in preference to the standard translation of 'administrative guidance'. On this choice, see Section 10.2 below.
37. For examples and further explanation, see the next two chapters, especially Section 10.2. Informal regulation is more frequently used in the financial sector, for which see Miwa (1993a, especially Section 5.6).
38. This applies not only to industrial policy but also to other fields of policies in Japan. The government seldom tries to evaluate, much less publish, *ex post* the effectiveness of a concrete policy.
39. Usually they stay in the same position for less than two years. Even for senior officials in a ministry, therefore, or officials who belong to different divisions or enter the division at a later date, it is impossible to know in detail the content of informal regulation.
40. This also applies to the impact of the postwar deconcentration policies such as *zaibatsu* dissolution. I argue in Miwa (1993b, pp. 147–8) that the deconcentration policies played no substantial role in strengthening market competition which was one of the main engines of Japan's rapid economic growth. The main reason for my revisionist conclusion is that most previous research did not seek to identify and evaluate the policy effects in isolation.
41. Most participants of the conference mentioned above share the view, I believe.
42. For instance, the Basic Issues Special Subcommittee of the Industrial Structure Council expressed support of the merger in its August 1968 report, *Opinion on Reforming the Structure of Industry and Mergers*.
43. See Section 8.4 above, which is examined in further detail in Section 10.3.
44. In Section 10.3, I conclude that 'the government did not play a role or have a substantial direct influence on output and price coordination within the list-price system'. And also, 'in evaluating intra-industry coordination as industrial policy, our conclusion must be that it was ineffective in the case of the list-price system in the steel industry'.
45. In such unsuccessful cases as the 1955 'People's Car' concept and the 1961 'producer group' concept in the motor industry, and the new industrial order debate on the Specified Industries Act, the problem is simple. The plan could not pass either the Council or the Diet and therefore was never implemented. By definition there were no policy actions. In the case of the *keiretsu* diagnosis of the Small and Medium Enterprise Agency in 1952–3 for Toyota and members of *Tokai Kyoho-kai* mentioned in Section 4.3, the problem of identification has critical importance. Though it was, after all, a big event and had a great impact on Toyota, one has to be careful not to overestimate the role of the government. Note, at least, that only Toyota's case is considered successful. If the government

could contribute greatly in the case of Toyota why not for other car manufacturers and firms in other industries?

46. 'You are emptying the baby out with the bath water' is one type of reaction to my two papers adopted in this volume as Chapters 9 and 10.

47. For details, see Section 10.5 below.

48. Many praise the superior capability of Japan's bureaucrats and argue that, because of their excellent advice and guidance, Japan has realized great economic success. Note, however, that many others agree with the comment of an official in the Ministry of Finance who said that frankly 'we should rather use "in spite of" instead of "because of", that is, in spite of their non-excellent guidance, the Japanese economy was a success'.

9 Economic Consequences of Investment Coordination in the Steel Industry

1. One cannot estimate the impact of regulation directly from what the regulator does or insists on doing. As Stigler and Friedland (1962, p. 1) argue, 'The innumerable regulatory actions are conclusive proof, not of effective regulation, but of the desire to regulate'. See also Caves (1964, pp. 180–81).

2. Coase (1964, p. 194) is an example of a sceptical view at an early stage: 'What the regulatory commissions are trying to do is difficult to discover; what effect these commissions actually have is, to a large extent, unknown; when it can be discovered, it is often absurd.' Also see Stigler and Friedland (1962) and Posner (1969). For an overall review, see Kahn (1988) and Vickers and Yarrow (1988) and Foster (1992) especially for the UK.

3. Recall the discussion in Section 8.4 that the new industrial order debate was fought on the common understanding of the necessity to avoid 'excessive competition'.

4. For instance, an attempt to build an econometric industry model and to use a policy dummy for identification seems to be too brave. There are three difficulties: (1) little information is available on what actually occurred in the coordination process, and the government's role; (2) it is very hard to model the investment behaviour of individual firms and the total industry in such an oligopolistic market partly because of the scarcity of information; in building a model there is hardly a persuasive way to select valid assumptions, for instance, on the reaction of rival firms; (3) little information is available to test the hypothesis. Therefore, even when an econometric study finds that the coefficient of the policy dummy variable is effective, little information is available for interpretation and it is dangerous to reach a conclusion with only the finding that the policy was effective.

5. Often this conclusion is contrasted with that of Imai (1976). See, for instance, Tsuruta (1988, p. 86) and Yamawaki (1988, p. 294). The fifth Section of the original version of this chapter, Miwa (1990a, pp. 263–76), is a critical review of the past literature, mostly the examination of Imai (1976). I argue there that Imai's (1976) conclusion–based on incorrect facts, unclear reasoning and unpersuasive empirical study–is wrong. In the original, I used this result as the third basis for the conclusion.

6. The discussion of this chapter is empirical, and I do not go into the normative side of the past controversy. Most of the past literature, see Imai (1976), focused on whether investment coordination was beneficial for the economy, on the assumption that it strongly affected investment behaviour of individual firms. My conclusion that there was no impact implies that such debate is useless.

7. *Toyo Keizai*, 6 April 1974. See also Imai (1976, pp. 140–1), and Section 9.3 below. Note, however, that whether the guide once was effective is another question. The Act is officially titled the Act Concerning Foreign Capital, and was enacted in 1950. Under this Act before the liberalization in 1969, coupled with the Foreign Exchange Control Act, 'technology import licences . . . were allowed preferentially to industries expected to contribute to heavy and chemical industrialization and attain comparative advantage as future export industries. Within the industries, the licences were granted to the firms with a high promise of developing into foreign exchange earners as future exporters by embodying the imported technology in equipment investment' (Goto and Wakasugi, 1988, p. 189).

8. On this occasion, eight firms participated in the coordination programme: Yawata Steel (Yawata), Fuji Steel (Fuji), NKK Corporation (Kokan), Kawasaki Steel (Kawatetsu), Sumitomo Metal Industries (Sumikin), Kobe Steel (Kobe), Amagasaki Steel and Nakayama Steel Works. Hereafter I use the abbreviations shown in parentheses.

9. Formally released as the interim report of the Heavy Industries Division on 2 November 1966. The Industry Rationalization Council was reorganized into the Industrial Structure Council in 1964. Hereafter, for simplicity, I use ISC for both.

10. In this chapter, the term 'demand' means not the domestic demand but the demand for the products of Japanese manufacturers, including export demand. Also the term 'supply' is that by Japanese manufacturers. Therefore, *ex post* 'demand' always equals *ex post* 'supply' or 'output'.

11. I use the term 'informal regulation' as the translation of *gyosei shido* in preference to the standard translation of 'administrative guidance'. On this choice, see Section 10.2 below.

12. The Industrial Finance Committee of ISC, for which the coordination was formally requested, was supposed to accept the conclusion of the Steel Committee.

13. As will be shown in Section 9.3, there was in substance no change in the coordination process.

14. For instance, the production share of three leading firms in hot-rolled coil and sheet was 50.2 per cent in 1963 and 51.8 per cent in 1966. Those for cold-rolled sheet was 46.8 per cent in 1963 and 44.7 per cent in 1966. Those for wide strips were 62.1 per cent and 50.3 per cent, and for pipes 53.5 per cent and 56.3 per cent. See FTC (1969).

15. Also in prewar Japan, steel manufacturers tried to maintain stable coordination. Because of the import pressure of pig iron, however, the stability of coordination was rather more limited than during the postwar period. (See Okazaki, 1993). With the advantage of a converter furnace over an open-hearth furnace, the conditions for coordination were established in the second half of the 1950s, which made it fairly successful.

16. The Sumikin (Sumitomo Metal Industries) Incident, which occurred in 1965 as a reaction against output and price coordination by MITI through informal regulation (*kankoku sotan*), came about because of a confrontation neither on whether output coordination was unnecessary nor on the amount of total output for coordination but on the allocation of shares. As Tachibana (1966, p. 19) argues, 'Sumikin did not insist on free competition. It is the problem of output share allocation, as they assert, "as repeatedly insisted, we are not against the raw steel output coordination. We are against its unequal and unfair method".' Also see Zadankai (1966, especially p. 28) and the statement of Mr. Hyuga, the president of Sumikin, in *Ekonomisuto*, 30 November 1976.

17. The steel manufacturer's views are symbolically revealed in the following statements: 'Mr Inayama, the president of Yawata: Almost always, the forecast of the government has been incorrect (laughing). A pessimist always underestimates the future demand.' Mr Hyuga, the president of Sumikin: 'The government's forecast was the worst, and the industry's was the second. The FY 1966 demand in fact is exceeding 50 million tons, which is 7 million tons larger than the forecast at the beginning of the year' (*Toyo Keizai*, 10 December 1966).

18. Output coordination of raw steel both in 1962–3 and 1965–6 are examples. See also fn. 108 of Miwa (1990a, p. 270).

19. Not all firms consistently stood on the same side, and often the side was chosen strategically (for instance, a firm constructing a blast furnace tended to stand on the weak forecast side in order to postpone the others' plans, which created room for its next capacity increase plan). However, in total, Yawata and Fuji were representatives of the former, and Sumikin of the latter.

20. It finally built five blast furnaces in the Wakayama mill. It is the custom to number them in this manner.

21. Note that FY begins in April in Japan.

22. This conclusion was summed up thus 'Sumikin conceded in the way of output coordination and Yawata in investment coordination' (*Toyo Keizai*, 31 July 1965). Note, however, that whether this MITI informal regulation had actual impact is another question. As shown in Section 10.3, the steel output coordination in the 1960s was basically through self-coordination and was not successful, and MITI's contribution to this attempt was minor. It was in the next quarter of the year, October–December, that the Sumikin Incident arose over the way in which output coordination was handled.

23. This conclusion had an exception clause, and for the consequences of this moratorium agreement see Section 9.4 below.

24. Mr Tokunaga, then a managing director of Fuji Steel, was a former vice minister of MITI.

25. See Tsuruta (1988, pp. 70–71).

26. This is a corollary to the general discussion on the stability of cartels.

27. See the note 2 above.

28. These two are officially, the Act on Temporary Measures for the Promotion of the Machinery Industry and the Act on Temporary Measures for the Promotion of the Electronics Industry. See Komiya (1988, p. 16).

29. See Tsuruta (1988, p. 71).

30. See Negishi (1975). Even in this case the government did not always use its power. In the case of the Petroleum Industry Act, for instance, it is the Petroleum Council that decides formal action against violators (see *Nihon Keizai Shimbun*, 6 November 1969 and Section 10.4 below). Also in the Banking Act, action takes the form of notification (*tsutatsu*) of the bureau director.

31. For instance, under the Act on Temporary Measures for Textile Industry Equipment and Related Equipment (New Textile Act) enacted in 1964, the capacity registration system was adopted, and machines such as spinning machines could be built up only via registration (Section 3) and a new capacity could be registered only for replacement of an old one (Section 7). In the petrochemical industry, the *Kanmin* Consultative Group was established in December 1964. It set guidelines for new naphtha facilities in January 1965, and the goal of the technology licence approval guidelines became ethylene production of 100 000 tons per year. See Tsuruta (1988, p. 72). But this is not based on an industry act, and is not included in the second category.

32. For instance, under the Act Concerning the Organization of Small and Medium Enterprises (1957), the Minister of MITI is empowered to issue an order to outsiders of a cooperative of small business and restrict or prohibit the construction of new capacity when their action impedes the stabilizing activities of the cooperative.

33. See Goto and Wakasugi (1988, p. 189). 'Until the liberalization of capital transactions, the Foreign Capital Council had approval powers over the importation of foreign technology. This licensing system continued until 1972, when capital transactions in the petrochemical industry were liberalized' (Tsuruta, 1988, p. 71). For instance, the production technology of high-density polyethylene, one of the most important petrochemical products, was at the start totally imported and under the control of the Foreign Capital Act. On this point, see Nakamura *et al.* (1971, p. 167).

34. For a general discussion of informal regulation, see Sections 8.4 and 10.2

35. The investment coordination based on the discussion within MITI in the ammonia industry in 1968 was an example. See Itoh (1968).

36. The role of this Committee was both to 'coordinate' the scale of the total investment of all industries, 15 major industries to which MITI was the *genkyoku*, and to allocate it appropriately among industries.

37. As shown above, following the 1966 ISC report, the Steel Committee was established within ISC for the steel industry and the Industrial Finance Committee was supposed to accept the conclusion of the Steel Committee.

38. On the *Kanmin* system, see Section 8.3 above. Chemical fibres and petrochemicals are famous examples, but the same type of groups, though with other names, were established in other manufactures such as vinyl chloride pipe.

39. As shown in the following example, some statements on the validity of the effectiveness of informal regulation are biased. I heard from a manager of a big heavy-duty electric equipment manufacturer that, in the 1950s when it planned to enter the home electronics industry, the Bank of Japan opposed the plan and it could not borrow from city banks because of the informal regulation of the Bank of Japan. But a manager of the other city bank explains differently: 'No such regulation did and could exist. The Bank of Japan had enough information to make regulation neither on individual industries nor on firms. In my view, the bank used the 'regulation' of the Bank as an excuse to refuse the loan proposal.' In fact, this firm entered the market and enjoyed significant success.

40. For instance, when Idemitsu refused the informal regulation of MITI on output quota in 1965, two years after the Idemitsu Incident, the company was said to have finally accepted the regulation because of two unrelated reasons. First, it needed a licence to borrow US$ 40 million from Gulf Oil. Second, it needed MITI's permission to initiate the second naphtha cracking facility for Idemitsu Petrochemical Industries, its subsidiary. See Kawasaki (1966, p. 54). For discussion of the Idemitsu Incident, see Section 10.4.

41. Mr Shigeo Nagano, the president of Fuji Steel and the most enthusiastic promotor of the steel investment coordination, proposed the enactment of a Steel Industry Act and explained the reason: 'In order to suppress the excessive competition in investment in the steel industry, the present self-coordination method through cartel and informal regulation is not enough. It needs to be backed up by an Act based on the national interest' (*Asahi Shimbun*, 30 March 1966). This statement suggested that the steel investment coordination programme was not ensured the effectiveness by enforcement power.

42. Recall the argument on 'signalling effects' or 'cowbell effects' in note 39 of Chapter 3.

43. Ogura and Yoshino (1988, p. 136) and Yamawaki (1988, pp. 283 and 286). See also Fukukawa (1964) and Nihon Keizai Chosa Kyogi-kai (1971, p. 146).
44. See Nihon Keizai Chosa Kyogi-kai (1971, p. 147).
45. See Tanaka (1975, p. 134 and Chapter 7)
46. To be precise, it was not the control of bunker coal but the allocation of foreign currency for imports, whose legal basis was Section 9 of the Trade Control Ordinance. See Zadankai (1966, p. 38). Throughout the 1950s, the foreign exchange allocation system under the Foreign Exchange and Foreign Trade Control Act (1949) was actively applied as an important means of restricting imports. With the June 1960 announcement of the overall Plan for Trade and Capital Liberalization, however, its use was gradually eliminated. From October 1960 for pig iron and June 1961 for ordinary semi-finished products and rolled steel, application of the allocation system ceased. See Yamawaki (1988, p. 289).
47. For this incident, see note 16 above and Section 10.3.
48. For a general discussion on this point, see Section 10.2 below
49. The Incident ended with the acceptance of the output quota by Sumikin, which was explained by Negishi (1977, p. 146) as 'MITI forced Sumikin to accept the regulation by allocating import licences according to the output quota'. But other explanations are also possible. The task of identifying the impact of an intervention is seldom easy, but many argue that the further price decline of steel products was one potential reason. See Zadankai (1966, p. 30), Tachibana (1966), Kawasaki (1966) and the statement of Mr. Hyuga, the chairman of Sumikin, in *Ekonomisuto* 30 November 1976, pp. 78–85.
50. As shown in the previous Section, the steel investment coordination for FY 1965 foundered. It is reported that MITI stuck to their basic procedure: 'First, we ask the firms to reach an agreement. In case Sumikin insists on the adoption of its plan, we judge the plan "inappropriate" in the Industrial Finance Committee, and request the Federation of Bankers Association of Japan to refuse their loan proposal' (*Toyo Keizai*, 17 April 1965). As mentioned above, however, the effectiveness of regulations based on coordination through the Committee was dubious.
51. See Komiya (1975, Chapter 3), Ogura and Yoshino (1988, pp. 129–32), and Yamawaki (1988, pp. 285–6).
52. *Nihon Keizai Shimbun*, 18 November 1970, and *Toyo Keizai*, 17 October 1970.
53. Mr Nagano, the president of Fuji, stated in an interview: 'After all, self-coordination in fact does not work well . . . Even in the past, we, Yawata and Fuji, had no power to force other firms to accept our will. No power to force Sumikin not to build a new capacity. The government had no legal power, either. We are not in a controlled economy' (*Toyo Keizai*, 22 June 1968).
54. Recall the argument in Section 8.5 on the bias of information available for outsiders from the insiders, including the government. However, Nakamura (1974, p. 60), for instance, took the case of the steel investment coordination as an example of effective informal regulation that intervened in actions of individual firms, and quoted the explanation of MITI (1969) quoted in the text.
55. For instance, in the FY 1965 investment coordination, there was a hot debate on the evaluation of the supply capacity of existing facilities and those already approved for construction. The debate focused on such detailed points as converter furnace ratios, pig-iron making capability of blast furnaces, reduction of work of blast furnaces because of repair and suspension, and their low-level operation at the start. See *Toyo Keizai*, 17 April 1965.

56. I use the term 'approve', but nobody had the power to refuse some of them.
57. For the character and role of the long-term forecast, recall the discussion in the second part of Section 9.2.
58. Note that terms such as 'excessive competition' and 'excess capacity', though so widely and frequently used, were ill-defined. The following opposite views on the same state expressed by two presidents of major steel firms were symbolic of the ambiguity: 'Mr Hyuga, the president of Sumikin: We increased production capacities competitively, and I don't think there is excess capacity. In fact, we are importing pig iron. Interviewer: You mean that there has been no excessive competition in a strict sense in the steel industry? / Mr Hyuga: In conclusion, I should say, "yes"' (*Toyo Keizai*, 8 June 1968); 'Mr Fujimoto, the president of Kawatetsu: I don't know what is the public's answer to whether there has been excessive competition in the steel industry. I do think there has been. Simply, production always exceeded demand. Production capacity is excessive, I believe' (*Toyo Keizai*, 13 July 1968).
59. Initially MITI proposed a plan to approve the initiation of construction in FY 1960 of two blast furnaces. See Kawasaki (1968, p. 600).
60. At the beginning of the coordination, MITI anticipated the FY 1960 steel demand to be 19.6 million tons (Kawasaki, 1968, p. 601), but the actual production was 23.2 million tons.
61. Statement made on 22 December 1960. See Shin Nippon Seitetsu (1970. p. 239). For the character of this material, see note 15 of the next chapter.
62. For instance, Yawata postponed the initiation of Sakai no. 1 construction and Fuji suspended the construction of Tokai no. 1. For further information, see Miwa (1990a, p. 256, fn.71).
63. On this point, see Miwa (1990a, p. 256, Table 9.3).
64. MITI (1969, p. 49), however, insists upon the effectiveness of the coordination:

> 18 blast furnaces have been completed since 1960, of which eight postponed the time of completion than the initial plan with the coordination programme. However, we needed output coordination of raw steel in 1962–3 and 1965–6. If we had not coordinated investment, we would have suffered from a larger capacity increase and more serious turmoil in steel product markets.

As shown above, however, many postponed the construction schedule not because of the coordination but because of the recession, for instance, in 1962.
65. Also Sogo Seisaku Kenkyu-kai (1963, p. 222), evaluating the result of FY 1962 coordination as 'a step for real coordination', insisted, 'Real coordination is to coordinate long-term plans, that is, to select some from individual firms' plant construction plans or to coordinate the order of their construction, including, as a part, the promotion of joint investment'.
66. Because of the character of the coordination mentioned in Section 9.2, whether or not to adopt a long-term allocation rule was a hot issue. Firms with a weak forecast position such as Yawata and Fuji, were enthusiastic about establishing a rule, and those with a strong position were against it. As mentioned also in Section 9.2, the final result of the FY 1965 coordination was that, for the two years of FY 1965 and FY 1966, firms were free to initiate new construction of blast and converter furnaces, but no new rolling mills. However, the two years' moratorium agreement had an exception clause, on which firms began to propose plans for new capacity construction in FY 1966. They finally cancelled the agreement in November.

67. Recall the statement of Mr Tokunaga quoted at the end of Section 9.2.
68. See *Toyo Keizai*, 27 July 1968.
69. The capacity increase with these seven blast furnaces was thought to be enough for the demand forecast of the Industrial Structure Council for FY 1973, 111.6 million tons in raw steel base (120 million tons, the historical peak, was the actual output).
70. To be precise, the FY 1965 coordination reached an agreement for FY 1965 and FY 1966 that firms were free to initiate construction of new blast and converter furnaces. But for FY 1969, industry members gave up the coordination. Of five for FY 1969, two were for Nippon Steel before the merger in 1970, and Ohita no. 2 for FY 1970 after the merger. Until then they coordinated only the time of initiation of construction. Since the FY 1969 coordination, the focus has centred on the time of completion with a condition that the time of initiation should be no more than 18 months before the approved time of completion.
71. For economic plans in Japan, see Komine (1993).
72. Ohita no. 2. Also Tobata no. 4 as a replacement.
73. The demand forecast for FY 1975 varied widely: 130 million tons in raw steel base by Nippon steel; 165 million tons by Sumikin; 145–55 million tons by MITI. *Toyo Keizai*, 19 June 1971.
74. *Toyo Keizai*, 19 June 1971.
75. Yawata and Fuji merged into Nippon Steel in March 1970. This was a merger between the two largest firms. As shown below in Table 9.3, the market share of the new firm was over 30 per cent, both in semi-finished products and in principal ordinary steel products. The new firm was relatively large compared to those of rivals, and became a dominant one. I believe this merger functioned as a strong support for the overall coordination of the industry and was by itself a part of the coordination. See Chapter 12 of Miwa (1990a) for my view of this merger. The relation of the steel investment coordination to the output coordination was expressed in the statement of Mr Fujimoto, the president of Kawatetsu: 'If each firm's plans for capacity construction has been approved, the output coordination would have been hard to maintain and each firm's profitability disastrous, which we feared and hated' (*Toyo Keizai*, 13 July 1968).
76. The completion of Ohita No. 2 was achieved in the autumn of 1976, later than that of Kashima no. 3 of Sumikin, adopted in the FY 1974 coordination.
77. Recall the above mentioned result of the FY 1971 coordination.
78. The steel production in FY 1967 was 2.75 times larger than that in FY 1960, which implies that most of the former was produced with capacities constructed under the investment coordination programme.
79. In my view, the largest impact of MITI on the steel investment coordination was to make more difficult, perhaps only slightly, an application of the Anti-monopoly Act to the coordination by providing the result of the coordination with a form of informal regulation and by concluding with FTC the understanding in November 1966 on 'The Application of the Anti-monopoly Act to the Use of Policies for the Reform of Structure of Industry.' For this understanding, see, for instance, Imai (1976, pp. 141–2).
80. The first five points are related to the direct impact of coordination policies. The sixth point suggests an indirect impact. By affecting the overall coordination which had an impact of each firm's behaviour including investment, the investment coordination might have an impact on each firm's investment. However, examination of such an indirect impact is beyond the scope of this chapter. For such an indirect impact, see Section 10.5.
81. Recall note 6 above.

10 Coordination within Industry: Output, Price and Investment

1. It is necessary to explain why the term 'intra-industry coordination' (coordination within industry), which is hardly ever used, is employed in this chapter. In the literature on postwar Japanese industrial policy, the terms, output coordination, price coordination and capacity (investment) coordination appear frequently. These are applied to an extremely wide range of industries, and it seems that such policies are often thought of as being the model of industrial policy, or at least a representative form. I am applying to these as a whole the term 'intra-industry coordination' and am analysing them together in this chapter for three reasons. First, these are all often closely linked in practice and can be observed to play complementary roles. Second, all of them have the common characteristic that they seek to coordinate the mutual interests of the firms that comprise an industry. Third, though to a varying extent, there is a common feature in that the government often participates in a variety of ways, although its role may not be obvious and it may often participate for some particular purpose.

   Thus in this chapter 'intra-industry coordination' is used as a general term for the various patterns referred to as output, price and capacity investment coordination. Whether or not each of these fits into this mould can be judged for each of the cases described in the following analysis. Instead of 'intra-industry coordination', the phrase 'intra-industry coordination policies' could be used, but this analysis as a whole, and in particular Section 10.2, should serve as an explanation why this has not been done.

2. The specific reasons why it is difficult to distinguish the impact of policy may be illustrated, as was done in Section 8.6, by referring to the example of the list-price system (*koukai hanbai seido*, literally open [public] sale system) in the steel industry to be discussed in Section 10.3.

3. For example, concerning the petrochemical industry, Tsuruta (1982, p. 186) states that, 'when there is government intervention based on legal powers of compulsion, then the performance of the industrial organization helps directly in evaluating the effectiveness of the government intervention'. However, it is not easy, for example, to judge the effectiveness of medical treatment by the course of a patient's illness following hospitalization, because a patient's demise may not imply that there were faults in his or her treatment. Hence this sort of reasoning cannot be thought appropriate. Even though there may be 'legal powers of compulsion', they do not extend to all facets of a firm's behaviour, and it is wrong to think that there are no restrictions on the use of these powers. Again, policy is not able to handle all the factors that affect the 'performance of the industrial organization'. For example, when it became possible to procure low-cost oil, it was inconceivable that some policy response could have been used to forestall a worsening of performance in the coal mining industry.

4. As mentioned in Chapter 8, it is instructive to consider the debate on the new industrial order and the failed Specified Industries Act in the first half of the 1960s, especially in 1962–3, and the 1968 debate arising from the merger of Yawata Steel and Fuji Steel.

5. See, for example, Harada (1983).

6. Recall the comment of Kyogoku (1983, p. 347) quoted in note 25 of Chapter 8.

7. Haley, however, emphasized 'its ubiquity' (p. 162) in Japan, and began his chapter, 'Conclusion: Command without Coercion', by stating: 'Words fail to convey the nature and process of governance in Japan. No commonly accepted paradigm of how policy is made and enforced seems to fit. Terms like "regulation", "control", "freedom" and even "autonomy" and "consensus"

seem oddly inappropriate' (p. 193). I cannot agree with him on these points, and readers of Part III of this volume must realize the reason for my disagreement.

8. Details of the argument are presented for the petroleum refining industry in Section 10.4.

9. For '*genkyoku*' and the industry–government relationship, see the second part of Section 8.4.

10. This situation reflects the nature of output coordination and the role of the government therein. Section 10.6 also touches on this point.

11. Fair Trade Commission (FTC) (1977, p. 99).

12. Imai (1976, p. 154).

13. Uekusa (1982, p. 209).

14. As mentioned in Section 8.4, the system remained in effect until June 1991, when it was finally abolished.

15. This volume is a compilation of the main Sections of the *Eigyo Junpo* (Ten-Day Operations Report) for the years 1959–62. I expect that there will be objections to using this source as the primary material for judging the actual functioning of the list-price system. However, this material is relevant for the following three reasons: (1) this company, particularly Yawata Steel before the merger with Fuji Steel in 1970, was always regarded as the leader of the industry, and was furthermore a continually enthusiastic leader of the list-price system; (2) these materials were drawn up for firms with which they had a long-term business relationship, so that one would expect them to be frank; (3) during this period the Anti-monopoly Act was in hibernation, and so one would presume that the opinions expressed in it are not biased by the existence of the Anti-monopoly Act or any concern with public opinion in support of the Act.

16. This statement is from a summary explanation by Inayama at the 26 July meeting of the Public Sale ('list price') Committee. See page 215 for the evaluation of the system by trading firms/wholesalers and steel consumers. See page 69 for the determination of prices before the change in the system.

17. Recall the figures in Table 9.1.

18. Mr Inayama, then Managing Director of Yawata Steel, stated at the 20 January 1959 Futures Committee meeting that, 'although there is such a thing as a depression cartel, the fact of the matter is that we are carrying out the list-price system under informal regulation, without bothering to request approval of a depression cartel' (ibid, p. 26). Section 24.3 of the Anti-monopoly Act authorizes the FTC to permit depression cartels in accordance with the requirements, such as that the price of the commodity in question must be below the industry average production cost for such commodity. When the requirements are present, the FTC may grant approval to a depression cartel for a limited period of time, usually for six months. A depression cartel approved by the FTC enjoys exemption from application of the Anti-monopoly Act.

19. This is part of the statement by Mr Abe, Director of the Sales Division of Yawata Steel, at the 24 October 1962 meeting of the Futures Committee.

20. Mr Inayama, the Chairman of the General Affairs Subcommittee, stated:

> If this is done, then because it is accompanied by financing for the full quantity of the products, there is of course no need to discount heavily. Until now, it was feared that the method of buying up unsold steel would lead to under-the-counter sales and the sales of many cheap products, along with it being very difficult to monitor. From now on, however, if all steel, including secondary products, is bought up by a specified trading firm/wholesaler, then not a single item will leave the factory. (Ibid., p. 448)

21. In this period, the 'proportional decrease in ingot production will be increased by 5 percentage points . . . and at the same time the product-specific output reduction system will be strengthened . . . with heavy and medium plates output to be cut by 40 per cent from the base level of January of this year' (ibid., p. 491).

22. The monitoring system consisted of 'industry members sending people to each other to monitor production' (ibid., p. 518).

23. Recall that it was stated in Section 10.2 that 'furthermore, there is no reason to presume that preventing excess capacity and "excessive competition" had always to be the primary goal for all participants'. Here we do not consider the issue of whether MITI considered this to be desirable, or whether it actually had sufficient power.

24. Tokunaga (1967, p. 58). See Section 9.2. Hisatsugu Tokunaga was at the time a Managing Director of Fuji Steel and a former administrative vice-minister of MITI. For a view of the outcome of the FY 1960 coordination, recall the evaluation by Mr Inayama, quoted in Section 9.4.

25. This can be viewed as an evaluation of the entire history of investment coordination. In contrast to this view, some would mention that the Sumikin (Sumitomo Metals) Incident arose over the way in which output coordination was handled in 1965. However, I do not feel it is relevant to the current discussion. There was a time lapse between the decisions on capacity investment coordination and the occurrence of the Sumikin Incident, and even the closing off of the allocation of import licences for bunker coal was not sufficient to force investment coordination (see Section 9.3 above). Upham (1986) studies the Sumikin Incident and emphasizes the government's active intervention in the private sector and the effectiveness of government policy. In view of how we saw industrial policy carried out in Section 10.2, however, this Incident is an example of the failure of industrial policy, and one which does not shed light on what the government could do, but can rather be viewed as useful in judging what the government could not do. As shown in the text, the government could not and did not participate actively in the output coordination programme in the preceding period even when self-coordination proved to be ineffective. See also note 49 of Chapter 9.

26. For the details of this, see ibid., pp. 22–3.

27. Ibid., p. 29. This is according to Section 10 of the Petroleum Industry Act.

28. This standard is set out in Section 6 of the Act

29. Later, in the summer of 1962, the Industrial Structure Committee made known its basic line of thinking on the new industrial order, which was the predecessor to the proposed Specified Industries Act. It should be noted that there were two main points in the industry's criticism of the Specified Industries Act. First, it was feared that the restrictions on the freedom of industrial activity that the Act would impose would result in a system of bureaucratic control. Second, it was feared that, if anything, the setting of promotion standards in line with bureaucratic-type thinking and restrictions on firm activities would lead to a weakening of competitive strength. This draws upon Tsuruta (1976, pp. 442–3).

30. This source is a compilation of the series of Tokyo High Court decisions during 1980–81 on the so-called 'Petroleum Cartel Case'. This is used here because it includes the 26 September 1980 decision on the Petroleum Association of Japan and two others in the Output Coordination Case.

31. This standard 'was based on a composite index, with weights of one-third each of the market share of fuel oil sales, the share of all imported oil processed for domestic consumption and the current share in total average capacity' (ibid., p. 212).

32. It ceased in the second half of FY 1966 (ibid., p. 217).

33. This was done from November 1962 to February 1966.

34. It is undoubtedly wrong to assume, however, that without government participation in this fashion such meetings would not have been held. This would be to overrate the effectiveness of policy.

35. For example, in the 1960s there were Idemitsu Kosan, Nisshin Spinning and Sumitomo Metal Industries and, more recently, Tokyo Steel Mfg.

36. The report of the government discussed in Section 10.2 states that one of the reasons for firms having followed informal regulation was that 'Japanese firms are organized into associations industry by industry, and it is difficult for them to act as outsiders. Larger firms in particular are strongly aware that they comprise an industry, and dislike threatening their own foundation by upsetting the order within their industry' (Administrative Management Agency, 1981, p. 107).

37. In particular, the situation described in the first point, particularly in the second half of the paragraph, had a deleterious effect on the maintenance and furthering of competition, and so this can serve as a basis for judging that 'coordination' itself is undesirable.

38. See Komiya (1975, pp. 327–8).

39. Tanaka (1980, pp. 34 and 37).

11 Corporate Governance in Japanese Firms: The Body of Employees as the Controlling Group and Friendly Shareholders

1. For these figures, see note 9 of Chapter 1.

2. By 'legal fiction' they mean the artificial construct under the law which allows organizations to be treated as individuals (ibid., p. 311).

3. This concept corresponds to Alchian and Demsetz's (1972, p. 778) 'centralized contractual agent in a team productive process'.

4. Dore (1992) does not assert that this community nature is peculiar to only Japanese firms. In the corresponding commentary, Harold E. Edmondson, a Vice President of Hewlett-Packard, wrote that '[w]hile the entity is important in Japan, . . . feeling is present in many American companies, too', and that 'I feel that there is a fair amount of the cooperative or Japanese approach to things in our industry' (Edmondson 1992, p. 26).

5. This relationship is what Simon calls 'authority'. See Simon (1976, Chapter VII).

6. This is only a result of the position of the body of employees, not that their stable position is by *antei-kabunushi*, as is often misunderstood. When the latter is the case, nothing prevents shareholders from deciding together to neglect the will of directors and managers and at least we would have observed some such examples.

7. All data are from the *Security Reports* (*Yuka Shoken Hokoku-sho*) (Ministry of Finance).

8. The corresponding figures for 20 firms with employees between 1 000 and 2 000 in 1990 were 58.47 per cent in 1980 and 55.25 per cent in 1990.

9. Directors are selected at a slightly higher age in Kayaba, and lower in Koito. The average age of the few directors selected from outside the firm was around 50. For instance, the two directors of Kayaba from Fuji Bank were both selected at the age of 52. Also the two directors of Aisin Seiki from Toyota were selected at 52.

10. The former top two remained on the board and occupied the newly created seats of chairman and vice-chairman (positions presumably only nominally higher than the president). At the time of the change, the former president was 88 years old and the former no. 2 director was 64 years old.

11. When Boone Pickens attempted a takeover of Koito, commentators and journalists represented this firm as a member of Toyota group both because of the large shareholding and because the president was once a manager of Toyota. This characterization is a matter of definition. Note the two points. First, Nissan appeared as a large shareholder at the same time as Toyota, and has been a stable, large shareholder. Second, Mr Matsuura, a former manager of Toyota, was selected as president of Koito in 1985 at the age of 59, after 13 years' experience as a board member of Koito. Mr Ohtake, who was the former president selected in 1979 at the age of 65, had been a board member since 1961 and remained as chairman thereafter. Another Mr Ohtake was the president from 1972 to 1979, and then became chairman at 68.

12. One may argue that corporation is based on the corporate law which assigns as the claim on the residual to shareholders, who therefore obviously control the firm. However, as Komiya (1990, pp. 168–9) argued, 'irrespective of legal definition of rights and responsibilities, ownership of the firm, in an economic sense, is not easily defined. "Ownership" is not a black-and-white affair' (quoted above in Section 7.4). When shareholders cannot decide the residual by themselves, the assigned residual claimants position does not make sense. One simple fact is that in Japan there has been no case where shareholders received positive returns from liquidating a firm listed on a stock exchange.

13. Thus Kaplan and Minton's (1993) finding that in Japanese firms the turnover of directors is higher when the shareholder's rate of return is lower can be interpreted also as a result of employees' criticism of the board's performance.

14. The four largest shareholders of these banks were all life insurance companies. The market value of these banks' equity in Toyota's portfolio was roughly 40 per cent that of Toyota's equity in their portfolio in March 1993.

15. The market value of each of these banks' stocks owned by Kayaba was about 40 per cent that of Kayaba's stock they held in March 1993.

16. As shown in Chapter 4, almost every *Kyoho-kai* member is also a member of other assemblers' suppliers association, and cross-holds the equity with Toyota's rival assemblers. For instance, Kayaba is also associated with Nissan, Mitsubishi, Suzuki, Hino and Mazda.

17. *Nihon Keizai Shimbun*, 20 June 1994, reported that recently some supposed friendly shareholders sold shares, especially bank shares, on the market, and commented that cross-holding of the equity between firms without close trade relationship would decrease steadily.

18. The above story of Japanese friendly shareholders is affected by two characteristics of the Japanese legal system. First, Section 9 of the Anti-monopoly Act stipulates that 'No holding company shall be established'. Also, Section 11 states, 'No company engaged in financial business shall acquire or hold stock of another company in Japan if by doing so it holds in excess of 5 per cent (10 per cent in the case of an insurance company) of the total outstanding stock'. Second, corporate law (Sections 222–1 and 242 of the Commercial Code) strictly limits the role of preferred stock, which results in almost non-existence of preferred stocks in Japan. For the roles of preferred stock, and more generally dual class common stock, see Gordon (1990).

19. Recall, from Chapter 4, that suppliers trust that assemblers will consider their interests. This trust has played a crucial role in the development of an efficient car production system.

20. For a critical review of the literature on corporate groups in Japan, see Chapter 7.

21. This view is compatible with Dore's second feature of the Japanese economy (1992, p. 20). 'One of the banks is generally considered a firm's lead bank. It may

provide only marginally more loan capital than other banks, but it will own more of the firm's equity, it will put more effort into monitoring the companies performance, and it will be the prime mover in any brink-of-bankruptcy reconstruction'. Often the supporters of this view proceed to suggest that this lead bank, usually called main bank, has significant power and even controls the borrower's management. However, why does the controlling group continue to choose a certain main bank? As shown in Chapter 6, I am quite sceptical on the current flood of literature on the Japanese main bank system which, instead of assuming a competitive market, implicitly assumes the existence of a tight cartel among Japanese financial institutions and its dominance in the Japanese capital market.

22. A similar view is often expressed for non-Japanese firms. For instance, Thurow (1992) pointed out that, among the four factors (natural resources, capital, technology, and skills, where skills include the management skills necessary to coordinate these factors of production) traditionally contributing to making individuals rich, companies successful, and nations prosperous, 'managerial and work force skills' are left 'as the critical strategic variable in the competitive equation' (p. v).

23. Like firms shown above in the Toyota Group, such as Nihon Denso and Aisin Seiki, even parent companies which hold more than half of the stock of their subsidiaries may not have the power to enforce their will. Because of the critical importance of management and workforce skills, it is in the interest of the parent company to be a friendly shareholder. Many cases of this kind are found in Japan, such as Hitachi Cable, Hitachi Metals and Toshiba Machine, discussed above in Section 7.6.

24. Another principal study was Gordon (1945). On this point, see Bain (1968, pp. 63–6) and Williamson (1964). As Gilson and Roe (1993, p. 873) rightly point out, before the recent basic paradigm shift,

> the 'traditional' model of American corporate governance presented the Berle–Means corporation – characterized by a separation of ownership and management resulting from the need of growing enterprises for capital and the specialization of management – as the pinnacle in the evolution of organizational forms. Given this model's dominance, the study of comparative corporate governance was peripheral; governance systems differing from the American paradigm were dismissed as mere intermediate steps on the path to perfection, or as evolutionary dead-ends, the neanderthals of corporate governance.

Hence the American system's characteristics colour the lens through which comparative studies viewed the rest of the world. They argue, however, '[c]omparative corporate governance . . . now enjoys important government and scholarly attention' (p. 871). With this observation, unfortunately, they study Japan's *keiretsu*, following the conventional view, shown to be totally false in Part II of this volume.

25. As mentioned in Chapter 7, Miyazaki (1976) followed Gordon. For the separation in Japan, see, for instance, Chapter 4 of Hazama (1989).

26. Recall note 12 above.

27. As mentioned above, this definition is from Simon (1976, p. 119).

28. Dividends first decreased to 6 yen per year in 1971, increased again to 7.5 yen in 1973, but returned to and stayed at 5 yen even when dividend payment exceeded the profit. The only exception was FY 1977 when dividend payment fell to 4.5 yen

as profit per share was only 0.9 yen. For the behaviour of banks, including main banks, see Chapter 6.

29. M&As, particularly those through takeovers, are not popular in Japan. Note, however, that takeovers, and in particular hostile bids, are not the normal form of corporate control. As Jenkinson and Mayer (1993) points out, outside the UK and USA, hostile takeovers are largely absent in most countries, including Continental Europe and Japan.

30. See *Toyo Keizai*, 4 June 1994, p. 18. *Nihon Keizai Shimbun*, 6 June 1994, reported that Nippon Steel's extra payment amounts to 60 billion yen (nearly US$ 600 million) this year. It can pay this amount because of its huge retained profits. I do not intend to argue that lifetime employment is prevalent in Japan.

31. Note that the dividend irrelevance theorem – dividend policy does not matter (see Jarrow 1988, Chapter 4) – does not hold here. Under the conditions we are discussing, the present value of the flow of dividend is not controlled by shareholders but by the body of employees.

32. For instance, Jensen and Mechling (1976, p. 311, fn. 14) emphasize the role which the legal system and the law play in social organizations, especially in organizations of economic activity:

> Statutory laws sets bounds on the kinds of contracts into which individuals and organizations may enter without risking criminal prosecution . . . The courts adjudicate conflicts between contracting parties and establish precedents which form the body of common law. All of these government activities affect both the kinds of contracts executed and the extent to which contracting is relied upon. This in turn determines the usefulness, productivity, profitability and viability of various forms of organization.

Technology, demand, competition, and transaction costs are on the list as examples of constraints and variables which affect the effective boundaries.

33. For example, in the field of marketing the same kind of mechanism is discussed as in Stern and El-Ansary (1988, p. 410):

> The ability of a channel member to exercise control stems from his access to power reserves . . . the accrual of such power generating resources to a channel leader may be the result of the specific characteristics, experience, or history of the firm and its management. Alternatively, power sources (or their absence) may reflect particular characteristics of the environmental forces impinging upon the channel (demand, technology, competition, legal constraints, etc.) and the channel member's ability to capitalize on these forces. Therefore, the power of a channel leader may reflect both the characteristics of his environment and his own characteristics.

34. Thus the significance of an inside–outside distinction, which is not a black-and-white affair, depends on the goal of the analysis. It therefore makes little or no sense to distinguish, like Williamson (1991), the third area between 'market' and 'hierarchy' and call it 'hybrid'. Like most actual markets located between pure monopoly and perfect competition, which are polar cases hypothetically formalized for analysis, actual organizations are typically 'hybrid'.

35. On this point, see the last part of Section 4.4.

36. As mentioned in this chapter and in Chapter 4, other types of relationships based on such factors as shareholding, loans and dispatching directors are not crucial.

37. Much of the literature emphasizes the importance of the discrepancy between actual behaviour of American corporate directors and assumptions embodied in

American corporate law. See, for example, Mace (1971, 1979). Also note the comment of Clark (1985, p. 56):

> [t]o an experienced corporate lawyer who has studied primary legal materials, the assertion that corporate managers are agents of investors, whether debtholders or stockholders, will seem odd or loose. The lawyer would make the following points: (1) corporate officers like the president and treasurer are agents of the corporation itself; (2) the board of directors is the ultimate decision-making body of the corporation . . . ; (3) directors are not agents of the corporation but are sui generis; (4) neither officers nor directors are agents of the stockholders; but (5) both officers and directors are 'fiduciaries' with respect to the corporation and its stockholders.

Also, taking a nexus of contracts view of the firm, Shleifer and Summers (1988, p. 45) warned against placing too much emphasis on the *ex post* consequences of unanticipated takeovers. Focusing on the *ex ante* welfare implications of breach of trust through takeovers, they stated:

> If potential stakeholders believe that their contracts will surely be violated whenever they collect more from the firm than they put in, they will not agree to implicit contracts. Potential suppliers will not invest in relation-specific capital, the young will shirk if they expect no raise in the future, and firms will be unable to reduce labor costs by offering insurance against uncertain ability to their workers. Even if breach via takeover is not a certainty but only a possibility, the opportunities for long-term contracting will be limited.

12 Inter-firm Relationships

1. Recall the comparison of Toyota with its rivals in Chapter 4 as a coordinating agent of the extensively divided production system, where as a result there exists a huge difference of productivity among Japanese car assemblers.
2. Even if this argument can be defended, whether it is a cause of the persistent trade imbalances between two economies is another question. Like most economists, I believe it is the result not of closed markets but of macroeconomic imbalances in each economy.
3. For more details on this point, see Miwa and Nishimura (1991, pp. 5–19).
4. '[A] conception of people as overwhelmingly sensitive to the opinions of others and hence obedient to the dictates of consequently developed norms and values' (Granovetter, 1992, p. 29).
5. The view that 'classical and especially neoclassical economics operate with an atomized human action' (Granovetter, 1992, p. 29).
6. Not all relations within networks for Japanese car production are long-term in character. As is reported in Takeishi *et al.* (1993), trade relations on the periphery of the production systems, for example, relations between subcontractors of parts suppliers and their subcontractors (third tier suppliers and fourth tier suppliers) are not so stable.
7. Dore's (1983) understanding of low transaction costs for large Japanese firms was inspired by the organization in the weaving Section of Japanese textile industry. He studied 'the small town of Nishiwaki . . . whose industry was almost wholly devoted to the weaving of ginghams chiefly for export to Hong Kong to be made up into garments for Americans' (p. 461).

8. Some industry members also comment that in Japan textile makers, rather than chemical firms like most fibre makers in other countries, produce synthetic fibres, which contributes much to this success.
9. I will return to this point in Section 12.9.
10. This Section depends totally on Nakamura (1979).
11. For more details on this industry, see Miwa (1994).
12. Data from *Wool Facts*, 1990, IWS.
13. See Bhagwati (1994) and Krugman (1994a), for more information about the 'closed nature' of the Japanese economy.
14. Fujitsu holds nearly 40 per cent of Fanuc's equity. Needless to say, firms outside Japan can purchase these core components from these firms, and they are widely exported. I do not suggest that every core component or all manufacturing equipment is provided openly by independent, specialized suppliers. This is a part of the make-or-buy decision which determines the firm size. In many cases each competing firm produces core components and manufacturing equipment for its own use. For instance, almost all Japanese car makers produce engines for their own use, and silicon wafers suppliers make their own silicon ingot manufacturing equipment.

References

Adelman, Morris A. (1963) 'A Commentary on "Administered Prices"', in Subcommittee on Antitrust and Monopoly of the Committee on the Judiciary, U.S. Senate, *Administered Prices: A Compendium on Public Policy*, U.S. Government Printing Office, pp. 22–4.

Administrative Management Agency (Gyosei Kanricho) (1981) *Gyosei Shido ni kansuru Chosa Kenkyu Hokokusho (Study Report on Informal Regulation)*, Tokyo: Administrative Management Agency.

Alchian, Armen A. and Harold Demsetz (1972) 'Production, Information Costs, and Economic Organization', *American Economic Review*, pp. 777–95.

Aoki, Masahiko (1990) 'Toward an Economic Model of the Japanese Firm', *Journal of Economic Literature*, March, pp. 1–27.

API Yearbook (Yearbook of the Association of Japanese Automobile Parts Industry) (annual). *Nihon no Jidosha Buhin Sangyo*, Tokyo: Jidosha Shuppan.

Arrow, Kenneth (1974) *The Limits of Organization*, New York: W.W.Norton.

Asanuma, Banri (1989) 'Manufacturer–Supplier Relationships in Japan and the Concept of Relation-Specific Skill', *Journal of the Japanese and the International Economies*, March, pp. 1–30.

Bain, Joe, S. (1968) *Industrial Organization*, 2nd edn, New York: John Wiley.

Bank of Japan (Nihon Ginko) (1964) *Money and Banking in Japan*, Tokyo: Bank of Japan.

Bank of Japan (annual) *Chusho Kigyo Keiei Bunseki (Financial Statements of Small Business in Japan)*, Tokyo: Bank of Japan.

Bank of Japan (annual) *Hikaku Keizai Kin'yu Tokei (Comparative Economic and Financial Statistics)*, Tokyo: Bank of Japan.

Bank of Japan (annual) *Keizai Tokei Nenpo (Economic Statistics Annual)*, Tokyo: Bank of Japan.

Bank of Japan (annual) *Shuyo Kigyo Keiei Bunseki (Financial Statement of Principal Enterprises in Japan)*, Tokyo: Bank of Japan.

Berle, Adolf A. and Gardiner C. Means (1932) *The Modern Corporation and Private Property*, New York: Macmillan.

Best, Michael H. (1990) *The New Competition*, Oxford: Polity Press.

Bhagwati, Jaddish (1994) 'Samurais No More', *Foreign Affairs*, 73(3), pp. 7– 12.

Calder, Kent E. (1988) *Crisis and Competition: Public Policy and Political Stability in Japan. 1949–1986*, Princeton: Princeton University Press.

Caves, Richard E. (1964) 'Direct Regulation and Market Performance in the American Economy', *American Economic Review*, May, pp. 172–81.

Caves, Richard E. and Masu Uekusa (1976) *Industrial Organization in Japan*. Washington DC: The Brookings Institution.

Central Cooperative Bank of Commerce and Industry (Shoko Chukin) (1983) *Shitauke Chusho Kigyo no Shin Kyokumen (A New Development of Small Business in Subcontracting)*, Tokyo: Shoko Chukin.

Clark, Robert (1985) 'Agency Costs versus Fiduciary Duties', in Pratt and Zechhauser (eds), *Principals and Agents: The Structure of Business*, Cambridge: Harvard Business School Press.

Coase, R.H. (1937) 'The Nature of the Firm', *Economica*, New Series, Vol. IV, pp. 386–405.

Coase, R.H. (1964) 'Comment', *American Economic Review*, May, pp. 194–7.

Coase, R.H. (1988) *The Market, the Firm and the Law*, Chicago: University of Chicago Press.

Daiwa Research Institute annual, *Analysts' Guide*, Tokyo: Daiwa Research Insitute.

Davis, Kenneth C. (1982) *Administrative Law Treatise*, Vol. 1, 2nd edn, San Diego: K.C. Davies.

Demsetz, Harold (1969) 'Information and Efficiency: Another Viewpoint', *Journal of Law and Economics*, 12 (April), pp. 1–22.

Dodwell Marketing Consultants (1992) *Industrial Groupings in Japan*, 10th edn, Tokyo: Dodwell Marketing Consultants.

Dore, Donald (1983) 'Goodwill and the Spirit of Market Capitalism', *The British Journal of Sociology*, 34(4), pp. 459–82.

Dore, Donald (1992) 'Japan's Version of Managerial Capitalism', in T.A. Kochan and M. Useem (eds), *Transforming Organizations*, Oxford: Oxford University Press.

Easterbrook, Frank H. and Daniel R. Fischel (1990) 'The Corporate Contract', in L.A. Bebchuk (ed.), *Corporate Law and Economic Analysis*. Cambridge: Cambridge University Press.

Economic Planning Agency (Keizai Kikaku-cho) (annual) *Keizai Hakusho (Economic White Paper)*, Tokyo: Ministry of Finance.

Edmondson, Harold E. (1992) 'Commentary', in T.A. Kochan and M. Useem (eds), *Transforming Organizations*, Oxford: Oxford University Press.

Fair Trade Commission (FTC) (Kosei Toriki Iinkai) (1969) *Nihon no Sangyo Shuchu: 1963–1966 (Economic Concentration in Japan)*, Tokyo: Toyo Keizai Shinpo-sha.

Fair Trade Commission (1977) *Dokusen Kinshi Seisaku 30 Nen-shi (Thirty Years of Anti-Monopoly Policy)*, Tokyo: FTC.

Fair Trade Commission (1983) *Kosei Torihiki Iinkai Shinketsu Shu (28), Sekiyu Karuteru Jiken Kankei Tokyo Kosai Hanketsu (Decisions of the Fair Trade Commission (28): Tokyo High Court Decisions on the Petroleum Cartel Case)*, Tokyo: FTC.

Fair Trade Commission (1986) *Wagakuni ni okeru Keizairyoku Shuchu no Jittai ni tsuite (A Survey of Concentration of Economic Power in Japan)*, 16 September.

Fair Trade Commission (1992) *The Outline of the Report on the Actual Conditions of the Six Major Corporate Groups*, February.

Financial System Research Council (Kin'yu Seido Chosa-kai) (1969) *Kin'yu Seido Chosa-kai Shiryo (Documents and Materials for the Financial System Research Council)*, Vol. 2, Tokyo: Kin'yu Zaisei Kenkyu-kai.

Financial System Research Council (1970) *Kin'yu Seido Chosa-kai Shiryo (Documents and Materials for the Financial System Research Council)*, Supplement, Tokyo: Kin'yu Zaisei Kenkyu-kai.

Foster, C.D. (1992) *Privatization, Public Ownership and the Regulation of Natural Monopoly*, Oxford: Blackwell.

Friedman, David (1988) *The Misunderstood Miracle*, Ithaca: Cornell University Press.

Fukukawa, Shinji (1964) 'Seifu Kin'yu Kikan no Kino to Sangyo Seisaku (The Function of Government Financial Institutions and Industrial Policy)', *Tsusho Sangyo Kenkyu* (MITI), No. 122.

Futatsugi, Yusaku (1977) 'Miyazaki Yoshikazu-cho Sengo Nihon no Kigyo Shudan (Professor Miyazaki's Corporate Groups in Postwar Japan)', *Economic Studies Quarterly*, Vol. 28, No. 1, pp. 90–92.

Gerlach, Michael L. (1992) *Alliance Capitalism: The Social Organization of Japanese Business*, Berkeley: University of California Press.

Gilson, Ronald J. and Mark J. Roe (1993) 'Understanding the Japanese Keiretsu', *The Yale Law Journal*, Vol. 102, pp. 871–906.

Gordon, Jefferey N. (1990) 'Ties and Bonds: Dual Class Common Stock and the Problem of Shareholder Choice', in L.A. Bebchuk (ed.), *Corporate Law and Economic Analysis*. Cambridge: Cambridge University Press.

Gordon, Robert Aaron (1945) *Business Leadership in the Large Corporation*, Washington, DC: The Brookings Institution.

Goto, Akira (1975) 'Daikigyo Taisei to Kin'yu Keiretsu (Dominance of Large Firms and Financial *Keiretsu*)', *Quarterly Chuo Koron*, autumn.

Goto, Akira (1983) 'Nihon no Kigyo Shudan (Corporate Groups in Japan)', *Bijinesu Rebyu* (Hitotsubashi University), Vol. 30, Nos 3, 4.

Goto, Akira and Wakazugi Ryuhei (1988) 'Technology Policy', in Komiya *et al.* (eds), *Industrial Policy of Japan*.

Granovetter, Mark (1992) 'Problems of Explanation in Economic Sociology', in N. Nohria and R. G. Eccles (eds), *Networks and Organizations: Structure, Form, and Action*.

Haley, John Owen (1991) *Authority without Power: Law and the Japanese Paradox*, New York: Oxford University Press.

Hannah, Leslie (1983) *The Rise of the Corporate Economy*, 2nd edn, London: Methuen.

Harada, Naohiko (1983) 'Gyosei Shido – Ho no Shihai to Nihonteki Gyosei Taishitsu (Informal Regulation: Judicial Control and Characteristics of Japan's Administration)', *Jurisuto Sogo Tokushu (special issue)*, No. 29.

Hart, Oliver (1989) 'An Economist's Perspective on the Theory of the Firm', *Columbia Law Review*, November, pp. 1957-74.

Hayek, F.A. (1945) 'The Use of Knowledge in Society', *American Economic Review*, September, pp. 519-30.

Hazama, Hiroshi (1989) *Keiei Shakai-gaku (Sociology of Management)*, Tokyo: Yuhikaku.

Holmstrom, Bengt R. and Jean Tirole (1989) 'The Theory of the Firm', in R. Schmalensee and R.Willig (eds), *Handbook of Industrial Organization, Vol. I.*, New York: Elsevier Scientific Publishing.

Horiuchi, Akiyoshi (1989) 'Informational Properties of the Japanese Financial System', *Japan and the World Economy*, Vol.1, No. 3, pp. 255–78.

Horrigan, J.O. (1968) 'A Short History of Financial Ratio Analysis', *The Accounting Review*, April, pp. 284–94.

Hoshi, Takeo, Anil Kashyap and David Scharfstein (1990) 'Bank Monitoring and Investment: Evidence from the Changing Structure of Japanese Corporate Banking Relationships', in H. Hubbard (ed.), *Asymmetric Information, Corporate Finance, and Investment*, Chicago: University of Chicago Press.

Hoshi, Takeo, Anil Kashyap and David Scharfstein (1991) 'Corporate Structure, Liquidity, and Investment: Evidence from Japanese Industrial Groups', *Quarterly Journal of Economics*, February, pp. 33–60.

Imai, Ken'ichi (1976) *Gendai Sangyo Soshiki (Contemporary Industrial Organization)*, Tokyo: Iwanami Shoten.

Imai, Ken'ichi (1989) 'Kigyo Gurupu (Corporate Groups)', in K. Imai and R. Komiya (eds), *Nihon no Kigyo (Japanese Firms)*, Tokyo: University of Tokyo Press.

Isobe, Koichi (1964) 'Jidosha Sangyo ni okeru Keiretsu (*Keiretsu* in the Automobile Industry)', *Chusho Kigyo Kin'yu Koko Chosa Jiho*, 6-3.

Itoh, Keiichi (1968) 'Toushi Chosei, Kajo Setsubi Shori to Dokkin-ho (Investment Coordination, Excess Capacity Disposal and the Anti-monopoly Act)', *Tsusho Sangyo Kenkyu* (MITI), No. 149.

Itoh, Taikichi (1985) 'Hashigaki (Foreword)', in Nihon Chusho Kigyo Gakkai (ed.), *Shitauke, Ryutsu Keiretsu-ka to Chusho Kigyo (Subcontracting, Distribution Keiretsu and Small Business)*, Tokyo: Doyukan.

Iyori, Hiroshi (1986) 'Antitrust and Industrial Policy in Japan: Competition and Cooperation; in G. Saxonhouse and K. Yamamura (eds), *Law and Trade Issues of the Japanese Economy: American and Japanese Perspectives*, Seattle: University of Washington Press.

Jarrow, Robert A. (1988) *Finance Theory*, Englewood Cliffs: Prentice-Hall.

Jenkinson, Tim and Colin Mayer (1993) 'The Assessment: Corporate Governance and Corporate Control', *Oxford Review of Economic Policy*, Vol. 8, No. 3, pp. 1–10.

Jensen, Michael C. and William H. Mechling (1976) 'Theory of the Firm: Managerial Behavior, Agency Costs and Ownership Structure', *Journal of Financial Economics*, October, pp. 305–60.

Johnson, Chalmers (1982) *MITI and The Japanese Miracle*, Stanford: Stanford University Press.

Kahn, Alfred (1988) *The Economics of Regulation: Principles and Institutions*, Cambridge: MIT Press.

Kaizuka, Keimei (1973) *Keizai Seisaku no Kadai (Basic Issues on Economic Policy)*, Tokyo: University of Tokyo Press.

Kaplan, Steven N. and Bernadett A. Minton (1993) '"Outside" Intervention in Japanese Companies: Its Determinants and Its Implications for Managers', *NBER Working Paper*, No. 4276.

Kawaguchi, Hiroshi (1962) 'Futatsu no Nihon Keizai-ron (Two Views of the Japanese Economy)', in Kawaguchi (ed.), *Nihon Keizai no Kiso Kozo (The Basic Structure of the Japanese Economy)*. Tokyo: Shunju-sha.

Kawaguchi, Hiroshi (1965) 'Chusho Kigyo heno Kin'yu-teki "Shiwayose" Kiko (Financial Burden-Shifting Mechanism toward Small Business)', in R. Tachi and T. Watanabe (eds), *Keizai Seicho to Zaisei Kin'yu (Economic Growth, Budget, and Finance)*, Tokyo: Iwanami Shoten.

Kawaguchi, Hiroshi (1966) *Nihon no Kin'yu–Yushi Shuchu Mekanizumu (Finance in Japan–The Loan Concentration Mechanism)*, Tokyo: Nihon Hyoron-sha.

Kawasaki, Hirotaro (1966) 'Gyosei Shido no Jittai (The Reality of Informal Regulation)', *Jurisuto*, No. 342, 15 March.

Kawasaki, Tsutomu (1968) *Sengo Tekko-gyo Ron (The Postwar Steel Industry)*, Tokyo: Tekko Shimbun-sha.

Kiyonari, Tadao (1973) 'Niju Kozo-ron no Sai Ginmi (A Re-examination of the Dual Structure View)', *Shoko Kin'yu*, November.

Kiyonari, Tadao (1982) 'Nihon Keizai ni Niju Kozo ha Fukkatsu shinai (The Dual Structure Will Not Revive in Japan)', *Ekonomisto*, 6 June.

Kobayashi, Yoshihiro (1980) *Kigyo Shudan no Bunseki (An Analysis of Corporate Groups)*, Sapporo: Hokkaido University Press.

Kochan, Thomas A. and Michael Useem (1992) 'Achieving Systemic Organizational Change', in T.A. Kochan and M. Useem (eds), *Transforming Organizations*. Oxford: Oxford University Press.

Kojima, Seiichi (1960) 'Tekko-gyo no Jishu Chosei Hoshiki wo dou Kaizo subekika (How Should We Change the Investment Self-Coordination Programme in the Steel Industry?)', *Tekko-kai*, March.

Komine, Takao (1993) 'The Role of Economic Planning in Japan', in J. Teranishi and Y. Kosai (eds), *The Japanese Experience of Economic Reforms*, London: Macmillan.

Komiya, Ryutaro (1961a) 'Dokusen Shihon to Shotoku Saibunpai (Monopoly Capital and Income Redistribution)', *Sekai*, March.

Komiya, Ryutaro (1961b) 'Dokusen Shihon to Shotoku Bunpai to Shakai Kozo (Monopoly, Income Distribution and Social Structure)', *Ekonomisuto*, 5 September.

Komiya, Ryutaro (1962) 'Nihon ni okeru Dokusen to Kigyo Rijun (Monopoly and Corporate Profit in Japan)', in T. Nakamura, H. Ohtsuka and K. Suzuki (eds) *Kigyo Keizai Bunseki (Study of Corporate Economy)*, Tokyo: Iwanami Shoten.

Komiya, Ryutaro (1970) 'Gendai Shihon Shugi no Tenkai (The Development of Contemporary Capitalism)', *Ekonomisuto*, 10 November.

Komiya, Ryutaro (1975) *Gendai Nihon Keizai Kenkyu (Studies of Contemporary Japanese Economy)*, Tokyo: University of Tokyo Press.

Komiya, Ryutaro (1988) 'Introduction', in Komiya *et al.* (eds), *Industrial Policy of Japan*.

Komiya, Ryutaro (1990) *The Japanese Economy: Trade, Industry, and Government*, Tokyo: University of Tokyo Press.

Komiya, Ryutaro, Masahiro Okuno and Kotaro Suzumura (eds) (1988) *Industrial Policy of Japan*, Tokyo: Academic Press.

Kosai, Yutaka (1981) *Kodo Seicho no Jidai (The High-Growth Era)*, Tokyo: Nihon Hyoron-sha.

Kosai, Yutaka and Yoshitaro Ogino (1980) *Nihon Keizai Tembo (The Contemporary Japanese Economy)*, Tokyo: Nihon Hyoron-sha.

Koto, Rikuzo (1963) 'Sangyo Tosei Zo–Sangyo-kai kara no Ichi Teigen (A View of the Industry Control: A Proposal from the Industry)', in Y. Chigusa (ed.), *Sangyo Taisei no Sai Hensei (Reorganization of the Industrial Order)*, Tokyo: Syunju-sha.

Kreps, David (1990) 'Corporate Culture and Economic Theory', in J.A. Alt and K.A. Shepsle (eds), *Rational Perspective in Political Science*, Cambridge, Mass: Harvard University Press.

Krugman, Paul (1991) 'Introduction', in P. Krugman (ed.), *Trade with Japan: Has the Door Opened Wider?*, Chicago: University of Chicago Press, pp. 1–8.

Krugman, Paul (1994a) 'Competitiveness: A Dangerous Obsession', *Foreign Affairs*, 73(2), pp. 28–44.

Krugman, Paul (1994b) *The Age of Diminished Expectations: U.S. Economic Policy in the 1990s*, revised and updated edition, Cambridge, Mass.: MIT Press.

Kurasawa, Motonari (1977) 'Sen'i Sangyo ni okeru Chusho Kigyo Seisaku (Small Business Policy in the Textile Industry)', *Kokumin Kin'yu Koko Chosa Geppo*, January.

Kurasono, Susumu (1960) 'Chusho Kigyo Kin'yu (Financing Small Business)', in M. Kajinishi, Y. Kobayashi, H. Iwao and T. Itoh. (eds), *Dokusen Shihon to Chusho Kigyo (Monopoly Capital and Small Business)*, Tokyo: Yuhi-kaku.

Kure, Bunji and Kinzo Shima (1984) *Kinri Jiyu-ka (Interest Rates Liberalization)*, Tokyo: Yuhi-kaku.

Kyogoku, Jun'ichi (1983) *Nihon no Seiji (Japan's Politics)*, Tokyo: University. of Tokyo Press.

Lawrence, Robert Z. (1991a) 'Do Keiretsu Reduce Japanese Imports?', paper prepared for the Japanese Economic Planning Agency's Conference on External Adjustments and the Changing Trade Structure of Manufactured Goods Since 1985, Tokyo, January.

Lawrence, Robert Z. (1991b) 'Efficient or Exclusionist? The Import Behaviour of Japanese Corporate Groups', *Brooking Papers on Economic Activity*, 1, pp. 311–41.

Lev, Baruch (1974) *Financial Statement Analysis*, Englewood Cliffs: Prentice-Hall.

Macaulay, Stewart (1963) 'Non-contractual Relations in Business: a Preliminary study', *American Sociological Review*, 28, pp. 55–67.

Mace, Myles L. (1971) *Directors: Myth and Reality*, Cambridge, Mass.: Harvard Business School Press.

Mace, Myles L. (1979) 'Directors: Myth and Reality – Ten Years Later', *Rutgers Law Review*, 32(2), pp. 293–308.

Maddison, Angus (1991) *Dynamic Forces in Capitalist Development*, Oxford: Oxford University Press.

Management and Coordination Agency (Sohmu-cho) *Jigyosho Tokei Chosa* (*Census of Establishments*), published every three years. Tokyo: Management and Coordination Agency.

March, James G. and Herbert A. Simon (1958) *Organizations*, New York: John Wiley.

Matsui, Toshiya (1985) 'Jidosha Sangyo ni okeru Gaichu Kanri Seisaku (Purchase Control Measures in the Motor Industry)', *Ritsumeikan Keieigaku* (Ritsumeikan University), Vol. 24, No. 2.

Milgrom, Paul and John Roberts (1992) *Economics, Organizations and Management*, Englewood Cliffs: Prentice-Hall.

Ministry of Finance (Okura-sho) annual, *Hojin Kigyo Tokei Nenpo* (*Financial Statement of Incorporated Business*), Tokyo: Ministry of Finance.

Ministry of Finance (annual), *Yuka Shoken Hokokusho* (*Security Reports*), each listed firm, Tokyo: Ministry of Finance.

Ministry of International Trade and Industry (Tsusho Sangyo-sho) (1955) *Kokogyo Seisan Shisu* (*Production Indexes of Mining and Manufacturing Industries*), Tokyo: Ministry of International Trade and Industry.

Ministry of International Trade and Industry (Tsusho Sangyo-sho) (1969) *Tsusho Sangyo-sho 20 Nen-shi* (*Twenty Years of Ministry of International Trade and Industry*), Tokyo: Ministry of International Trade and Industry.

Ministry of International Trade and Industry (annual), *Kogyo Tokei-hyo* (*Census of Manufacturers*), Tokyo: MITI.

Mitsubishi Economic Research Institute (Mitsubishi Keizai Kenkyu-jo) (1965) *Buhin Mehka Senmon-ka no Jittai Bunseki* (*Study of Specialization among Car Parts Manufacturers*), Tokyo: Mitsubishi Keizai Kenkyu-jo.

Miwa, Yoshiro (1976) 'Shin Sangyo no Mebae (An Emergence of New Industries)', in H. Arisawa (ed.), *Showa Keizai-shi* (*Showa Economic History*), Tokyo: Nihon Keizai Shimbun-sha.

Miwa, Yoshiro (1988) 'Dokusen to Kigyo Rijun (Monopoly and Corporate Profits)', in K. Iwata and T. Ishikawa (eds), *Nihon Keizai Kenkyu* (*Studies of the Japanese Economy*), Tokyo: University of Tokyo Press.

Miwa, Yoshiro (1990a) *Nihon no Kigyo to Sangyo Soshiki* (*Firms and Industrial Organization in Japan*), Tokyo: University of Tokyo Press.

Miwa, Yoshiro (1990b) 'Book Review of Saxonhouse and Yamamura (eds), *Law and Trade Issues of the Japanese Economy*', *Journal of the Japanese and International Economies*, 4, pp. 93–5.

Miwa, Yoshiro (1991) 'Mein Banku to Nihon no Shihon Shijo (Main Banks and Japanese Capital Markets)', *Kin'yu*, August. pp. 11–19.

Miwa, Yoshiro (1993a) *Kin'yu Gyosei Kaikaku* (*Financial Administration Reform*), Tokyo: Nihon Keizai Shimbun-sha.

Miwa, Yoshiro (1993b) 'Economic Effects of the Antimonopoly and the Deconcentration Policies in Postwar Japan', in J. Teranishi and Y. Kosai (eds), *The Japanese Experience of Economic Reforms*, London: Macmillan.

Miwa, Yoshiro (1993c) 'Policies for Small Business in Japan', *Economic Development Institute of the World Bank Working Paper*, Number 93-39.

Miwa, Yoshiro (1994) 'The Retail Market for Wool Products: the Case of Men's Suits in Japan', in C. Findlay and M. Itoh (eds), *Wool in Japan*, Pymble (Australia): Harper Educational.

Miwa, Yoshiro and Kiyohiko G. Nishimura (1991) 'Nihon no Ryutsu: Josetsu (Japanese Distribution System: Introduction)', in Y. Miwa and K.G. Nishimura (eds), *Nihon no Ryutsu (Japanese Distribution Sytem)*, Tokyo: University of Tokyo Press.

Miyazaki, Yoshikazu (1962) 'Kato Kyoso no Ronri to Genjitsu–Keiretsu Shihai Kiko no Kaimei (The Logic and the Reality of Excessive Competition: A Study of the *Keiretsu* Control Mechanism)', *Ekonomisuto*, 10 October.

Miyazaki, Yoshikazu (1972) *Kasen–Gendai no Keizai Kiko (Oligopoly: The Structure of Contemporary Economy)*, Tokyo: Iwanami Shoten.

Miyazaki, Yoshikazu (1976) *Sengo Nihon no Kigyo Shudan (Corporate Groups in Postwar Japan)*, Tokyo: Nihon Keizai Shimbun-sha.

Miyazaki, Yoshikazu (1979) ' "Keieisha Shihai" Saiko (Re-examination of "Manager Control")', *Keizai Kenkyu* (Hitotsubashi University), Vol. 30, No. 3.

Miyazaki, Yoshikazu (1980) 'Kigyo Shudan Bunseki ni tsuite (On the Study of Corporate Groups)', in Mori *et al.* (eds), *Gendai Shihon Shugi (Contemporary Capitalism)*, Tokyo: Nihon Hyoron-sha.

Miyazawa, Ken'ichi and Hirotaka Kato (1965) 'Karite no Niju Kozo (Dual Structure among Borrowers)', in H. Kawaguchi and I. Kawai (eds), *Kin'yu-ron Koza (Lectures on Finance) Vol.5*, Tokyo: Yuhi-kaku.

Morita, Minoru (1960) 'Chusho Kigyo no Kin'yu to Zaisei (Finance and Budget for Small Business)', in Chusho Kigyo Chosa-kai, *Chusho Kigyo no Tokei Bunseki (A Statistical Analysis of Small Business)*, Tokyo: Toyo Keizai Shinpo-sha.

Morozumi, Yoshihiko (1966) *Sangyo Seisaku no Riron (Theory of Industrial Policy)*. Tokyo: Nihon Keizai Shimbun-sha.

Mutoh, Hiromichi (1988) 'The Automotive Industry', in Komiya *et al.* (eds), *Industrial Policy of Japan*.

Nakakita, Toru (1993) 'Trade and Capital Liberalization Policies in Postwar Japan', in J. Teranishi and Y. Kosai (eds), *The Japanese Experience of Economic Reforms*, London: Macmillan.

Nakamura, Hideichiro (1964) *Chuken Kigyo-ron (Medium-sized Vital Enterprises)*, Tokyo: Toyo Keizai Shinpo-sha.

Nakamura, Hideichiro (1975) ' "Miyazaki Yoshikazu" Taikei ni tsuite (A Critical Review of the Argument of Professor Yoshikazu Miyazaki)', *Kokumin Keizai*, No. 134.

Nakamura, Hideichiro (1985) *Chosen suru Chusho Kigyo (Challenging Small Business)*, Tokyo: Iwanami Shoten.

Nakamura, Hideichiro, Hajime Yamashita and Kimihiro Masamura (eds) (1971) *Gendai no Kagaku Kogyo - Kozo to Dotai (Modern Chemical Industry: Structure and Dynamics)*, Tokyo: Toyo Keizai Shinpo-sha.

Nakamura, Koji (1979) 'Kohaba Orimono Senshoku Kako Kogyo no Sanchi Hikaku Bunseki Shiron (A Comparative Study of *Sanchi* in the *Kohaba* Dyeing Industry)', *Shakai Kagaku* (Doshisha University), No. 25, pp. 63–124.

Nakamura, Koji (1993) 'Sen'i Risosu Senta Koso to Kyoto Senshoku-gyo (The Conception of the Textile Resource Centre and Kyoto Dyeing Industry)', *Shakai Kagaku* (Doshisha University), No. 50, pp. 101–32.

Nakamura, Takafusa (1974) 'Nihon ni okeru Sangyo Seisaku no Tokushoku to Hyoka (The Characteristics of Japan's Industrial Policy and its Effectiveness),' *Toyo Keizai Rinji Zokan* (Special Issue), 18 June.

Nakamura, Takafusa (1981) *The Post War Japanese Economy*, Tokyo: University of Tokyo Press.

Nakamura, Takafusa (1993) *Nihon Keizai (The Japanese Economy)*, 3rd edn, Tokyo: University of Tokyo Press.